The Future-Ready Leader

Peter Lorange • Karin Mugnaini

The Future-Ready Leader

Accelerated Learning for Business Success

With Contributions by Jan Peter Balkenende, Peter Brabeck-Letmathe, Anders Endreson, Dennis Jaffe, Jean-François Manzoni, Arnoud de Meyer, Mitzi Perdue, Bjørn Rosengren, Risto Siilasmaa and Hermann Simon

Peter Lorange
IMD
Lausanne, Switzerland

Karin Mugnaini
IMD
Lausanne, Switzerland

ISBN 978-3-031-45089-1   ISBN 978-3-031-45090-7   (eBook)
https://doi.org/10.1007/978-3-031-45090-7

© The Editor(s) (if applicable) and The Author(s), under exclusive license to Springer Nature Switzerland AG 2023
This work is subject to copyright. All rights are solely and exclusively licensed by the Publisher, whether the whole or part of the material is concerned, specifically the rights of translation, reprinting, reuse of illustrations, recitation, broadcasting, reproduction on microfilms or in any other physical way, and transmission or information storage and retrieval, electronic adaptation, computer software, or by similar or dissimilar methodology now known or hereafter developed.
The use of general descriptive names, registered names, trademarks, service marks, etc. in this publication does not imply, even in the absence of a specific statement, that such names are exempt from the relevant protective laws and regulations and therefore free for general use.
The publisher, the authors, and the editors are safe to assume that the advice and information in this book are believed to be true and accurate at the date of publication. Neither the publisher nor the authors or the editors give a warranty, expressed or implied, with respect to the material contained herein or for any errors or omissions that may have been made. The publisher remains neutral with regard to jurisdictional claims in published maps and institutional affiliations.

This Springer imprint is published by the registered company Springer Nature Switzerland AG
The registered company address is: Gewerbestrasse 11, 6330 Cham, Switzerland

Paper in this product is recyclable.

Foreword

When Peter Lorange asked me to write the foreword to the new book he was working on with his longtime associate Karin Mugnaini, I was both honored and moved; Honored to contribute to yet another thought-provoking book by someone I regard as a role model predecessor and colleague; And moved by the opportunity to look back on our relationship and shared commitment to lifelong learning.

I have known Peter for the better part of almost 20 years, since I was fortunate to be recruited by him in 2003, then to serve under his leadership as part of the faculty at IMD, where he had been President since 1993. He is a visionary leader who shaped IMD into what it is today: a lighthouse of world-class education and continuous learning for business leaders, from aspiring students eager to impact the world to accomplished CEOs and Board members who may have already left their mark on their organizations and on the ecosystems surrounding these.

During his 15 years at the helm of IMD and more generally a career that spans five decades, Peter very successfully combined three roles that tend to require very different sets of skills: He was a very successful academic in his own right, he was a transformational leader at several academic institutions, and he was a very successful investor and business operator. That is a very rare combination! Along the way, Peter built an impressive network of business and thought leaders. There are many benefits to this, two of which come to mind today, not least because they illustrate the lasting bond between IMD and its Honorary President.

The first is that (part of) Peter's network literally became the Lorange Network, where 3500 leaders from prominent organizations, business-owning families, entrepreneurs, etc. shared insights, built up their skillsets, and pursued new growth opportunities, both on the business and personal side. Most recently, we at IMD were fortunate to integrate the Lorange Network, thus offering its members access to an even wider set of development pathways, another sign of the synergy between Peter's lifework and IMD's raison d'être.

The second is this book. While over the years Peter worked on more than 30 books and led countless interviews with business leaders, he took the time, with Karin's help, to marshal these insights into a true reference guide. The value of this enterprise to you as a reader comes in part from the collection of book reviews and practitioner discussions herein brought together into one convenient volume. But what makes the whole greater than the sum of the parts is that, as you read on, you do not just scratch the surface of business literature or that of the executives' profiles. Nor do you only learn about the editors' own perspectives, whose decades-old experience with these exercises already tops off the stock of stories and content with their fine take on them. More importantly, you may learn about yourself and your own learning journey as these pages may resonate with your very own mental frameworks, forged during your personal trajectories (consciously or not), thanks to the mediation of a brilliant curator.

What makes Peter and Karin particularly suited curators is that they combine pedagogical excellence with entrepreneurial success, theory with practice. Under Peter's three terms as the institution's longest-serving president, IMD grew fourfold in size, and more than half of the buildings on our Lausanne campus today were constructed during Peter's tenure. About 30 years ago, he set IMD on the course to flourish into a powerful, agile, and unique institution driven by the purpose of challenging what is and inspiring what could be to develop leaders who transform organizations and contribute to society. Before that, he had his own shipping business, followed by a family office setup to manage the consequent investment portfolio. During and after, he continued to write to impact the way we do business. Seeing this book come together is another motivating illustration that IMD stands for the lifelong education of business, by business, for business.

We do so in a number of ways, shapes, and forms fitting different needs and profiles. When you come to our campus, you are drinking from a proverbial firehose of content with incredible faculty and classmates. In this book, you are biting into smaller digestible nuggets. Accelerated learning. Business success.

At IMD lately, we made huge progress on cracking the nut of piecemeal learning thanks to the design of the first-class technology-mediated interactions enabling our participants to take in content at their pace. I like to think that Peter and I share, in addition to immense respect and friendship for one another, this same passion for continuous learning, unlearning, and relearning. We believe it is key for successful business leaders to pause, observe, and take stock of where they stand in this cycle, as opposed to keep up with trendy theories and skills through second-hand readings. It is with that conviction that IMD, as an executive education institution, and Peter, as an educator and executive himself, focus on real learning and real impact on business and society.

This book is one very good place to start and/or continue down that real-world-focused path. In part, because it covers virtually all or most of what modern executives ought to know and think about, from the role of strategic management and (self-) leadership to political and world affairs that constitute the external environment informing a firm's strategy and investments. In part also, because of the authors' characters and own leadership stories.

Karin has been working with Peter for many years, and she, too, must have heard him say something he used to say often to the IMD faculty and staff: Good can always be done better. Illustrating this very principle to himself, Peter attended several programs at IMD last year, 14 years after leaving office. After each program, he shared with me his insights and feedback, and I was impressed yet again by Peter's curiosity, openness of mind, and acute insights.

And yet Peter was also a very nurturing leader, encouraging us to join him on this path of continuous improvement and striving for more real world, real learning, real impact. Along the way, he gave me and my colleagues an example that continues to inspire me to this day: As focused as he was on "good can always be done better," Peter was also able to help hardworking individuals to feel good about their efforts and their results. During the four years, I was fortunate to walk into his office as my boss; every single time, I walked into his office six feet tall and I came out of it feeling seven feet tall. Already back then, Peter was displaying and nurturing the combination of "challenging what is and inspiring what could be" that has become part of IMD's purpose statement.

Peter's wisdom and positive energy permeate this book, but they would not have come to the fore as clearly without Karin's insight and writing. I am glad the two of them took the time to put together this great collection, and I hope that you will enjoy reading it as much as I did.

Leadership and Organizational Development　　　　　　Jean-François Manzoni
IMD,
Lausanne, Switzerland

Preface

Acceleration is a concept that has been studied by mathematicians, physicists, and mechanics, to name but a few. Generally defined as the rate of change in velocity with respect to time, speed and direction clearly play critical roles. Acceleration has evident implications in business too. We speak of accelerated changes in markets, acceleration of demand or output for example, accelerating one's career, and so on. We chose to call our book "Accelerated Learning for Business Success" for several reasons. To begin with, we sensed an urgent and strong call from the business leadership community to determine the best way to address, understand, and solve burning challenges that will affect them in the future, some even that are affecting them already today. Also, we assume that learning is not just paramount for business leaders but should be lifelong. These two elements of timing, namely the immediate need and the pull for a long-term commitment, shape the way we have thought of, structured, and written this book. In other words, we need to learn quickly, accelerating our grasp of new tools, perspectives, solutions, and so on, yet we need to assure that the accelerated way of learning continues in intensity and frequency.

We also observe that there are different ways, speeds, and directions to learning. We know that certain forces, impulses, and inspirations can affect when, where, why, and how we learn. And, with the amount of changes we are facing today in our business environments, we live in a fast-paced world, full of acceleration. We also understand how critical it may be for learners to learn faster, besides better.

Additionally, we recognize the need for cross-functional thinking. This type of thinking plays a central role in our type of learning. This cross-functionality implies a way of reflecting that is unconventional and one that brings different disciplines together. This is in strong contrast to the classical perception of discipline-based knowledge in business positions and, above all, in academic circles and classic academic departments. We hope therefore that our book will encourage cross-functional thinking, and we praise many of the technological advances we witness, in particular AI, which boosts and enhances this approach to reflection and analysis.

Since our connections to practitioners have been so strong, we made a conscientious decision to turn our questions and dialogues back to these leaders. What are the issues today about tomorrow that are keeping you up at night? What challenges do you anticipate as the primary ones in the coming years? How can you anticipate solving or overcoming those, and what do you need in order to do so? What skills and tools do you identify as critical to obtain? We therefore left the academicians aside and chose, through our reflections, book reviews, and executive interviews, to lend the voice and the exchange to these leaders themselves to shed light on the process of learning, to address innovation and advanced technologies such as AI, augmented reality, virtual reality, holograms, and ChatGPT, and to integrate models and processes with information and knowledge. In other words, we aim to offer our readers a guide or manual to help them accept or adopt change, adapt to that change, to thus be able to align visions, missions, purpose, and goals to the future they face.

Initially, we had given the book the working title "Sprint Learning." In the end, we decided to move away from this, mostly because the term is currently being used and branded at IMD for its short, fast-paced deep-dive topical courses on cutting-edge topics, but simultaneously because we wish to suggest that it may not be so much about the movement we "sprint runners" or learners are undergoing, but rather the intricate relationship between us, the actors, and our environment. We therefore feel more comfortable with our final selection of title.

A bit about sprints though, before we begin to reinforce the concept that moving forward, and thus learning, can be done at different speeds, and not always regularly. We know of fast-moving, i.e., "sprints" or sprinting from track and field, athletics. Sprint running races are short-distance competitions whereby the athletes aim to run at maximum speed for the full race distance, starting from a crouched position. Interestingly, sprint racing is among the oldest sports competitions, going back to the original Olympic Games in the seventh century BC and also included in the first modern Olympic Games back in 1896.

It is no wonder, therefore, that when any skill is learned or executed at an extremely quick pace, or a target or goal is to be reached very rapidly, we tend to term it "sprinting," and in our case here, "sprint learning." Here, we could even interchange the words sprinting and accelerating.

Although in our book, we do not delve into the different "distances" the sprint (learning) can cover (in track and field these are 100 meters, 200 meters, and 400 meters), we do liken our learning process to an intense commitment to reach a learning target over a reduced or short period of time, through a quick process or series of fast-paced and shorter programs.

There are some other facts and analogies that also have relevance in this comparison. For example, running sprinters begin their races in starting blocks (these could be the companies where our learners are working) before they drive powerfully forward (trying to improve their business skills and competence) and then move into an upright running position in order to *accelerate* (this, in turn, could be the first phase of learning that kicks off the learning journey). Also, as the runners reach the finishing line (have completed their learning nugget or program), they walk or stand to cool down, check performance results, and perhaps reflect on their sprint and the next race (all of these can be compared to the review, analysis, and new goal setting that learners undertake when moving forward with their own executive education). Coincidentally, in the concept of accelerated learning, we also must appreciate that moment or those moments, when the learning pauses, even stops, and what happens in the non-accelerated, no-motion, or slow-motion process. Much more occurs cerebrally than that which we can imagine!

Racers speak about the importance of training, discipline, force, muscles, body alignment, concentration, and endurance. All of these hold a place too in our world of sprint learning—where we propose learning quickly, in smaller nuggets (race distances), but with the same intention to reach the target successfully. We suggest, using our new title, to learn with acceleration, using perhaps time more assertively, more wisely, and more intentionally.

The concept of learning in sprints within the area of executive business education is not new however, nor does it stand alone. There are many other sectors that have clearly understood the importance of continuous and lifelong learning, as well as the moving in and out of study and work to specialize further, to keep up with "the world." For instance, the case method, heavily in use at Harvard, and to some extent also at IMD, is indeed an example of the same, i.e., learning "does," practice learning, learning in smaller "doses" or cases.

In one way, the way we describe sprint learning, as an example, is similar to what the medical world "does" in terms of education (medical school), training during the learning process (additional required residency training), certification, regular exams and courses in many cases obligatory in order to maintain the degree or license, conferences, professional societies, publications, and obligatory retraining to keep up with innovation, etc. Doctors use both formal and informal learning to foster continuous development and improvement of knowledge and skills for both employment and personal fulfillment. There are times when they thus learn more intensively and have to push themselves to learn more quickly.

Another interesting aspect in medicine is the concept of "incremental learning"—the adding of responsibility gradually. Here too, there is relevance to our learning. Incremental learning allows doctors, or in our case, business students, to see as many permutations of a problem as possible so that they have a good chance of working it safely on their own when the time comes. We would only highlight the difference in the speed chosen—in our case, we push for quick learning, small nuggets. In the medical world, there is less pressure on time and velocity.

Another example used in many sectors, including executive education and medicine, includes using evidence-based tools (and these evolve over time, so they must be learned continuously) to assist with day-to-day decision-making. Often, vocational professions use these.

Thus, we have asked leading practitioners what they consider to be the key topics they are facing now, and which may continue to be important, and also how they think business schools can better address these in their curriculum development. We hope that this book may be seen as an eye opener or guidebook for progressive senior executives, as well as an inspiration to leading business schools in order to create the most appropriate educational offering for the future, one that captures current challenges, covers main issues, and provides solutions. It should be noted that we have deliberately not included aspects from any business school faculty members in our sample. The reason is that we have strived to come up with a "fresh view" regarding the ways leading business schools might be going, and this view should be more mind-stretching, or so we hope. Faculty members, on the other hand, are often bound by their disciplinary expertise, grounded in the past—initial doctoral training, research, and teaching. We have thus been deliberate in attempting to avoid this "bias from the past."

In line with this, we have reviewed 70 recent books written by leading practitioners, totaling more than 15,000 pages. The choice of books has of course been subjective, although we have tried to identify a portfolio of book reviews that might yield some answers when it comes to our search for curriculum topics for the future.

To attempt to further verify our findings, we have also approached 21 senior executives and business leaders, through interviews, by asking them to provide short inputs under their own names. Our aim has been to come up with further verification regarding what could be curricular trends, or at least possible needs or requests, for the future.

We have a fairly wide assortment of perspectives, from an organizational point of view, in both the books we selected to review and the executives we chose to interview. Our aim was to be quite broad. Clearly though, it would be important to note that each of these may cover a unique angle based on whether the topic or executive is from a corporate, SME, family business, start-up, or other type of organization. Not only are the views therefore different, but also for our readers, whichever type of organization you come from will also influence the interpretation and lessons taken from our selected reviews and interviews.

We readily admit that we have been "learning as we go." The process of reviewing books and interviewing has therefore been influenced by the choices of new books to review and additional executives to interview. While we have attempted to come up with articulations of what we see as some of the main conclusions that might be drawn, at the end of each of the book's Parts, it should be stressed that there are undoubtedly other conclusions to be made. It is up to the individual reader to study the materials, however, in order to draw his/her own conclusions.

While one of the authors has been writing several books featuring business schools of the future (Lorange, 2002; 2019; 2021), these are primarily focused on management processes and institutional design issues as they relate to business schools of the future. The present book, in contrast, is focused on emerging curricular content instead.

Finally, we think it is critical to mention that accelerated learning must be out-of-the-silo and collaborative. The best learning comes from going outside one's comfort zone, from new and fresh perspectives often found in other positions or departments within a company or in other industries, countries, and systems.

Please note that all the positions and companies attributed to the executives interviewed are correct at the time of the interview (and not at the time of book publication). Some have since moved on to new positions and/or new companies, and we wish them success in their new roles. The interviews and book reviews were originally published on the Lorange Network and appear as well on Peter Lorange's own thought leadership website (www.peterlorange.com).

Both authors would like to thank all of the authors who contributed to this manuscript, as well as all the reviewed book authors and executive leaders interviewed for their inspirational thought leadership. We are deeply grateful for your time and contributions.

We wish to thank Lizzie Schwegler-Ellis for her tremendous assistance. We are also grateful to Jim Ellert and Jean-François Manzoni for their inspiring input, and finally heartfelt appreciation to the team at Springer and Prashanth Mahagaonkar for the constructive feedback and their publishing wizardry.

Face your future! Enjoy the run! Win your race!

Zurich, Switzerland Peter Lorange
Lausanne, Switzerland Karin Mugnaini
September 2023

Contents

1	**Prelude**	1
	The Modern Business School Might Be Seen as a Development Platform	3
	The Program Offerings	3
	Marketing in a Business school's Network	4
	Emerging Structural Changes when it Comes to Program Offerings (Structure of the Apps): More Modulization	4
	Combining Job Career and Studies	5
	"Freshness" of Content ("up-to-datedness" of Apps)	6

Part I Political and World Affairs: Where We Are Today

2	**Practice Insights from Jan Peter Balkenende Former Prime Minister, External Senior Advisor to EY**	11
3	**Introduction to Political and World Issues: Where We Are Today**	15
4	**Essential Books to Learn About Political and World Issues: Where We Are Today**	19
	Bill Browder, (2015), Red Notice, Simon & Schuster (Reviewed March 2022)	19

John Plender, (2016), Capitalism: Money, Morals and Markets, Biteback Publishing (Reviewed February 2022)   22
James Breiding, (2019), Too Small to Fail, Harper Collins, (Reviewed January 2020)   24
Andrew McAfee, (2020), More from Less, Simon & Schuster (Reviewed November 2019)   27
Bill McKibbon, (2020), Falter, Henry Holt & Company (Reviewed May 2019)   30
Javier Blas and Jack Farchy, (2021), The World for Sale, Penguin Random House (Reviewed July 2021)   32
Nicholas Wapshott, (2021), Samuelson Friedman: The Battle over the Free Market (Reviewed March 2022)   36
Bill Browder, (2022), Freezing Order, Simon & Schuster (Reviewed May 2022)   39

5 Closing Remarks for the Part   43

Part II Adapting the Firm's Strategy to the External Environment: Getting Started

6 Practice Insights from Risto Siilasmaa, Chairman, F-Secure   47

7 Introduction on Adapting the Firm's Strategy to the External Environment: Getting Started   49

8 Essential Books to Learn about Adapting the Firm's Strategy to the External Environment; Getting Started   51
Michele Gelfand, (2018), Rule Makers, Rule Breakers, Simon & Schuster (Reviewed April 2021)   51
Steven Pinker, (2018), Enlightenment Now: The Case for Reason, Science, Humanism and Progress, Allen Lane (Reviewed November 2018)   54
Hans Rosling (2018), Factfulness, Sceptre (Reviewed August 2018)   56
Tara Westover, (2018), Educated, Penguin Random House (Reviewed February 2020)   58
Muhammad Yunus, (2018), A World of Three Zeros: A World of Social Engagement, Public Affairs (Reviewed December 2017)   60

Andrew Hill, (2019), Ruskinland: How John Ruskin Shapes our World, Pallas Athene (reviewed September 2020)	61
Risto Siilasmaa, (2019), Transforming Nokia: The Power of Paranoid Optimism to Head through Colossal Changes, McGraw Hill (Reviewed in October 2022)	64
Howard Thomas and Yuva Hedrick-Wong, (2019), Inclusive Growth, Emerald (reviewed May 2020)	67
Peder Anker, (2020), The Power of the Periphery, Cambridge University Press (Reviewed August 2021)	70
Klaus Schwab and Thierry Malleret, (2020), Covid-19: The Great Reset, Agentur (August 2021)	74
Ian Bremmer, (2022), The Power of Crisis: How Three Threats—And our Response—Will Change the World, Simon & Schuster (Reviewed June 2022)	77
Yascha Mounk, (2022), The Great Experiment, Penguin Random House (Reviewed May 2022)	79

9 Executive Profiles of Business Leaders 85
Jan Egeland, Secretary General of the Norwegian Rescue Council (NRC) (Interviewed April 2019) 85
Klaus Wellershoff, Chairman Wellershof and Partners (Interviewed January 2019) 89

10 Closing Remarks for the Part 93

Part III The Business: Your Company

11 Practice Insights from Hermann Simon, Founder and Honorary Chairman, Simon-Kucher & Partners Strategy and Marketing Consultants 99

12 Introduction to the Business: Your Company 101

13 Essential Books to Learn About the Business; your Company 103
Eyal Nir, (2014), Hooked: How to Build Habit-Forming Products, Redline (Reviewed March 2020) 103

Robbie Kellman Baxter, (2015), The Membership Economy, McGraw Hill (Reviewed March 2020) — 105
Anil Sethi, (2016), From Science to Start-up, Springer (Reviewed April 2021) — 108
Anne Janzer, (2017), Subscription Marketing: Strategies for Nurturing Customers in a World of Churn, Cuesta Park Consulting (Reviewed June 2020) — 112
John Carreyrou, (2018), Bad Blood: Secrets and Lies in a Silicon Valley Start-up, Alfred A. Knopf (Reviewed June 2022) — 114
Frank Lavin, (2021), The Smart Business Guide to China E-Commerce, Independent Publishing Group (Reviewed October 2021) — 118
Paul Polman and Andrew Winston, (2021), *Net Positive: How Courageous Companies Thrive*, Harvard Business Review Press (Reviewed October 2021) — 122
Ali Tamaseb, (2021), Super Founders: What Data Reveals about Billion-Dollar Start-ups, Redline (Reviewed August 2021) — 125

14 Executive Profiles of Business Leaders — 131
Hermann Simon, Founder and Honorary Chairman, Simon-Kucher & Partners, Hidden Champions, Presentation Given at the WHU Family Business Conference (September 2019) — 131
Markus Laenzlinger, CEO Migrolino (Interviewed April 2020) — 134
Kristian Jebsen, CEO Gearbulk (Interviewed January 2019) — 137

15 Closing Remarks for the Chapter — 143

Part IV Strategic Options: Strategy Means Choice

16 Practice Insights from Björn Rosengren, President and CEO, ABB — 147
Where We Come From: The Matrix! — 147
Creating an Entrepreneurial Culture: Through Accountability, Transparency, and Speed — 148
Driving Performance in a Decentralized Business Model — 148
The "Glue" that Holds ABB Together — 149

17	Introduction to Strategic Options: Strategy Means Choice	151
18	**Essential Books to Learn About Strategic Options; Strategy Means Choice**	153
	Reid Hoffman and Chris Yeh, (2018), Blitzscaling, Penguin Random House (Reviewed May 2021)	153
	David Epstein (2019), Range: How Generalists Triumph in a Specialist World, Penguin Random House (Reviewed March 2020)	157
	Patrick Flesner, (2021), Fastscaling, Self-Published (Reviewed September 2021)	160
	Reid Hoffman, June Cohen and Deron Triff, (2021), Masters of Scale, Penguin Random House (Reviewed October 2021)	163
	Ro Khanna, (2022), Dignity in a Digital Age: Making Tech Work for All of Us, Simon & Schuster (Reviewed March 2022)	168
	Shameen Prashantham, (2022), Gorillas Can Dance, Wiley (Reviewed March 2022)	171
19	**Executive Profiles of Business Leaders**	175
	Mirjam Staub-Bisang, Head of BlackRock Switzerland, (Interviewed November 2020)	175
	Oliver Blume, CEO Porsche AG (Interviewed December 2020)	178
	Jan Jenisch, CEO Holcim (Interviewed September 2020)	182
	Morten Hannesbo, Former CEO AMAG Group AG (Interviewed February 2019)	186
20	Closing Remarks for the Part	191

Part V The Family Business: An Inspiring Source

21	Practice Insights from Dennis Jaffe, Senior Research Fellow, BanyanGlobal Family Business Advisors	195
22	Introduction to Family Business: An Inspiring Source	199

23	**Essential Books to Learn About the Family Business: An Inspiring Source**	201
	Roy Williams and Vic Pressier, (2010), Preparing Heirs, Robert Reed (Reviewed June 2019)	201
	Joachim Schwass and Anne-Catrin Glemser, (2016), Wise Family Business, Springer (February 2017)	203
	Tom McCullough & Keith Whitaker (2018), Wealth of Wisdom: The Top 50 Questions Wealthy Families Ask, Wiley (Reviewed April 2019)	205
	Paul Hokemeyer, (2019), Fragile Power, Hazelden (Reviewed March 2020)	206
	Philippe J. Weil, (2019), Woes of the Rich, Self-published (Reviewed April 2020)	208
	Melissa Mitchell-Blitch (2020), In the Company of Family: How to Thrive when Business Is Personal, Eredita Consulting LLC (Reviewed April 2021)	210
	Josh Baron & Rob Lachenauer, (2021), Family Business Handbook, Harvard Business Review Press (Reviewed February 2022)	211
	Amy Hart Clyne and Dennis Jaffe, (2021), Finding Her Voice and Creating Legacy, Pitcairn (Reviewed January 2022)	214
	Mitzi Perdue, (2021), The Frank Perdue Way: Simple Steps. Super Success, Tremendous (Reviewed December 2021)	218
	Tom A. Rüsen, Heiko Kleve & Arist von Schlippe, (2021), Managing Business Family Dynasties, Springer (Reviewed December 2021)	220
24	**Executive Profiles of Business Leaders**	225
	Carole Hübscher, President Caran d'Ache (Interviewed April 2020)	225
	Carl Elsener, CEO of Victorinox (Interviewed May 2019)	229
25	**Closing Remarks for the Part**	233

Part VI Investing to Maximize Wealth: Value Creation and Growth

26	**Practice Insights from Anders Endreson and Peter Lorange**	237

27	Introduction to Investing to Maximize Wealth: Value Creation and Growth	243
28	Essential Books to Learn About Investing to Maximize Wealth: Value Creation and Growth	245
	Max Gunther, (1985), The Zürich Axioms, Harriman Classics (Reviewed January 2022)	245
	David F. Svensen (2005), Unconventional Success: A Fundamental Approach, Simon & Schuster (Reviewed September 2021)	247
	Mohnish Pabrai (2007), The Dhandho Investor, Wiley (Reviewed September 2021)	249
	Joel Greenblatt (2010), The Little Book that Still Beats the Market, Wiley (Reviewed October 2021)	251
	Guy Spier, (2014), The Education of a Value Investor, MacMillan Education (Reviewed October 2018)	254
	Jacob Goldstein, (2021), Money: From Bronze to Bitcoin, Atlantic (Reviewed July 2022)	255
	William Green, (2021), Richer, Wiser, Happier, Simon & Schuster (Reviewed July 2021)	259
	Peter Lorange, (2021), Reinventing the Family Firm, IMD (Reviewed December 2021)	261
29	Executive Profiles of Business Leaders	273
	Martin Stadler, CEO of Altoo (Interviewed May 2020)	273
	Alisée de Tonnac, Cofounder and Managing Partner, Seedstars Group (Interviewed October 2019)	276
	Brigitte Baumann, Founder and co-CEO of GoBeyond Investing (Interviewed June 2020)	282
	Thomas Dübendorfer, President, SICTIC (Interviewed December 2020)	287
	Urs Wietlisbach, Cofounder of Partners Group (Interviewed April 2019)	293
30	Closing Remarks for the Part	297

Part VII Leading the Organization: Towards Fulfilling the Mission

31 Practice Insights from Mitzi Perdue, Entrepreneur & Author — 301

32 Introduction to Leading the Organization: Towards Fulfilling the Mission — 303

33 Essential Books to Learn About Leading the Organization: Towards Fulfilling the Mission — 307

Daniel James Brown, (2013), The Boys in the Boat, Penguin Random House (Reviewed November 2019) — 307

Yvon Chouinard, (2016), Let My People Go Surfing, Penguin Random House (Reviewed May 2019) — 310

Ray Dalio, (2017), Principles, Simon & Schuster (Reviewed November 2017) — 312

Satya Nadella, (2017), Hit Refresh, Harper Business (Reviewed March 2018) — 313

Sam Zell, (2017), Am I Being too Subtle? Straight Talk from a Business Rebel, Portfolio (Reviewed April 2018) — 316

Steven Johnson, (2018), Farsighted: How We Make the Decisions That Matter the Most, Hodder & Stoughton (Reviewed August 2019) — 317

Stephen A. Schwarzman, (2019), What It Takes, Simon & Schuster (Reviewed November 2019) — 319

Eric Schmidt, Jonathan Rosenburg and Alan Eagle, (2020), Trillion Dollar Coach, Hodder & Stoughton (Reviewed June 2019) — 322

Dorie Clark, (2021), The Long Game, Harvard Business Review Press (Reviewed November 2021) — 324

Oleg Konovalov, (2021), The Vision Code: How to Create and Execute a Compelling Vision, Wiley (Reviewed October 2021) — 326

Jim Mattis & Bing West, (2021), Call Sign Chaos, Penguin Random House (Reviewed October 2019) — 329

Carolyn Dewar, Scott Keller, Vikram Malhotra, (2022), CEO Excellence, Simon & Schuster (May 2022) — 333

David Gergen, (2022), Hearts Touched with Fire: How Great Leaders are Made, Simon & Schuster (Reviewed July 2022) — 341

Gideon Rachman, (2022), The Age of the Strongman: How the Cult of the Leader Threatens Democracy Around the World, Bodley Head (Reviewed July 2022) — 343

34	**Executive Profiles of Business Leaders**	347
	Joël Mesot, President, ETH Zürich (Interviewed March 2020 and June 2023)	347
	Laurent Freixe, EVP Nestlé, CEO Zone Americas; Global Youth Initiative Program (Interviewed March 2019)	353
	Peter Brabeck-Letmathe, Chairman Emeritus Nestlé (Interviewed February 2019)	357
	Gillian Tett, Senior Editor, US, Financial Times (Interviewed November 2022)	361
	Conclusion	364
	Annika Falkengren, Managing Partner, Lombard Odier Group (Interviewed January 2022)	364
	Long-Term Focus	364
	People Focus and Clear Values	364
	Knowledge Bases	365
	Sustainability	365
35	**Closing Remarks for the Part**	367

Part VIII Leadership and Self: Now to You

36	**Practice Insights from Peter Brabeck-Letmathe, Chairman Emeritus, Nestlé Group**	371
37	**Introduction to Leadership and Self: Now to You**	375
38	**Essential Books to Learn about Leadership and Self: Now to You**	377
	Warren Berger, (2016), A more Beautiful Question: The Power of Inquiry, Bloomsbury Trade (reviewed March 2020)	377
	William MacAskill, (2016), Doing Good Better: Effective Altruism, Avery (reviewed October 2019)	379
	Petter A. Stordalen, (2019), Endelig Mandag (Finally Monday), Pilar (reviewed January 2020)	381
	Erling Kagge, (2021), The Philosophy of an Explorer, Penguin Random House (reviewed June 2022)	383
39	**Closing Remarks to the Part**	387

Part IX Conclusions

40 Practice Insights from Arnoud De Meyer, PBM, Business Academic at Lee Kong Chian School of Business, Singapore Management University — 391
How to Steer Universities and Business Schools Through Turbulent Times — 391

41 Conclusions on Accelerated Learning for Business Success — 395

References — 401

1

Prelude

This book has one main mission encompassing two primary purposes. Starting with the mission: the authors have assessed a need to help leaders to adopt, adapt, and align with the future. As the readers will quickly see from the start of the book, the overall picture of the world at hand is one of polycrisis. And as a consequence of the ongoing onslaught of multiple crises after crises, readers today may benefit from guidance. Modestly, alone we cannot be this guide, but rather we turn to business practitioners and educational establishments to help one another to understand how best to learn, in order to be able to adopt new knowledge and insights, to then better adapt to continuous change, and to more smoothly and strongly align to the future.

The first purpose is to offer general and practical support to students and participants at modern business schools or elsewhere who are keen to receive a faster but still cutting-edge and firsthand input from various authors and business thought leaders, perhaps different to those they may have been exposed to in their previous learning experiences. The typical modern business school differs from what might have often been seen as traditional in at least six radically different ways. These are the modern business school as a development platform, program offerings, marketing in a network, modulization, combining career and studies, and content freshness (discussed later in this introduction). And this book, a collection of 70 short book reviews, as well as 21 interviews with senior leaders, can complement the programs that students are following at such contemporary, future-oriented institutions.

The second reason is to highlight to all readers the importance of using short, simple summaries of often complex business ideas, principles, frameworks, or cases. There is something to be said about the power of simplicity.

Keeping oneself informed through brief nuggets of material can easily be worked into any busy daily or weekly routine. Such streamlined book reviews and interviews can serve to expand understanding and allow us to make an important comment regarding where "cutting-edge" new ideas often seem to be published. Who are the publishers of these types of books, with delineations of truly novel strategic concepts? Perhaps surprisingly, many of the books to be reviewed are published by less well-known authors and firms rather than by more well-known publishers and authors. Many breakthrough ideas seem to originate from relatively lesser-known individuals. The above observations do not of course always reflect the reality, however, but nevertheless, it should be made clear that to choose relevant authors and publishers has been quite demanding, perhaps more so when it comes to compiling more "normal" anthologies. Another observation may be that the selection we have made, both in terms of interviewees and book authors, tend to be highly specialized individuals with deep knowledge in their area or sector and with clear ideas about today's main challenges and relevant business topics. It seems that gone are the days of broad generalists.

While this book does not pretend to be confluent with the specific strategy of any concrete business school among today's leading ones, it should be no surprise that the International Institute for Management Development (IMD) in Lausanne is top of mind when it comes to both the book's reason for being and its structure. Both of the two editors are quite familiar with this institution. IMD has recognized the importance of shorter-term programs (i.e., 2–3 days, 5 days, a couple of weeks, etc.) both on campus and online. Its fairly recent launch of "Sprint" programs is a perfect example of its ability to bring even more learning efficiency into business education, as well as the concept of speed into learning. IMD Sprints allow students to refresh and upskill with the latest business concepts and tools, with top professors who have distilled the solutions to business challenges into condensed, accelerated learning, helping participants to acquire critical knowledge and skills with minimal disruption. These can be combined well and easily with any other learning programs. So, in one way, this book aims to highlight how one can sprint or accelerate through a diverse set of readings to support business learning in a "reader-friendly" way.

The book is organized into eight sections, which we call Parts, each with some relevant input from a leading executive in this given area placed at the beginning of the particular section. There are also introductory comments from us about the section topic, as well as on each book review and executive interview. At the end of each section, we conclude with summaries of the main business factors presented.

Let us once more briefly focus on each of the six strategic dimensions that we consider to be central for modern business schools.

The Modern Business School Might Be Seen as a Development Platform

In this case, a development platform is the collection of professors and staff at the business school, interacting with the students/participants. A development platform is more comprehensive when it comes to generating new knowledge than the more conventional types of platforms commonly considered: cost value, experience value, or platform value platforms (see Wade, Bonnet, Yokoi & Obwegeser, 2021). For such a platform to function, it needs to be supported by the so-called sensors. Such sensors might stimulate those in the platform to consider new trends and thoughts. The various reviews provided in this book and the executive interviews offer examples of such new concepts and ideas, indeed important sensors. Additionally, the forewords are also sensors.

There are also specific applications, commonly labeled *apps*. Various programs offered at a given business school are examples of such apps. These may typically also drive specific new research output. Noteworthy, though, is that not all apps have to be software programs as such. What is important is the recognition that there is emphasis to perform a specific function directly for the user. And as in the smartphone world of apps, these must be customer-oriented in terms of need and practicality and, of course, user-friendly (very easy to use!).

Modern business schools are indeed networks. The network strategy that is being pursued might be described as incorporating the three interrelated dimensions just alluded to, i.e., being a (development) platform, with sensors and apps (see Wade et al., 2021).

The Program Offerings

These tend to be relatively more condensed, shorter programs, also often more specialized than general, as typically was the case in the past, and often consisting of a combination of virtual e-learning occasions (online, either live and/or streamed, or replayed) and physical get-togethers, for face-to-face discussions among students and professors. A high degree of intensity characterizes this.

Marketing in a Business school's Network

Participants might typically be seen as members in a business school's network. They interact with the development platform. There is therefore a more direct relationship between students/participants and the business school. This relationship is focused on marketing rather than transactional marketing. Participants typically look for support when it comes to their longer-term managerial development, for example, critical knowledge to grow or scale their start-up, compile their board, or to seek investors, for instance. They may be looking for relevant program offerings (apps) being offered to them on an ongoing basis. Thus, each member in the network (student/participant) might rely on a given business school in a different way than in the past when it comes to the fulfillment of his/her lifelong learning needs. The given business school may attempt to develop a series of program offerings (apps) that meet this need, usually to be attended over time. Sensors, to pick up on emerging needs, sometimes even pain points, are thus of critical importance.

While business schools have always had their groups of alumni, the network strategy that now emerges represents something more active, with relatively much closer, multidirectional relationships between the platform, with its apps, and students/participants. In the most efficient networks, participants and business schools are connected, linked, sharing, engaged, and communicative. We are truly in a new era of education.

Emerging Structural Changes when it Comes to Program Offerings (Structure of the Apps): More Modulization

As discussed in the program offerings above, the educational offerings tend to be relatively shorter than before, being a mix of virtual, distance learning, and physical get-togethers, and are typically more intensive as well. Such offerings might be "combined" into longer programs, such as an EMBA or a diploma of Digital Strategic Transformation. These programs are commonly characterized by a high degree of flexibility regarding which modules to include in a given longer offering and in what sequence to take various modules. There may also be an "organic" element present, in the sense that programs initially taken can at times lead to unexpected yet opportunistic options for later learning. For example, a student initially choosing a Board program can then go on to an EMBA for a more comprehensive experience, followed by specific, more narrowly defined programs such as Leadership in Networks, Sustainability, or, say, Finance with a cryptocurrency focus. In one way, therefore, modulization can continue long term and be highly personalized.

More structured classical offerings, such as many MBA programs, may normally not lend themselves to becoming modularized and to stimulate such learning journeys. We might perhaps therefore expect a relative demise or total transformation of classical MBA program offerings, with a relative increase in dynamic EMBA program offerings instead. It is the editors' overall assessment that dynamic changes in our business world are triggering a similar dynamism in business education. This is seen as a positive phenomenon.

Combining Job Career and Studies

Many students/participants today might not be prepared to give up their jobs to enroll in full-time study positions. There may be several reasons for this—economic, career related, and/or family. Many such students/participants, though, could be prepared to combine studies with their job, say, through studying virtually from home, often combined with physical learning sessions over a few days, on weekends and/or vacation periods.

Convenience is a key factor when it comes to making and implementing this emerging way of learning, particularly when it comes to where physical gatherings for learning are to be held. Locations near major airports, for instance, rather than at more remote conventional campuses seem to be a trend. Also increasing in popularity are study or discovery tours entailing learning abroad, with multiple company and factory visits in cities away from the campus and/or student's home base. Another recent and highly creative example is "speed-dating" type programs where professors from business and academia are matched to students and/or a program, come in for highly intensive and extremely short learnings. Formal and continuous mentors or educational coaches are also additional examples of growing stimulants to modern learning.

Also, combining job career and studies can, in some institutions, also be applied to the professors who may run multiple programs and consult at the same time as they research, publish, teach, advise, and at times also "work," invest, or manage a company on the side. In summary, both students and professors are now increasingly able to work while learning, or learn while working.

"Freshness" of Content ("up-to-datedness" of Apps)

There seems to be a clear acceleration of many things. Physical features are changing faster and faster (for example, from conventional gas-driven automobiles to electric cars to self-driving cars), or technologies (i.e., from 3G or 4G to 5G networks, the artificial intelligence chatbot ChatGPT). Knowledge of how to manage our businesses is also evolving, typically through specific phases, and at a more rapid pace than ever. Business books, for instance, frequently have to have been published relatively recently so as to realistically reflect such emerging cutting-edge trends (it is no longer uncommon to have new editions a couple of times a year or frequent updates available online in the case of e-books). Another proof of content freshness is the increasing numbers of blogs, newsletters, whitepapers, reports, links, and apps that get released and "refreshed" constantly, not to exclude the often daily posts, tweets, and commentaries shared online by thought leaders and other content providers. "Day old bread" is no longer a bargain nor an interesting offer: content can only be up to date!

Executives now run firms that tend to be rapidly transitioning—hence, what executives might see as cutting-edge today may be "old hat" a few years from now and, in some industries, even a few months or weeks from now (in the tech areas, the pace of change can evenly be daily). Professors too shall have to deeply commit to doing research in their fields of specialization, as well as nurture their own networks of business contacts (real-world!), so as to be able to stay on top of things, constantly! They must, however, be more open-minded, more agile, and less silo oriented than ever before in order to pick up on emerging best practices from students/participants as well as from other leaders. The business school development platform might become more and more similar to "fresh produce" in a grocery store, with a limited life span only, or a financial market's trading floor (high speed, quick exchanges, and constant back-and-forth). As argued, the roles of key actors tend to change. For many professors in particular, perhaps, such changes might become particularly dramatic. Classical, in-depth disciplinary competences, while still important, shall now become relatively less dominant. Those professors who are less able to cope with this shift (for many, rather a serious "transformation") might increasingly risk becoming obsolete. Some business schools are indeed fast becoming outdated, none-the-least due to this phenomenon.

Finally, as we near the end of this prelude Part, let us bring up two issues that readers might keep in mind when it comes to combing through this book.

First, while we have always attempted to review books that we judged relevant to our topic, we readily admit that, through reviewing 70 books, ploughing through some 15,000 pages, clarity comes to us only gradually, over time. We have gained insight as we go, one might say. A similar argument shall be made when it comes to 21 interviews with the various executives that we have undertaken. More clarity came gradually as we went through the interviewing. This is also what happens in the learning model we discuss in this work—namely, that exposure to something does not always automatically and instantaneously yield comprehension or realization. Instead, learning absorption may take time too.

Second, while we have attempted to highlight some implications for leaders when it comes to the conclusions this book might have to offer, we make no claim that these attempts at synthesis available at the end of each Part are exhaustive. There are clearly additional implications that our readers may come up with on their own. Given the incremental nature of this book's development, this is indeed not a surprise!

The structure of this book, as already alluded to, has been organized into eight distinctive sections. The first, Part two, discusses political and world issues in general. Increasingly, we seem to be living in a world characterized by rapid change, even turbulence—politically, technologically, socially, ecologically, …. We all now talk of VUCA, Warren Bennis and Burt Nanus's leadership theory from 1985 volatility, uncertainty, complexity and ambiguity—as our current reality. Part three covers how organizations may adapt their strategy to the external environment.

Part four addresses business overall, and Part five addresses the firm's strategic options and how these may evolve. From where to where has business strategy developed? The sixth part of this book then discusses how these business strategy trends apply to a family business setting. We have argued elsewhere that family businesses often might find themselves to be in better positions than publicly traded firms when it comes to adopting long-term horizons. It thus becomes important to look at the specific ways that such family firms invest to maximize their shareholder values and to be able to learn from them. This is covered in Part seven.

In the end, much comes down to the main characteristics of the leader(s) in charge of a business. What matters? These issues above all shall be dealt with in Parts eight and nine.

Have a good "journey"!

Part I

Political and World Affairs: Where We Are Today

There is nothing permanent except change.
—Heraclitus, Greek philosopher

Without order, nothing can exist. Without chaos, nothing can evolve.
—Oscar Wilde, Irish poet

2

Practice Insights from Jan Peter Balkenende, Former Prime Minister, External Senior Advisor to EY

Challenging world issues for business leaders: Responsibility, responsibility, and responsibility!

Business leaders have to play a key role in today's world challenges, and they have to act! In a world in which autocrats are busy with national or even purely personal interests, democracies are losing trust among people, many societal issues are not being solved and coherent future strategies are failing, business leaders play a vital role to build a better future for all. This means the time of "business as usual" is over and fundamental new orientations are required. Let me mention three important aspects.

- The implementation of the global agenda is key. If we really want to achieve a world wherein no one will be left behind and where the goal is to improve the quality of life for everyone, we must implement the UN Sustainable Development Goals. The key question is: Are we able to realize these goals in 2030? The answer today is clear: no, not all. And even worse, circumstances are deteriorating. After the time of COVID-19, we are confronted with a totally unjustified and illegal war of Russia in Ukraine, with terrible consequences for the people in Ukraine and elsewhere, with huge implications for food supply in poorer regions in Africa and with horrible effects on energy supply, energy prices, and inflation especially in Europe. This also shows the UN seems to be powerless. Too many countries, although not supporting Russia, leave room for terrible Russian aggression—killing, raping, and destroying—instead of stopping these attacks on humanity. The UN is confronted with losing credibility and trust. The big issues of today and tomorrow—climate change and its immense consequences, worrying scarcity of natural resources and materials and the enormous risks of inequality—require, however, the opposite: a meaningful and highly relevant UN. We are running out of time in the implementation of the SDGs. When the world started in 2015 with the SDGs, the then UN Secretary-General Ban Ki-moon stated that the SDGs will never be realized without the private sector. He was right. Business leaders are extremely important to realize the global agenda, in the interest of our planet—"Our Common Home"—and of future generations. They have a huge responsibility.

- Bridging the gap between sustainable business intentions and traditional, short-term business measurement practices. A lively debate is taking place throughout the world about the future of market economies and capitalism and about reorienting business models. The Belgian historian Jonathan Holslag was very clear in his book *World Politics since 1989*: The West has failed in 30 years' time to build up a real sustainable and inclusive economy. Too much self-interest and too much inequality. More and more people do understand that a fundamental reorientation of the organization of economies is necessary. For that reason, it is understandable that the current debate is about stakeholder, progressive, moral, conscious, responsible, and inclusive capitalism. Different orientations but with three common elements: choose for long-term orientations instead of short-termism, serve all stakeholders and not only the shareholders and realize a much better balance between economic, social, and ecological interests. Professor Rangan of Insead mentions three shifts in this regard: from output to outcome, from minimum means to minimum harm and from competence to character (care, commitment, and courage). Other works, such as the report on the future of market economies in Europe for generations to come, to be published in the first half of 2023 by Professor Buijs, also discuss the new required market environment to withstand today's global challenges. There is a debate about economic growth, the quality of growth, and de-growth. Read books such as *The value of everything* by Mariana Mazzucato or *Doughnut Economics* by Kate Raworth. The focus on growth as a goal in itself is under attack. Stop ignoring externalities. These orientations are clearly connected with the reorientation of business models. Sustainability and the SDGs should be fully integrated into business models. Rethink business activities, purposes, and goals. That is the message of people such as Paul Polman (in his and Andrew Winston's book *Net Positive*), Professors Robert Eccles, Michael Porter, Mahendra Chouhan, Mervyn King, and many others and of organizations such as UN Global Compact, OECD, World Business Council for Sustainable Development, the Dutch Sustainable Growth Coalition, and more. Against this background of changing realities for market economies, businesses, and business leaders, it is key to be aware of the tension between new orientations and old-fashioned business practices. People are advocating long-term value creation, but business measurement is predominantly focused on short-termism, quarterly results, turnover, profits, and cost-saving measures. ESG is on the agenda, but much has to be done regarding concrete implementation. Fortunately, there is progress as well: Integrated reporting is becoming more and more essential, and in the European context, the Corporate Sustainability Reporting Directive (CSRD) and other EU instruments will have great influence on companies, just to mention some important examples. Business leaders should be agents for change, with another mind set, with new views on creativity and societal engagement, with redefining economic, social, and ecological success, and this means much more than only compliance. Game changers will be the winners of tomorrow. All this is about a changing world for business leaders and their responsibility.

- Values—no matter we are talking about the global agenda, redefining capitalism or reorientation of business models—are always key. The fundamental issues of today and tomorrow such as climate change, the circular economy or combatting inequality are not just matters of technique, policy proposals and new measurement tools. These issues are predominantly moral issues. In which world do we want to live, are we taking care of the most vulnerable people, what about our responsibility towards younger and future generations? The golden rule of treat others like you want to be treated by others can be found in almost all religions. Mahatma Gandhi was very clear when he said: The best way to find yourself is to lose yourself in the service of others. Pope Frances made very important remarks in his Encyclical *Laudato Si'* about taking care of our planet, "Our Common Home," and people who suffer. You never can be successful in a world that fails, in the words of the Dutch business leader Feike Sijbesma. Therefore, values are so important: human dignity, human rights, solidarity, freedom, stewardship, justice, and responsibility. It is remarkable that there is so much attention for the purpose of organizations, their values, the Why-question. The Noble Prize Winner Professor Jean Tirole wrote a book with the title *Economics for the Common Good*. The Dutch economist Professor Lans Bovenberg is convinced that the economy should not be about transactions but about relations. The founder of modern economic thought Adam Smith underlined the connection between the invisible hand and moral sentiments. Also, business leaders have to rethink their own position and their own strategies. Take into account new views such as expressed by Paul Hawken in his book *Regeneration. Ending the climate crisis in one generation* or listen to critical voices in *The Climate Book* created by Greta Thunberg. Business leaders have to understand their moral responsibility, not only in good statements but especially in new business practices. In my opinion, business leaders should read and practice Professor Rob van Tulder and Dr. Eveline van Mil's *Principles of Sustainable Business. Frameworks for Corporate Action on the SDGs*. Guidance by values among business leaders is an expression of responsibility.

One of my favorite books is *Why Nations Fail* of Professors Acemoglu and Robinson. Success of nations depends on three key factors: innovation, the rule of law and the necessity of having inclusive institutions. People must be able to share in the revenues of economic well-being and not just the elites. There is no future for business leaders if they do not contribute to finding solutions for the global challenges of today and tomorrow. Instead, business leaders can make the difference when they change fundamentally: from value based to values based, from short-termism to long-term value creation and from economic and financial self-interest to the will to really serve society. These leaders have a world to win, just by being and acting responsibly.

3

Introduction to Political and World Issues: Where We Are Today

The socio-, geo-, and political contexts in which the firm finds itself shall always evolve. World affairs will tend to change, often dramatically and at a rapid pace. The COVID-19 pandemic and the Ukrainian war are just two examples. So, how do we deal with such events? How do we make sure to observe, analyze, react, sometimes even predict or foresee these types of changes, in order to be sure that we might withstand and perhaps even "master" this type of change? In this Part, we shall simply observe current world and political events and trends.

First, a short explanation about why and how we have chosen to start with this broad topic and work our way, throughout the book, "inward" so to speak. In other words, it made sense to us, based on conversations, readings and interviews, that we first examine the external environment in its broadest sense—the world in which we are living (Parts 2 and 3, Political and World Affairs, Adapting the Firm's Strategy to the External Environment), and then work to the business (Parts 4 and 5, The Business, Strategic Options), then the family business as one inspiring example (Parts 6 and 7, The Family Business, Investing to Maximize Wealth, this section showing how to build, grow, and preserve value and wealth), the organization (Part 8, Leading the Organization) and then the leader (Part 9, Leadership and Self). This may not come as a surprise, since professions from business to psychology often start with a big picture look and analysis, or the "outside" to "inside," in order to be able to move to more detail and more personal. Getting an accurate picture of the situation allows us as leaders to make sound observations and consequently changes and improvements to further growth. With this structure to our book, we hope to open up exciting learning opportunities for our readers.

As an example of a present political and world issue, the current war between Russia and Ukraine at the time of the writing of this book represents an unfortunate case, with severe business ramifications impacting most of us and our companies globally, regionally, and locally. The human sufferings on both sides, in this war, are of course both immense and tragic, but we shall not delve further with this at this point. Instead, let us consider some of the economic repercussions of this conflict, as examples of how an explosive, dangerous situation in one area might have ripple effects on the entire world and thus on our international business context as well. As a starter, let us consider the economic Russian boycott, which seems to have led to reductions of oil and gas exports in turn. As an immediate consequence, prices of gasoline have increased dramatically, both in the US as well as in most European countries. The shortage of gas and oil has also led to problems for the generation of electricity, with electricity prices going up in many European countries, including in traditionally electro-energy rich countries such as Norway. And, the inflation which appears to have come about has put additional strains on people and companies.

Further, the traditional export of grain, both from Ukraine as well as from Russia, has had to be drastically trimmed back, due to the now increased danger of operating out of Black Sea ports and of sailing in the Black Sea. The direct result of this has been acute shortages of food, coupled with significant price increases in many countries, perhaps particularly alarming when it comes to regions in the Middle East and Africa. The continued effects of these price increases, driven by shortages and all of these disruptions traceable back to the adverse political events in Ukraine, do, of course, further add to the increased inflation pressure. This has in turn has led to higher interest rates in many countries. There are also other effects, such as on freight rates for ships and transportation, as well as for the acceleration of the installation of equipment for alternative types of energy generation. We might go on and on listing such secondary and tertiary effects.

Let us, however, stop here. What suffices to stress in the fact that most industries have faced disruption, directly for those companies operating in the energy sector, as well as perhaps indirectly for companies in such diverse areas as manufacturing of fertilizers (shortage of gas), shipping companies (revised routings), real estate firms (interest rates), retailers (increased prices), as well as for the general increase in uncertainty facing all firms. We see how important seemingly isolated political events can disturb our global order. Fundamental revisions of how value chains have traditionally been working, must result.

We have also identified specific business factors that are linked to the topic of this Part—world and political affairs: overall risk scenario monitoring and

3 Introduction to Political and World Issues: Where We Are Today

planning, speed of change as well as the need for speed in possibly adjusting strategy and tactics based on those changes and possible organizational configuration adjustments. Many of our readings touch upon these themes.

In the following, we shall present several books that discuss factors that may disrupt, at least surprise or possibly catch off guard, established world balance. Further, we shall see how firms may be able to adapt. Needless to say, business schools face large challenges to adequately respond to all of this.

Here are some takeaways that you might expect from this Part:

1. How to reach compromises? How to develop a willingness to settle, so that there might be a "win-win"?
2. There may be one or several environmental "crises": ("pollution, air, oceans, beaches, rain forests…"). How might one come up with ways to ameliorate these? I.e., "progress in the small" rather than seeking unrealistic "global" solutions?
3. Social conflicts often manifest themselves as focus on free markets versus regulation. How can "modern capitalism" work?

Finally, before we begin with our book reviews here, a comment about the ordering we chose. Initially and in one way, we did not wish to be locked into a specific "order" for the book reviews in each of the Parts, as well as for the order of executive interviews. Each book chosen or each executive interview shared has much to offer. And, every one of the authors or leaders have shared their own studies, observations, research or experiences in unique ways that we believe can help our understanding of today and most importantly of the future. Yet, in the end, perhaps more for conventionality, we have listed them in chronological order.

In some cases, the geographies, sectors, or experiences may be connected from book review to the next or from interview to the next. Yet, we advise our readers to not look so much for those connectors, or the "logic," but rather to be openminded and accept that we have distinctly different viewpoints that on their own can benefit our journey. Impulses, as we shall call them, may come perhaps somewhat randomly. This is also how life works. As does learning. Businesses do not always foresee what is next, nor do leaders predict tomorrow. Again, the idea of cross-functionality in thinking and in this case in how we have chosen and laid out the book reviews and interviews proves its point. Diverse topics, different perspectives and sometimes even randomness or lack of connectivity can help us thrive to become broader, more agile thinkers. Leave rules and expectations slightly behind. Openness and curiosity should take their place.

4

Essential Books to Learn About Political and World Issues: Where We Are Today

Bill Browder, (2015), Red Notice, Simon & Schuster (Reviewed March 2022)

The author was the largest foreign investor in Russia, through his investment fund Hermitage Capital, capitalizing on imperfections in the Russian economy due to non-rational, at times even illegal moves by oligarchs and members of government. When such moves became exposed, there were inevitable reactions from the Russian government, perhaps even sanctioned by Mr. Putin himself. Not only was Mr. Browder expelled from Russia, but also some of his closest allies were put in prison, some even tortured to death. Russian courts ruled against Hermitage and Mr. Browder, dishing out huge fines based on false, fabricated evidence. Lack of predictability seems to be at the center of all of this. Humiliation of those perceived as threatening is also present. There is much brutality. Mr. Putin seems to be squarely behind it all.

This book attempts to shed more light on the Russian regime, on Mr. Putin himself and the apparent psyche of the Russian elite. There seems to be a high level of organized crime in Russia, augmenting what might elsewise be assessed as "Putin's actions." It is thus probably a combination of Putin and organized crime, which are at play.

The author lived in Russia for more than a decade and was the founder and CEO of Hermitage Capital Management, the largest foreign investor in Russia for several years until 2005. He was declared a persona non grata by Russia on November 13th, 2005, and was deported from Russia. Thereafter, his so-far highly successful investment company went into a tailspin. Browder gradually became what we might label, a human rights activist. The book is "a sizzling account of Browder's rise, fall and metamorphosis from investment banker to renowned human activist" (The Economist).

The book deals with the author's "agenda," first as a successful business executive in Moscow and later as a proponent of various human rights measures in Russia, and above all the passing in the US of the so-called Sergei Magnitsky Rule of Law Accountability Act on December 14th, 2012. A similar law was also later passed by the EU parliament on April 2nd, 2014. The gist of these legislations was to deny some 20 named Russian individuals deemed to have been directly involved with the jailing and murdering of Sergei Magnitsky.

Red Notice, and the author's career. Red Notice is issued by Interpol requesting the arrest of wanted persons, with a view to extradition. An Interpol Red Notice is the closest instrument to an international arrest warrant. So, let us assess what happened to the author after December 2015, before articulating what he sees as prototypical sides of Putin's Russia. Before going further though, what prevailed after 1995 as he became an activist? His activities over the last few years have been largely focused on human activism. He has spent considerable efforts to clear the name of Sergei Magnitsky, the former head of legal at Hermitage Capital Fund. The author seems to have been "attacked" by various Russian initiatives, typically relatively ill-conceived and propaganda-driven, but nevertheless calling for responses. While the author is free to move around in North America and Western Europe, he has of course not visited Russia since 1995.

So, what seems to be a few fundamental sides to how Putin's Russia functions?

To save face. Russians seem to always look for ways to save face. President Putin especially never appears ready to back down from a fight. He simply does not want to show any sign of weakness. Still, he is known for keeping options open as long as possible. When Putin gets humiliated, he retaliates by lashing out against the person who humiliates him. Being publicly humiliated is the worst. So, for him, it is all about launching counterattack after counterattack, rather than accepting defeat. The author said about Putin, (CNN 17/3/2022) "he does not have a reverse gear, only forward ones." In those cases where Putin is forced to retreat, it is typically only temporarily so, in order for him to get time to regroup and get renewed strength so that he can attack again.

Lack of predictability of Russian Actions. As Sir Winston Churchill said as early as 1939 about Russia, then Soviet, they are "a riddle wrapped in a mystery, inside an enigma." This black hole still seems to represent the dominating reality today, with a lack of predictability and much secrecy.

Cover-ups. Denial seems to be the norm and Russian state-sponsored lying, the standard. Known for fabricating evidence, to make own actions more acceptable and according to their own logic, this made-up "proof" is often less convincing, however. There are frequent glaring inconsistencies and lies.

Protests. Putin seems to largely ignore protests, cultivating an aura of invincibility. Those who might protest tend to then be called "scum." Restrictive laws and brutal Putin-controlled police make most protests almost unheard of, anyhow.

Russian "stories," empty talk. The Russians are skilled in talking without actually saying anything. Some say that Russian stories almost never have happy endings.

Humiliation. Putin seems often try to humiliate opponents, to put them in their places. He appears to be satisfied only when an opponent has failed and is miserable.

Putin himself. He has perhaps become more and more brazen over the years. Judging him in 2002, he seems to have been quite liberal. Today, however, he looks totally changed.

Is there an end point? Perhaps not since organized crime is part of it all and is likely to continue even after Putin's departure. Mr. Putin himself may have much to gain by attempting to stay in office by hanging on to power.

Russia's system of justice. This is often violent, at times even barbaric. Rather than being based on more or less objective criteria, the legal system seems subject to largely direct manipulation by the ruling elite. White is black; up is down; etc. There are negotiations within the legal systems where neither law nor logic seems to play a role.

Putin's judgment regarding his contemplated actions. Russians may be nasty, but they are still only human. They will make mistakes, just like everybody else. One key error might be failure in realistically judging consequences of their actions.

Domestic misinformation campaign. Russia's reaction to US' enactment of the so-called Sergei Magnitsky Act is a case in point. Russian children were no longer allowed to be adopted by US foster parents. Russians at large generally have soft hearts when it comes to children, and there were considerable, unexpected domestic reactions to this, which seems to surprise the central leadership.

Sanctions. To what extent do they work? Might the cost of sanctions be so high that Putin may ultimately back down? There were sanctions imposed on Russia in the 1970s and Russian restrictions when it came to allowing Jews to emigrate. Ultimately Russia relented, and 1.5 million Jews were allowed to emigrate. The sanctions were then lifted.

Putin's view when it comes to Russia today, its geography and its role, seems to be that the ancient harmony enjoyed during the Imperial and Soviet periods should be largely re-established. The issue of how the Russian regime seems to operate to make this happen is perhaps rather complex, however, and harder to understand. This book sheds important light on this.

John Plender, (2016), Capitalism: Money, Morals and Markets, Biteback Publishing (Reviewed February 2022)

This is a well-written book from a few years ago, still highly relevant today. Above all the author addresses two inherent dilemmas concerning capitalism:

- Its unstable nature, typically driven by the following cycle: profits, speculation, then irrational exuberance, followed by stock market panic, and, finally, recession.
- Its ethics, perhaps above all regarding its reinforcement of a widening gap between boardroom and workplace rewards. Greed is indeed a key element in capitalism!

Also, the author offers an impressive set of quotes from key literature sources throughout history. This remarkable collection of scholarly quotes from relevant literature references makes the book itself a primer for viewing and understanding the history of ideas around capitalism, important for most business leaders to capture.

The book is organized into twelve chapters, each pinpointing key dilemmas that have come to be associated with modern capitalism. In chapter one, "The Root of all Evil," the author discusses various dimensions of ambivalence towards moneymaking, in a market-based capitalist system, fundamentally built on private ownership. Many leading thinkers over the decades behind us have expressed reservations. Still, the author points out that our capitalistic system, in general, has largely been successful.

In the next chapter, "Animal Spirit," the author stresses how the instinct to make money typically is a key driver for an entrepreneur. Keynes had reservations here, but Schumpeter basically liked it. Excesses, as exemplified by robber barons, does not seem to be acceptable, in the end.

"Hijacked by Bankers" is the third chapter. Here, the author discusses the basic business model for operators within this industry, lending out money that for the most belong to a bank's depositors. Regrettably, there are plenty of examples of "sloppy" lending—too risky, too "expensive," even though capital reserve requirements on banks have now been introduced: stress tests, capital reserve requirements (Basel I, II, and III), new legislations, new overseeing bodies....

In chapter four, "Industrial Shrinkage, Financial Excess," the author presents the stressful shift of going from a predominantly manufacturing-based economy to now more services, to a large extent driven by shifting financial conditions. Successful banks have indeed been profiting from supporting the shift!

"Sophisters, Economists and Calculators" is the name of chapter five. Why is it so hard to predict economic crises? Are we seeing a shift towards behavioral economics here, away from more traditional market-economy thinking?

Trade has indeed become a main driver for global economic success, covered in chapter six, "Trade and the Fatal Embrace." The author points out that trade does appear to stimulate price, as long as a basic balance is maintained among trading partners. China's recent successes, coupled with US demises, may increasingly lead to trade problems and political instability!

Chapter seven, "Speculation—the Missing Shame Game," highlights how speculations around price/market cycles may impact trade. To take advantage of such cycles is indeed important when it comes to most products and businesses central to trade, raw materials, and shipping above all: in/out, long/short.

Debt/leveraging is of course critical here, discussed in the following chapter, "The Dynamics of Debt." There is a profound ambivalence about debt imbedded in many of us. Still, to take advantage of high leverage is a principal part of capitalism, as pointed out by many leading economists, including Schumpeter. The element of speculation was associated with increased debt, and the risk of when taking on too much debt does represent a stark reality, of course. Modern rules in our capitalist system may, however, make leveraging slightly less risky.

"Gold: The 6000-Year-Long Bubble," chapter nine, is seen by many as creating a "safety," by having a counter-cyclical effect, i.e., representing value in offsetting risks of high leverage. However, there is more gold now, and it is becoming cheaper, driven by more effective mining and refining. There are many skeptics of gold, including Warren Buffett.

Another asset class that might ameliorate excessive leverage-related risk-taking is art, discussed in chapter ten, "High-Minded about Art." The proposal here seems to be that investing in prominent artists (such as Warhol, Koons, and/or Hirsch) and to store/hold these assets is rewarding! In contrast to buying art because of the personal satisfaction of "having such pieces hanging on the wall," it seems beyond doubt that art as an investment class does tend to be rather non-cyclical.

But then, there are taxes. In his chapter eleven, "Tax and the Division of the Spoils," the author discusses the redistribution effect of taxes. Many economists find this acceptable, including David Ricardo, and there are no taxes on gold or art! Taxes are, of course, needed as a means of financing the public sector. But, there are indeed global restrictions when it comes to how high a given country's taxes can be, before becoming uncompetitive! The so-called tax farming, i.e., outsourcing of tax collection to various private institutions (such as banks in Italy, until 2006) may clutter up this assessment of how to maintain a country's competitiveness.

In the final chapter, "Capitalism, Warts and All," the author summarizes the key arguments of the book in a brilliant way: He points out that the inherent challenge of economic instability associated with capitalism is still with us. And, key ethical conundrums are still present, such as increased income differentials and underinvestment in a cleaner/safer environment. However, despite all of these dilemmas, capitalism is indeed the best system we have.

This is an impressive and clear book and timely when it comes to many dilemmas associated with capitalism. Above all, the book reflects insightfulness! Complex issues are dealt with in a way that most readers can understand! And, as an "extra bonus," the many quotes from earlier generations of experts are illustrative of the author's raised points and are enjoyable to read!

James Breiding, (2019), Too Small to Fail, Harper Collins, (Reviewed January 2020)

Three key issues are seen as particularly critical, especially perhaps for firms that might be relatively minor and/or coming from fairly small countries: To fight dysfunctional effects from bureaucracies may be relatively easier when "smallness" defines the context; innovation and flexibility—likely so, and this seems to be the case also for enhancing responsible ownership. Smaller countries, as well as smaller firms, often outperform larger ones. The concept of "constructive destruction" is also discussed.

In his new book "Too Small to Fail: Why Some Small Nations Outperform Larger Ones and How They Are Reshaping the World," the author argues that smaller nations often do better than their larger counterparts. Many of the arguments the author puts forward may have relevance when it comes to why some smaller companies often outperform larger ones.

Smaller firms often have "less bureaucracy," "more flexibility and a strong innovation orientation," and "ownership by management ensuring skin in the game." It should be noted that the author applies these "success factors" to countries, i.e., differently than what we propose. We took the principles behind Breiding's analysis and applied them to private enterprises, based on our own experience as investors.

Bureaucracy. Both large countries and large firms can be characterized by bureaucracy, depending on established routines, standardized modes of communication, formal guidelines for decision-making, and clear delegation of responsibilities. As a result, large size entities, countries as well as firms, often experience a lack of drive that undermines their initiatives, dynamism, and speed! In such an environment, a particular behavioral style often develops: "play it safe." It may be relatively more important to avoid mistakes than to take initiative and get things done. There might be little incentive to take risks.

Here are three examples, one from the corporate sector and two from the public sector:

- Example 1: A large, diversified firm, headquartered in the US, was making a significant acquisition in Europe. The acquisition was led by the SVP Europe, who was located in Paris and had more than 10,000 persons reporting to him in the European division. There was wide media attention surrounding the acquisition. The SVP found himself on local TV several times per day, as well with the press even more frequently. When the SVP wanted to hire someone to assist him with these activities, it took a staggering nine months before he got the green light to make the hire from the US headquarters. An abundance of staff and others, with consulting powers within the firm's complex organization, had to give their consent. The result was that the dynamic European manager in the end gave up. Even worse, he eventually quit his job, and is now in charge of a small, but highly successful investment bank. He felt that all of this bureaucracy was simply too demotivating for him.
- Example 2: There is a small town on the border between France and Switzerland, with about half of the town being on each side of the border. Each side of the town has its own mayor—one for the Swiss part and another for the French. When an issue came up concerning the town on both sides of the border, the Swiss mayor was able to decide on the matter swiftly and assertively. The French mayor, in contrast, was obliged to consult with Paris. In the end, he came to the same conclusion as his Swiss

counterpart, but it took excessively longer to reach a decision. This illustrates how bureaucracy might disrupt action. It may also be evident that there is more bureaucracy in large countries such as France versus in smaller countries such as Switzerland.

- Example 3: In 2016, Mr. Trump won the US presidential election, in part based on his "cleaning up the swamp" slogan, i.e., attracting the established mode of doing business in Washington, D.C. Routines in Washington were well set, and, perhaps even more so, the decision-making bureaucrats, elected politicians as well as career professionals, seemed quite comfortable within the resulting culture with relative inaction. Regrettably, entrenched bureaucracies frequently make up the central governing bodies, in large countries and in large firms alike.

Innovation and flexibility. The underlying factors entailing innovation and flexibility appear clear: Bureaucracy does not usually go well with innovation and flexibility. But, there may be more to it. When you are small, being innovative and flexible is perhaps largely a matter of survival. On the positive side, new opportunities may be quickly explored. More innovation may come about in the smaller settings!

There is also another side to this, however. Smaller entities have to come up with innovative solutions to thwart threats. If they are not sufficiently fast and flexible, they run the risk of extinction. In his case studies of smaller countries, the author demonstrates this in a couple of ways: For example, how the educational system in Finland was relatively rapidly overhauled to allow this small country to develop a significant competitive advantage, or how the small nation of Singapore was able to implement an effective health care system in record time, while debates regarding how to deal with this issue in larger countries, such as in the US, seem to go on forever.

Responsible ownership. Another important factor in determining performance is the alignment of interests between the individual in leadership and the entity itself. This alignment is generally easier in smaller entities. Individuals in leadership positions at a small firm or in a small country often tend to take long-term perspectives. These individuals tend to invest in research and development. They build new infrastructure in their communities, even though a more short-term focus could have entailed lower taxes, thus making it easier for the politicians to be reelected.

In a large firm or country, a shorter term view is often taken. Most senior management know that they will hold their positions for relatively brief periods of time only. At large firms, the incentives are bonuses and/or stock options, values that are impacted by increased profits and/or sales. To increase profits, senior management may cut spending in research and development or in marketing. Furthermore, rather than fixing the businesses that might be dampening down performance, they might simply sell under-performing businesses. Short-term profits will thereby increase.

To further boost growth at large firms, senior management may look at increasing the rate of acquisitions, often financed through increased borrowing. Such excessive acquisition behavior could be counterproductive in the long run. What is the strategic rationale driving an acquisition?

Responsible ownership is typically more feasible in relatively smaller business entities. When it comes to larger firms, it may be hard for management to own significant parts. The capital needed to purchase a significant level of shares may also be too high. The positive effect from having significant "skin in the game" may simply not be there.

We also see a similar pattern that applies to firms in communities, where the leaders in charge of smaller communities may know that they shall typically remain part of this particular context for a long time. As a result, they usually take a long-term point of view. On the other hand, in larger communities, there may be a much weaker link, if any at all. It is easier for leaders to cut corners, and those responsible know that they will not "get caught" by their irresponsible short-termness.

So, small might tend to outperform big, true for firms as well as countries. Size, growth, profitability, and scale may no longer be as central to success. Whether we are talking about countries or firms, "small is beautiful!"

Andrew McAfee, (2020), More from Less, Simon & Schuster (Reviewed November 2019)

This book delivers a rather optimistic picture when it comes to how macro-trends are shaping, in particular the concept of man versus the nature. While most of us tend to be quite pessimistic about the possible evolution of our world, this author is optimistic. His optimism is based on an assessment that peoples' attitudes in general are changing fundamentally. People are now calling for relatively broad worldwide agreement on the reduction of greenhouse gases, acceptance of nuclear technology, current and cutting edge, protection of rare species, accelerated research efforts to better understand these issues, as well as the promotion of relevant competition, such as to create markets for CO_2 deposition.

Investments in projects that reduce our usage of Earth's natural resources, as well as those that help address climate change, are increasingly accepted by the private sector. Firms are investing more to alleviate present crisis. This is the context of the book.

Global warming and the deteriorating global climate—largely attributed to greenhouse gases emissions—have arguably become one of the most contentious policy issues in the world today. Good reasons to be concerned abound. Wildfires, for example, caused largely by extensive periods of draught, have become a severe threat. Wildfire emergencies in Australia, California, Brazil, and elsewhere are indeed very severe, with loss of human and animal life as well as the destruction of dwellings and forests. Also, dramatic increases in the numbers and strength of tornados (US, Caribbean, the Philippines, etc.); floods and melting ice in the Arctic are just a few of the calamities that the present climate crisis seems to have provoked.

None of the global climate conventions organized by the United Nations have led to any tangible progress so far. Many of the world's leading politicians have expressed little commitment to acting on climate change. There is still considerable denial that we are facing global climate problems.

At the core of this skepticism and inaction is the notion that containment of emissions to limit climate change may be very costly. In developed countries, the coal and oil industries are represented by the powerful lobby against restricting CO_2-generating fossil-fuel burning. Shipping companies, automotive firms, airlines, and other heavy CO_2 emitters have worked consistently to block the adoption of pollution restrictive policies. At the same time, many developing economies see such control measures as unacceptable, also putting too heavy burdens on their economies and slowing down economic development.

The trend to deal with this environmental challenge seems to be gaining momentum despite the resistance. The world has witnessed the rise of the "green" movement, most notably in Europe (e.g., Germany, Scandinavia, and others), but also elsewhere. Modern youth, in particular, are taking leadership of this movement. The young Swede Greta Thunberg, for instance, is the most famous of them. But, some key politicians still state that the "green" side comes off as "doomsday-er" and "too pessimistic."

Yet, this important wave of optimism cannot be ignored. Recent research and books by authors such as Steven Pinker and Hans Rosling leave us with an optimistic outlook. And now, Andrew McAfee, a faculty member at MIT Sloan School of Management, published the present book, also with a positive twist. Things are getting better. We are using less resources!

As noted, the author makes the claim that we are using fewer natural resources than before, while production in general is increasing. We are thus better able to satisfy the needs of an increasing world population and increase their standards of living. This increase in productivity might largely be attributable to new technological advances, especially digital ones, to the increased role of private capitalism, to stronger public awareness and to more responsible governments.

Clearly, the author disagrees with Malthus pessimistic outlook of stagnation and crisis. He underlines instead how several technological advances within an array of different areas seem to show that Malthus' predictions were incorrect. While we have come a long way, he there are also transgressions, some made as far back as the early industrial era, above all the still common practice of child labor and the senseless exploitation of some natural resources, taking place even today, especially through wasteful mining, unacceptable forestry practices and the brutal killing of many animal specimens, including whales.

Pollution remains excessive, air quality is deteriorating, global warming is increasing, sources of some types of possible fuel are running out, a gloomy picture indeed. The CRIB approach (Consume less, Recycle, Impose limits, Back to the earth) to curtail this deteriorating situation simply does not work. But again, the author comes in positively, acknowledging that some of CRIB's various sub-components may have value, including significant reversals in mindsets regarding the use of some natural resources, such as several rare metals, in agriculture, and when it comes to certain wood products. The growth in CO_2 emissions seems indeed to be flattening out.

The author further examines the main causes for the encouraging trends he has documented, labeled "the Four Horsemen." These factors fall in two groups: the combined positive effect from new technologies and from capitalism, i.e., productivity gains from private firms investing in new technologies, and an increase in public awareness combined with policies from more responsive governments.

Capitalism may have a negative connotation to it for many when linked to the environment. However, the author argues that such capitalism could be more than willing to invest in sustainable ways, must not be selfish, amoral, oppressive, nor to foster inequality. But as the author points out, socialism such as that in Venezuela for instance, and in the former Soviet Union and in China, does not seem to yield enough capital for investment in new resource-saving technologies. It seems to be clear, in general though, that private investments are part of the solution and not the problem.

The author observes that having all "Four Horsemen" present at the same time might provide a good context for positive evolution. Many things are improving globally, even though excessive emission of climate-changing gases is not. Why is that? The author argues that it is mainly because it is so expensive to remove. Reducing excessive emission may thus decrease economic wealth, induce an economic slow-down, an issue which could be of particular concern for developing nations, such as India.

So, in order to make this difficult tradeoff work—the costs associated with restricting emissions in the short term versus a gain in the long-term by reducing emissions—the author calls for strong mobilization of public opinion. This is difficult, of course. Concentration of wealth seems to be on the rise, for instance, resulting in more disconnection, less social capital. While to build a broad coalition to handle the emission tradeoff problem is not easy, things are nevertheless improving! And now, the CO_2 emission challenge appears to have solutions. Optimism is perhaps justifiable!

What can we do as individual citizens to make our planet better? The author calls for several actions, all of which to be linked by a broad shift in our attitudes: Reduce pollution through the reduced emission of greenhouse gases, and instead start promoting nuclear energy again; preserve species and habitats, including promoting genetically modified organisms (GMOs); fund basic research on pollution-control, and finally promote open markets, competition and efforts by all.

Some of these factors, such as promoting nuclear energy or embracing GMOs, are not yet typically endorsed by environmentalists or "greens." There is probably still some way to go before a more broadly based coalition of progressive opinion-makers can be established.

Our earth is by far the best of all planets in the solar system. We now have the ability to control pollution and thus impact our planet positively. It is up to us to ensure that there are ever more reasons for such optimism! The role of business is key here!

Bill McKibbon, (2020), Falter, Henry Holt & Company (Reviewed May 2019)

The author is a prominent proponent of "saving our earth" through tougher restrictions on greenhouse gas emissions and restoration of more "normal" climate. While McKibbon draws a crisp clear picture of where we seem to be going, he appears more in remiss when it comes to proposing means that might effectively ameliorate the present climate crisis, i.e., not very different from what we seem to find in much of today's debate on the issue. The author dismisses certain approaches that have often been suggested as parts of potential solutions: Laissez faire shall simply not work! And, relatively short-term moves by politicians are equally largely dysfunctional; artificial intelligence shall also not offer a solution. In total, a rather bleak outlook!

Bill McKibbon, the well-known environmental activist and a Distinguished Scholar in Environmental Studies at Middlebury College (Vermont, USA), attempts to shed light on our planet's development over the coming decades, a rather gloomy outlook! The author calls for a dramatically increased emphasis on climate change issues, given how out of control the world's climate have developed. The effects of climate change increasingly impact us. This growing pressure derives from the increased accumulation of CO_2 now not only in the Earth's atmosphere, but also in its oceans. The results from the consequent climate change will be devastating:

- We can expect stronger heatwaves, to the extent that it will become increasingly difficult—if not impossible—for humans to continue to live in some traditionally inhabited areas of the world.
- The world's oceans will warm, leading to accelerated melting of ice in the Arctic and Antarctic regions. As a result, water levels will rise, threatening the very existence of many of our world's leading cities (London, Shanghai, Boston, New York, Miami, and Kolkata, to name a few only) and leading to the disappearance of several island nations (e.g., the Seychelles and the Maldives) and low-lying regions (e.g., large parts of Florida, Denmark, and Holland). Thus, the space available for humans to live will shrink. The author calls this a lessening of the size of the board. In all likelihood, it will also lead to major population displacements and geopolitical tensions.

Climate change will also bring the plight of the major oil- and coal-producing companies. McKibbon argues forcefully that the continued intensive burning of fossil fuel—primarily coal and oil—is the main cause of all of climate change. The author further argues that short-term economic gains may lead to a suppression of these facts among leading oil and coal producers. McKibbon calls this "the leverage argument," i.e., the burning of fossil fuel is of such critical short-term importance to the world's economy that not much may be done to curtail the use of fossil fuels.

Several major societal developments may also have an effect on this course of events. And, the author reaches the fundamentally pessimistic conclusion that the world's course will not be corrected.

- Ayn Rand's philosophy, as well as that of other leading laissez-faire thinkers, seems to underscore that, in their opinion, governmental intervention would be largely inappropriate.
- The short-term nature of most political activities may largely be dictated by the fact that politicians face short-term reelection pressures and thus may not realistically be expected to act on longer-term climate change issues?
- Artificial intelligence is clearly here to stay, but the author does not see how this could realistically help to address our climate change challenges either.
- Gene manipulation may similarly have questionable value. Here, too, the author does not foresee much help.

Humanity might nevertheless have an outside chance of averting catastrophe, perhaps above all due to the emergence of a more effective solar power technology. In the author's opinion, this development could lead to a more realistic optimism that climate change may curtail. He also sees the emergence of a nonviolent protest movement as critical. In this respect, say, the Sunrise Movement, may prove to be successful.

The author draws an analogy with the impressive advances that mankind has made in space exploration and concludes once more that some hope might exist after all. But is there still time? The gravity of the climate change threat is high. A call to action is critically important! Are the supporter movements of climate control too fragmented?

Javier Blas and Jack Farchy, (2021), The World for Sale, Penguin Random House (Reviewed July 2021)

A group of actors who appear to be taking relatively extreme views on acceptable exploitation of various types of natural resources (oil, minerals, corn, …) are the traders practicing in leading trading firms, many of which are located in the Swiss cities of Geneva or Zug. Much of the success that the bulk of these seem to have may be based on "pushing the limits" for what society considers permissible. Individuals such as Mark Rich and Ivan Glasenberg stand out, and so do their firms. Most of these individuals and their companies' success may rest on the fact that they are allowed to enter into options, whereby they lock in the price now, but take delivery later, at the locked-in price level, which in the meantime may hopefully have gone up. We all have much to learn about taking advantage of the option price phenomenon.

This book discusses how successful commodity traders operate, not only with regards to oil trading by firms such as Vitol, Trafigura, Glencore, perhaps the most well-known area of commodity trading, but also when it comes to coal and metals trading (Glencore, …) as well as trading in agricultural products (Cargill, …). Trading has developed significantly from pre-World War II until today. A relatively small group of traders revolutionized international trade and also came up with a clear way to link trading to the financial markets. Countries rich in natural resources, but often isolated and run by dictatorial regimes, thereby became linked to the global economic system.

The book also discusses the darker side of trading, with a world of immense wealth and political power, often gained by pushing legal systems to the limit, and perhaps with little-to-no concerns for ethical dysfunctionalities. As also discussed, there are many examples of overstepping boundaries between what might be considered legal versus what might be illegal.

The book thus recounts the actions of a large array of traders, ranging from Marc Rich to Ivan Glasenberg, from Philips Brothers and Cargill to Glencore. It is about a mix of big money, strategically important resources, and a willingness to operate close to the edge of what may be considered legal. The book also addresses the lack of transparency and the resistance to cast light on the often-opaque world of privately held trading companies, with little to no public disclosure of information.

The pioneering of commodities trading can largely be traced back to firms such as Philips Brothers and Cargill, as well as to individuals such as Marc Rich, who spent more than 20 years at Philips Brothers before starting his own firm, based in Zug, Switzerland. The pipeline across Israel, from Eilat (Red Sea) to Ashkelon (Mediterranean Sea), was central to how Marc Rich's success was built, allowing oil, primarily from Iraq, to be distributed in the world markets. This also contributed to the breakup of the so-called "seven sisters" cartel of major oil companies, which had controlled the oil business so far. A good example of how Marc Rich was able to develop barter trade deals might also be exemplified by the 10-year contract with Jamaica, allowing the country to supply alumina at a fixed price, in exchange for oil. There were indeed also considerable financial aspects in this arrangement, and the French bank Societé General played a prominent role here.

But, in the end, Marc Rich ran out of luck. A big bet to "corner" the market for zinc failed. The financial strains increased dramatically. A new trading company emerged from the turmoil and partial collapse of Marc Rich + Co., namely Glencore.

The book also details how traders took advantage of the collapse of the former Soviet Union, with massive aluminum trading as well as oil trading, largely with oligarchs who had been able to acquire large physical assets in Russia for much less than their intrinsic values. Cuba's ability to continue to function after the Soviet's collapse by trading sugar for oil, all organized by the large Geneva-based trader Vitol, is also covered.

Major strategic shifts fundamentally changed the nature of commodity trading, such as when the trading houses started to acquire physical mining assets, for instance mines, to control more of the value chain and improve trading performance. Ivan Glasenberg, the CEO of Glencore, was the main proponent for this strategy. First, he and Glencore made a series of coal mine acquisitions meant to support one of Mr. Glasenberg's special areas of competence, coal trading. It goes without saying that the volume of coal eventually controlled by Glencore was considerable. Glencore also acquired a controlling stake in Xstrata, a diversified mining company also headquartered in Switzerland. Eventually the two companies merged. Major copper deposits in Congo were also acquired. The underlying rationale for all of these moves was to be in a better position to trade.

It should, however, be noted that to acquire physical assets to trading activities seemed to be possible only in cases with a possibility to consolidate some ownership, in order to gain more market power, such as for coal and some minerals. For agricultural products, on the other hand (corn, wheat, soybeans, coffee, cocoa, juices…), there were typically too many independent producers (i.e., farmers) to make such consolidation possible. And, when it came to oil production, interests were of course so considerable that takeovers by traders would have been totally unrealistic, and unacceptable for most oil-rich nation governments as well.

A second shift was brought on by the expansion of derivatives, futures and options markets for commodities. These financial vehicles further linked commodity trading to the broader financial markets. Thus, it was now possible to trade in commodities without physical transfers of these. All that was needed was a contract to deliver a particular commodity sometime in the future, or to have an option to pick up a particular commodity sometime in the future. The "old" style of trading had been mostly physical, with physical repositioning of commodity assets and thus also exposure for the traders to adverse price developments during the period of the holding of such assets. Many old-style traders were unable to make the transition to paper-based trading and subsequently eventually failed.

A third fundamental change in commodity trading had to do with an increasing emphasis on fundamental analysis of patterns of supplies and demands, including a better factoring in of political analysis. For instance, the rise in oil prices stemming from the embargo of Iranian oil led to a considerable windfall gain for Phibro Energy (the successor of Philips Brothers), which had forecasted this, even to the extent that the company had chartered in 11 large VLCC crude oil tankers to store oil in the interim. These was by now a strong shift towards protecting, maintaining and further building one's reputation in contrast to the "wheeling and dealing" mentality of past years' trading. Sophisticated analysis was now the modus operandum in contrast to the typical traveling by trading executives to various "hot spots" around the globe of the past.

Yet, there was still some reminiscence of the "old" way of doing things. Bribing continued to rather common, even though this practice was of course typically denied by the various traders. Iranian oil was widely thought to be traded as an extension of the so-called "oil-for-food" program. Russia was suddenly in a financial squeeze due to a wide array of price collapses among several other commodities. The country was forced to export more oil, and the new Geneva-based trading company Gunvor handled most of this. Another company, Vitol, handled the sale of crude oil from eastern Libya on behalf of the rebels, in exchange from refined products such as gasoline. The African Republic of Chad entered into a long-term contract to sell most of its oil with Glencore, receiving considerable financial support in return. There are many examples of such "shadowy" deals in the book. It becomes clear that while many traders rose to fairly prominent positions of political power, the way that this had come about may often raise questions.

Most trading firms were initially privately held, but in 2011, Glencore became the exception by going public. Perhaps, this could be seen as symptomatic of the immense amounts of wealth that had been created through commodity trading, now being distributed to the firms' key executives.

Commodity trading is of course a good example of how so-called "asset-light" strategies might work. To become more asset light is perhaps a trend that others may be interested in exploring. Options and futures are perhaps particularly important keys to this, and the book provides very good insights regarding how to deal with such derivatives. Trading in stocks, currencies and even commodities are becoming interesting tools for many corporations' financial officers.

Nicholas Wapshott, (2021), Samuelson Friedman: The Battle over the Free Market (Reviewed March 2022)

This book chronicles discussion between perhaps the two greatest economists from the end of World War II to the beginning of this century. These took place for nearly five decades, for eight years (1965–1973,) through columns written in the weekly magazine, Newsweek. Remarkably, although the two tended to have dramatically opposite views, they always remained friends on a personal level, with deep respect for each other. What is a certain takeaway here for our business leaders is the healthy, mind-stretching advantage of debating constructively about topics, and even working through what may appear as highly conflictual or opposing viewpoints. In other words, just because someone thinks differently, do not exclude their perspective—rather use it to learn more.

The author of this remarkable book, Nicholas Wapshott, has written many books that all fall into the genre of economics/ political science, such as the biography of Margaret Thatcher and the widely acclaimed Keynes Hayek: The Clash that Defined Modern Economics. He lives in New York City.

Paul Samuelson was of course the world-known liberal economist from MIT, noted for his strong beliefs in Keynesianism and thus considerable amounts of governmental intervention in the economy—a true liberal. He is also acknowledged for his textbook Economics, the most widely sold textbook of its kind ever sold. He received the Nobel Prize in Economics in 1970.

Milton Friedman, almost equally famous, was a University of Chicago-based conservative economist, fiercely opposed to the interventional ideals of Samuelson. His mantra, instead, was to prescribe the amount of money supply in a society, i.e., its liquidity situation, as the critical factor to drive economic progress. Friedman was indeed brilliant, and conservative, a non-interventionalist. Friedman received the Nobel Prize in 1976.

Both were trained as mathematical economists, comfortable not only to work with mathematical equations but also with modern statistical methods. Wapshott's piece is full of economists' and politicians' names, anecdotes and events. Some might perhaps say that there might be too much detail. The authors here do not share this view. The book gave Lorange a vivifying reminder of what he once found to be such stimulating economic science, a true tour!

The first three of the book's 17 chapters detail the careers of Samuelson and Friedman, as well as how Newsweek's ownership shifted hands from the Astors to the Grahams (Washington Post). Then in chapter four, there is a brief review of Friedman's two key writings: Essays in Positive Economics and A Monetary History of the United States, 1867–1960, the latter turning on its head the causes for the crash of 1929 and the Great Depression, namely that this was primarily caused by the tightness of money in circulation.

The following chapter builds up to the fundamental dilemma: to intervene in the economy or not to intervene. Hayek's highly influential book The Road to Serfdom provided plenty of inspiration for the conservative side. Leading economists lined up on both sides, Robert Solow and others with Samuelson, George Stigler, Gary Becker, Theodore Schultz and others on the side of Friedman.

Keynes was by many considered one of the major economists who ever lived. Samuelson even considered him the greatest. Number two was Adam Smith according to Samuelson; number three was Leon Walros, the Lausanne-based economist of the eighteenth century. But, Friedman was unstoppable when it came to questioning Keynes. Economics was about money. His just mentioned A Monetary History of the United States, gave him what he felt was ammunition, further supported with arguments from Hayek. As Friedman's monetarist ideas gathered momentum, Samuelson tried to stop this anti-Keynes counter revolution in its track using cold, clear logic. He described the hyperinflation that came about during the Vietnam period, for instance, as producing a classical demand-pull inflation, i.e., "too much spending chasing a limited supply of goods, with labor markets tight and under backlogs high as overtime production could not produce as much as needed" (Newsweek, Dec. 1970). Aren't we seeing much of this today too?

But, the inflation was not stopped. Nixon, then president, hesitated to curtail government spending—he was more interested in being reelected than initiating unpopular moves. The number of new government agencies mushroomed for instance. Again, are not we seeing the same today?

The next chapter, chapter 10, provides details around both Samuelson and Friedman's Nobel Prize awards, in 1970 and 1976, respectively, as already noted. It is worthwhile to observe that there were demonstrations in the streets of Stockholm when Friedman got the prize, none the least due to allegations that he might be close to general Pinochet of Chile. Perhaps, such demonstrations may have been expected anyhow, in light of the largely left leaning political norms of the Swedish society at the time.

The battle against inflation went on, and President Carter appointed the charismatic former banker Paul Volcker to now lead the battle. His "miracle prescription" was to increase the money supply, coupled with high interest rates. Inflation subsequently came down, and Volcker and Friedman received full credit for this remarkable achievement.

Then enter the new president, Ronald Reagan, and the young Chicago-based economist Arthur Laffer, with his so-called bell-shaped curve indicating that overall tax return would not necessarily go up when the tax rate would be raised beyond a certain point. Accordingly, taxes were reduced!

The next two chapters, 13 and 14, are both relatively peripheral to the main body of this text. The first has to do with how the two heroes of the book, Samuelson and Friedman, stopped writing for Newsweek around 1983. Fatigue and frustration with having to live up to weekly deadlines, always with constraints regarding the permissible length of their writings seem to have been the reasons. In the UK, Margaret Thatcher was a firm believer in Friedman. She initiated several important changes to enhance deregulation, many of them having had lasting transformational impacts on the UK society.

Then comes President Bush, the elder. The September 11th, 2001, terrorist attack represented a shock to the US. Are we no longer secure at home? But also, the economy suffered. To stimulate the economy the new Federal Reserve Chairman, Alan Greenspan, initiated a drive to lessen the cost of money. Cheap money was not what Friedman had prescribed, however. But, it seemed to work!

Following, Ben Bernanche became Federal Chairman. He was initially a "brilliant MIT graduate," although relatively conservative. When the economic crisis hit Wall Street so hard in 2008, he did not hesitate to intervene, using large amounts of government funds to bail out several banking or insurance firms that elsewise might have risked defaulting. This was truly Samuelson-style thinking! Bernanche was indeed comfortable!

The last chapter of this remarkable book covers several "post happenings" after the deaths of both of these giant economists (first Friedman in 2006, then Samuelson in 2009). Partly, this deals with where the two wanted their collected writings to be placed, in the end Samuelson at the MIT archives, Friedman at Stanford's Hoover institution. And, there were some departing shots between the two camps. Since Friedman passed away first, these came largely from the Samuelson side, but not from Samuelson himself. Lawrence Summers, ex-President of Harvard University and ex-Secretary of the US Treasury, Samuelson's nephew and tennis partner, was quite critical of Friedman, and so was Robert Solow, the other MIT economist of world fame.

Wapshott appropriately raises the question at the end of the book: What were the lasting legacies of each of these two giant economists? He seems to feel that Friedman's legacy might perhaps be stronger than Samuelson's. Keynesian thinking is no longer as solid as it might have been, Wapshott writes. This might perhaps have more to do with the political "pain versus pleasure" in practicing Keynesianism and, typically calling for a rather robust political determination versus conservative, with the laissez faire of such politicians commonly involving relatively less political guts. There is possibly a clear trend towards "baking the cake before you eat it." But, there is probably not a steady state balance between the two extremes here. The pendulum goes back and forth! Thus also, it is likely far too early to declare Friedman more influential than Samuelson or vice versa.

We are left with a lot of admiration for what the author has accomplished in putting together this book. As already pointed out, there are numerous names and anecdotes—perhaps too many! Yet, this does not detract from the overall impressive message of this book, namely that the battle over the free market has been going on for a long time, and it is rolling back and forth and likely to continue. To gain further insight into this core dilemma, the book offers indispensable insights. It is indeed also interesting reading for anyone preoccupied with modern economics, which all business leaders should be.

Bill Browder, (2022), Freezing Order, Simon & Schuster (Reviewed May 2022)

In many ways, this book could be seen as a continuation of Mr. Browder's previous book. Here the focus has now shifted towards how Russian officials seem to be attempting to extend their powers to outside their own country. Many countries have by now included stricter legislation dealing with white-washing, "Magnitsky legislations." These legislations are named after Sergei Magnitsky, a Russian lawyer who worked for Mr. Browder, and who was at the center of exposure to much whitewashing when it came to trying to poison key persons outside of Russia. This, as well as some of Russia's attempts to influence elections in various western countries, is discussed. The overall implication for business is to be careful when it comes to operating with Russia!

This book relays the author's truly unusual and first-hand experience of how Russia is managed from the top, and how this country now seems to be run under President Putin's power.

The author, a successful equity investor, was the largest foreign investor in Russia until early this century. He was then also actively pursuing various money laundering schemes by Russian oligarchs and government officials, particularly ones that involved tax evasion scams, where funds were diverted out of Russia through complex systems involving a myriad of foreign banks.

One particular such scheme was an attempt by several Russian criminals, all having positions within the Russian government, to sift off USD230 million that technically belonged to a Russian steel manufacturer, having been paid to them by the author's firm, Hermitage, as taxes owed on stock speculations that his firm had done involving the firm's steel stocks (totally legal, of course). These funds thus <u>de facto</u> belonged to the Russian government. Mr. Sergei Magnitsky, who worked for the author as a legal advisor, exposed much of these illegalities. He was soon imprisoned, and subsequently beaten to death.

The author and several other Russian advisors followed up when Magnitsky's life was cut short. This turned out to be a complex path of moves, including legal advisors, government legislation, murder, as well as several attempts on the author's security. This present book provides a telling narrative of all of this. It is becoming entirely evident that the Russian government, under Putin's leadership, seems to shy very little when backing these types of criminal acts.

So, in addition to sharing with us how the Magnitsky Act for curtailing Russian money laundering was adopted in around 30 countries, the book also discusses how the USD230 million was embezzled, by whom in the Russian hierarchy, and how the Russian authorities attempted to fight this, including going after the author.

The book's narration largely takes place between 2008 and 2018, providing shocking details into the inner workings of Russia. Its leaders seem to have nothing to spare when implementing cover-ups, not only through assassinations, torture and imprisonment, but also through further mobilizing the already corrupt Russian legal system. Even the US legal system was being targeted.

It is worthwhile noting that it might have been to protest the enactment of the US Magnitsky legislation that was a key factor behind Russia's attack on the 2018 US presidential election. Also, surprisingly, would be the pro-Putin leaning of Prince Albert of Monaco. Interpol is apparently also notoriously known for being lax on Russian extradition requests.

It is also worthwhile to consider that several prominent US individuals and institutions sided with the Russians when it came to working against the Magnitsky legislation, notably a well-known New York law firm, several prominent lawyers, some leading politicians and a well-known lobbyist. On top of this, a judge presiding at the New York Court of Appeals that heard the author's case was an 84-year-old, and not on top of things.

A collection of good lawyers, a fact-orientated judge, and a US Government'Affairs expert, were, however, all supportive of the author's case.

Two Russian activists/informers were mysteriously killed. Another activist was poisoned but survived.

Putin himself was not directly involved in this all. His official profile has usually been to stay clear of any dubious financial transactions, but rather to work through others. Key legal officers on the Russian side were Russia's general prosecutor, and a senior lawyer in charge of the Magnitsky case, however.

It becomes abundantly clear that the author was indeed a tough fighter. Perhaps the most important conclusion from the book is that the Russians never seem to want to back down, and that only a strong, uncompromising person, such as Browder, might be something that the Russians would understand. The author had unusual support from his CFO, Mr. Kleiner, an exceptionally effective "snooper," in addition to the many persons that were on his side. Still, there is no doubt that the author's exceptional and imaginative fighting spirit seems to have made a difference. None of the efforts by the Russians nor by their US collaborators were successful! So, while in the end, the success of the Magnitsky legislation became a reality with almost 30 countries adopting the legislation thus making it much harder for illegal payments be made, and increasing the risk of Russian assets to be "frozen"—there is still no complete clarity when it comes to the specific person responsible in the fraudulent scheme involving the "stealing" of tax deposits to the tune of USD 230 million, paid in by the author's firm. This shall perhaps never be known.

5

Closing Remarks for the Part

To say the least, it is difficult not to agree that the world seems to be in a certain state of disarray. However, maintaining positivity and practicing solution—and opportunity—mindsets can prove beneficial.

While some of us may suffer, wallow, or complain about the current state of affairs, others might see opportunities and reply courageously. "So then, let's keep on moving forward," relying instead on hope, resourcefulness, innovation, creativity, and openness with others to "get out of the mess." What is clear to all though is that the world is increasingly inter-related, inter-connected. And, the key to the future is heavily based on our ability to understand, share, and communicate such forces for progress, which may have multitudes of effects, for good and for society. The key thus seems to be to think and act multidimensionally!

This book is not meant to focus on political science in its own sense, but rather on what might be some major implications from political science and world affairs for leaders to consider and simultaneously for the curricular considerations of leading business schools as they face the future. In line with this, we see an overriding concern: stability. What does it take for a political region to ensure the kind of stability that business tends to want? How might we assess this?

We shall indicate some factors that we see as essential when it comes to this:

Human freedom and dignity. Some political regimes, typically authoritarian, may score relatively low when it comes to these factors. Iran, Afghanistan, China, and Russia come to mind. And, there are also other regimes, such as NATO-member Turkey or EU-member Hungary. Many business leaders will stay away from starting or building up activities in such countries, fearing that political instability may be inevitable.

Economic weakness. Many countries may be faced with relatively weak national economies, heavy national debt burdens, in particular. And, this might also, in the end, lead to lack of political stability. Examples may be countries such as Argentina or several African republics, but economic weakness does not necessarily always have to lead to chaos. A case in point might be seen in Greece, which was able to turn its economy around through self-discipline, and which today enjoys impressive economic growth. To be able to come up with accurate judgments when it comes to this seems paramount. The Chinese bought the Greek port of Pirceus at the depth of this country's crisis. In retrospect, this turned out to be a very good investment. But, in contrast, China seems to have invested heavily in several African countries where turnaround seems unlikely!

Military. Some regimes seem to be embarking on relatively aggressive military paths, threatening neighboring regimes or even invading. Russia comes to mind, with its invasion of Ukraine. China is another example, with its threats to invade Taiwan, its expansion into the South China Sea, and so on. Boycotts and other restrictive legislation impositions are often the result. The economic climate in such countries typically suffers.

Nuclear. Some countries appear relatively more ready to actively pursue nuclear threats, India and North Korea come to mind. India and Pakistan also seem to offer relatively unstable economic business contexts due to this.

Part II

Adapting the Firm's Strategy to the External Environment: Getting Started

The difference between what we do and what we are capable of doing would suffice to solve most of the world's problems.
  —Mahatma Gandhi, revolutionary activist

If world problems feel too big to tackle, think small. Step by step. Small wins build confidence, lead the way to change.
  —Rosabeth Moss Kanter, Professor, author

6

Practice Insights from Risto Siilasmaa, Chairman, F-Secure

Clarity of thinking is critical for today's leaders that want to navigate the unusually complex environment they have to operate in. The classical waterfall process of planning will produce a plan, but we can be quite certain that we are failing to account for some unknowable unknowns quickly rendering the plan, if not obsolete, at least suboptimal. Therefore, we need to complement the planning process with a culture of healthy suspicion regarding the plan's underlying assumptions coupled with constant experimentation.

While the leader relies on the organization's built-in agility of experimenting and challenging the plan to deal with the unknowable unknowns, we can and should also do a much better job regarding the knowable unknowns.

When we are surprised by something that, in hindsight, seems perfectly obvious, we are dealing with a knowable unknown that we ignored only due to not having built the capability for thinking clearly—and, perhaps, a little bit of mental laziness.

Examples of knowable unknowns are many. In geopolitics, consider Putin's attack on Ukraine, a surprise for many when it happened, but in hindsight, indeed one of a short list of actions that Russia had for many years clearly signaled, in both words and actions, would take place. Or think about the COVID-19 pandemic that many societies and organizations were rather unprepared for despite the fact that scientists had been warning us of the certainty of a pandemic over the longer term. Failing to acknowledge the certainty of something in the long term due to the low probability of the event at a specific moment is one of the typical reasons enabling knowable unknowns. Or consider Kodak, the original inventor of digital photography that despite the overwhelming evidence of rapid and constant improvement of digital cameras, decided to bet the company on film photography just a few short years before digital cameras surpassed film cameras in performance leading to the bankruptcy of the iconic company. The examples are endless.

Consider the politicians, business leaders or academics that had the mental discipline to challenge the status quo, gather and look at the data, and take action. They were the winners in the fight against the pandemic, they were the first movers in digital photography, and solar power, and cloud services, and smart phones. For every losing party, there is someone gaining advantage.

By building and constantly exercising the capabilities for scenario planning, identifying outcomes at multiple levels, gathering relevant data, endless simulation of the operational environment and real-world experiments on the results of the most successful simulations a leader can eliminate many of the knowable unknowns and gain a significant competitive advantage over her competitors.

The challenge in creating an organizational capability for revealing and acting on the knowable unknowns is that the leader cannot simply patch that capability on top of the existing organization. For instance, the typical organization may not be built for experimentation. The access and expertise required for multiple levels of leaders to create simulations based on corporate data typically does not exist. The empowerment to take action on the possible outcomes may not exist. Even the job titles and roles natural for this mode of operation may not have been established. The change is not easy, but just like in the examples above, the ones that move first and fast will have the advantage. My guess is that, for many, the advantage will be sustainable and the value creation opportunity immense.

The change starts from the acknowledgment of the need for the change. The creation of the capability starts from the first action taken. Both can happen today.

7

Introduction on Adapting the Firm's Strategy to the External Environment: Getting Started

So, with world spinning, with daily, sometimes hourly significant change in markets, and with often dramatically new customer demands on markets, what do we do? We may of course obtain some solace and assurance from knowing that life is impermanent—and in a flux, that change is constant—but we also need to understand how to act even react! Resilience can help, "paranoic optimism," as Siilasmaa (2019) says. But specifically, what can we do? How can we as business leaders lead and grow through these storms?

Acceptance of this basic of "constant turbulence" plays an important role in this: live with the situation. We might focus on things that are within our control, prioritize appropriately, stay aware, be alert, link up with positive people or companies as inspiration that might serve as role models, expand our networks, accordingly, know when to recharge, as well as when to rest, for then get started again. Some term these "hacks," and others call it traits. We believe that many companies have succeeded in riding the waves and surviving the worst, and we have included in this section some examples that will hopefully provide fuel to others. Constant change!

Similarly, try to continue with the above, and suitable approaches for business sometimes include "keep going," observe the environment, "read the room," stay focused on clear goals and tasks, support your teams, keep morale high in your troops, bring your people together, look at the facts, use time to rethink and re-strategize, cement the relationships that work, reduce and manage stress, and go outside the box to explore the new. Keep on learning. Obviously, the learning can come from the experience itself, your own initiatives, your employees, a mentor or coach, and an educational organization. It is all about "hanging in there," practicing paranoic optimism!

In this Part as well, we can consider a few business factors that are woven throughout the book reviews and executive interviews selected: keeping an eye on disruption to carefully observe and try to understand it, long-term thinking mixed with significant short-term agility (be in there for the ride!), and speed in that agility (be ready to move quickly!).

Here are a few conclusions which can be drawn from this section:

- What does "responsible" mean? Regarding growth? Regarding humanitarian aid? Regarding the closing-down of facilities?
- Cooperation between the public (government) sector and the private (business) sector? How? What if one side dominates?
- Confront mistakes early. Willingness to take ameliorating action, especially in light of environmental shifts (inflation, COVID-19…).

8

Essential Books to Learn about Adapting the Firm's Strategy to the External Environment; Getting Started

Michele Gelfand, (2018), Rule Makers, Rule Breakers, Simon & Schuster (Reviewed April 2021)

The author makes the distinction between tight ways of managing and controlling in contrast to loose approaches. This could be applied to corporations (Daimler, Chrysler, Mitsibushi—tight, versus Microsoft—loose), as well as to countries (Germany—tight; France—loose) or even to regions (California—loose; Texas—tight). The author develops this distinction further, to distinguish between flexible tightness and structured looseness. There seem to be at least three classes of issues that could determine which side of this tradeoff to settle on: norms and preferences applying to oneself: am I cautious, controllable or rather adventurous and impulsive, and do I prefer good order or do I prefer less structure and more tolerance for ambiguity. For businesses that operate internationally in particular, to run operations relatively decentralized so that each country might be allowed to run itself in a fairly tight way, while other countries in the same firm may be run relatively loosely.

In this book, the author argues that in so-called tight societies with clearly stated rules, versus loose societies (countries, regions, and even families), behaviors may vary, influenced by different perceptions of threats. Reactions to conflicts may be metered out in different ways, to a large extent dependent on degree of societal tightness.

The author, Professor Michelle Gelfand, has studied this phenomenon widely. She is a social psychologist and teaches at the University of Maryland. Her study sheds light on why cultures differ, depending on the strengths of their cultural glues. Tight cultures, with strong social norms and relatively little tolerance for deviances, might be seen as rule makers, while societies with relatively weak societal norms and a high degree of permissiveness are rule breakers.

Foundations: In the first phase, with the power of primal social forces at play, there seem to be relatively fewer norms in loose societies than in tight ones. However, there appears to be a continuum between these two extremes. Amongst her vast array of examples of norms that might differ between tight versus loose societies, she cites: the phenomenon of receiving help from strangers (less so in tight societies), gambling (less so in tight societies), political demonstrations (less so in tight societies), usage of profane words (less in tight societies), ... even less waste in tight societies. She goes on to discuss particular conditions regarding when we may find an over-abundance of tightness: not only threats, but also over-crowdedness, propensity for natural disasters (droughts, floods, earthquakes…), as well as likelihood of scarcities, such as lack of food, unstable contexts for dwellings, etc. In contrast, looser societies might often be associated with a relatively open view when it comes to coping with the above types of issues, and also the propensity to debate and to protest.

Analysis: Tight-loose here, there, and everywhere. The author starts off with a compelling analysis of differences among various US regions—relatively tight in the south, with rather explicit behaviors and rules, versus relatively loose in the north-east as well as in California. She argues that such differences might, at least in part, be traced back to how the regions were colonized—more law-abiding from Scotland and Ireland in the south versus more individualistic "protestors" in the north-east and California. The author then extends this analysis to discussing the contrast between working class versus upper class, with the former generally having to fight for survival, with relatively little opportunity to take chances/initiatives and experiment. In short, this setting is "tight." In contrast, upper class people tend to operate in somewhat safer contexts, being able to take more risks and to appreciate societal diversity (loose).

Moving onto corporations, the author analyzes the failed acquisition by Daimler of Chrysler and concludes that cultural incompatibility may have been the apparent reason for the breakdown. This incompatibility made it particularly arduous and complex to integrate organizational structures. And, there may have been a colossal underestimation of this tight-loose divide between Daimler and Chrysler.

Based on an analysis of several other corporate combinations, she also indicates that a large tight-loose divide could be associated with more difficult negotiation processes, often a significant fall in stock market values too, as well as lower ROA than hoped for. Above all, a tight-loose gap might typically lead to substantial, unexpected setbacks.

The author indicates that in loose cultural settings (e.g., Israel, California …), there may be a strong resistance when one is told what to do, the propensity to take risk might be relatively high. Labels such as flexibility, initiative, and innovations may apply. In contrast, there may be more tight business settings in countries such as Germany, Singapore, Japan, and Korea, with strong formalities, many rules and more hierarchical/organizational firmness. Cooperative attempts might be more difficult with such different loose-tight contexts existing.

The author does not analyze it, yet the overriding vision at Daimler seems to have been to develop a *global* automotive entity comprising Chrysler (US), Mitsubishi (Japan), and Daimler (Germany), with Daimler in the lead. Large cultural tight-loose differences reflected in irrevocable leadership style differences seem to have been an overriding reason why this combination did not work. Stresses, even breakdowns, when it came to the failing cooperation between Nissan (Japan) and Renault (France) point in the same way: Japan, tight, versus France, loose.

Leaders might also tend to be primarily tight versus loose, of course, with Jurgen Schrempp and Dieter Zetsche of Daimler being examples of the former versus Ricardo Semler (Brazilian; CEO of Semco Partners) and Bill Gates being examples of the latter—discipline, obedience, autocratic, command-and-control versus relatively more, risk taking, innovations, and openness to change.

When digging deeper into this dichotomy, the author finds that there could be differences even within a given firm, say, R&D being a looser versus a tighter manufacturing function. We may see this not only in firms such as Deloitte, but also in some pharmaceutical firms.

The author also builds on the concept of differentiating between structural looseness versus flexible tightness. This balance between the two extremes might be renegotiated on a more or less continuing basis.

What type of mindset is dominant for each of us—tight or loose? The author sets out three questions to determine this:

- The extent one might notice specific norms that may relate to other expectations regarding oneself (tight)?
- The extent to which one is cautious/controlled (tight) versus adventurous/impulsive (loose)?
- Preference for structure/social order (tight) versus enjoying less structure and tolerance for ambiguity (loose).

The author finally discusses the so-called negatively "u"-shaped curve, the "goldilocks curvilinear principle," for how too tight as well as too loose positions settle on in order to avoid chaos, apparent in biology as well as our own society. Avoiding extremes might be better in creating order, happiness, and desirable outcomes. While every culture may have their own optimal tradeoff between tightness and looseness, extreme positive should be avoided.

The author then delves into how global disorder can be analyzed, pointing out that when cultural norms collapse, then extremism may fill the vacuum. Clearly, there are cultural divides. The collapse of looseness-tightness paradigm might help to explain why international confrontations seem to be on the rise, largely due to this.

How then might social norms be harnessed? She argues that over-crowding on our planet, getting CO_2 emissions under control, to return to a more normal climate, and so on, might be better understood when considering them through the loose-tight lenses. While all of this may be good, it nevertheless sounds rather speculative.

Above all, the "tight-loose" conundrum may not only help to create realism when it comes to mergers, but also help to better understand how to develop more effective operations in multinational settings, with a wide array of operations, and in different countries. In this context, it is interesting to observe the strong emphasis that many unsuccessful firms with global operations, such as Nestlé, for instance, seem to put on managing each country, quite separately as well as also each geographic region. Such firms appear to recognize the importance of country-specific differences, between tight and loose, and seem to be ready to modify their managerial practices accordingly. For family-owned business portfolios too, it is probably important to pay close attention to tailoring the corporate level interaction with each entity in a firm's portfolio in terms of structured looseness versus flexible tightness.

Steven Pinker, (2018), Enlightenment Now: The Case for Reason, Science, Humanism and Progress, Allen Lane (Reviewed November 2018)

Dr. Steven Pinker is a Professor of Psychology at Harvard, and one of the world's most influential thinkers on the evolution of our world. The author has a fundamental optimistic view about how things evolve but says "I am not an optimist. I'm a very curious possibilitist" (page 345). While this book may be complicated to follow, it straightforwardly argues that enlightenment seems to be on the rise today. There is thus a key reason for optimism!

The author makes a fundamental argument for his positive view on the world's development, namely that enlightenment prevails. He does not give a concise definition of what this is, beyond stressing that it is based on reason, which is non-negotiable! Other labels for enlightenment are humanism, the open society, or classical liberalism (page 4). Pinker attempts to restate the ideals of enlightenment in his book, what enlightenment means, how it works, and an overall defense of enlightenment.

So, enlightenment is explained as reason. Science may be there, or not! How might entropy or disorder be counterbalanced by evolutionary trends that bring in energy. Any relevant information helps to better know how forces of entropy might be compensated for. Pinker is realistic, too, regarding what might be realistic forces of counter-enlightenment: populism, authoritarianism, contemptuousness, nostalgia regarding the past.

There are some 15 phenomena that in particular may demonstrate through facts, that the state of the world is moving forward in a positive way. There seems to be evidence, beyond reasonable doubt, that enlightenment is working. Key scientific findings are confirming this, investors and entrepreneurs are pursuing opportunities that are emerging due to this, new legislation is strengthening this, and even activists are contributing to the strong evidence coming from these tales of reality.

There may also be a strong defense for all of this progress, based on enlightenment. A synthesis could be built on reason, arguing that there may still be some room for some irrationalism such as believing in conspiracy theory. But, a belief in fundamental logic and reason shall still prevail. And, it is built on science, i.e., the power of irrefutable scientific discoveries. Finally, it all comes down to humanism! In the end, enlightenment is fundamentally built on this.

There is here a convincing rebuttal of the commonly presented bleak assessment of the world. What we get from much of the press and TV might simply not be correct. Things may be evolving in a fundamentally better way. Encouraging!

Hans Rosling (2018), Factfulness, Sceptre (Reviewed August 2018)

This book provides insights on how to handle ten common misconceptions, misguided instincts, regarding how to handle basic facts that can be critical for us. Based on these ten sets of factual analyses, the author concludes that things are often better in this world than we typically believe, a good thing to keep in mind for many of us inundated with negative news from the media, by politicians and different ideal institutions.

A Swedish medical doctor, Rosling was a professor of international health at Karolinska, the world-renowned medical school in Stockholm. He was also an advisor to WHO and UNICEF and a well-known speaker on the global stage. Rosling also developed several world-known TV series.

The ten misguided instincts, and the author's suggestions for coping with these are:

- The GAP Instinct. Recognize when a story talks about a gap between two extremes and look for a majority position instead. Thus, beware of comparisons of averages and of extremes.
- The NEGATIVITY Instinct. Expect bad news. Also, understand that good news and/or gradual improvement may typically not be considered news. More news is not equal to more suffering however, and beware of glorified positions, by people as well as nations (glorified history!).
- The STRAIGHTLINE Instinct. A line will seldom continue to be straight. Expect curves, such as S-Bands, slides, or lumps. Lines may eventually bend!
- The FEAR Instinct. The world usually appears scarier to us than it actually is. Risk equals danger times exposure. Get calm before you carry on. Calculate the risk.
- The SIZE Instinct. Single numbers on their own are always misleading. Thus, always look for comparisons among numbers. Focus on the few key items first! Look at the rates per person, when comparing between countries or regions. Take and put things in proportion!
- The GENERALIZATION Instinct. Question your categories and look for differences within groups as well as for similarities across groups. Beware of "the majority" (it may mean 51%, which is different from 99%), as well as so-called rigid examples, which are typically the exceptions rather than the rule.
- The DESTINY Instinct. Slow change is nevertheless change! Keep track of gradual improvements. Update your knowledge. Keep in mind how values

have changed and challenge the idea that today's culture may be the same as yesterday's and shall also be the same in the future.
- The SINGLE PERSPECTIVE Instinct. Test one's ideas. Recognize one's own limitations. Remember that no one analytical approach is the best in every instance. Use numbers and qualitative analysis. Simple ideas and simple solutions should be viewed with suspicion. Use the entire "toolbox."
- The BLAME Instinct. Resist finding a scapegoat; look for causes instead! Look for systems, not heroes! Resist pointing your finger!
- The URGENCY Instinct. Control the urgency instinct by taking small steps! Take a break! Insist on data and be skeptical to fortune tellers. Try to avoid drastic actions!

The final chapter of this key book analyzes factfulness in practice when it comes to:

- Education, i.e., what we should teach our children when it comes to the 10 principles of this book.
- Business. We should avoid Euro/US-based stereotyping, i.e., not fall into the trap that everything that originates from the US and/or Europe is the only answer.
- Journalists, Activists, Politicians. They will always compete on presenting news of interest. Thus, they will typically also be biased. It would be up to us consumers, however, to become more facts driven and to pursue a more realistic analysis.
- Organizations. Promote balance, so that the public is afraid of the right things, and do not promote fears. This might imply meaningful regulations!

This book is highly welcome, perhaps now in particular, when there seems to be growth in populism and biased axiomatic thinking. Proper balanced analysis of the data is more important today than ever, so that over-simplistic conclusions can be avoided. It is worthwhile to pay attention to Bill Gates' recommendation of this book on its dustjacket: "One of the most important books I've ever read—an indispensable guide to thinking clearly about the world."

Tara Westover, (2018), Educated, Penguin Random House (Reviewed February 2020)

The author grew up in a remote Mormon-dominated center of Idaho, and then went on to Harvard and Cambridge for her education, earning a PhD from Cambridge as the culmination. She emphasizes the power of hard work, to "stretch" oneself, to take advantage of crises, to be better at receiving feedback, to listen, to not tolerate any types of sexual or racial discrimination, and to adopt the latest available technology with enthusiasm. These lessons are critical for business. The author offers three additional lessons: Allow employees to have a strong sense of their own work and careers; avoid favoritism at all costs; take a balanced view regarding customers, so that demands coming from new customers are adhered to while also respecting existing customers' needs.

This book presents the author's life recollections. Her upbringing, in a remote corner of Idaho where she spent a tumultuous time in an orthodox Mormon culture, is then shifted to her time at Brigham Young University in Utah, and later to Cambridge (UK), where she obtained her PhD. The author's central tension is how to follow one's own ambitions and desires for education without alienating her family.

Here are some key business implications for the author's fascinating autobiographical stories. Ideology and culture can lead to things easily becoming rather static and fixated. We also see how fear of not conforming to culture might also play a key role, to run the risk of being excluded! Conformity is expected! Opposition to such strong ideology and culture typically provokes significant conflicts. The world of business is full of these issues too, of course!

Constructive dialog might be difficult to have when a set ideology is allowed to dominate. How can meaningful innovations happen? Extraordinarily strong individuals, such as the author, are perhaps the only ones who may have the strength to break this cultural conformity and thus spearhead innovation. Regrettably, veering away from conformity might often come at a high personal cost, as often seen in business. An organizational culture may be so tight that it becomes nearly impossible for any individual to pursue innovation, which might, in turn, threaten the status quo. Fear, friction, even violence may be commonplace. Some family businesses regrettably fit into this typology.

The author's experience at BYU point towards several business implications:

- Hard work is called for, to stretch oneself! This gains respect and support from higher levels in an organization including getting good recommendations and positive reviews.
- Paradoxically, a severe crisis may change key individual actors in several positive ways, for instance, a better ability to listen or to give positive feedback, all as a result of broadening and strengthening self-confidence.
- Tolerance of sexual or racial discrimination is highly dysfunctional in any organization, even if presented with humor. People on the receiving end of such comments are typically more sensitive to such behavior than one might think. Business can learn!
- Making use of the latest commercially available technology is crucial. However, here again we often experience that a set organizational culture could lead to resistance against such adaptations.

Now to the author's experiences at Cambridge, also presenting several critical lessons for business:

- Employees should have a strong sense of control over their own work and the direction of their careers. Proponents of a more traditional culture may find it hard, if not impossible, to allow for this, possibly necessitating management reshuffles. We see a mushrooming staff size in some firms due to the fact that some executives might have been sidelined but not fired, to "soften" a firm's culture and thus the possibility of innovation.
- Favoritism should be avoided at all costs. Similarly, established processes associated with an outdated culture may have to be modified.
- While we know that "the customer is king," perhaps, a balance is needed here too, between established, often customer-blind culture, and a novel customer focus.

How far might an executive be expected to go before encountering too much conflict with his or her family when it comes to this? One might be able to build on experiences from other firms when it comes to coping with this type of dilemma.

Muhammad Yunus, (2018), A World of Three Zeros: A World of Social Engagement, Public Affairs (Reviewed December 2017)

The Nobel Peace Prize Laureate, Muhammad Yunus from Bangladesh is the founder of Grameen Bank, a key developer of the micro-finance concept. Micro-finance has had, and is having, a major positive impact on economic development among many poor and has helped lift millions of families around the world out of poverty. Dr. Yunus received the Nobel Peace Prize in 2006.

The three zeros he discusses in the book are:

- Zero poverty. His focus lies on tackling poverty, but he also addresses the topic of income inequality. This issue is, a difficult one in all societies. The relative low-income inequality that can be found in the Nordic countries or Switzerland, for instance, has been attributed as a contributing factor to the economic success of these countries.
- Zero unemployment. Here he looks at how to create jobs, how to get people involved in active work. There are lessons to be had regarding the potential dangers of allowing new technologies to become too efficient in eliminating jobs. People should be employed, rather than out of work (even if society might have to offer financial support to facilitate the employment). In Switzerland, for instance, low-income persons are doing active work in cleaning up the environment, parks, and streets. They receive salaries for this, rather more than passive financial compensation. Jobs are thus created. Self-esteem is on the rise!
- Zero net carbon. Dr. Yunus argues for the need to create a more sustainable eco-economic system, including through taxing pollution, creating carbon-trading systems, and providing economical support for technological advances that may curtail pollution, such as solar power or windmill generated electricity, electric cars, gas-driven turbines, buses and ships, etc.

The author goes further, however, by discussing another three key factors that he feels may help to speed up these transformations:

- Youth. He stresses the importance of a "young" demographic profile (in contrast to what we find in countries such as Japan and in Western Europe, where lack of economic growth has been attributed to aging populations). Dr. Yunus underscores that this younger generation must be energized and empowered.

- Technology. Dr. Yunus points out that advances in technology might also be a key factor to make life better for many. As an example, he points out mobile telephony, which has dramatically opened up for communication among many. However, as already discussed (under zero unemployment), technological advances can become a double-edged sword, when indiscriminately eliminating jobs.
- Good governance. He points out that good governance is also important, in national societies as well as for corporations, plus raises the issue of corruption and how to ameliorate it. Even more fundamentally, he covers the awareness of dysfunctional consequences from power imbalances and gender inequality. He calls for a strengthening of the human rights for all.

In order to impact financial infrastructure and to influence world leaders to speed up major changes, Dr. Yunus calls for closer cooperation between government and private sectors. He mentions companies such as Renault, Essilor and Danone as positive examples. Impact investing comes to mind!

How do we measure returns on philanthropy? What are the philanthropic goals? But what are philanthropic goals actually? There may perhaps not be any right way to be a philanthropist, to give nor to measure! These comments are worth keeping in mind when reading Dr. Yunus' book. Although he is convincing, what he proposes may certainly not represent the only way!

Andrew Hill, (2019), Ruskinland: How John Ruskin Shapes our World, Pallas Athene (reviewed September 2020)

Mr. Ruskin, a world-famous English philosopher and author who lived during the Victorian era, greatly impacted business, universities and us as citizens. His major contribution was on doing, i.e., action rather than procrastination. "Today, today, today," as he said. Focus on education is key, none the least when it comes to learning ("try it"). Principles are delineated, perhaps most critical being to avoid "laissez faire."

John Ruskin's motto, "To-day, to-day, to-day," and his words, "things are either possible or impossible," have relevance today. If things are impossible, do not trouble yourself about it: if possible, try for it! Clearly, these could be central leadership principles for today's organizations and for its successful leaders. John Ruskin died in 1900. He was an artist, rather than a business leader. It is remarkable, however, how relevant much of his thinking still seems to be now almost a century and a half after his contributions were formulated.

Andrew Hill is an associate editor of Financial Times and a world-leading expert on leadership in business organizations. To explore how a thought leader from the nineteenth century might still be a source of inspiration for today's leaders, is undoubtedly a key reason why the author has embarked on this book.

Mr. Ruskin may have been largely forgotten, even though he was perhaps the most influential thinker in UK's nineteenth century world. Who was John Ruskin? His primary ambition was to be a leading art critic, combined with being an important artist himself (drawings above all). But, he spanned over a much broader area of influence than this, being also a prolific writer (39 books, thousands of articles and letters) as well as a teacher (Oxford; Working Men's College).

He was hands on but tried to combine the inspirational with the practical. He was both eclectic and eccentric! And, he was comfortable with teaching adults, of various races, both genders and different social status. Ruskin encouraged his students, both at Oxford and at Working Men's College, to build links between different items, so as to develop a broader understanding regarding how art and other disciplines, such as geology, for instance, might be seen together. He expertly covered art, history, science, economics, politics, biology, geology… you name it! He was a universalist par excellence!

Eclecticism resounds here. Similarities with another artist who lived more than a century later, the world-famous Danish painter Asger Jorn, may come to mind. The most striking similarity is that such eclecticism, these broad interests, characterized them both. And, both men were politically radical and philosophically radical, and Jorn was indeed a devoted communist. While Ruskin was not radically outspoken politically, his thinking has no doubt been an early inspirer for the welfare state concept.

There are many positive ways for leaders (and all of us) to live a better life:

- Seeing, observing, and understanding, i.e., to try to see things more clearly, so that they lead to a better understanding. To be good at seeing relationships between often seemingly rather different phenomena, thus coming up with new insights. The focus might primarily have been on "small data," but minutely observed, understood and linked together with great attention to detail.
- Reflection i.e., being a proponent of "slow" living, typically away from the big cities, taking the time to "understand" and being highly disciplined when it came to how to spend time and energy. Ruskin was exceptionally

hard working but was seemingly not driven by what might have been seen as a dysfunctionally hectic agenda.
- Provenance, "local," focusing on what was unique from a local perspective. While respecting the "local," Ruskin was in fact what we would today call "global." (Ruskin did indeed spend more than 50% of his life outside of his home country.)
- Humans and their environments. Ruskin had a strong interest in conserving buildings, and the environment—to preserve the original context, dictated by physical architectural layout and the nature the way it was. Ruskin may indeed be seen as the driver behind the UK's first national park and as a forerunner for UK's national park system.
- Ethical leadership and meaningful work.
- Connectedness. To "connect the dots" among many people, representing different fields. Today, we label this a "network." To cultivate links in such a network was critical. This is also the way leading organizations work today.
- Quality and quantity. Ruskin was highly prolific, but always with quality and insightfulness, rather than quantity, even sloppiness. Perhaps, we might characterize him as having an anthropological mindset, with a focus on "having done it," confident but not arrogant. Ruskin was a celebrity for much of his life, but he did not act that way. This could be contrasted with a sociological mindset—talking about things, in the way many consultants and academicians do, but without having sufficient hands-on understanding, and often with a lot of arrogance! Ruskin was the anti-thesis of this.
- Economics. When it came to criticizing traditional economics, Ruskin was clear, having an aversion to "laissez faire," and instead believing in commitment. He was a social critic, objecting to the fact that some had received ill-acquired gains, and a somewhat negative relationship with wealth. Ruskin felt that wealth could positively influence the lives of others, however. He had inherited a large amount of money from his father, a successful wine merchant, and gave most of it away.
- "A little too many irons in the fire." Overwork eventually started to drive Ruskin to the edge of sanity. His mind bubbled over with so many ideas that could have required several lifetimes to adequately follow-up on all of them.
- What came afterwards? Ruskin, a giant in his lifetime, has basically faded away after his death. There is a Ruskin College at Oxford, and a permanent Ruskin collection at Sheffield Art Museum, as well as a city in Florida named after him. Yet, there is little left among his thoughts today. Indirectly, he seems to have inspired many, however. Many good practices in modern leadership can be traced back to Ruskin.

A networking approach is hard to pull off but is powerful and can potentially lead to outstanding results. This requires hard work and energy, as most leaders know. It is a matter of practicing "today, today, today" but with an eclectic balance.

Risto Siilasmaa, (2019), Transforming Nokia: The Power of Paranoid Optimism to Head through Colossal Changes, McGraw Hill (Reviewed in October 2022)

This is an important book, detailing how Nokia changed its strategy, by exiting the hand-held mobile phone business, where it was once the global leader, for then to expand into the business of networks to support mobile telephony through base stations, pivoting to global leadership here, after Ericsson and Huawei. It was a transformation that could be considered one of the most dramatic makeovers in modern business today and can easily serve as inspiration for other companies busy or aiming for their own transformations. The book, written by Nokia's chairman, Mr. Risto Siilasmaa, illustrates how the company's board of directors, above all lead by its chairman, played a key role when it came to successfully achieving this strategic transformation. This represents another theme that can benefit any business leader— effectively utilizing board talents and guidance in times of extreme change. As Siilasmaa himself shares on his blog, "the ultimate role of the board is doing whatever it takes to maximize the leadership team's success."

The author details this transformation, driven by his, the board's and the management's *paranoid optimism*. Interestingly, much of the transformation was built on cooperation with business giants such as Microsoft, Siemens, and Alcatel-Lucent. In the end, a new culture had to be created, above all, built on trust, according to the author.

The author explains how Nokia came back from being almost eliminated, to a new success. Learning seems to have been central, and the author outlines how learning may have shaped the "new Nokia" in several ways. Thus, the power of paranoid optimism and the precepts of "Entrepreneurial Leadership" built sustainable success.

The book falls into two parts. During part one, the first eight chapters, the author discusses possible major lessons for how a firm's board of directors and its top management may or may not be able (or willing) to see danger clouds on the horizon, even when a storm is brewing! In the second part, the remaining 11 chapters, the author outlines how Nokia actually went about to reposition itself. The author had become chairman of Nokia's board then and provides useful summaries of learning points throughout as well as practical wrap-ups at the end of several of the chapters.

The author summarizes main learnings from previously having been hugely successful to becoming unable to admit or even see upcoming mistakes:

1. Bad news does not reach you or your team.
2. Your team does not appreciate negative news, even when based on facts.
3. Ameliorating decisions are postponed and watered down.
4. There is often a plan A, but no alternative plans B, C, or D!

A culture that is driven by data analysis and regular deep dives is called for!

The rest of the book, detailing Nokia's actual transformation, is the part that was the most interesting to this reviewer. When taking charge in a crisis, the author and chairman sees ten key, critical aspects of entrepreneurial leadership:

- Hold yourself accountable.
- Face facts.
- Be persistent.
- Manage risk, i.e., with open eyes and in a deliberate, analytical way.
- Be a learning addict.
- Build a team of people you like and respect.
- Ask why.
- Never stop dreaming.
- Maintain focus.
- Look to the horizon.

The three last dimensions here might sum up what paranoid optimism entails!

The author further reflects on what paranoid optimism might entail when he looks back at the negotiations with Microsoft, which ultimately lead to the sale of the hand-held telephony business to Microsoft—a bold move indeed! Over time, it also turned out that this became one of Nokia's best moves! Here is the essence of a successful paranoid optimist's negotiation tactics:

- Maximize face time, in contrast to virtual communication.
- Build a small negotiation team.

- Meet counterparts, i.e., chairman to chairman, CEO to CEO, CFO to CFO, etc.
- Prepare negotiation tactics in advance.
- Be systematic and clear.
- Keep the board on board!
- Maintain negotiation momentum.
- Ask boldly what is needed.
- Build relationships.
- Avoid being trapped by one's own ego.
- Create trust.

The issue of creating trust is of course equally relevant inside the company's own organization. Critical issues here are:

- Never lie.
- Admit openly that you cannot talk about a given topic, and explain why, if possible.
- Say the most you can! Get across that you are doing your best.
- Discuss the upcoming process that might be taken.

It is paramount to develop an organizational culture which drives the way one is operating, built around being paranoid optimists, of course:

- Accountability.
- Scenario-based thinking.
- Trust.
- Calmness.
- Laughter.

Nokia's leaders deserve high marks for entering into strategic alliances with several of the world's most prominent corporations, such as Siemens, Microsoft, and Alcatel-Lucent. Here are a few observations:

NSS (Nokia Siemens Networks). This merger between the two companies' network businesses, created in 2007, was largely driven by the fact that the investments needed in 3G and 4G was too large for each company alone. Yet, the two companies' cultures differed dramatically, with Siemens being much more formalistic, perhaps more bureaucratic, one might say.

Microsoft was understandably driven by its aspiration to develop a viable business for hand-held phones to realistically compete with Apple and Samsung. For them, a wholly owned strategy was probably more attractive than to build such a strategy on a joint venture with Nokia. Hence, in the end, Microsoft bought out Nokia, on quite favorable terms to Nokia, it might be said.

Alcatel-Lucent. By combining with this group, Nokia's new entity may be in a better position to compete against Ericsson and Huawei in network businesses. But, this added immense additional cultural challenges, with the company effectively now being Finnish, French, American, Chinese, etc. Only 1% of Nokia's 1999 workforce were still with the company! So far though, it seems to work!

In conclusion, this reviewer is left with a deep sense of admiration for what Nokia seems to have successfully undertaken and completed. Paranoid optimism seems to work! This seems to be a main element in successful entrepreneurial leadership! Open-mindedness, learning and a "can-do culture" also seem necessary—Finnish sisu (determination, purpose and grit, bravery and resilience)!

Howard Thomas and Yuva Hedrick-Wong, (2019), Inclusive Growth, Emerald (reviewed May 2020)

Both economic and social inclusion seem important for allowing individuals as well as firms to grow, based on creating the necessary access to the economic resources that growth might take. The authors formed four specific factors regarding this: interaction/trust-building, more inclusion (above all through mobile telephony) training and including more women. It is a matter of bonding, within the networks, bringing diverse interest groups together and lining, i.e., developing ties to entities with power and influence. So, for corporate leaders one should always recognize that enhancement of growth implies many other things than simply having lined up financing.

The gap between the wealthy and the poor around world seems to continue to grow, above all perhaps caused by lack of access to some fundamental inputs required to create value. Social impact investing is a tool which could reverse this trend. The authors have conducted a multi-year research project to explore effects on socio-economic inequality of such social impact investing, the topic of this book.

This research project was carried out at the Singapore Management University (SMU), where Dr. Thomas served as the Dean of the business school. The co-author Dr. Wong is a former Chief Economist at the

MasterCard Inc. company, which contributed the majority of the funding for this study.

A central concept of the book is that inclusive growth consists of two components: Financial and social. There needs to be access to basic inputs such as electricity, healthcare, and education, which in turn enable input such as IT networks, financial services, and property rights to come about. Complementary asset input, such as social capital, professional networks and skill networks, shall also become more available now.

To experience this inclusive growth should be a basic right for all. It is a matter of having access to the necessary resources to be able to participate in modern economic value creation processes. This comes down to financial as well as social inclusion. Uncovering what are the main routes to breaking down the barriers to inclusion:

- More interaction and trust-building.
- Effective adoption of mobile telephony, making inclusion easier and less expensive.
- More effective training.
- Empowerment of women, a key for cracking this inclusion conundrum.

So how might we define financial inclusion? The authors do not come up with a clear definition but rather indicate what financial inclusion might entail. They discuss opening up for various ways of digitalization: payments, credit, saving, and insurance. The mobile phone is key, a powerful enabler of all of this. Financial exclusion in these areas results in a lack of such formal financial services—a particular problem when it comes to developing economies in Asia and Africa.

Social inclusion entails:

- A certain element of financial literacy.
- Digital capabilities.
- A minimum of trust with regards to financial institutions.

The book clarifies the often-used term social capital, arguing that the use of the word capital might be misleading. Instead, we are perhaps talking about capabilities in society, especially to stimulate various forms of entrepreneurship. Are the entrepreneurial networks in a particular society effective? Only then will the social capital be sufficient to spark entrepreneurship. Key characteristics of an effective network might be:

- Bonding: are the various networks and sub-networks sufficiently interwoven?
- Bridging: tying together different social network components might be key, such as acquaintances and interest groups.
- Linking: ties to people or organizations with power, social clout or influence.

The authors then outline how social entrepreneurship can take place within an effective social capital context. Social entrepreneurship is what happens in the overlap between profitability and social goals, i.e., entrepreneurship and the effort to change the negative aspects of a society. Social entrepreneurship, often labeled social impact investing, is thus the instrument to improving differences when it comes to wealth creation, among countries as well as among smaller groups of individuals.

What seems to be the main role of women in all of this, specifically female entrepreneurs? They make the point that in many cultures women are often excluded from becoming effective members of economic growth-enhancing efforts. Such exclusion of women may represent a major indicator that a particular society in general suffers from low financial and/or social inclusion.

So, the importance of access seems critical, in particular perhaps categories of critical core resources to improve productivity:

- Networks for basic inputs: electricity, water supply, transportation, health systems and education.
- Additional input regarding logistics, information (communication networks, financial services networks, legal systems, and intellectual property frameworks).
- Complementary input such as social capital, knowledge, and professional networks.

The research also evaluated ten case studies to illustrate various aspects of furthering inclusive growth. These add weight to the research findings, and a few which we found particularly illustrative are:

- Veriown (India), an enabling platform in the areas of solar energy and micro-finance—the two work well together!
- iCare (Vietnam), an electronic payment system for digital financial services.
- Fullerton Financial Holding (Myanmar), an innovative lending solution with administrative structures.

So, inclusion and entrepreneurship can help to flatten differences between wealthy and less wealthy countries, societal groups, as well as individuals. More effective financial inclusion as well as social inclusion thus lie at the heart of tackling this challenge. This approach is clearly much more appealing than various forms of societal revolutions and tries to modify the context for economic value creation in a given society, Totalitarianism is clearly not the only way, nor preferred!

Peder Anker, (2020), The Power of the Periphery, Cambridge University Press (Reviewed August 2021)

This book deals with environmental changes, and specifically how corporations may become impacted by legislation in this area, enacted by various governments. The author, a historian at New York University, claims that relatively smaller countries, in this case, Norway, could be effective proponents for the introduction of pertinent legislation to establish new norms. He points out the pioneering efforts by Norway's former Prime Ministers Gro Harlem Brundtland (climate; the Rio Conference; ban on cigarette smoking) and Jens Stollenberg (NATO). For business leaders, it may make good sense to scan trends emerging in smaller countries, to detect/take advantage of novel practices for doing business.

This book discusses how pioneering environmental policies were developed in the relatively small country of Norway. The author, Dr. Peder Anker, a professor at New York University, claims that the evolution of environmentalism in this relatively small "peripherical" country might serve as an example for larger countries, worldwide.

The book's topic is of course central, namely, how to find more effective ways to cope with environmental deterioration, perhaps above all, air pollution-related issues leading to adverse climatic changes, as well as the degradation of our world's water resources, and so on. We are faced with severe climate problems throughout the world: record high temperatures, forest fires, torrential storms, flooding, strong rainfall, mudslides, and so on. And, at the same time, there seems to be a broad realization that little has been agreed upon so far when it comes to controlling these issues, primarily perhaps those relating to the emission of CO_2 gases. There simply does not appear to be a strong political will to prioritize climate control, at the expense of further economic growth. The political will to make such a tradeoff does just not exist.

But may we perhaps be at a point of change? Can our plant still be saved? Specifically, are we able (and willing) to transfer faster from fossil fuels (coil, oil, …) to renewables? And, is it possible to find an agreement on this especially among the world's largest players, in particular the US, China, India, and EU? It might be noted, for instance that while China looks to be coming along well in their process of phasing out coal-fired power plants, this country is nevertheless offering funding for construction of new coal-fired electric plants to several developing countries in Africa.

Let us summarize six factors that might represent "prerequisites" for environmental changes:

- Is there a strong and broad opinion that these issues matter? While previously nothing seems to have changed since the first global conference on climate in Rio de Janeiro in 1983, there may currently perhaps be a growing realization that time may now be running out, and thus, the time is now!
- Can we observe further deteriorating effects on our environment such as forest fires, heavy air pollution, floods, etc.? The answer may now increasingly be "yes!"
- Are we ready to accept that cooperation across national borders may be critical as well as necessary? We saw that this worked well when it came to curtailing acid rain in Northern Europe. Hopefully, we could see more of this.
- Specific actions are called for, rather than endless discussions leading to nothing. Perhaps this was one of the key lessons one might draw from the climate chatter this far, not much action!
- Is there a sufficiently strong political willingness to act? The book points out that this appears to have been the case in Norway when the labor party was in charge for over two decades, from 1945 onwards. And, this increasingly seems the case today when it comes to key countries, such as China or the US.
- Tensions and stress among key stakeholders might indeed be a "prerequisite" for progress. We see this when it comes to opposing views between countries that appear willing to accept more sustainable realities, such as in the US as well as in many European countries, versus those countries putting higher focus on continued economic growth, such as perhaps India and many African nations. And, we see how tensions among academic disciplines as well as between many high profile individuals have led to ultimate progress, in the end.

A key proviso needs to be stated now, before doing this: The book's main focus is on how Norway "journeys to develop a more sustainable environmental stance. Is this putting limits on the book's conclusion? We think not.

The book's introduction reports on the Global Seed Vault, constructed by Norway's government deep inside a mountain in Svalbard, at the world's northernmost city, are able to store seeds from various plants in the world over long periods of time. This might be interpreted as an example of Norway's willingness to commit to broader environmental issues. The book further details contributions from several Norwegians when it comes to enhancing environmental insights, highlighting an extraordinary exposé to various aspects of ecological issues, rooted on expeditions, back to nature, studying indigenous people, anthropological studies of Sherpa villages in Nepal, and so on.

Ecological concerns came into the forefront after the publication of findings relating to dysfunctional effects from DDT. Biologists now sat at forefront when it came to research on various aspects of ecological issues, with an aim to try to determine when a new steady state might be reached, i.e., with environmental degradation possibly "flattening out." This also led to an increased interest in ecological issues among philanthropists, the emergence of principles of environmental ethics for how to be good to the world. While some of these eco-philosophers might seem rather pessimistic in their outlooks, others took a more optimistic stance, perhaps inspired by Mao or Ghandi. Protests against the construction of new electric plants were usually peaceful.

This eco-philosophic movement evolved into what the author has labeled "deep ecology." This was broadly based, with eclectic focus, study groups, and with inspiration primarily from "oriental ecological wisdom," as opposed to "accidental stupidity." University courses were introduced to focus on environmental studies, such as at University of Oslo from 1972. Over time, this movement became more politically left wing, although building more on Marxist's ideology, and it gradually also lost importance. Instead, so-called "shallow" ecology became more prominent, with less focus on left wing social analysis. Perhaps, an important learning here may be those ecological institutions, relatively closely linked to specific political dogmas, tend to be less easily "acceptable" as examples to be followed more broadly in societies. The "shallow" ecological findings outlined in the report Limits to Growth, as an example, seem to have had quite a broad impact.

The link to religion might be critical too. This meant a new focus on nature, not only wilderness in a narrow sense, but also on plants, insects, and animals, i.e., on the "life necessities society," in contrast to "industrial growth society."

The primary focus was on to do good, to find harmony. Action research sprawled, with the aim being to find eco-friendly solutions. Unfortunately, some of these solutions might be labeled as having missionary overtones and with a "do-gooding gaze." Again, we see that too strong links to theology could weaken broad acceptance of various types of ecological actions. This being said, it seems important to recognize that environmental topics have become vital to most Christians.

The church as a whole seems to have moved more towards eco-theology. But science, not religion, should be at the core of new knowledge. This brings us back to what might be seen as a sustainable society. Sustainability could be considered normative, a vision for how an environment of the future may be. And, a Christian perspective might be key here. Moral strength seems to be important to drive sustainability.

So-called "shallow" ecology focusses on pollution control and depletion of natural resources, more than enough for the development of new ecological norms. The earlier described "deep ecology," on the other hand, concentrates perhaps on too many factors to actually achieve a real sense of realism, say on our ways of life, economic systems, societal power structures, and national differences.

The acid rain phenomenon provides a good example of what new norms might lead to. Mrs. Brundtland, then Minister for Environment in Norway, came up with a system for measuring the emission of CO_2 from coal-fired power plants in various northern European countries, and these countries then agreed to limit their emission levels in line with what became agreed on as new norms. As a result, emissions from Poland and, in particular, the UK were scaled down. The result was immediately noticeable: less acidity in rivers and less damage on forests.

So, what does the author see for our common future? The climatological side of the ecological equation seems more and more under control, with cost-benefit analysis, to come up with "solutions" for climate changes. How might a peripheral country such as Norway be a driving force, a world pioneer, regarding environmental changes, especially those that relate to the emission of CO_2, acid rain, and depletion of the Ozone layer? We have already covered the need to come up with cross-national accepted new norms, such as the one that specified maximum acceptable emission levels from coal-fired power plants, which led to a reduction of acid rain. Another approach pioneered by Norway is so-called trading in carbon emission certificates between producers and countries. Norway, for instance, would finance clean development mechanisms in various relatively poor countries, for then to purchase the resulting carbon emission certificates that these countries would then be able to sell.

These certificates would then off-set dysfunctional effects from Norway's burgeoning off-shore oil industry.

Perhaps, this is an example of trying to avoid a binary thinking regarding "life necessities" societies versus industrial growth societies. Perhaps, there are ways to combine the two as we saw when it came to carbon emission certificate trading. There exists nevertheless a potential tension between the two sides, for good and bad. Norway's "do-good" profile focused primarily on climatological issues, emission issues, rather than broader ecological issues seem to have led to positive results! Good! But, this "do-good" profile has also provided incentives for various Norwegian firms to pollute abroad. Bad! There is of course no end to this saga of more versus less effective environmental initiatives. More will clearly come.

Klaus Schwab and Thierry Malleret, (2020), Covid-19: The Great Reset, Agentur (August 2021)

The recent pandemic has led to several fundamental changes in how firms articulate their strategies and how executives work. The authors identify five such changes, resets as they say: Social—how societies are learning how to be more effective in handling such pandemics. Economic—increased use of robots, working from home aided by technology. Geographical—China versus Europe versus US versus the rest of the world, the role of WHO and of the assistance from the more developed world to the less developed. Environmental—Speed of diseases from animals to human, none the least due to diminishing space for animals. Technological—accelerating trends regarding digital transformation. The authors also point us towards how changes in creativity might happen, how the concept of time could change, how consumer trends might be impacted and how increases in mental health issues may become new realities, all of which have important implication for business.

The COVID pandemic represents the most important public-health challenge that our world has faced. This book discusses ways to address this, so as to hopefully be able to alleviate some of its impacts going forward. The authors are Dr. Klaus Schwab, Founder and Executive Chairman of the World Economic Forum (WEF), and Dr. Thierry Malleret, economist and Founder of the Global Risk Network at the WEF.

That the pandemic has put our world in a serious crisis is beyond doubt. Many changes had to come about. The authors make the strong point that we should take advantage of this. But, it was indeed hard to come up with a clear set of actions because the present pandemic-induced crisis seemed to be quite different from any other crisis. Thus, history may not be able to provide us with relevant guidance. The authors have however nevertheless been able to comprehensively analyze what the world has faced. The authors state that several "pillars" would have to be adhered to, namely widespread interdependence, high velocity (speed) as well as large complexity. Based on this, they suggested several "resets":

- Economic reset. They made the vital observation that, the inevitable economic reset did indeed entail a labor market crisis; people were in part replaced by robots and "smart" automation. We have seen a shift, from focus on growth in economies' gross national products (GNP), swinging towards the "care economy" (health, welfare, education, …). The power of massive fiscal stimulation "packages" to keep economies was also introduced. And, the relatively stable US dollar was seen as a precondition for gaining successful economic reset.
- Societal reset. Societies that were more effective in handling this pandemic crisis were usually characterized as being better prepared, able to make faster, decisive decisions, having well developed healthcare systems, enjoying good leadership with high emphasis on widespread trust and societal acceptance, and with solidarity being a common societal denominator. The crisis often led to a relative spike in governments' powers, manifested largely through increased funding to the public sector. This made it even more paramount that the governmental sector be competently run. In line with this shift, the so-called social contract within many societies emphasized more social assistance and more protection of those most vulnerable in society.
- Geographical reset. The authors discussed the geopolitical "trilemma" of only two of the following three critical success factors being mutually attainable: economic globalization (such as free trade and non-protectionism); political democracy (i.e., in contrast to dictatorial regimes); and nation state (nationalistic policies). Two important trends seemed to be reversing—global supply chains "shortening," with relatively more regionalization instead, and more nationalistic policies rising, such as imposing restrictions on foreign owners buying into what a nation might consider to be strategic companies, for them and/or to prevent foreign takeovers. Even though the World Health Organization (WHO) may have been saddled with much inefficiency, this institution nevertheless represented a potentially positive force for combatting COVID-19. Direct as

well as secondary effects from the pandemic led to national instability, not only when it came to the burden of handling the significant increased costs, coupled with a lower taxable income, but also due to significantly less income from tourism, due to travel restrictions. Prices on fossil fuels also hurt many countries' economies.

- Environmental reset. Diseases, spreading from animals to humans are on the rise. Growing urban sprawl and significant deforestation have brought animals and humans more closely packed together. More effective environmental policies were called for, appealing for changes in our behavior, so as to seriously increase our prioritization of better environments.
- Technological reset. The pandemic seemed to have induced an accelerating trend regarding technological progress and digital transformation. Three major stakeholder groups searched for new technologies to cope with the pandemic: the customers with online shopping and home delivery; the regulators with more liberal payment approaches; and the firms with more automation. A dilemma arose, namely, how to protect personal freedom while also stimulating technological advances, analogous to protecting public health benefits while not infringing on personal freedom.

Resets were also seen at the micro level of society, for business firms as well as for various industries. Firms tended to cope with this in four ways: First, to take advantage of acceleration of digitalization, such as implementing O2O (online to office). Secondly, shortening and simplifying supply chain. Third, increasing salaries, including minimum wage levels. And, finally, implementing a broadened stakeholder focus, such as ESG (environment, social, governance).

Resets within various industries are driven by three major factors:

- The extent to which social interaction may have changed, for instance, in much of the entertainment industry i.e., theaters, cinemas, concerts, and sports.
- Are key behavioral factors changing? We saw this, for instance, when it came to the increased frequency of shopping, for instance, vacationing, and so on.
- Resilience: To what extent were industries able to thrive in different circumstances?

Finally, the resets for us as individuals were also significant. What were typical effects from self-isolation and/or disarrays of personal and professional plans? The authors delineated several areas where the pandemic seemed to impact individuals: Creativity; how we spent our time; how our patterns of consumption changed; and how our mental health and sense of well-being changed. Is there now a stronger move back to nature?

So, the pandemic crisis led to significant resets, at the macro-, micro-, and individual levels. This book was a quest to better understand how complex crises may be coped with, and also to lead to new insights potentially supporting how mankind can deal with future critical global challenges that could also become crises, for example, nuclear threats, climate shifts, the seemingly uncontrollable extraction of natural resources (mining, forestry, fishing, …), and dangerously widening income differences, and so on.

Ian Bremmer, (2022), The Power of Crisis: How Three Threats—And our Response—Will Change the World, Simon & Schuster (Reviewed June 2022)

This book offers hope on how we might face with the following three critical problems currently present in our world:

- Global health emergencies (such as the one we experienced with COVID-19).
- Transformative climate change (global warming; CO_2 emission).
- Artificial intelligence (AI) revolution.

The author explains that the coming crises likely to face us as listed above may actually drive many of us, to an extent, politicians and normal citizens alike, to come up with workable solutions. Serious crises, felt by so many, may actually catalyze us to positive actions!

Dr. Ian Bremmer. Boston-born, and with a Ph.D. from Stanford, is the President of Eurasia Group, a leading consulting and research firm dealing with major global socio-political issues. He also teaches at Columbia University.

According to Dr. Bremmer, we are facing two major collision courses which shall "shape" the way we face with the above three emerging major worldwide crises. The two collisions are "us versus them," i.e., the increasingly dysfunctional and polarized America, and "at home and abroad," i.e., the rivalry between America and China. While the first might be seen as quite obvious to most of us and may be relatively easy to understand, the second may require some further elaboration. There seem to be three major reasons why China appears to be "drifting away" from America: China's reluctance to open up more of its market, its readiness to subsidize many of its companies, often quite heavily indeed, and its disrespect for rules protecting intellectual property, at times even manifesting itself as outright stealing. But there is also hope. Above all, the interrelationship between China and America when it comes to trade is strong, indeed much more so than the case of US-Soviet relationship during the Cold War. So, there are opportunities, even though the rising trends towards more Chinese nationalism do lead to concern.

The first major dilemma facing the world is pandemic politics. Generally, the worldwide experience in coping with COVID-19 was not good—lack of resolute early handling in China during the outbreak period, no global coordination of vaccination, and so on. What can we learn, to be better prepared to handle the next pandemics certain to come, perhaps even more infectious than COVD 19? Dr. Bremmer offers six areas of action: Invest significantly now, so that we all (politicians and "ordinary people") know what to do; exchange information, above all based on a more systematic global approach to testing; share burdens more equally (a good example might be the so-called COVAX project that brings together governments and vaccine manufacturers to ensure more equal access to vaccines worldwide); and more effective learning from COVID-19 (testing, restrictions on mobility, use of marks, …).

The second major source of crisis seemingly facing us is climate change. What is driving global warming, and the excessive emission of so-called climate-impacting gases, above all $CO2$? Dr. Bremmer discusses six factors: water, too much and too little(!); competition (resistance by many countries to impose restrictions and thereby impeding their abilities to catch up with more wealthy economies); migration (so-called "climate refugees" due to rising sea levels, excessive heat, and so on); unrest and conflict; "climate apartheid" (the richer parts of the world simply ignoring the poorer ones); and dangers of geo-engineering (such as climate manipulation, "cloud whitening," and so on). Dr. Bremmer points out several courses of action against climate emergency: setting rules, joint R&D, schemes for "managing" carbon, planting more trees and better forest protection, above all. But who pays for all of this? A "green" Marshall Plan might be needed. National approaches to this global problem may simply not suffice!

Disruptive technologies represent the third major source of global conflict. A "digital divide" appears to exist, and a race, above all between the US and China, to be ahead, as witnessed for instance when it came to the controversy over 5G (fifth generation) in mobile telephony, which offers much faster and more powerful features than earlier types of networks. There are indeed new risks emerging: autonomous weaponry, cyber-war technology, and drone-based technologies above all. Perhaps, a world data organization might be called for?

The concluding chapter of the book starts with a quote from Louis Pasteur, which is highly appropriate: "Change favors only the prepared mind." So, what are the major "pillars" of such "preparation"? We may revert to more effective ways of cooperation within already existing organizations, such as United Nations, the World Trade Organization, NATO, and the European Union. Dr. Bremmer has suggested a four-part agenda for cooperation here:

- A global COVAX.
- A binding agreement on reduction of carbon emissions.
- A green Marshall Plan.
- A world data organization.

Large corporations, with their leaders, may have their own definite views when it comes to these factors. Fundamentally, there could be only three outcome scenarios:

- The state reigns supreme, and so-called national champions win.
- Corporations capture the state, and globalization wins.
- The state fades and techno-utopians win.

While none of these scenarios probably offer "ideal" outcomes, the first one does seem to provide at least some degree of stability. More effective cooperation seems to be the key. A positive vision would be called for so as to shape the world order. Fear alone is not enough, i.e., what might come about from the severe crisis facing mankind. The challenges ahead are plentiful, but the author is a guarded optimist!

Yascha Mounk, (2022), The Great Experiment, Penguin Random House (Reviewed May 2022)

This important book discusses possible paths for the various societies of this world towards more authority and intolerance, or towards more all-inclusive, tolerant democracies. How do we turn a mono-ethnic and conventional democracy into a multi-ethnic one? And, how might such a vision of the future be something that members of both majority and minority groups in society embrace? There are indeed plenty of examples that imperialism may be on the increase. Examples abound: Russia (Putin), China (Xi), Brazil (Bolzanaro), US (Trump), Hungary (Orban), and Philippines (Marcos), just to mention a few.

The author recognizes, in full, that the outcome of the evolution we are in does not seem to clarify whether more tolerant multiracial democracies shall become the future norm or not.

The core topic of the book is of course of critical importance, also for us in business. As Anne Applebaum, political historian says: "anyone interested in the future of liberal democracy should read this book." The author is a German-born social scientist who has lived in the US for the last decade and a half. He is now a professor at John Hopkins University. The author is an optimist, which we find to be encouraging when attempting to grapple with this complex book. Having rather radical political views, which the author shares without hesitation, the book is nevertheless truly balanced, seemingly objective. It does indeed provide a winning pattern for the future. Most of us, including those active in business, might appreciate this, and we should all read, read, read!

The author sees two main overriding reasons why it may be particularly hard to achieve effective diverse democracies: economic stagnation and mistrust/disinformation stemming from the rise of social media. Ironically, the author also points out that a certain degree of diversity can be a stumbling block, where the role of a majority may deepen the exclusion of some minority groups. A major strength of the book appears already in the introduction, namely, to analyze the challenge of achieving diverse workable democracies from both an optimistic evolutionary viewpoint as well as from a pessimistic one. The positive reality seems to be underscored by the fact that we are making strides when it comes to incorporating diversity. The negative reality, on the other hand, is founded on the fact that white, rich men often still seem to have a hold.

A discussion of why everyone cannot just get along provides the start of this section. Important words: different races, religions, and levels of income. This analysis is taken further by examining ways that societies might fail. Anarchy is the first, with chaos arising, stemming from the absence of state power. The original work of Thomas Hobbes, the seventeenth century English philosopher, provides the basis for the argument here. Then, domination is introduced as another factor associated with failure of diversity. Interestingly, such failure due to domination may also come from dominating minorities! (Syria, South African's apartheid, …). Fragmentation represents a third source for achieving effective diverse societies. Often arbitrarily set borders are a key source here, particularly in Africa, but also elsewhere (Europe: Belgium, Ireland/Northern Ireland, …). Power sharing may often be difficult!

The first section concludes with a discussion of how to keep the peace. Several prepositions are stated. Provide equal status to all groups, emphasize common goals, build on initiatives that feature intergroup cooperation, and be absolutely clear and consistent when it comes to support from authorities.

This part of the book discusses four foundational questions, each often being quite contested.

- What role should the state play in diverse democracies? There are of course different ways in which citizens of diverse democracies should be able to lead their lives, the degree of state intervention being the determinator.
- Should diverse democracies embrace patriotism? Ethnic patriotism and focus on ethnic "purity" are indeed seen as dysfunctional. But, civil patriotism is seen as normally good, i.e., citizens should be proud of their countries!
- To what extent should immigrants and members of other minority groups be expected to "integrate" into mainstream society? Must many become one? The author discusses the so-called "melting pot" vision, and rejects this, as not sufficiently respecting original national traits, including languages, and religion. The opposite, labeled "salad bowl" by the author, is of course not good either—simply too much fragmentation, no integration at all! The author then introduces his own ideal: "the public park," open to everyone, with freedom to pursue various options, and a functional "meeting place." These are all ideals that one might agree with, but are they too utopic?
- Finally, what kind of informal rules should structure how people lead their daily lives? Can such shared lives be meaningfully built? The author provides several propensities regarding this, including to emphasize what people basically share, showing empathy rather than being overly rash, and to pursue solidarity as much as possible.

To what extent might it be realistic to push for such democratic diversity, what are some particular potential obstacles and what are the costs of failure when it comes to this? The author's view is that cost of failure may be too high. So, why should we be optimistic? A major factor is that most diverse democracies have without a doubt made meaningful progress over the last decades. Most believers of the Islamic faith, for instance, are moderate, and so they do their best to become integrated in the social and economic lives of countries where they have immigrated. But, there are of course also examples of the opposite, i.e., typically involving individuals with a more fundamental faith. Conservatives, in particular, are often quick to blame these groups. The left is frequently in passionate disagreement when it comes to this. The author cites these key factors in this respect:

- Will immigrants and minority groups forever remain second-rate citizens, not being fully accepted into society? While we may be likely to find political and linguistic enclaves, there seems to be no doubt that integration indeed is taking place. The old notion of "Gastarbeiter" in countries such as Switzerland and Germany, for instance, appears on the way out.
- Are immigrants and minorities underperforming in schools, in universities as well as in the job market? Here, it should be noted that many immigrants are indeed highly skilled. Progress when it comes to education, i.e., achieving exams and degrees, is clear. But is it correct that crime and terror tends to be associated with immigrants in particular? Most immigrants clearly embrace the core values of the societies in which they live. And, those who still might have a propensity to practice violence should be firmly opposed by all the rest of us, not accepting that such groups "return to their own tribes" where violence might be tolerated.
- Are such fears of terrorism and propensities to undertake criminal acts forever remaining fundamental threats to the rest of us? Demographics lead to a higher proportion of representation of new citizen groups. But interestingly, these new groups are not necessarily pursuing unique, distinctive agenda items. They often pick up on already well-established political ideas, but frequently while maintaining their own "shades of gray." The new mainstream might be growing more inclusive. Demography is not destiny!

The author makes a good point when he asserts that books about big ideas may typically suffer from "letdowns" when it comes to the challenges raised. Often ameliorating suggestions might be more or less utopian, lacking realism to a considerable degree. He offers four major suggestions for how to pursue societal change, building further on the fact that rapid economic progress may help, giving us reason for optimism.

- It is easier to cheer for the success of different groups when one feels that one's own future is likely to go the right way. This is worthwhile considering that financial crashes seem to benefit the right in particular, while "steady" economic growth seems to benefit the left. The challenge is to find ways to pursue "inclusive growth."

- Low socio-politic standings continue to be a problem for some groups. Universal solidarity is critical here; how do we build on this? Public policy can do a lot. The so-called "welfare state," perhaps pioneered above all in the Scandinavian countries, may be crucial here.
- How might all (or at least most) groups be included when it comes to making key decisions? How can effective inclusiveness be achieved? To welcome immigration, to invite such groups to participate in democratic processes, seems important. Paradoxically, perhaps, a tight border control seems to be more closely related to such welcoming of immigrants.
- How can people with whom one might be in disagreement, be seen in a more agreeable light? To try to push for more mutual respect seems necessary—avoid polarization, avoid "them" versus "us." The author suggests that while sticking to personal principles, one should not only be willing to criticize one's own but also to try to engage and persuade opponents rather than ridicule them.

The author maintains that there are indeed several reasons for optimism, as seen by various developments around the world—more inclusiveness, more acceptance of all, more widely shared economic benefits, and so on. There will always be pessimists, in contrast, but advocates of diverse democracies must have the courage to fight these groups. Various dysfunctional views peddled by pessimists must not be allowed to dominate. A faith in a shared humanity, based on a diverse democratic movement, is what we should be committed to.

9

Executive Profiles of Business Leaders

Jan Egeland, Secretary General of the Norwegian Rescue Council (NRC) (Interviewed April 2019)

The need to think ahead is a key driver for the NRC organization and its Secretary General, and this manifests itself in four core areas where the NRC works: (1) refugees, relief, and resettlement; (2) stimulate impact investing by leading corporations, to create new job opportunities, for youths in particular; (3) fuel innovations in the humanitarian sector, by promoting new technologies and digital transformation, to enhance more efficient running of humanitarian organizations; and (4) better identification documents as a part of enhancing human mobility and fight corruption. NRC's success is clearly linked to its organizational independence, not being associated with any country's foreign policy, nor branded by financially driven biases from where its funds might be sourced.

Nearly 70 million people are escaping violence and conflict facing being displaced by climate change and disasters. Not since the aftermath of World War II, have we seen as many people fleeing their homes in search of safety. Mr. Egeland runs what is known as one of the most effective refugee relief organizations in the world.

The NRC is an independent humanitarian organization focused on helping displaced people in emergency situations across the world. Founded in 1946, has helped 8.5 million displaced people with services such as protection, food, shelter, water, sanitation, education, and livelihood programs. It relies on the efforts of more than 14,000 humanitarians, many of whom are refugees themselves across 31 countries, with several NRC operations located in some of the world's most dangerous and unstable areas. The NRC currently collaborates with several companies and foundations, such as Equinor, BCG, Microsoft, Kluge, and the Grieg Foundation, and is also actively looking to extend such collaborations to more actors from the private sector to reach even more displaced people.

Mr. Jan Egeland has been Secretary General of the NRC since 2013. He has served as the special advisor to several UN relief efforts. From 1990 to 1997, he was State Secretary in the Norwegian Ministry of Foreign Affairs, where he co-organized and co-initiated the Norwegian channel that led to the Oslo Agreement between Israel and the PLO (1993), as well as peace agreements in Guatemala (1996) and elsewhere. He has received a number of international awards, and in 2006, Time Magazine named him one of the "100 people who shape our world."

The NRC's humanitarian principles identical to those articulated by the founder of the Red Cross, Henri Dunant, are:

- Independence. NRC is ready to serve any person in true need, irrespective of international relations, making it independent of all governments.
- Impartiality. NRC is solely driven by human need and is in no way motivated by other factors, such as political considerations, ethnicity, or religion.
- Neutrality. NRC is not "for" nor "against" any particular political regime.
- Humanity. NRC is solely focused on meeting human needs.

NRC's mandate is thus to protect the rights of displaced and vulnerable people during grave crises. It does so by providing emergency assistance, contributing to more durable solutions and attempting to prevent further displacement. Crises today produce millions of displaced people, many living in dire conditions. These crises are often in conflict areas with little to no access for international organizations. Here, civilians are often left to their own devices and typically desperately fight for their own survival. To help others may not be high on their agendas.

A particular problem is often the lack of access to civilians caught in crossfire. With the increasing number of complex and dangerous conflicts seen around the world today, the NRC has decided to focus on gaining access to areas that are cut off from the rest of the world. This seems to be paying off. The organization has reached displaced people in areas where few other organizations are present. Much of the success can be attributed to Mr. Egeland's and the NRC's strong reputations as principled humanitarians, a reputation which has proven to be essential for the NRC when negotiating access with local and national governments, civilians, and even armed groups.

Protracted crises may be the new normal today. Crises now typically last for many years, if not decades. It is thus imperative that organizations shift their focus from short-term emergency relief to durable solutions. For the NRC, this means providing displaced people with the opportunity to rebuild their lives through education and livelihood programs. A life in limbo is not only devastating to people who have been displaced, but it is also costly to our societies. As Mr. Egeland puts it, "There are millions of extremely capable displaced people out there that can and want to contribute to society; they just need to be provided the opportunity to do so. By investing in them and their capacity, everyone will benefit from it." Also "the severe lack of opportunities for the displaced population is a major cause of disruption in the world today. By changing the way we think of refugees—from a problem to a solution—giving them a chance to contribute to their local and national economies, we give them their lives back, and we help stabilize whole countries and regions. Ultimately, this effort will contribute to creating a safer and more predictable world with stable economies, a cause both NRC and the private sector should be and are interested in." Building on its success, NRC provides vocational training and creates job opportunities to the millions of displaced youths who are left behind. "The lack of opportunities for millions of displaced youth is, in many places, a looming disaster. The enormity of the situation calls for an immediate reaction from both the private and humanitarian sector."

In many humanitarian aid and development programs, supporting children is the main priority. Because they are not prioritized, many young people are likely to end up more or less permanently unemployed and often feeling hopeless. This youth challenge is a massive problem we face today. "If you're a young person who has been fighting for an armed group, earning the respect of your peers, earning money, and giving you a sense of purpose, what do you do when peace time comes and there are no opportunities? We need to give people a real chance to become productive members of their communities. However, because governmental donors are more willing to fund so-called "lifesaving" relief or traditional development projects, funding start-up projects for rootless youths in conflict areas has proven to be difficult. Assistance from private-sector partners may not only help to fund this gap, but also often brings in a wealth of knowledge and expertise on how to help develop human capacity and businesses."

The international community is urged to adapt a more holistic approach to solve the many complex crises the world faces today. Private-sector partners may often help: "Let's sit down, discuss, find a common goal and work together. Imagine reaching one million displaced young people, say, from

Colombia or Myanmar, and provide livelihood programs, offering them hope and a sense of purpose. Such a feat would set an impressive precedent for what can be achieved when businesses and humanitarian organizations come together."

New technologies, digital transformation, and several forms of emerging innovations are crucial for humanitarian organizations to increase their efficiency, to improve even more support, say, for hard-to-reach communities. NRC has a strategic aim to become a leader in using data and technology for humanitarian services and is developing partnerships to build in-house skills and infrastructure for this. For example, NRC and Microsoft have a partnership that includes grants for software, funding for technology education specialists, and access to experts in artificial intelligence to support development of humanitarian-focused initiatives.

Fighting the scourge of corruption is often essential. NRC has implemented a rigorous system of control and documentation to address this, involving physical checks, monitoring, internal and external auditing, evaluations, and verifying in real time that various items are actually being used. Most inventory items are also bar-coded. Moreover, the extensive internal revision is documented and analyzed in annual reports. These reports show minimal corruption in NRC's programs. When evidence of wrongdoing is found, it is dealt with swiftly. Thanks to such practices, the NRC is highly regarded by several watchdog institutions, such as Transparency International, for instance.

NRC is entirely a non-governmental organization, with no political or religious affiliation. In 1946, the NRC's original name was Europahjelpen, reflecting its then principal focus on supporting European war refugees, a massive challenge during the years after World War II. NRC's attention has since shifted toward addressing the global refugee issue, a change that took place in the 1950–60 s. Being based in a Scandinavian country is an asset for NRC, none the least since none of the Scandinavian countries have any significant colonial pasts. A Scandinavian way of managing also seems to be regarded as generally positive, with its informal and nonhierarchical perspectives. Possessing valid identification documents would typically be a main determinant for allowing people to move around more freely and to get better access to education, work, and government services. NRC has emphasized making such valid identification documentation available. Indeed, the NRC considers enhancing a person's mobility a particularly valid way of ameliorating the dysfunctionality of being a refugee.

The NRC's status as one of the leading refugee organizations seems to be closely linked to the leadership's direction and the positive and principled drive that Mr. Egeland and his colleagues have provided. The NRC's values are indeed consistent with its top management's values, a key to its success. Clearly, donations are always needed, but today, impact investing is also necessary for the creation of private-sector jobs for displaced youths in conflict areas. A more holistic approach is indeed necessary in the displacement crises, and here, the private sector not only has the financial means to contribute but also relevant know-how. "We are facing a global crisis, the means and expertise of the private sector is needed more than ever."

Klaus Wellershoff, Chairman Wellershof and Partners (Interviewed January 2019)

Dr. Wellershof was chief economist at UBS before starting his own economic consulting firm in 2009, advising corporations on impacts from shifts in economic trends. His messages are four-fold: (1) Be self-critical, when it comes to forecasts given—be ready to make revisions. Prestige and over-confidence should not come into it; (2) speed is critical—unfortunately, there is often excessive bureaucracy and complexity, both in countries' administration, as well as in many large corporations. Such bureaucracy tends to slow things down; (3) to break social norms is also important, but can take a long time—for instance, many of us seem to believe in relatively low inflation as a "reality for life." Such a norm may have to be broken in today's settings; and (4) the economics profession must be fully prepared to become more eclectic in its focus, perhaps with a relatively stronger eye on economic history. Overly mathematically formulated theories may also have to be presented in more broadly understood ways.

To be a successful economist, it is most important to be honest with oneself and to be self-critical and fast. Be honest because one should never oversell oneself or the services of one's company. Be self-critical because that is the only way to improve oneself and one's products. And be fast, because time waits for no one, and speed can be a great competitive advantage, particularly in a world of many complacent large businesses.

In the business of economics, honesty means understanding which forecasts seems more feasible versus which that might be less so, when you analyze the world economy and financial markets, or when one gives advice on investing strategically or tactically. For example, nobody knows where an exchange rate will be at the end of a given year, but most banks and economists still produce such forecasts, probably knowing that this implies knowledge they do not possess. Obviously, this cannot be a basis for good advice.

We shall thus have to be honest about our abilities, as well as our limitations, to advise our clients. Fascinatingly, even though we do not know many things, we economists do nevertheless possess potentially very powerful elements of knowledge about the future. "At our company, we focus on the little things we seem to know, which prepare us for the future of the world economy and of financial markets."

To be self-critical implies analyzing forecast errors, being empirical at every step. Take the theoretical relationship between an exchange rate and the interest rate differential as an example. What good is this theory, if it does not explain the future, particularly if it has never worked consistently in the past? A safe conclusion might be: Not good at all! All our hypotheses and all the advice we give have to pass empirical tests. Otherwise, wishful thinking could taint our recommendations. Unfortunately, this happens quite often. One instance is the Euro currency discussions. Most economists, including Wellershoff, would say that the Euro is not an optimal currency area. He would even venture that it is ill-constructed. But does that mean the Euro will fall apart and should thus be avoided? Of course not, as a look at other ill-constructed currencies will tell us. To separate ideology or political preconceptions from analysis and advice is critical to success in the field of economic advising.

Speed: Consider for instance the research process in large banks where it might have, on average, up to two weeks before a bank's investment committee decisions might be communicated to clients via flagship publications. But in the period of fifteen days, financial markets might turn upside down! Wellershoff advises that once you reach a conclusion, you need to act immediately. Otherwise, you might as well not do research or money management at all!

An economic policy is implemented by government institutions. All large institutions exhibit inertia. In many ways, this is good, provided that such institutions provide stability. If they are supposed to cause change, however, things start getting difficult. They get even more difficult if long-standing population habits, such as smoking, are affected. Breaking a social norm, in particular, can take a long time.

In the field of macroeconomics, we are often confronted with beliefs that change take place at a glacial pace. Sometimes, this is beneficial, such as when inflation expectations are low and well-anchored. Changing such beliefs, however, can be very difficult. In the US in the early eighties, Fed president Paul Volker resorted to double digit rates for Fed funds to bring incredibly high inflation expectations to more tolerable levels. In the process, he triggered a major recession. Many of these considerations are at the center of focus once again, not only at the federal, but also the European commission, Bank of England, Japan's Central Bank and others.

A clear vision is key for high-performing organizations today. This vision needs to be succinct and clearly communicated. In the past, a clear vision was maybe not as important as it is today, given the hierarchal organizational structures we typically had. In today's organizations with flatter hierarchies, a clear vision is central to the business' success. Wellershoff adds, "You must be able to communicate the "why" of your organization well. Otherwise, you might not be able to motivate your younger talents to give their best."

In today's world, you need strong, inspired teams bound together by a vision. Without this vision, you might never see a "go for it" attitude in your employees. Endless debates on why and how, are the death of the agility of an organization. Academia and business economics face their individual challenges. Much of today's business economics has degenerated into sensationalism, almost to the point of entertainment. Just look at the economics section of an airport bookstore. He believes it is a disgrace.

In universities (and perhaps in corporations), we waste our energy on educating too many students. Only the few top talents matter when it comes to advancing our academic understanding of economics. "Do not get me wrong—it is still important to teach students basic economic insights in business school, but the scientific part of economics produces too much absolutely useless information. We do not need tens of thousands of PhD economics students who must publish three articles in scientific journals before receiving their degrees. We need a broader education of our top talents. Nobody should get a higher degree in economics without strong knowledge in a wide range of subjects, such as the history of economic thought, advanced programming skills or a thorough understanding of financial markets and political processes."

10

Closing Remarks for the Part

Adapting a firm's strategy to the external environment is perhaps an issue of being sufficiently open-minded, so as to squarely observe, capture, and reckon with critical shifts that may be more or less apparent. It is perhaps worthwhile to consider the most valuable corporations on Standard and Poor's list of top ten, a generation ago versus today. Classic corporations such as Exxon, General Motors, and General Electric were previously on the list, but are no longer be found on today. High tech, software-driven firms have taken over. Why did Exxon and other energy-producing firms not see the shift towards the increasing prominence of alternative sources of energy? Why did General Motors not see the shift towards electric propulsion? Also, why did General Electric not see the shift towards asset light business activities? There seems to be one overriding conclusion when it comes to this, namely a strong propensity to stick to one's traditions. To question this would typically not be on the agenda.

But, there are exceptions of course. IBM, for instance, successfully exited from hardware manufacturing, then from software to support traditional hardware, and is now primarily a service firm. Its Watson artificial intelligence tool is part of this. Another example is the Danish energy production producer DONG, which used to be the major player in Denmark's oil and gas offshore exploration activities. It has since exited this and is now the world's largest operator of offshore windmills for electricity generation.

In terms of concluding thoughts, let us discuss three overriding factors that often may challenge conventional ways of doing business:

Atmospheric emission issues. These lead to climate change, primarily emission of CO_2. We have already highlighted the emergence of cars with electric propulsion, thereby reducing CO_2 emissions from conventional engine substantially. Tesla is perhaps the pioneer here. We see dramatic increases in the installation of windmills and solar panels for electric energy generation, thereby reducing emissions from coal-fired electric electricity plants. Airlines are increasingly making use of biofuel in their jet engines now much more energy efficient anyhow. And, cement manufacturers and steelmakers are coming up with new ways to operate. One example is the Norwegian producer of fertilizers, Yara, a world leader. This company has been able to develop a fertilizer produced by electricity and not conventional natural gas. A competition among value chains seems to exist—fertilizing to farming to food manufacturing to retail. Major food companies such as Nestlé and Unilever may be expected to compete, through being part of the competing value chains.

Excessive waste, recycle, repair. These can be revisited to increase quality. There seems to be a clear trend towards avoiding waste and practicing recycling, upscaling, sharing, repairing, and so on. Secondhand stores for clothing and more are flourishing. The sale of sewing machines is increasing. Biodegradable packaging is on the rise. New types of glue for fastening of components allow for better recycling of valuable parts of mobile phones and electric cars, and so on. Old items are converted or fixed into near-new or given another life through a new use or exploitation. Items not frequently used can be shared amongst communities, for example skis or cars—things with higher price points and not always in use.

These trends largely reflect value shifts amongst an increasing number of consumers. Thus, it is becoming a true necessity for firms to adopt measures such as those above, both to allow for the attraction of the most qualified employees, as well as to ensure more favorable financing. The majority of the banks, for instance, are adhering to these principles. Wealth funds are increasingly adhering to these types of principles also. This might, in turn, impact firm stock prices.

What is clear is the preponderance of dramatic changes—we might label this business transformation, which includes digital transformation—especially for the sake of adapting and succeeding, important for both leaders and firms.

It goes without saying that our world has become largely virtual. We are active digitally as individuals, through our various organizations and communities, privately as well as in the business world. Web-based elements are part of most value-creating activities both for us as individuals as well as for most businesses. Here are some reflections regarding this:

<u>Wider reach</u>. Executives from all over the world are logging in to work and to communicate with their constituencies. The digital transformation of our businesses and organizations allows us all to reach wider audiences, and more

deeply. Clearly the benefits of digitization are many, from access of information, income generation, to brand building, business preservation and growth, customer and shareholder interaction, to name a few. There are both benefits when it comes to increased quality as well as lower costs.

As for self-studying, this added width, depth, and breadth also applies. Executive education students can study with online modules, developed by specialists, participate live in virtual classrooms, enjoy virtual breakout sessions with their professor and fellow student, even with hologram professors and participants, take exams online, receive mentoring online, dive into augmented and virtual reality scenarios and communities, and much more. While previously what tended to be available online would be the videotaped versions of conventional lectures from classrooms, since, however, there has been rapid evolution when it comes to virtual learning modules. Some examples are:

- Tailored, typically relatively short sub-modules that cover "the basics," with clear definitions, delineation of core concepts, etc. Typically, such sessions are centered around a specific element of a broader subject at a time.
- Tests and exercises, for participants to be active in how well they have understood the concepts in question. This typically includes feedback, providing the "correct" answers, and often even possibilities to ask an expert online, if in doubt.
- Virtual question and answers as well as discussions, allowing participants to dialog with the teacher, as well as to dialog with other students.

<u>Scale and cost efficiency.</u> Since the learning goes on online, with no limitation when it comes to the number of participants, in existence earlier due to availability of classroom spaces or not, there are few limitations of size—better economies of scale for the learning can be reached! And, the participants may also come from a broader variety of sources, geographically. All continents, many countries and cities, as well as different genders, races and ages, and of course, diverse employment backgrounds and pre-class experiences—all of this making the experience richer. More diversity typically benefits the learning.

Better learners, better leaders, better performance.

Part III

The Business: Your Company

There is no such thing as the average customer.
 —Jos Burgers, marketing consultant, author

Good is the enemy of great.
 —Jim Collins, business management consultant, author

11

Practice Insights from Hermann Simon, Founder and Honorary Chairman, Simon-Kucher & Partners Strategy and Marketing Consultants

What is currently robbing entrepreneurs and managers of sleep? First and foremost, it is inflation. Inflation does not only affect price management; all functions are affected. Central, of course, is pricing power. Companies without sufficient pricing power run into trouble because they cannot pass through the cost increases. Purchasing also has a difficult task. Not only does it have to ensure favorable purchase prices, but in view of the supply bottlenecks, it also has to make sure that the required goods are available at all and on time. In other words, purchasing assumes a kind of overall responsibility under the prevailing conditions.

Both in the short and longer term, the recruitment of qualified specialists remains a huge challenge. The simple fact is that over the next few decades, only half as many young people will enter the labor market as retire. That is where the moment of truth comes in terms of employer attractiveness.

The reconfiguration of the global value chain must be addressed. COVID-19, climate, and political conflicts have revealed that the risks of the globalized supply chain have been underestimated. Exports are increasingly being replaced by direct investments. We already see this at Tesla in Berlin or Intel in Magdeburg. But, it also goes in the opposite direction, with German hidden champions, for example in mining technology or artificial intelligence, setting up competence centers in China. All Chinese automakers have a design center in Germany. The global value chain is being completely reorganized.

Finally, I want to mention the problem of Russia and Ukraine, without giving a timeline here. It is clear that we have to help rebuild Ukraine. Turkish companies, by the way, see this as a huge future growth opportunity. But what about Russia? Right now, the West is driving a Morgenthau Plan with the sanctions. At some point, probably after Putin, we will have to rebuild Russia, that is, set a Marshall Plan in motion. However, it cannot be ruled out that the Ukraine war will end in a Korea situation that could last for a long time. That would be fatal for Europe. If Russia is not brought to an acceptable level of prosperity, we will have a Burkina Faso with nuclear bombs in our immediate neighborhood.

12

Introduction to the Business: Your Company

What is a business really? Why do we establish them? How can we grow our own businesses, or those we work for? Our efforts and activities can benefit from observing and learning from business success stories, as well as those companies who have struggled or failed.

We typically create a business if and when we have identified a market need, demand, or opportunity and have hopefully also achieved a good product (or service) to market fit. Add on top of that, a good team fit so that the equation becomes product-team-market. Purpose and vision evidently play a key role in our "why, how, and what," yet they do not always have to be the same.

In the process of selecting the book reviews and executive interviews for this book, we spent quite a bit of time going through factors. The factors we identified are many and directly involve the various sections we have organized. For example, on the topic of business, we identified that certain choices made, such as those of organizational configuration—whether to scale up or down, vertical or horizontal integration, sourcing and outsourcing, external cooperation—have a huge impact. Secondly, the "what"—branding, quality, exporting, and pricing—also define the business. Finally, how one chooses to distribute the product or service—value chains, manufacturing processes, and the technology a business will choose to use and develop these—all come into play here and are somehow addressed in the readings we have chosen.

The eight book reviews and three interviews with business leaders reproduced in this part showcase a few examples of business activities in order to highlight the vision, entrepreneurialism, business initiatives that may serve helpful as we seek to acquire deeper understanding and mastery of our own business efforts.

Therefore, let us give you brief impulses through the book reviews and executive interviews to follow. As already alluded to, for full exposés to the various concepts that are being raised, readers must refer back to the specific books that are being reviewed, or further search for more information about the leaders spearheading remarkable programs in their firms from whom we have been so fortunate to hear.

Let us already now, however, share with you what might be some three main insights that we might distill from the book reviews and interviews in this part:

- Focus on new ventures, start-ups, and to "capture" new technology early on.
- The membership/subscription economy is coming, i.e., to secure cash flows through repeat payments from members in networks.
- The customer is always key and must be served. Is one's offering relevant? Cost/benefit ok? Are we able to shape new habits in our customers?

13

Essential Books to Learn About the Business; your Company

Eyal Nir, (2014), Hooked: How to Build Habit-Forming Products, Redline (Reviewed March 2020)

To develop habit-enhancing products/services is an important approach for keeping competitors out—less brand-switching—and/or renewal rate up, less "churn." Good to take away is to aim for a deeper commitment to observing the behavior and psychology of the customer, in order to be able to work it to the favor of the business. Are we really "creatures of habit?" Let's look in the mirror.

How might one create a product or a service that can become so essential and form a strong habit in the life of the customer? To put it in business terms, how does one achieve minimum churn for one's service or subscription model? Using his background from the video gaming industry, the author has developed a four-step model for getting customers "hooked" on a product:

- To start with, a description of how strong user habits can be cultivated is key. For instance, modern IT systems and cloud-based technology facilitate the forming of habits by means of a convergence of data, access to the data, and speed of said access. A key objective for a business is to come up with products or services that fall into the so-called habit zone, characterized by a high usage rate as well as high perceived utility from using the product. Some products or services can be thought of as "pain killers." However, as the usage rate increases and the habit forms, the product may become a

"vitamin pill," thus also enabling the manufacturer or service provider to raise prices.
- The next step is to develop the so-called "trigger." There are two types of triggers, external and internal, both intended to lead the customer to take action. External triggers—advertising, e-mails, and relationships—those that contain information the customer takes in and registers. Later, internal triggers, manifested as emotions, take over and further help to form the desired habits.
- The next step is to move from the trigger towards the desired action, employing a behavioral model that represents desired *b*ehavior as the function of *m*otivation, *a*bility, and strength of *t*rigger, or B = MAT. The likelihood of desired actions taking place can thus be increased by attempting to reinforce any of the three factors.
- Variable rewards are then the extent to which potential customers feel that they benefit from a given action. There are three types of variable rewards: tribe, which has to do with whether a customer feels that he or she is benefiting from connectedness with other individuals, typically other users; hunt, which implies that the customer will get material resources and/or information; and self, which has to do with how an individual gets satisfaction from mastering, added competence and/or seeing the completion of a given task.
- The final step has to do with investing in one's product through making regular use of it, thus increasing the anticipated rewards in the future.

To develop a so-called "manipulation matrix" is then discussed. This matrix helps analyze customer behavior in two ways: Does the product materially improve the user's life or not? And does the producer use the product him/herself or not?

The four archetypes of products in the matrix are then: "facilitator" products. These products are used by the producer and to improve the users' life; "peddler" products, where the producer does not use the product him/herself, but where the product nevertheless delivers positive benefits to the user; "entertainer" products, where there is no benefit to the user, but the product is nevertheless used by the producer; "dealer" products, the least attractive, as they bring no benefits to and are not used by the producer.

Finally, there are various aspects of consumers' habit testing. Three recommendations are given: identify how people are using a given product, isolate users who are driven by strong usage habits, and modify a given product so that more users might be converted into developing strong usage habits.

There is perhaps a fine line between a genuine effort to come up with better products and manipulating customers. But are we seeing examples of such devious manipulations?

With the dramatic proliferation of the subscription-based service business models, developing products with reduced churn propensity might be more important than ever.

This concludes the book review section in this part. Let us now share with the reader three interviews with executives, also with focus on business.

Robbie Kellman Baxter, (2015), The Membership Economy, McGraw Hill (Reviewed March 2020)

To purchase a renewable membership in a network, rather than to take an ownership position in an asset (through purchase) seems to be an important trend, closely associated with so-called network strategies. It could be interesting for us to look at our own initiatives or businesses from this network lens and to see how subscription can complement, enhance, or stretch these. The consideration of setting up subscription-based offerings as extensions of business (new services, new markets) can be a welcome and powerful growth vitamin.

Although Robbie Kellman Baxter's book "The Membership Economy" is not new, it represents, perhaps, the most comprehensive overview to date of the increasingly important challenge of developing an effective membership-based strategy, also known as a subscription strategy, sharing strategy, or, simply, service strategy. The key idea behind such a strategy is that in order to benefit from the use of an asset, one does not necessarily have to own it, but instead can simply subscribe to it. This business model has been around for a long time—a classic newspaper is an example. Readers subscribe to this newspaper and by so doing also become members of the of the newspaper's daily readership. A key advantage for the business that employs this strategy is a typically steady stream of annual subscription fees, most of which are renewed every year. However, some users may decide not to renew, and drop out, creating what is called "churn."

Today, there is a wide and growing variety of firms that adopts a membership strategy. It appears that these firms tend to grow faster and be more profitable than most of their more conventional counterparts. The primary message of the book is how can one create a stronger sense of belonging among one's users (members). Mutual respect stands out as particularly important because it helps to clearly delineate benefits for all parties. A loyal membership community definitely has value! Being a member in this case evokes a sense of privilege!

The author, Robbie Kellman Baxter, is a consultant and speaker based in the Silicon Valley. She is the head of the successful consulting firm Peninsula Strategies. The four sections of her book focus on what one might need to know about a membership economy, specific delineation of membership economy strategies and tactics, discussion of membership organizations of all shapes and sizes, and finally how a membership economy might cope with transformation.

The book discusses several basic principles and issues central to the membership economy model. Netflix is used as a comprehensive case example.

What is a membership economy? The author has indicated the following five characteristics: annual subscription, community of users, clear communication among the users, strong sense of belonging among members, and these members who play critical roles, perceived as an association!

Those whom we traditionally saw as customers are now members. How do we build a strong social capital and create more meaningful connections among members? What motivates members who are now target buyers? How do they buy? How do we earn their loyalty? The central aspect of the book is the conceptual model for building a firm's strategy in the membership economy, consisting of several elements:

- Organization: Instead of discussing organizational structure, the author focuses on three tactics organizations must adopt to now be successful, promote a culture of marketing innovation and technology, avoid too much complexity, and strive for success, particularly at the start.
- Acquisition funnel: Acquisitions might perhaps be compared to an hourglass, more so than a funnel, with a wide "top" and narrow "bottom." The top "half" of the hourglass describes the steps to generate loyal members in the same way and sequence as a funnel might do: awareness, trial, sign-up, and loyalty. An interesting additional aspect of the process is then presented in the "bottom" half of the hourglass. It provides context in which acquiring and retaining loyal members may be easier. For example, the source of referral is an important part of this context. Depending on the quality of a source, engagement may increase.
- Onboarding: This pillar deals with what might be done to create a strong usage habit among members. How can this process be made as effective as possible? It is critical to make usage as easy as possible, in order to deliver immediate results. To make onboarding even more effective, rewarding

desired behavior is helpful. The ultimate purpose of onboarding is to create a group of super-users.
- Pricing: The author acknowledges that setting the price "right" may be difficult. Price must always be consistent with the perceived value that the members of a given membership community see as reasonable. A good policy is not to change it too often. It is also important to avoid an excessive number of different price points. An additional perspective might be, however, that one might want to develop a higher price for those who use the membership service infrequently. Super-users, in contrast, should get a better price, especially when the price of all available services is bundled together, and paid for, say, once per year. The higher the overall usage, the lower the price!
- Freemium: The author discusses how to provide a so-called "freemium," that is, to specify what might be such a "for free" level. This can be a good tactic, in contrast to entirely free, open trials.
- Technology: Technology is a fancy word for software packages, developed through open or closed sourcing. Nowadays, there are many open-source software packages available. It is of course important to invest appropriately in this area. A particular challenge might be to link software programs together that have primarily been developed for different applications (e.g., for marketing automation, for billing and renewal of subscription, and so on). In the end, open sourcing tends to become significantly less expensive than closed sourcing systems.
- Customer success, less churn: The final dimension of a membership economy strategy deals with how to be more effective in retaining members. It is important that members feel that they are linked and connected. Such network of contacts might be a good way to build loyalty, lessen the churn! And this is not only a matter of focusing on free trials or giving favors (hopefully that are relatively inexpensive).

There are perhaps six different types of membership organizations:

- Digital subscriptions. Here, it is particularly critical to encourage annual subscriptions, with less churn.
- Online community models. Leveraging the know-hows of members is particularly key here.
- Loyalty programs. In this case, the members themselves essentially promote this type of program.
- Traditional membership economy companies. Scalable solutions are particularly important.

- Small businesses and consulting firms. These typically represent relatively inexpensive ways for achieving one's goal.
- Nonprofit organizations, for example, societies and trade organizations. The broader community might be encouraged.

How might membership organizations might evolve and transform?

- From idea to start-up: Here, one must be quite clear about the benefits. And it is beneficial to keep a relatively narrow focus and a tight budget.
- From start-up to mature company: Perhaps, the biggest challenge when it comes to this transition is how to evolve from a one-single-big-idea-focus, to now a more continuous innovation. New skills will be needed, likely as well as another culture.
- From offline to online: To be able, over time, to provide one's offering online is key. Most members expect that things are online. Specific technical skills are needed, for this, however.
- From ownership to access: The stream of relatively small membership payments can be expected to grow over time. It is important to understand the specific priorities and interests of each membership cluster subsegment, as the network evolves.
- From "business as usual" to "competitive disruption": One's business model should evolve proactively through the launching of new "disruptive," innovative features, thus keeping competition at bay.

This book, in summary, provides practical techniques and insightful new examples to guide organizations in building powerful, ongoing relationships with their members.

Anil Sethi, (2016), From Science to Start-up, Springer (Reviewed April 2021)

When it comes to launching successful start-ups, to be able to link up with incubators is critical, and most of such incubators tend to have strong technological sides. Many technical universities, in this case, ETH in Zurich, tend to nurture such spin-offs. This may serve to open our eyes to looking for collaborations, partners, multipliers, friendships, and/or connectors at universities, research labs, and other locations and, equally, to think digital and tech from start to growth.

13 Essential Books to Learn About the Business; your Company

This book is written by one of Switzerland's top serial entrepreneurs, Anil Sethi, who founded Flisom in 2006 and led the company through 2012, when it went public (IPO). Sethi is an "Entrepreneur in Residence" at ETH Zurich and has been honored as a Technology Pioneer by the World Economic Forum. His company, Flisom, has also received numerous prizes, including the Pioneer Prize (from Zurcher Kantonalbank) and the Red Herring Award. Flisom's business niche: the making of ultrathin photogenic film for electricity generation. This book's main focus is on how to build on unique technological insights so as to develop sustainable business. And the author draws heavily on his own experience.

The dictum of clarity for what to do as well as what not to do seems primary! In line with this, personal vision and aspirations tend to be relatively more critical than strategic plans and financial projections!

Are you meant to be an entrepreneur? While many of us shall undoubtedly prefer to answer affirmatively to this, the author raises several "requirements," which may make one's answer less obvious: Do we have a sufficiently clear vision? Are we predisposed to move sufficiently quickly? Are we ready to break conventional rules? Business people might be distinguished from technology "owners"/scientists, the latter group typically lacking in understanding what makes customers tick. And scientists may also resist leaving their laboratories!

In addition to clarity, the readiness to scale up (versus "remain" in the lab) as well as to explore the geography is key. B2B is probably more relevant to this book than B2C, as long as one does not fall in love with technology, and customers' needs might therefore be suppressed! Patience and team involvement are critical. Many individuals may not be up to working effectively this way!

Is one's technology ripe for commercialization? One good way to assess this might involve observing how a given technology works in one setting, for the entrepreneur then to simply transfer this to another geographic setting. A famous example is how the Austrian businessman and entrepreneur Dietrich Mateschitz discovered the basic concept of a power drink in Thailand, for then to transfer the concept to his own country and develop it further, so that it became Red Bull. A more general approach to evaluating a technology might be to assess the degree to which a given technological approach could be replicable. Is there a "proof" of concept? And it might be wise to pursue several technological options when it comes to this, as long as one keeps in mind that technology-people, "techies," often prefer to do more research (and more, more, more, …), at times failing to see that manufacturing and/or marketing might impact the validity of a chosen approach.

Now to the team. To have a strong team in place is always important. The entrepreneur's spouse should indeed be in the extended team, so that she (or he) might more readily support all the hard work, personal sacrifice, and "blood, sweat, and tears." Some team members, perhaps founders in particular, may be impatient, perhaps also greedy, and ask "when can I exit?." Good teams, in contrast, must have a long-term commitment.

There are often of course changes, and at times even rather fundamental shifts, that might test the basic commitments of team members. There might be dilutions and loss of control, at times coming from conditions imposed through new financing, such as loans (even "soft" loans from the public sector). There may also be a need to change the overall vision. Backup technologies might make this more feasible. Again, however, the team members must be comfortable with this or resign!

Team members might typically be willing to settle for relatively low ongoing salaries and instead be willing to settle for stock options. Retired executives, often with an abundance of experience, may be good team members, as long as they do not contribute to "over-engineering." Steady, honest, open communication is critical. Any type of friction within a team should be avoided, or at least minimalized. There is always the option to opt out.

Patents may be important for protecting one's discretionary technology, but they provide freedom to operate for only 20 years maximum! Ironically, it might be that protection of proprietary technology may have to be developed not only to oppose competitors, but also with regard to past team members who may have since departed. It could also be that one would decide to choose the route of developing trade secrets (such as Coca-Cola, for instance, with more than 120 years trade secret associated with its formula!). Normally, the more patents the better! This might not only disenchant competitors but also keep more options open and also generate more liquidity when selling.

Choosing good investors is also paramount. Whom to target should be carefully planned for. To avoid "quarrelsome" investors, who might have histories of conflicts representing red lights! Archetypes of investors are: angel investors (early; typically, relatively small investments), venture capitalists (often somewhat later in a venture's evolution, and often also with relatively larger investments), strategic (when a venture fits into the strategy of the financing entity), funds (these might typically have set time horizons for exit, hence typically having strong focus on exit), and foundations (these often tend to put relatively lesser focus on exit).

To come up with a proper valuation is crucial for all these types of investors. While there does not seem to be an exact formula for coming up with this, a combination of idea, plan, growth expectation, technology, team, prototype, and customers might do it!

To close the deal and thus to secure funding are key. To be realistic seems particularly important here, especially not to take any tentative commitments from various investors for given until a deal is signed. One should keep in mind that investors frequently evaluate many deals and that they incur low risk by saying no! To shop around may be acceptable or the usual practice for them. One should be aware of the transparency that is quite common among investors and thus the risk of involving too many prospective investors. To have two realistic investor lead candidates is perhaps optimal. "Hang in there," never give up.

When a letter of intent is drawn and signed (a milestone!), several new issues seem particularly critical:

- An investor will typically ask for exclusivity during the period that now follows, until final signing. It is important not to promise too much at this stage!
- Eventual liquidation is an issue. Most investors shall prefer to be paid back before others. What is fair?
- Ethics. The entrepreneur should be clear regarding what he/she is ready to accept. Is it fair for all involved?

Now comes the exit and the opportunity to convert equity to wealth. Until now, imaginary values may be considerable, but since nothing shall actually be realized, what is it worth? There is not much to contribute here, except perhaps to add that some funds might be more or less forced to sell at some predetermined point, in line with the given funds' bylaws. There might be good opportunities for others to take advantage of this and secure favorable "discounted" deals for themselves.

What seems to be some recurring features associated with the successes? It seems as if those who succeed all tend to be flexible, with a willingness to revise plans and visions, and seem to have had particularly strong contacts with their customers. Additionally, on the revenue-generating side, it is to have secured strong growth, nonetheless.

Anne Janzer, (2017), Subscription Marketing: Strategies for Nurturing Customers in a World of Churn, Cuesta Park Consulting (Reviewed June 2020)

The power of subscription, with the challenge of keeping renewal rate up ("churn" down), is well documented here. Herein is a strong advocacy for true customer relationship management—trust building, communication, listening, finding storytellers, and acting on customer feedback are just a few concepts to take away. Think about customer value, value, value, from the beginning!

Over the last decade, we have seen a massive tectonic shift from the traditional model of selling products or services toward a subscription-based model, and marketing imperatives that underpin subscription-based models are inherently different from those in the traditional marketing model. There are several important changes in our behaviors: greater appreciation of valuable content, more frequent instant gratification, and an added sense of convenience. Advanced connectivity, digitalized supply chain, and "Internet of Things" are the technologies that allow us to have seamless access to products and services without the necessity to own them. Here are three incremental ways to facilitate the shift of one's offering to the subscription model: As a first step, try out the subscription model in a small part of the business, make use of the subscription model to come up with new ways to segment, and pivot toward the subscription approach by gradually abandoning the old way of doing business.

The overriding issue when it comes to the switch to a subscription model might stand out as central: how to provide meaningful incentives to ensure good continuing performance, that is, minimizing churn? Perhaps, one might start by having a better idea of how much revenue is generated per customer. This in turn can help to understand how to attract and keep the most relevant customers. A good test of potential success of a subscription model is to examine the extent to which valuable existing customers see value in complementary offerings, which they might now subscribe to. Cultivating customer trust is key in this regard. In fact, one can think of marketing in the subscription context as a tool to develop more trust and to create and deliver on a promise! This focus on the development of trust should be maintained also after the customer has decided to subscribe. Value marketing is essential and is built on: The support of a customer's way of being successful is to make it absolutely clear to customers that one particular model offers good value; create additional value dimensions, such as developing social networks of subscribers; add more in-depth thoughtfulness in interactions with subscribers, if possible, of course; and try to align one's subscription offering as much as possible with particular values of subscribers.

Creating a customer launch plan might represent a good step toward communicating value. Essential here is to understand what motivates a person to become a customer. Then, it is key to identify ways to make it easier for customers to use the service, that is, to build on their positive confirmation bias. Early success can be guided, through development of support materials, such as videos or other tools (e.g., diplomas and certificates), to help educate and train the customer. The point is to create new, identifiable customer values!

Another way to communicate additional value is to share relevant stories with customers. Thus, also, it is essential for a business to pick the most relevant storyteller and the best propagandist. Who has the best reputation? Who is the most credible? Whom are customers listening to? Salient relevant stories may attempt to focus on the core values that one's subscription model is offering. And customers' success should be applauded! To that end, one may consider sending out congratulatory emails or letters or making personal phone calls to successful customers. So, in the end, it is all about creating relevant subscription value, as experienced by the customer. One should strive to create a community of like-minded users. Podcasts, for example, and other social media channels can be an effective tool.

If a community of users and customers is created, the business can then tap into that, to nurture relationship and develop "brand advocates" from within the customer base. This tactic is called "advocacy marketing." It is important, however, to approach the customer community with honesty and humility: one should stay away from flattery but strive for "honest" advocacy, which must be "earned!" Some traditional customer loyalty tools, like reward programs, club memberships, or gifts, might be useful. However, it may be more effective to engage customers directly, ask for feedback, and listen carefully to what they say.

Regrettably, some subscribers may decide to leave. This process should be handled gracefully, without clinging to customers who have already made up their mind. To reduce the likelihood of such "breakaways," some noncontroversial values need to be shared with the customers. One such value, for example, may be "practice what you preach." Hopefully, such core values might be relatively noncontroversial and might thus be shared. One possible way to illustrate showcase core values is to offer free trials, so that prospective customers may experience what the business truly stands for. To manage the challenge of minimizing churn thus might many forms.

Putting strategies into action is fundamental! The aim may be to pursue so-called "high-value customers." High-value customers are those who spend more on subscribing to higher margin products, less likely to cancel the subscription (i.e., lower churn). To generate, develop, and nurture relationships with such customers, a long-term focus is critical. Organizational silos typically represent major roadblocks in cultivating these relationships. At times, there may be a conflict between nurturing deep relationships and going for ultrarapid growth. Growth at all costs, at the expense of added value, should be avoided!

For subscription-based models, scale is of key importance. At the core of operating at scale is software. Still, non-scalable dimensions such as customer meetings, answering e-mails, etc. are also important.

Three of the most common "traps" of a subscription model tend to stand out: to avoid unnecessarily complicated pricing and stay away from complex discount schemes and to upsell meaningfully. Add only those services that truly can add value to the customer. And avoid non-related services; as a rule, remember that value always starts with the customer.

Ultimately, a main implication of the shift toward a subscription business model implies a shift in customer orientation. The new model demands that an entire customer journey must be embraced as a long-term priority, as opposed to most traditional marketing models that tend to see customer interactions as leading up to sales transactions, which must be maximized short term. But a long-term focus on the customer helps build a relationship, the primary focus of which is to create value on an ongoing basis. In a subscription business context, marketing is different! The classic marketing focus on trying to influence a purchase decision is no longer "it!" Instead, long-term relationships, concentrated on building trust, are what matter the most.

John Carreyrou, (2018), Bad Blood: Secrets and Lies in a Silicon Valley Start-up, Alfred A. Knopf (Reviewed June 2022)

This book brings our attention to fraudulence in the start-up world and can perhaps serve useful to developing our own ways to detect potential bad investments from the good, as well as to wisely spot unethical or greedy founders from the solid and reliable.

This book reports on the start-up of the Silicon Valley firm Theranos in 2008, a company offering blood tests through a simple, small sampling of blood from the individual's fingertip, rather than from the slower, much more expensive conventional method of drawing larger blood samples from the arm, to then sending them to a regular laboratory. The four main types of blood tests might thus be performed cheaper and faster, offering potential benefits to patients, medical doctors, and pharmaceutical firms undertaking clinical trials of new drugs alike. The company was founded by Elisabeth Holmes, a Stanford University undergraduate biochemistry dropout, who was reported, in October 2014, to have a net worth of USD 4.5 billion and the world's youngest self-made female billionaire. But Theranos did not work as expected, producing often erratic, unreliable "answers." A patient's health might indeed be put at risk, due to such inaccurate diagnoses. So, the estimate of Holmes' net worth was revised to zero in 2016, and the company was ultimately dissolved in 2018.

Carreyrou, this book's author, is a Pulitzer Prize-winning investigative journalist at The Wall Street Journal (WSJ). The work, highly acclaimed, became the winner of The Financial Times/McKinsey Business Book of the Year Award for 2018. The author has painstakingly pieced together this remarkable story of how Elisabeth Holmes, a 19-year-old college dropout was able to successfully launch Theranos, to become by age 29, Silicon Valley's first female billionaire entrepreneur. The book provides, however, a clear warning about what could happen to a person who tries too hard, say to replicate the accomplishments of a Steve Jobs or Bill Gates. Elaborate corporate fraud could have been at the center of it all, a company actually willing to gamble with people's lives! But this tale of Theranos is not just full of corporate fraud and not just a biotech company with a seemingly relatively plausible, although far-stretching business model. Greed, pride, vanity, lust, and anger are central parts of what is reported through the author's investigative journalism. It is a story of breathtaking rise and shocking collapse.

We are struck by the feeling that to assess the potential viability of these types of firms may prove difficult, at least for nonspecialists. Most of us lack the specific biotechnical and medical insights to assess the plausibility of a business strategy such as that of Theranos. Having invested in a biotech start-up myself some years ago and yet not seen many tangible results, I wonder whether there may be fraudulent behavior at work there too. This book has, however, provided me with several insights regarding how to probe into the reality of this type of start-up. The following points seem particularly important:

1. The founder, Elisabeth Holmes in the case of Theranos, should have a multitude of deliberate strengths, that is, be more than a one-dimensional

specialist with convincing abilities in a number of areas. Ms. Holmes, for instance, seems to have an exceptional drive, being self-assured to a high degree and having an extraordinary ability to convince potential investors. Her strong mind and apparent beauty also clearly played parts in her effectiveness.

2. Super-marketing seems to be central, in the sense that the Theranos team consistently claimed that the firm's testing equipment was able to deliver fast, valid tests, underscored by reliable data from such tests themselves, when this was clearly not the case. This was indeed extreme overselling, even actually bluffing! But a common dilemma when it comes to marketing in high-tech firms is that there is a need to do some overselling, to capitalize now on performance features likely to be realized in the future. But how much of such "stretch marketing" might be acceptable? Where to draw the line, so as not to market outright lies and bluffs? Super-marketing is indeed part of many start-ups' success stories, but where is the limit?

3. Are there clear streams of revenue coming in? Can specific customers be identified? In the case of Theranos, this was certainly the case. The large drugstore chain Walgreen's had entered into an agreement with the company to set up "test stations" in their various stores. Incidentally, Theranos had told Walgreen's that it had a commercially ready laboratory with capability to undertake 192 different blood tests, all from its proprietary testing devices. And revenues were coming in. But Theranos was nevertheless far from breakeven. Ms. Holmes further claimed that there were contracts with several pharmaceutical companies to add support to clinical testing in such firms. A trip to Novartis in Basel seems to have led to no new contract however, apparently because of the lack of reliable data from the testing equipment being documented.

4. Who has already signed up as credible supporters? At Theranos, there seemed to be at least four central supporting groups:

   – Dignitaries on the company's board. These included important ex-politicians such as George Schultz and Sam Nunn. Elisabeth Holmes appears to have put much energy into cultivating contacts such as these. Clearly, their high status and reputation added a lot of clout to the firm.
   – Strong scientific support. The pre-eminent supporter here was Professor Channing Robertson, Associate Dean of Stanford's School of Engineering, and one of Stanford's star faculty members.

13 Essential Books to Learn About the Business; your Company

- Endorsement from venture capital experts. Perhaps, the most prominent one here might be Mr. Tim Draper, the head of DFA, known for lucrative early investments, including the e-mail service firm, Hotmail.
- Investors. The list of major investors in Theranos was very impressive and included DeVas, Cox, the Waltons, Carlos Slim, and Rupert Murdoch (who invested, and lost, USD 125 million). All told, investors in Theranos have lost nearly USD 1 billion.
- Poor advisors. Ms. Ramesh "Sunny" Balwani, a Pakistan-born entrepreneur whom Elisabeth Holmes had met in Beijing, was Theranos' number two executive and Elisabeth Holmes' boyfriend, although around 20 years older than her. Sunny appears to have had a generally bad influence, both on Holmes and on the firm, which he co-led: lack of moral fiber, overly aggressive with employees (bordering on paranoiac when it came to company secrets), and so on.

Mr. Carreyrou had put together an article, published on the front page of The Wall Street Journal on October 15, 2015. Its title was "A Prized Start-up's Struggles." This signaled the beginning of the end for Theranos. It is remarkable to read aloud the extent to which the company tried to block the publication of the article. Former employees were threatened with litigations and potential lawsuits, including the grandson of board members George Schultz, Mr. Tyler Schultz, who worked for Theranos for 8 months in late 2013 and early 2014. There were endless meetings between the firm's lawyers and the editorial leadership at WSJ. A main argument was that the lawyers were questioning the journalistic objectivity of Mr. Carreyrou. Ms. Holmes even seemed to try to include Rupert Murdoch, the owner of WSJ and a major investor in the firm to interfere, which, to his credit, he declined to do.

Rather than specifically reviewing each of the 24 chapters of the book, we shall conclude our book review with a general observation that have come about to recognize not only as a reader of this great book but also in our capacity as investors in various start-ups through our own portfolio investment firms. This insight has two aspects:

- The honesty and integrity of the leader at the top must be impeccable. As you perhaps saw in this book, to assess the above may perhaps often be quite difficult. Not only are many such leaders very good at camouflaging this side of what they stand for, they may be "smooth salespersons!" And the degree of dishonesty may grow over time, as many such leaders become "trapped" or addicted to the success of their own falsehoods.

– It is often difficult for nonspecialists to assess the true merit of the business strategies of many start-ups. I do, in fact, often find myself in such an uncomfortable situation. It does help, of course, to reach out to specialists and to make some inquiries, such as Rupert Murdoch did before investing in Theranos (he listened to Yuri Milnar, the Russian technology investor, and called Toby Cosgrove, the CEO of Cleveland Clinic). But there is often little time!

For this reviewer, it has been revealing to read this book. There are clearly some "inappropriate business practices" going on in many aspects and perhaps particularly when it comes to making investments in start-ups. As an investor myself, I felt that careful reading of this book has given me several new insights for how to review such start-up investments. These are inherently risky, of course, but some aspects of the risk may perhaps be avoided.

Frank Lavin, (2021), The Smart Business Guide to China E-Commerce, Independent Publishing Group (Reviewed October 2021)

China does of course represent an important opportunity for growth, perhaps, above all, when it comes to new waves of virtual technology, and how these are used for business development. New ways of envisioning what seems to be effective marketing may be particularly worthwhile pursuing. We hope this book can be inspiring to anyone involved in selling products or services online, wherever they may be or to whomever they are trying to sell to. E-commerce represents a must-know for most of our businesses today, whether being in actual selling or in marketing, customer support, or distribution.

The author has more than 30 years of experience helping companies succeed in China, the last 10 years as owner and founder of his own consulting firm *Export Now*. He has had a distinguished career both in the private sector (with Bank of America, Citibank, and others) as well as in the public sector (former US Undersecretary of Commerce for International Trade, former US Ambassador to Singapore, former Chairman of the Steering Committee of the US Pavilion at the Shanghai 2010 World Expo).

As background for the book, the following conundrum seems be at play. On the one hand, many of the restrictions on free trade between China and the United States, as set out by former US President Trump and largely continued by President Biden, might be scrutinized and judged inefficient. The author might even say that open trade with China is the only way forward, also to ease the tension between these two world powers. On the other hand, the rapid military buildup in China, coupled with aggressive stances regarding Taiwan, Hong Kong, and in the South China Sea may call for a firmer, non-compromising stance by the United States. This critical dilemma concerns most of us!

The author claims that it is nevertheless appropriate to follow the strong advice that the Chinese market represents an exceptional opportunity. Should private business be embracing China in such an unconditionally positive way that this book seems to propose? Should we endorse "good China" as the most positive way to maintain the strengths of the United States and Europe, in contrast to a much more defensive "bad China" approach, which might not bring us forward in significant ways. The issue is "how fast can we run in this marathon?" As Mark Schneider, President, Nestlé says "if you want to see the future, look at China."

For business leaders not yet active in China, they may need convincing about the attractiveness of this huge market. "Why" China and "how to" China, with its more than 1 billion consumers, seems to have a virtually insatiable demand for product innovations, above all from international lifestyle brands. Well-developed e-commerce platforms who are also at the center of much of China's evolution are supported by powerful networks of social media and electronic payment systems.

China is notorious for major shopping "days," namely, singles day (November 11), the 18th of June shopping festival, and the so-called "Double 12 s" festival on 12th of December. Sales on each of these days, primarily through e-commerce, is staggering! Everything is big in China! Many Chinese consumers spend considerable time online. The luxury goods segment seems to be particularly "hot," but, as indicated, new models, shapes, tastes, and features have to be clear.

Consumer tastes, in contrast, seem to be more or less the same all over the world, whether a Starbucks or a Mercedes. There is a "law of convergence" at work here. There are mistakes being made all of the time, of course, some of which may be grave! Lack of sufficient focus on growth is one! Social experiences are also important, and most consumers search for reviews, endorsements, and comments by other purchasers, before purchasing. Perhaps, the biggest mistakes that prospective actors in the Chinese market could make may be to underestimate the convenience of online shopping—is it all about e-commerce! So-called "single brand" outlets seem to be the easiest ones for consumers to handle.

Market research may normally be needed, and one's own field research seems particularly major here. A clear Chinese strategy should come out of all of these market-related deliberations. This should typically break with the so-called MOTS approach (More of The Same). The key headings in a China plan should emphasize how to get to more revenue, how to attract more consumers, how to build a higher market share, and how to take home more bottom-line contribution! The China strategy should also have a long-term focus. Pricing is typically not a constraining issue. And if one's strategy does not work, it may in the end be more of a problem with the specific actor behind a strategic plan, rather than a more general China problem.

China is different! Tailoring of product and/or service offerings appears even more critical in this market than in others, so that consumers might be delighted, that is, indeed feel that they are part of a successful movement. An effective e-commerce strategy should reflect all of this. It should ideally be driven by exclusivity. To analyze what the main competitors may be doing seems essential to achieve this.

In the end, the ability to purchase something depends on the ability to produce and thereby generate income seems to apply in the Chinese market—supply creates its own demand! Say's Law!

Many businesses might already have an initial experience in China and may hope to expand. A major topic continues to be how to court the Chinese consumer. To build up one's sales strategy with the three one-day sales events as a basis (18/6, 11/11, 12/12) seems to be a solution. There are however risks here, surprises, and unexpected changes. To manage risks, the "safe" approach is critical—a low break-even point, relatively little debt, and quick responses to currency shifts. Then, there are potential intellectual property infringements and counterfeits. The best defense is a strong offense. Tracking, reporting, complaining, and following up are sine qua non!

Regulatory and compliance risks are of course also real. The best advice seems to be to adhere closely to all rules, including to have one's paperwork in order.

Then, there is a political risk. The author notices that retailing and trade do not seem to have been subject to too much regulation in general. Such trade problems seem to have been relatively short term. And the author should know! But there are of course macro-political realities that might be hard to understand, as well as unforeseen fluctuations.

The art of marketing in China is focused on how to come up with a connected network of consumers and especially what they say to each other about one's brand, that is, word of mouth marketing par excellence! There seem to be three dominating e-commerce platforms that one might draw on (Alibaba,

JD, and PDD) as well as three prominent advertising channels (WeChat, Weibo, and Little Red Book (for luxury and beauty products)).

It is important to overhaul the product content that one might have, so that it is truly relevant for the Chinese market, and to possibly revise this very frequently. Digital reviews must be honest and focus on authenticity. Live streaming seems to be a much more central part of the marketing mix in China, with celebrities demonstrating one's products and answering core questions from prospective customers. There seem to be five different livestream platforms that above all might be enlisted to handle this (Taobao Live; Douyin, Kuaishou, JD.com, Pinduoduo). Livestreaming is thus paramount, but not "hard selling."

Mini apps seem to be special, for the Chinese market also, providing a quick introduction to one's brand. There seem to be three major mini-app platforms (WeChat, Alipay, Baidu). Co-branding appear potentially important, as evidenced by the author's discussion of Dermalogica, a Unilever-owned brand out of California, which first promoted a skin care product and later a broader range of cosmetics.

When it comes to logistics, a so-called cross-border model might apply, where products are made, packaged at home and then shipped to China. Specialist companies such as Cainao or JD might be of support. Then, at a second stage, a designated fulfillment center in the region may be called for. And as a third stage, local manufacturing might be established. Thus, the risk might be relatively small. To shift from shipping products from airfreight to later making use of container ship service is also part of this.

Now to the finance dimension. Every e-commerce strategy needs a finance strategy. To work closely with one's established bank seems central. And so as to have a clear legal recourse, one's CFO should be non-Chinese, or at least reside outside of China. When it comes to consumer credit, Chinese shoppers might use Alipay, Taobao, WeChatPay, or Huabei.

Failure to agree on realistic China goals typically rather long term and/or to adopt a China strategic plan once more seems of importance. And central here might be not to blame lack of success on factors that would be outside a firm's own control. The counterpart to failures is of course how to get started in a way that might lead to success. To simply do it seems key! And to develop a network of friendly relations to draw on would be advisable.

Insights gained through workable experiences in the Chinese market, perhaps particularly when it comes to e-commerce, are likely to be of benefit also in other markets. So, while the Chinese market is demanding and may call for significant funding as well as a great deal of dedicated time from one's top management, the benefits can be more than financial, also becoming insightful for other markets.

Paul Polman and Andrew Winston, (2021), *Net Positive: How Courageous Companies Thrive*, Harvard Business Review Press (Reviewed October 2021)

How did the large multinational company, Unilever, address the challenge of achieving more environmentally friendly growth, that is, less emissions, healthier products, more environmentally friendly packaging, etc.? Let us possibly exploit many of the suggestions made towards increasing courageousness and altruism in our own firms or those for whom we work. Setting the agenda in your companies towards helping improve the future is not just a fluffy "do good" now, rather a strategic priority deserving acceptance from the top.

In this seminal book, former Unilever CEO Paul Polman and sustainability expert Andrew Winston explore how corporations might fix world environmental issues, instead of adding to these problems. Companies must become net positive they argue, that is, "giving more to the world than they take." They advocate five key principles for a company to become net positive:

– Take responsibility for one's company's full impacts
– Work for the long-term benefit of society
– Create positive outcomes for all stakeholders
– Improve shareholders' return
– Embrace transformation partnerships

Paul Polman is the outgoing CEO of Unilever. Before this assignment, he was CFO and then Head of North America at Nestlé. He is/has been very active in a number of organizations focusing on the environment and sustainability. Andrew Winston is a leading thinker on sustainable business and author of several books on this topic, as well as many articles on sustainability.

This book focuses on how Unilever managed to become closer to being net positive under Mr. Polman's tenure, an impressive chronology! But why, for instance, are key competitors such as Nestlé and P&G seldom discussed?

Also, while it can be no doubt that Mr. Polman deserves the reputation of being "a standout CEO of the past decade" (Financial Times), one might nonetheless and perhaps appropriately ask whether his focus on environmental/sustainability issues might simply have been too much. As the authors themselves acknowledge, did he perhaps "take his eyes off the ball," perhaps failing to a degree, to perform the full plethora of CEO duties? He must indeed have spent a lot of his time and energy on sustainability also being a member of a variety of environmental initiatives and "championing broader societal causes." And few leaders, if any, can point to such impressive successes!

The book's introduction gives us a backdrop to Mr. Polman's efforts at Unilever. For a number of years, he seems to have been busy setting in motion an impressive array of environmentally friendly, sustainability-enhancing strategic initiatives, only to experience the threat of a hostile joint takeover bid from 3GC, the majority owners being Jorge P. Lehmann (Brazilian/Swiss entrepreneur) and Berkshire-Hathaway (Warren Buffet, CEO). This seasoned team was obviously impressed with what had been achieved at Unilever. Ultimately, this takeover attempt failed, however.

A short-term focus on sustainability that seems to dominate corporate and government lives does not give us much room for optimism. The short-term focus is driven by many factors. Corporations' strategies are driven by top management's renumeration and bonuses, as well as stock options. Expectations of short-term gains in stock markets add to this. Societies are similarly increasingly being driven by "short-termness," through reporting quarterly on GNP growth, as well as with impact coming from legislature, political election concerns, and lobbying efforts. Even corruption may be at play to enhance societal short-termness.

Yet the authors convincingly argue that long-term focus may nevertheless often pay off, Unilever's 10 years of improvements in both top-line and bottom-line during Mr. Polman's tenure. Shareholder values grew significantly as a result of such long-termness! A long-term focus, and likewise culture, is of course key here. Employee's attitudes need to be in line with such a long-term value set. A net positive corporation, one that gives more than it takes, does indeed seem to be more attractive, for both employees who choose their workplaces more carefully, as well as investors who increasingly decide where to commit their funds long term.

The authors stress that an effective leader might typically be net positive too. Key words here are "purpose-driven," decency, and self-confidence (relying on others who may be smarter than the leader itself). It is important for a leader to be courageous enough to act in a long-term way. And inspirational leadership is part of this!

Let us mention two critical procedural elements here, followed at Unilever:

- The Compass: A short document for how to come up with a winning long-term strategy and sustainability targets.
- The Unilever Sustainable Living Plan (USLP): This brings Unilever' strategies and the company's sustainability targets even more closely together. Net positivity is a primary word to describe the USLPs!

It seems to have been critical to send consistent signals to all parts of Unilever's global organization, in order to get broad buy-in from employees as well as from major shareholders. Unilever thus also developed a corporate specific leadership development program to enhance a strong implantation focus.

All large companies are faced with sets of boundaries, of course. These may partly have to do with the way such firms are organized. Unilever attempted to centralize its formal organization, to make things simpler, as well as to weaken silos. Importantly, to break down boundaries might also add to bolder, more flexible thinking!

To be transparent and more open seems to be paramount. This is a crucial condition for building effective trust. Data-driven transparency plays a principal role here. The authors state "when in doubt, do the right thing," a saying credited to General Norman Schwarzkopf, the commander of the US forces in the successful first Iranian war campaign (Schwarzkopf, 1993).

Partnerships seem critical, so also to achieve relatively easy synergies (1 + 1 = 3)! The authors distinguish between two forms of synergistic partnerships, namely, on the one hand those that might focus on bringing together stakeholders within one's current terrain of operation versus, on the other hand, those where stakeholders may have to work together to change a system itself. The former may entail enhanced partnering within one's value chain, within one's industry, while the latter might entail integration across sectors, with various societal realities as well as with governments.

Partnering with various groupings of multistakeholders might lead us into the other archetypes of synergistic realities, namely, for creating entirely new contexts, new systems, as the authors write. Also, central here are line-ups to limit corruption, even bribery.

The authors are, of course, keenly aware of the fact that there shall typically be a strong short-term focus in place that might jeopardize progress towards an environmentally unfriendly way for firms to operate, making it hard to overcome the short-term bias that is so often at play. This might include a poorly delineated tax regime, corruption, executives (over-)pay, and unprepared boards.

The end of the journey takes us back to a discussion of corporate culture, and it all comes together here. Culture is always changing of course. This seems to be quite analogous to the famous example from quantum physics, set forward by the Nobel Prize recipient Werner Heissenberg: "Matter changes form when you attempt to observe these matters!." The so-called infrastructure of culture changes continuously too, especially when in finance and with budgets, R&D as well as M&A. What we call "purpose-driven brands" evolve. (They also tend to be more profitable than other brands, hence, also the need to utilize brands!)

Ali Tamaseb, (2021), Super Founders: What Data Reveals about Billion-Dollar Start-ups, Redline (Reviewed August 2021)

Another major factor when it comes to launching start-ups seems to be proper timing, the topic of this review/book. Timing is a crucial theme in all businesses, and from this book, we can draw intelligence and awareness about timing, management of timing (as opposed to time management), and optimization of timing.

Ali Tamaseb is a partner in a successful venture capital firm in San Francisco (DCVC). He has spent over 4 years collecting and analyzing more than 30,000 data points on start-ups and has also conducted 15 case studies, interviewing many players involved in such start-ups. The aim of his work is to be better able to understand what characterizes successful start-ups. The author's goal is thus to come up with a list of critical success factors for what characterizes those start-ups that have subsequently grown to have more than a billion dollars in sales. Examples of what tends to drive such successes might be for start-ups to offer highly differentiated products and for founders to have a solid education. Whether to be first to market or not does not seem to matter, however.

What are the characteristics of successful founders: backgrounds, education, and experience? Several myths about what constitute successful founders are debunked. Age does not seem to matter, nor whether a founder is operating solo or whether there are several co-founders. Whether a founder's background is technical or commercial does also not seem to matter. But to have experience from an earlier start-up does seem to be a great plus. Similarly, to know a lot about the business in which a start-up is operating is key, that is, to know what one is talking about businesswise! And to be able to attract good talent is equally critical, that is, to be able to create a strong, hustling team. To be inspirational, supporting one's team is paramount.

Most successful founders seem to have university degrees. College dropouts are typically rare, but there are indeed success examples here too, such as Bill Gates or Mark Zuckerberg. In general, successful founders tend to come from top-ranked schools, with Stanford in the lead, perhaps also because of its location in Silicon Valley. It all seems to translate into the critical importance of having strong credibility.

When it comes to having relevant work experience, this seems to be particularly important for entrepreneurs operating in health/biotech businesses, but less so if in consumer businesses. An ability to effectively handle computers seems critical.

It is essential for a successful founder to be a strong communicator, as well as to be an effective networker. The ability to raise necessary funding is typically also a function of this.

Beyond this, what seems to characterize so-called super founders? An almost obsessive propensity to build, even tinker, and to plan, so that "the billion-dollar business idea" pivots into something that solves real world problems seems paramount. A main aspect here is an ability to scale, to move fast! And be willing and ready to work hard is, of course, an evident given.

The author now shifts to analyze specific ventures, especially what it might take to come up with good timing in markets where a start-up firm operates, how to handle competition, and the creation of defensible positions. A fundamental starting point seems to be open and ready to conduct a careful, rigorous analysis of one's own business. To be able to identify how to enhance speed appears to matter particularly.

To be effective when it comes to experimenting "trial an error" seems critical, that is, having an organization that can undertake so-called pivoting. To have no vested interests, no personal emotions at stake is a precondition for effective pivoting. And to be relatively small also appears to be an advantage. The aim would be to pivot it all into something that works even better, and faster! And so-called "pain killer" products are seen to work better than "vitamin pill" products, that is, solving problems that customers might be faced with.

Better, it is said, to focus on big, existing markets where one might aim at capturing a growing market share, rather than to try to create a new market. Many business ideas have been tried before. To be the first may not be optimal, but rather to be as close as possible to an inflection point. Timing is all!

To have competitors is not only the norm but might also even be good. This could lead to even deeper focus, so as to explore weaknesses when it comes to competitors, to enable a further driving down of costs, and additional enhancing of one's product quality. To develop a more defensible business might come out of this, above all having better engineering capabilities, as well as creating positive network effects (you often become stronger as you grow!), in total, brand building. Patent protection, that is, creation of intellectual properties may also be important, but the implicit protection from growing fast seems to be relatively more important.

In summary, successful start-ups seem to entail early pivoting to fine-tune product-market fit and developing "pain killer" products aimed at helping one's customers to save time and money. Hopefully, such products might be highly differentiated. And to compete for market share in already established markets appears the way to go, rather than to attempt to create a new market. To develop a defensible position can of course protect from competition.

A final issue is with fundraising for start-ups. The dynamics seem to be important here too, namely, to start out with the little amount of capital that one might scrape together, so-called bootstrapping, while one is developing a viable business concept. Venture capital from outside sources may then relatively easily be found later on. Rapid growth might thereby be financed. And a sequence of initially bootstrapping, for then later to find venture capital, also tends to cause less dilution of a founder's ownership share than if he/she might have attempted to try to attract significant amounts from outside at an earlier stage. And with too much dilution a founder might easily start feeling that he/she in essence might now in essence be working for the venture capitalists!

What about impacts from the state of the economy? How do funding issues differ when there is a bull market versus a bear market? It goes without saying that fundraising tends to be easier when the general financial market is strong. A firm's valuation can then be set much higher and, to take one's firm public through an initial public offering (IPO), can more easily be done. Even selling one's firm might become easier, enjoying a good price!

But recessions might also offer positives. First of all, valuations may be lower, opening up for venture capital to secure larger ownership shares to their investments. And for a firm itself, it may be relatively easier to hire good talent. A firm's business concept must be strong and realistic, however, in order to be able to secure new venture capital.

Usually, it is of course relatively easier to raise whatever capital might be needed when a business is capital light. Various service businesses, without manufacturing and inventories, and with distribution primarily drawing on the internet might fall into this category. Most software companies tend to have very high margins also! It is well known however that to finance a start-up in the next rounds can often be hard, especially if the firm's performance is not as high as perhaps promised. (The "Death Valley" challenge!)

There are many so-called accelerator or incubator programs available, to support start-ups. Accelerators will typically support start-ups with the knowledge and funding to accelerate customer acquisitions, including grow faster. Incubators are normally longer term in focus, typically providing knowledge and funding for products and idea development, including for pivoting. All time founders may benefit from these forms of support.

Angel investors typically provide much of the funding that comes with accelerator and incubator programs. Angel investors may themselves have a portfolio of early start-ups where they have taken stakes. Many angel investors evolve into leaders of venture capital funds later on, leveraging their expertise to assess start-ups by being able to draw on funding also from several other investors, in addition to their own funds.

Venture capital funds may be looking for different types of characteristics than "normal" investors in the firms where they are investing. A common factor for most venture funds is to assess the quality of the particular management team in a given firm. Important additional factors might be the fit within the given business field (medical, for instance), as well as the strength of a firm's products and technology. And the "proposer" of a company is likely to matter. "Why is this firm growing?," "why is this company likely to become an important part of the future in ten years?." Venture companies tend to prefer to invest in strengths, not focusing on ameliorating lists of weaknesses. They do not necessarily focus much on valuations either. For them, the upside potential longer term tends to be of greater significance.

Fundraising abilities are in many ways an "acid test" regarding the viability of a start-up. Successful start-ups tend to find it relatively easier to raise funds through fairly larger first rounds. A simple, well-formulated pitch by the founder of the firm is crucial, as well as being able to change one's thinking along this way.

The author offers a set of critical issues that may be particularly important to keep in mind in order to achieve perceived as well as real success, among which the following six seem to stand out:

- Speed of learning is key, particularly when it comes to effective successful pivoting. To listen to the market is clearly a major issue here.
- To develop "pain killer" products/offerings seem important.
- Such product offerings should be differentiable.

- To be close to the "takeoff" point is significant.
- It is critical to go for so-called network effects, that is, to become stronger as one grows.
- To get started ASAP, to build experience is a must.

14

Executive Profiles of Business Leaders

Hermann Simon, Founder and Honorary Chairman, Simon-Kucher & Partners, Hidden Champions, Presentation Given at the WHU Family Business Conference (September 2019)

This is a summary of a presentation that Dr. Hermann Simon gave at Otto Beisheim School of Management (WHU) on September 20, 2019. He argues that many of the relatively unknown, but no longer so small, German-based export companies seem to become and remain successful due to their closeness to the customers as well as a strong emphasis on quality. Business-to-business strategic settings seem to be particularly well suited for this approach. What may we bring away here is how steady, solid growth, and development can pay off. It is not always about being so visible, rather to commit to performance using a very practical, grounded long-term approach to business, sometimes discreetly, and understanding that time is an ally rather than a source of pressure.

"Hidden Champions" is a term coined by Hermann Simon, a German academic and business leader, and used later in the title of his best-selling book *Hidden Champions. Lessons from 500 of the world's best unknown companies*, Harvard Business School Press in 1996.

A Hidden Champion (HC) is defined as being among the top three globally in sales in a particular market niche and/or number one in the firm's home market. It will usually earn up to 5 billion euros in sales. However, it is "hidden" because it often falls under the radar of being well-known, quietly becoming a leader in its field instead.

Simon first identified a large swathe of such firms in Germany, companies that typically are not household names but that often enjoy world market shares of over 50%, that is, with the majority of their products being destined for export. He points out that Germany was by far the leading exporter in the world for many years (until surpassed by China in 2009) and that much of this success typically derives from the relatively little-known "mittelstand" companies, small- and medium-sized enterprises in German-speaking countries. Typically, only few businesspeople, academics, or journalists know the names of such companies or are aware of the products and services they offer.

Exploring the reasons for the German HC phenomenon, Simon notes that Germany is a relatively decentralized country, with an open educational system that allows for upward mobility and individual advancement. This contrasts with more centralized countries, such as France, for instance, with a more elite educational system, less upward social mobility, and relatively little capital available for investments in new businesses. High property taxes mean that investors often rely to a larger extent on the government, as individual effort does not generate the necessary capital surplus. Simon contrasts the typical longevity of German HCs with the situation in China, where emerging business leaders tend to go for an IPO relatively early on in order to obtain the necessary funds to enable continuous fast growth and to fund greater levels of R&D. Conversely, German family-owned HCs may at times fail to realize that it might be time to relinquish some of their ownership control in order to go for more rapid growth from "fresh" capital injected through IPOs.

There are several of key differences between Hidden Champions and many more well-known companies: The first is exhibited in their ambition for market leadership.

– Ambition for market leadership. HCs exhibit an often "relentless" ambition to be market leaders. They want to be world leaders in their field, and they set high benchmarks! Their leaders often possess a single-mindedness and attention to doing one thing better than anyone else. Their absolute focus on their missions makes them "unbeatable."
– Market-driven. This takes the shape of having a relatively narrow range of specialized products, then investing in the global marketing and sales of these. Specialized products are usually based on unique know-how, improved over time through incremental innovations. This continuous improvement—"evolution not revolution"—is a major sales argument for

- such firms, selling based on performance/quality, rather than competing on price.
- Digitalization. Hidden Champions seem to be at the forefront when it comes to digital transformation, particularly in the area of B2B. Their use of analytics and the long-term perspectives of these predominantly family-led firms have been advantageous in this respect. In addition, HCs tend to employ qualified staff with the expertise to drive forward their digital programs.
- Customer satisfaction. This may occupy as much as 65% of HC's management attention, compared to 19% in other firms. HCs usually work closely with their customer bases in order to better understand their needs.
- Workforce. The workforce mix is often different than in many other firms. HCs tend to employ highly qualified workers, many of whom are graduates, and there is normally very low turnover in their workforces. The CEOs themselves often have long tenures. This stability is achieved by unqualified support from the owners, to enhance enthusiasm for the company's mission, encouraging all to deliver the best performance.
- Leadership style. HCs are often family owned. HCs frequently exhibit a distinctive leadership culture, which is frequently rather participative. However, there seems to be a dichotomy here: HCs are often authoritative at the macro level, with clear focus, goals, and priorities, but more flexible when it comes to the detail of their day-to-day operations. Employees have the freedom to do what they consider and to make use of their full potential but, equally, must take responsibility for ensuring that their actions do not damage the long-term vision of their firm.
- Self-reliance. HCs tend to be wary of management fads and will often stick to their own paths. They tend to be far less likely to outsource, or to engage in strategic alliances, and will often manufacture all the key components required for their products, typically to very high standards. They rely on their own strengths and prefer to "go it" alone.

A successful strategy for an HC might often be compared to three intersecting circles:

- Outer circle, which specifies the HC's focus, its closeness, and value offered to customers, its commitment to globalization, and how it is taking advantage of unique know-how features.
- Middle circle (digitalization), indicating degree of "depth" (in contrast to superficiality), how to maintain a highly motivated workforce, and how to spark relevant innovation.

- Inner circle, which articulates a HC's leadership and which major ambitious goals, is being pursued.

Perhaps, we have here a model for winning strategy and viable strategic management in the twenty-first century: digitalized processes, exploiting close customer relationships, delivering real customer benefits. And a strong degree of patience? We can all learn from Hidden Champions!

Markus Laenzlinger, CEO Migrolino (Interviewed April 2020)

Here, a new store concept is discussed with super-fast convenient shopping, easy parking, and so on. The product/service range is relatively small but offers what people normally need. Remember to always look at patterns and trends in consumer behavior and consider that customers usually seek convenience.

Migrolino, a wholly owned subsidiary of Migros, the Swiss retail giant, was started in January 2009 as a result of the de-merger of the joint venture between Swiss Federal Railways, Valora and Migros. Mr. Markus Laenzlinger has been the CEO since the start. As of April 2020, Migrolino counted some 325 stores and has a turnover of close to CHF 1 bn.

The Migrolino store concept is, above all, built on convenience, initially by co-locating relatively small Migrolino stores together with gas stations, so that customers might make their necessary purchases while they were filling their cars. This has since evolved into Migrolino stores located also elsewhere. Parking is however always key! Carefully stocked Migrolino stores are also critical, to be able to cover most of the average persons' daily basic needs in a simple, convenient, and fast way!

Mr. Laenzlinger was formally reporting to Mr. Beat Zahnd, who was heading up the largest countrywide unit in cooperative Migros and leading the commerce division of the Migros Federation, consisting of 5 units and a turnover of 7.3 bn. The main store structure of Migros was embedded in ten regions, covering various parts of Switzerland, quite similar to the cantonal structure of this nation itself. Migros' 28 product-producing entities were part of another nationwide Migros division.

Some outsiders may perhaps feel that the structure of the Migros group might perhaps be too complex. Mr. Laenzlinger did not feel so. While the Migros organization could be seen as somewhat political and complicated,

Mr. Laenzlinger did not believe that this would hamper him when it came to Migrolino, neither for its ability to be innovative nor for growth.

Most of Migrolino's gasoline-station-located stores did very well during the pandemic, perhaps with the exception of a few stores in the canton of Ticino, close to the Italian border. Stores located in railway stations were also doing rather badly. The sourcing/supply of goods/logistics function did fine.

Germany. Mr. Laenzlinger was not given approval from Migros headquarters when it came to expansion into the German market. He had observed that prices in Germany, in general, tended to be even higher than in Switzerland! The Frankfurt-Rhein-Main area might have been a good starting target, to be served by a relatively small local logistics center, sourcing around 50–60 outlets. The Migros-Zurich organization (from the Zurich region) was already active in Rhein-Main aera. Eventual expansion into the rest of the German market would then be region by region, following the Frankfurt model.

Migrolino worked with McKinsey on developing a new store concept, very simple, with a higher share of fresh products and with no Migros-branded products, in order to start an even more rapid expansion and also to be more attractive for landlords. Migrolino had also run the "pick me" experiment, which involved semiautomated sourcing for each customer. This did not seem to work as intended, above all because of the need to tailor this function specifically to every individual store location. But this trail continued for another year at two outlets, before being abandoned.

Mr. Laenzlinger was in general able to open new stores across Switzerland but with consensus from the regional organizations. A rare exception was a lack of such consensus when it came to a potential new store in Baden, which was only 100 meters from a Migros own outlet. Mr. Laenzlinger noticed that the sister organization, Denner (with much larger turnover), was allowed to decide independently on its new store locations, without any such consultations with the regional organizations.

Mr. Laenzlinger is a member of the international board of directors of the US-based NACS organization. Over 400,000 smaller stores worldwide are part of this organization, which is a source of many new and innovative retail concepts.

Competition. Pronto (owned by COOP) is the major competitor. Migrolino and Pronto tend to copy each other to a considerable degree. Migrolino has recently surpassed Pronto in terms of locations and sales even though they started 10 years later. Migrolino has a potential advantage over Pronto in that it can lean on the Migros Group's products, produced by the Migros Group itself, that is, a "private brand" advantage. As noted, the Migros Group owned 28 different manufacturing entities. Migrolino is, however, free to buy from these or not, depending on price and quality. These products are however well recognized in the market.

Valora had recently won a contract to establish around 220 stores located in SBB railway stations but had to pay double the rent it had paid in the period before. As part of this bid, Migrolino lost some ten stores. In general, Valora was following an "ultrafresh" concept under the brand "avec" as well as a rather standardized so-called "box concept." The latter did not give the customer much choice in the sense that narrow and similar price/product choices, etc. could be found in every store.

To stimulate a high frequency of purchases was seen by Mr. Laenzlinger, as absolutely critical, based on adopting the idea of "wheel of retailing": relevant products; a competitive price, to give the customer several choices combinations; and finally store layout and cleanliness.

Mr. Laenzlinger was very much involved in these decisions. He often visited his stores as well as the competition and also generally talked extensively with customers.

Migrolino has three supply chains, one for frozen food, one for nonfood, and one for "night logistics," that is, sandwiches and salads. These were completely automated.

To sell fresh products has become central to Migrolino's competitive advantage. The unique sourcing issues from this, which are handled as follows: The stores put in its orders for fresh products in the afternoons, and fresh food is then prepared at night through various sub-suppliers. This was then sent out early in the morning, via light trucks, and left in boxes outside each store to be ready for its opening hours that morning.

Migrol is the gasoline-filling station chain owned by Migros Federation and is a sister company of Migrolino. They traditionally saw themselves as supplier of fuel. However, later they consider themselves more as supplier of energy (gasoline, electric, hydrogen others). Migrolino might play a role here, regarding the attractiveness of Migrol, by being located in many Migrol facilities. Migrol's CEO has joined Migrolino's board, and Mr. Laenzlinger also joined Migrol's board.

Mr. Laenzlinger believes that hydrogen-driven cars will gradually take over. These are <u>de facto</u> electric cars. Trucks would be too heavy to be run using electricity, however. He sees this happening over a ten-year time horizon. So, most filling stations for petrol and diesel will still be there in the future (for hydrogen), and parking will thus typically still be good!

Cash and cards. There will always be a societal demand for cash—without cash, the government's ability to monitor might make them potentially too strong! A possible "Octopus" card might function almost as cash! The Migrol and Socar cards relate to gasoline purchases only. Cumulus (Migros' loyalty card) is now accepted in all Migrolino stores. A clearer strategy for the Cumulus card might be needed, with this card intended to become associated with all purchasing activities within the Migros Group in the future.

Packaging. In general, there tends to be a lot of throwing away of packaging, say, of plastic bottles, packaging, etc., often by the youth. Perhaps, relevant education might help ameliorate some of this. The fresh products of Migrolino are also often wrapped in biodegradable packaging, again ameliorating some of the throwaway problems.

What can we learn from the Migrolino story? To serve the customer better seems to be, above all, a question of coming up with more convenience. Migrolino seems to have hit a "nail" here: Save time for the customer, provide convenient parking, and offer good quality products at a reasonable price.

Innovations might often be more effective when one is able to build on an already existing infrastructure. Existing gas stations were the perfect structural support for Migrolino. Many new waves of changes in retailing might not necessarily impact Migrolino's business model. There will likely always be a need for energy-filling stations for cars, perhaps hydrogen, rather than petrol or diesel, and modern customers may tend to do their daily shopping while their cars are charging/filling up, that is, convenience and accessibility. Migrolino should continue to be well-positioned!

Kristian Jebsen, CEO Gearbulk (Interviewed January 2019)

This shipping firm with around ten large-bulk carriers, practices "cycle management" where timing is of the essence (in/out, long/short). The emerging role of China when it comes to bulk shipping commodities is also discussed. Cycles exist in all businesses, and leaders must not forget: beware of ups and downs and their repetitions. Also, watching out for strong geographic competition, at times from the obvious, and at other instances from surprising areas, is something to always keep in mind. Additionally, take a close look at the impact of culture as it makes a huge difference to performance and legacy, or at least the future. And least but not least, examine how alignment of values at the leadership level can strengthen a company.

Shipping is by definition an international business, and the shipping business has been known to create, and destroy, large fortunes around the world. Names such as Møller, Li Ka Shing, Kuok, Fredriksen, Oetker, and Aponte rank among some of the most successful family names in the shipping industry.

Kristian Jebsen is also part of a global shipping family phenomenon, Gearbulk. What makes Jebsen's experience and perspective unique is his own international outlook, education, and experience, as well as how he has added his own strong sense of major business principles to operate the world's largest fleet of open hatch gantry and jib crane vessels.

Kristian Jebsen has grown his company and taken it into new waters through an almost relentless customer focus; he has a strong and intuitive understanding of the open hatch bulk carrier business and its market cycles, and a firm commitment to organizational quality, hard work, and social issues.

Mr. Jebsen, is the chairman and principal owner of Gearbulk Holding AG. His company specializes in the transportation of paper and pulp and maintains a fleet of around 65 large-bulk carriers. Mr. Jebsen and his three children control 51% of the company, while the Tokyo-based shipping group Mitsui O.S.K. controls the remainder.

Mr. Jebsen's father, Mr. Kristian Gerhard Jebsen, founded Gearbulk in 1968. When he passed away in 2004, the company was initially co-managed by Mr. Jebsen and his brother Hans Peter, until 2011, when Mr. Kristian Jebsen took over the open hatch bulk carrier business, while his brother stayed with the firm's tankers, OBOs, and cement carriers. Mr. Kristian Jebsen retained the name Gearbulk.

Mr. Jebsen received his undergraduate education from the University of Lausanne and his MBA from Thunderbird in Arizona. He has accumulated diverse job experiences, all within the Gearbulk group: in Bergen, Norway; in Tokyo; and in Vancouver. He spent 14 years at Gearbulk's new headquarters in London before moving to Switzerland, transferring its headquarters to Pfäffikon outside Zürich in 2015, and moved a large part of its operations to Singapore.

Mr. Jebsen is known to be a hands-on CEO with a firm grasp of his B2B business, including a close link to many of its customers. He is known to make decisions relatively quickly, which are often based on, say, an 80–90% completed analysis, while also acknowledging that eventual remaining issues might have to be addressed before concluding a deal. This fast management style, a trademark of Gearbulk's culture, can be traced back to Mr. Jebsen, who also embodies the following traits: entrepreneurial, hardworking, a strong customer focus, as well as being very private and discreet.

In particular, this strong customer focus is considered to be particularly key. Gearbulk has often been known to seek out new ways to serve its key customers, almost as being partners. Gearbulk's large size gives credence to its ability to offer such superb service. Mr. Jebsen feels that Gearbulk's culture is a major strength, not only in terms of its speed, entrepreneurial attitude, customer focus, and reputation for hard work but also for its professionalism. Mr. Jebsen places heavy emphasis on attracting new talent, who tend to be typically rather young, often strong in challenging key assumptions and unafraid to ask difficult questions. Still, he feels there could be even less bureaucracy in the organization. To maintain agility is increasingly important!

Gearbulk's culture is worth further consideration. Mr. Jebsen and his younger brother have been known to apply rather different management styles—that is, fast, intuitive, and entrepreneurial versus highly analytical but, at times, slower. This style difference at the helm of the company was one reason why the company was split between them.

Gearbulk's corporate culture has also clearly changed over time. Moving the headquarters from Bergen to London in 1993 led to a more international culture. The move also allowed the Jebsen family to maintain a fairly low profile, by being "relatively small players in a big place, rather than big players in a small place." One important motivation was to be able to plan more firmly, in a way that was often not possible in the politically less-stable Norway. Tax-planning issues, wealth, inheritance, etc. were also particularly important.

Then, as noted in 2015, Gearbulk moved its corporate headquarters to Switzerland and some of its operations to Singapore. This relocation was partly driven by cost considerations and partly by tax considerations plus a desire for even more political stability. The operational entity's relocation was primarily a function of the fact that the world's economic gravity had moved to Asia; hence, Gearbulk wanted to increase its presence there.

Mr. Jebsen considers the following aspects of his business context particularly important:

– Acting on major trends (indeed, mega-trends) is crucial. In most business segments, price dynamics and operations have become increasingly commoditized and mature. Price is becoming the dominant factor for winning business, as opposed to coming up with additional unique or brain-driven special service approaches. To understand these shifts, Mr. Jebsen emphasizes maintaining a large network of resourceful people with whom to discuss business, not only shipping. He also stresses the importance of strategic retreats where lead experts can challenge commonly accepted beliefs. It is imperative to understand what is happening in the technology sector and what impact technology may have on shipping and the company's customers (and on their customers, in turn). Needless to say, following international

and local news in business and politics and reading often are highly prioritized.
– Mr. Jebsen strongly believes in an open management style with a broad sharing of key facts. He does, however, perceive a certain diminishment in ethical standards, with more and more executives taking an egocentric approach to decision-making, that is, to primarily benefit themselves rather than the firms by which they are employed. Mr. Jebsen feels that factors such as the above have led to a decrease in the "joy of doing business."

Over the years, Gearbulk has been a consolidator in its segment, open hatch bulk carriers. The most recent consolidation move occurred in 2017 when Gearbulk initiated a strategic alliance with Grieg Star, another player in the open hatch business and a former competitor. Gearbulk has taken a 65% ownership in this joint-venture pool—G2Ocean—which now controls about 60% of the global open hatch fleet. Although technical management, ship management, and corporate functions have remained separate entities, the commercial and operational sides are now fully integrated. Other functions, such as purchasing and IT, have also been integrated. Needless to say, aspects of the two companies' cultures differ. Some of these differences have been reconciled, and some will take more time to align. These organizational frictions are the biggest challenge of the merger so far.

Mr. Jebsen views his firm as a family business and finds inspiration in this view. He also finds it crucial to preserve financial flexibility and to avoid major drawdowns. To remain so heavily invested in an increasingly mature and capital-intensive shipping segment may not be commensurate with such family financial wealth preservation, however. It might actually be more sensible to bring in another strong partner, which Mr. Jebsen's father did in the early 1990s.

Through the creation of G2Ocean, Gearbulk has become more of a holding company and a more "interesting" player in its segment, which again opens up for the possibility of further liquid shareholding for the Jebsens.

While all three of Mr. Jebsen's children have shares in Gearbulk, he still retains control. Growing up, none of them appeared very heavily involved, nor very interested. In retrospect, Mr. Jebsen regrets that he did not involve them more. One of them has worked in the company and is presently completing an MBA. The other two have chosen educations in teaching and journalism.

Hobbies. Mr. Jebsen is a keen photographer. He has found that it is relatively easy for him to combine this hobby with the extensive travel schedule he typically undertakes. He uses state-of-the-art digital cameras. For his 60th birthday, his wife Ana published a book featuring a collection of his best photos that cover inspirations from all over the world, including Antarctica.

The Kristian Gerhard Jebsen Foundation's[1] primary focus is on health, education, and social issues but also supports culture and art. Mr. Jebsen is its chairman. Nutritional health is of special interest to him. This includes not only research but also education and advocacy. For instance, the foundation has sponsored two professorial chairs: one at EPFL (the Federal Technical University in Lausanne) in nutrition and metabolism and one at CHUV (the University Hospital in Lausanne) in palliative care.

As of recently, the foundation has also focused on the reduction of single-use plastic waste in the oceans. Its cooperation with eight other foundations in the Plastic Solution Fund is a major initiative in this area. Mr. Jebsen has a strong social commitment and would like to spend more time on his philanthropic and social entrepreneurship activities going forward.

Key Strengths. The following key strengths might, in particular, provide an accurate snapshot of Mr. Jebsen and the Gearbulk Group: A strong customer focus, which is the centerpiece of his hands-on business philosophy; a unique understanding of most aspects of the open-hatch bulk carrier business, with particular emphasis on taking advantage of the industry's market cycles, due to supply versus demand imbalances; a working style that might be summed up simply as "working very hard," with a total commitment to Gearbulk's business; a recognition that the core qualities of Gearbulk's organization are professionalism, internationalism, openness, entrepreneurship, and agility. Mr. Jebsen "lives" these strengths himself; and finally, a strong social commitment, primarily through leading the Kristian Gerhard Jebsen Foundation. This latter reflects a good work–life balance, where his other life interests play key roles.

---

[1] It should be noted that there is a second foundation with the same name as Mr. Jebsen's father, based in Bergen, however the two are independent of each other.

15

Closing Remarks for the Chapter

It is not always simple to split the topic of business from strategy. You cannot have a business without a strategy. We might see from the wide span of foci in the books reviewed as well as in the executive interviews that there typically are many viable ways forward. We have chosen to split the two in order to provide a logical foundation for our discussion— namely, by starting with a look at the product or service offered by the organizations selected herein, we can then afterwards reflect on the firm's strategic options. Strategy means choice (Lorange, 2005). And strategy is much more thinking and execution than planning (Lorange, 2009). So, as we move from a look at business to a discussion of strategy, let us acknowledge the necessity for clarity, structure, and foundations when establishing a business. An explicit, straightforward, and relatively simple sense of which strategy and direction to be taken seems critical. That seems to be a consistent "message" coming out of the book reviews and interviews alike.

So, while an overriding conventional view regarding business has been that a financial focus, profit maximization, should be the sole center objective for a business, the readings suggest that there be a need for a broadening of this view. Other factors that come to mind include national values, political beliefs, legal realities, and even shifts in many executives' values. Let us briefly comment on each.

National values often impact a business. For we who live in Switzerland, for instance, it may be beneficial to reckon with the (what may be seen as a typical) work ethic found in this country. This might imply that sole belief in the virtues of high salaries and high financial bonuses have only a limited effect. To the contrary, the basic work ethic of a business could be weakened, in the face of excessive financial rewards for the employees. A case in point may be the large international bank, Credit Suisse, headquartered in Zurich and founded by the legendary Swiss entrepreneur Alfred Escher some 150 years ago. Aggressive increases in salary levels, as well as high bonuses, even when the bank's financial results were down, seemed to be the bank's way up until things collapsed. Over time, this not only corrupted the entire value system of the bank but led to excessive salary costs for many other banks, thus weakening the traditionally so strong Swiss banking sector. Needless to say, Credit Suisse's approach failed, and it has now become part of UBS. We can only watch and wait for what comes next.

Moving now to having to adhere to overriding political trends, let us simply notice an ever-increasing need for business to operate with social responsibility. It may not only be harder and harder for such firms' employees, that is, reducing a firm's work force. Other political trends might call for fuller attention to emission constraints and excessive pollution control. And there may be emerging national political shifts, such as the growing skepticism that has to do with Russia, say, in the wake of the Ukrainian war. The Verbier Festival, for instance, indeed a business, went the step of terminating the contract with its, until recently, Artistic Director, the St. Petersburg-based world-known conductor, Valery Gergiev.

Legal realities do, of course, also come into play here. Boycotts, not only of countries such as Russia, but to a lesser extent also nations such as China, North Korea, and Iran, typically led to restrictions for many businesses, changing how they ran or still run their international operations, where they invest, their export policies, and so on. If a business does not follow such nationally set regulations and instead is lured by trying to generate even more profits, then they may be typically fined by various national authorities, or by supranational ones such as EU.

There are clearly shifts in the value sets of members of the business' workforce, often among younger employees. So-called "green values" are frequently strong. So is the belief that "small is beautiful." Again, we see that many firms not only find it necessary to modify their environmental practices, but perhaps also pursue entirely new ways to do business, such as Tesla with its electric cars or Yara with its "clan" fertilizers. And companies break themselves up, to act smaller. An example is GE with its breakup into three separate firms and sell-off of several other now "peripheral" businesses. A similar argument might be raised when it comes to companies such as ABB, which has reorganized itself into some 21 freestanding business divisions, each to run autonomously, quite analogous to being small companies. To attract the best talents is of course a key factor when it comes to all of this.

Part IV

Strategic Options: Strategy Means Choice

In real life, strategy is actually very straightforward. You pick a general direction and implement like hell.
—Jack Welch, business leader, chemical engineer and writer

The real challenge in crafting strategy lies in detecting subtle discontinuities that may undermine a business in the future. And for that there is no technique, no program, just a sharp mind in touch with the situation.
—Henry Mintzberg, academician, author

16

Practice Insights from Björn Rosengren, President and CEO, ABB

This foreword describes ABB's strategic choices and my experiences with the restructuring process of the Swiss-Swedish technology company that I am currently serving as CEO. It will highlight the leadership principles I truly believe in and that have been key in driving the transformation towards a more entrepreneurial company.

Where We Come From: The Matrix!

How do you define the success of a company? From my perspective, it starts with being able to deliver superior value for customers. When I became CEO of ABB in 2020, my conclusion was clear: ABB has, over many years, created a complex matrix organization with strong central control but only little entrepreneurial spirit in the operating businesses. In fact, this complexity was not at all good for creating entrepreneurship. In today's fast-changing world, speed and agility are critical for business success. At a time of rapid technological advances, sudden shifts in demand, and increased market uncertainty, companies need to be close to their markets and customers, as well as adaptable, flexible, and fast. In short, they need to be entrepreneurial.

For large companies in particular, this is a challenge. What do you focus on when you have multiple businesses competing in many different markets? How do you decide what actions to take in the face of new technologies and global challenges like climate change, labor and skills shortages, and supply chain disruptions? How do you compete with smaller, more nimble competitors? Can you successfully compete with them at all?

Many people think to be a big company means to be slow and unwieldy—to have long, complicated approval processes, to lack focus.

Creating an Entrepreneurial Culture: Through Accountability, Transparency, and Speed

In fact, there is no reason why large companies cannot be entrepreneurial and innovative. Large companies are well positioned, because their operating divisions can pool resources and capabilities among each other where they benefit (e.g., in digital, R&D) and benefit from lean and consistent corporate governance. So, if set up right, the operating businesses of large companies can focus more on their customers, innovation, and performance delivery. The keys to creating an entrepreneurial culture are accountability, transparency, and speed. This is where I believe entrepreneurs become successful: being close to the customer (i.e., truly "understand" the customer) and able to respond quickly to changing market conditions. This turned out to be highly motivational for our employees in ABB, especially in our operating businesses ("divisions").

Today, when it comes to running the business, our 20 divisions are the highest operational level in the company. They have full ownership and accountability for their respective strategies, performance, and resources. We have eliminated the matrix organization: country-holding managers are nowadays only taking care of fiscal and fiduciary duties but do not interfere with managing operating businesses locally. We have decreased resources in the central organization—from 18,000 to 800 people centrally and in the country organizations. ABB's operating divisions are defined so that they are as much as possible distinct from each other: specific customers, unambiguous offerings, unique technology, etc. Electric motors, drive products, and robotics are only some examples of the 20 ABB divisions.

Driving Performance in a Decentralized Business Model

In a decentralized company, the role of the corporate headquarters is very different to that of a centrally controlled corporation. Because operational decisions are taken in the divisions, the headquarters can be much leaner. At ABB, our corporate center focuses on performance and portfolio management, capital allocation, governance, and the ABB brand.

We manage divisional performance through a transparent scorecard system, based on a set of common key performance indicators. Our divisions are required to deliver stability and profitability before investing in growth. They drive value creation with the clear aim of being the no. 1 or 2 in their respective market segments.

Once our divisions are in the growth phase, they are expected to focus on organic growth by collaborating with customers on innovation, investing in R&D, sales and service, and continuous improvement. They are also encouraged to seek out value-creating acquisitions to expand capabilities, offering, and market coverage. We insist that our divisions aim for market leadership because it is the key to profitability. Market leaders have more resources to invest in R&D, are in a better position to achieve premium pricing, and can take advantage of benefits of scale.

The "Glue" that Holds ABB Together

In a decentralized organization, the challenge is making sure that the company holds together. At ABB, with our 20 divisions, four business areas, and a lean corporate center, we have a common purpose and operating model—the "ABB Way"—which defines "who" we are and "how" we create value. Our purpose is simple: to enable a more sustainable and resource-efficient future with our technology leadership in electrification and automation.

Under the ABB Way, we drive performance through active portfolio and performance management, focusing on people development, maintaining a strong culture of governance and integrity, and building and protecting our brand and reputation. The ABB Way consists of a set of rules, policies, and procedures that must be followed by the divisions. The ABB Way is like a glue that keeps the group together and that makes sure that we as a group are stronger than being separate businesses—after all, ABB is not a conglomerate.

In a decentralized company, collaboration is crucial. In ABB, we refer to the benefit of collaboration as "smart leaders collaborate." This means that we encourage our divisions to work together where it makes sense from their perspective—and find synergies to create competitive advantages. Today, our divisions are collaborating in many areas as for instance, by working jointly on serving key customers, pooling resources for research or digital platforms, changing best practices in pricing, etc. And we can see a positive result:

working together helps the divisions to be more cost-efficient and effective when serving the customers.

What has once been a merger between Sweden's ASEA and Switzerland's Brown Boveri is today a truly global technology company with strong entrepreneurial divisions.

The transformation we initiated in 2020 went very smooth despite several external headwinds. My experiences from similar restructuring processes, both in Atlas Copco and Sandvik, is that it is much easier to drive decentralization with full accountability than the opposite, centralization. What we have seen and learned is that when people and organizations are empowered, they can achieve incredible things.

17

Introduction to Strategic Options: Strategy Means Choice

Now to the book reviews and interviews. This part discusses some key strategic options for businesses. We shall pay particular attention to how business strategies seem to be evolving and especially in today's rapidly changing world. As commonly accepted, the first step in business is to define a strategy that sets the direction of business through its clear definition, goal setting, values, and purpose. Thus, we too shall begin with the topic of strategy.

IMD Professor Knut Haanæs, along with Martin Reeves and Janmejaya Sinha (2015), proposes distinct ways to critically consider strategy and how to choose and execute the right approach. From assessing business environment to predictability, malleability, and harshness, their book, Your Strategy Needs a Strategy, shows five categories of strategic approaches as already discussed in the foreword (Warren & Nanus, 1987) and slightly re-labeled here—Be Big, Be Fast, Be First, Be the Orchestrator, or simply Be Viable. Their main emphasis is how today's volatility, uncertainty, complexity, and ambiguity (VUCA) environment makes it ever more important to select the right approach to strategy. And much of our selected content supports this necessity, perhaps urgency. We both believe this will continue to accelerate over the next years.

Additionally, as in the previous part, we wish to point out that we went through a list of main business factors when selecting the book reviews and executive interviews to include herein. For the topic of strategic options for the firm, factors such as (a) the financial management systems set up and the mix of treasury and financial instruments to employ, (b) digital strategies including customer growth and management programs, membership/subscription and community engagement building models, and (c) ESG / impact and green strategies, for example, are all part of a company's strategic options with distinct implications. Directly or indirectly, these get presented in this section.

A long-term focus, but not one that eliminates or overshadows a company's ability to be agile and flexible in the short-term, still prevails as advisable when defining the business strategy and emphatically underlines the very critical topic of human resource and talent management. Pick up any dictionary and we see that the word itself, *strategy*, comes from the Greek, *strategia*, *strategos*, and *stratos*—all referring to the office of command of a general, commander of an army, multitude. *Stere* is a proto-Indo-European root meaning to spread or spread out; *agos*, leader; and *ag*, to drive out or forth, move. So, resources and talent for leadership are engrained in strategy.

What are some of the key takeaways from this part? Let us highlight the following three:

– Joint ventures and cooperative arrangements are paramount.
– Rapid scale-up, speedy expansion is key.
– Sustainable growth. Are we "safe?"

18

Essential Books to Learn About Strategic Options; Strategy Means Choice

Reid Hoffman and Chris Yeh, (2018), Blitzscaling, Penguin Random House (Reviewed May 2021)

How to scale up rapidly is being discussed in more detail, with a "warning" about factors that might derail this process, such as financial constraints and excessively detailed management processes. Seductive and exciting, scaling your business in a blitz intense way may get you to where you want to go. But beware the demands! It is not for the fearless.

Growth is in many ways the most critical success factor when it comes to several aspects of business today:

- It is seemingly the most straightforward way to create value in a business.
- It is a key condition for successfully raising new capital.
- It represents a prerequisite for favorable valuation of a business in case of sale or merger.
- It is possibly the most reliable yardstick to guide investors when it comes to navigating where and how to invest.

Blitzscaling addresses how corporations might achieve ultrarapid growth. Fast growth is a matter of getting in early and quickly. This can make a big difference! Blitzscaling is one of the latest concepts when it comes to strategy, with a set of techniques that allows both start-ups and established companies to build dominant, world-leading businesses in record time. It is a matter of speed and intensity!

The authors, Reid Hoffman and Chris Yeh, are credible experts when it comes to this new approach: Reid Hoffman is a successful and famous Silicon Valley-based internet entrepreneur, investor, venture capitalist, and author. He has been among the founders of PayPal, LinkedIn, and SocialNet and has also invested in AirBnB, Facebook, and Zynga. Further, he is on the board (or has been) of AirBnB, Microsoft, Mozilla, and Zynga. Chris Yeh is a writer, investor, and entrepreneur and has developed a highly successful consulting practice focusing on the topic, which has benefitted companies from his knowledge and insights to accelerate their businesses. Both of them have offered a highly successful course on blitzscaling at Stanford.

The book clearly lays out the "how to do it" as well as the "key potential pitfalls," with many useful examples, which shed further light on it all.

The book is comprised of six parts, plus introduction and conclusion. In the introduction, the authors provide a clear outline of what is to come:

"Blitzscaling is an aggressive, all out program of (rapid) growth." To achieve this, a company must have a "killer product," as well as a well-defined market and a clear distribution channel. Management must be ready to take the additional risk and discomfort of blitzscaling their company. Yet this could go wrong! The authors point out that speed is central to it all (i.e., to ultrarapid growth), rather than efficiency as such. And they argue convincingly that such rapid growth is perhaps the best predictor for business success and greater return.

There are three distinct types of innovation that seem to drive blitzscaling:

– A growth-orientated business model
– A growth strategy itself
– Management processes, that is, to instill a "do it" culture in the firm that embraces blitzscaling

The term "blitzscaling" is linked to the "blitzing" concept that the Germans practiced during WW2, perhaps exemplified above all by General Heinz Guderian's attack on France with his "panzer" tanks brigade in 1940. While the authors' choice of name "blitz" might perhaps be somewhat unfortunate for this reason, the notion of blitzscaling nevertheless adds to the clarity of the concept of driving for ultrarapid growth.

Now to business model innovation. In addition to the three conditions that need to be present for successful blitzscaling (business model, strategy, processes), the authors also highlight the importance of the potential for positive so-called network effects, that is, that growth might lead to expansion of one's group of customers (through word of mouth, market dominance, …). The authors infer that we typically tend to talk about businesses that might be characterized as "bits," that is, software, rather than as "atoms," that is, hardware, distinguishing between offerings that are free (grow fast, increase the network) versus "freeism" (value customers but nevertheless with slower growth).

The authors also identify several "conditions" that may make blitzscaling more achievable. The first is whether the so-called Moore's law might be in effect. Clearly, companies that are pursuing blitzscaling might benefit when this "law" applies (named after one of Intel's founders, Gordon Earle Moore), where the speed of technological change leads to an ever-accelerating array of new technological opportunities—new models, more advanced components, smaller and more powerful parts, etc. Clearly, blitzscaling might be easier when such conditions apply.

A second "condition" lays out the degree to which a business might lend itself to automation. Blitzscaling assumes that automation might be done. A third condition is whether it is possible to follow a different path than the majority. This might normally take a great discipline, however. It can be hard to do the opposite of everyone else, to break one's natural flock mentality. There is an interesting analysis of the business models of four well-known and highly successful firms: LinkedIn, Amazon, Google, and Facebook.

Strategy innovation is it! A review of the biggest potential opportunities by starting blitzscaling emphasizes that an early start usually might represent a big new opportunity to go faster. There are typically learning curve effects that can be had by being the first to blitzscale, relative to competition. The early advantage of high speed might be formidable.

Should one ever stop blitzscaling? Many of the managerial principles of this approach shall of course remain valid under most conditions. Stopping might thus make little sense! When slowing growth, increased overheads and worsening economic performance might set in once the intensity of one's efforts is eased.

The authors underline that a blitzscaling strategy process typically is iterative, and that one's strategy thus will change at various stages. This might also be the case when it comes to the role of the founder, changing perhaps from personally leading the super-growth efforts, through managing other super-growth prone people, through working out an organizational design to enhance blitzscaling, to finally managing a portfolio of business lines, where the blitzscaling intensity might be higher in some parts than in others.

Managerial innovations associated with blitzscaling are key. Several of these have to do with how managerial focus might have to change as high growth evolution takes place, away from so-called "start-up-people." Also, there may be an evolution from more informal data sources to formal data applications. A single business focus may become a portfolio. The authors give us an interesting analog here, namely, to evolve from being pirates to being a navy and then going from being captain to becoming admiral. A detailed analysis of how Uber's top management might have missed out here follows.

There seem to be several counterintuitive rules for good management practice when blitzscaling. One would be to embrace chaos and to hire the best people that might be comfortable with this, with no procrastination! Various aspects of one's business might not be perfect but, and one should still move on. Ignore occasional fires! Further, one should not be "distracted," slowed down by occasional outlying customer complaints.

The authors point out that when new capital shall have to be raised, one should always attempt to go for a higher amount that what might be needed in the short term, even though this might imply a higher degree of ownership dilution. Blitzscaling costs money, and a liquid resource of at least 18 months might be prudent.

To evolve one's culture is a major challenge when blitzscaling. It might not be all that easy to maintain a highly action-orientated culture as one's firm grows. Blitzscaling requires a clear understanding of one's cultural context. The leader shall typically have a particular challenge to transmit the essence of this, and he/she must take the time to do this. And since one's culture more-or-less continuously will change, the leader must be comfortable with the so-called "ship of Theseus" principle, which states that over time, every original plank of one's ship shall have to be replaced. And so, it may be also with an evolving organizational culture. To increasingly open up for more diversity might be particularly important. What is termed "cultural hypocrisy" should be avoided.

Blitzscaling might also have broader implications. One is how independent investors might benefit from a better understanding of blitzscaling. This group of stakeholders cum investors are always striving to manage their investment portfolios and are thus having to cope with where and how to invest and also considering potential exits. Growth represents perhaps the safest predictor for finding attractive investments. The many factors associated with successful blitzscaling might indeed be used as checklists for investors, to help them identify growth.

A second key implication might be how the blitzscaling approach should ideally impact societal policymaking. Ultrarapid corporate growth is key. What might be done when it comes to national policies to enhance such growth? What is the relevance of blitzscaling for policy makers in the public sector? To provide favorable conditions for firms to grow represents a critical challenge for policymakers. To keep taxes and public fees at reasonable levels is one factor, to make it more worthwhile for blitzscalers to take the risks that the approach implies. To avoid restrictive regulations to provide the blitzscalers sufficient freedom to evolve the business, as well as to minimalize bureaucratic slowdowns, and to provide safe patent protections for blitzscaling firms' core technologies do clearly also represent key public policy dimensions.

Further, the authors discuss the geographic spread of blitzscaling. While the approach was developed in Silicon Valley, it is evidently relevant on a much larger geographic scale. Are there some possible geographic areas that stand out when it comes to incubating blitzscaling? Unexpectedly, Silicon Valley comes out on top of the list. Above all, there seems to be a confluence of people with the requisite attitudes (creativity, open-mindedness, willingness to take risk, tolerance of "chaos"), risk capital, and innovative technological approaches. Yet, as the authors point out, there is nothing sacred about Silicon Valley's position as the blitzscaling location for excellence. Other locations are coming up in the rest of the United States (Seattle, Boston, NYC, Denver, …), in Europe (Berlin, London, Stockholm, …), and Asia (Chechen, Shanghai, Seoul, Taipei, Hong Kong, Singapore, …). The key conditions relating to people, capital, and technology are footloose!

A final potential dilemma with blitzscaling is that high growth might raise ethical dilemmas when it comes to social networks' concern for limiting some individuals' access to use of their network—curtailing free speech because of potential risk of gross misuse (Facebook). Clearly, such ethical dilemmas seem to have no immediate solutions.

Occasionally, new refreshing approaches emerge in our field of strategy, such as the focus on market share in the 1960s, the competitive forces in the 1970s, and/or the integral role of innovations in the 1990s. The blitzscaling concept of this book adds to this list. Without a doubt, this represents another landmark when it comes to the evolution of our understanding of corporate strategy as of the 2010s!

David Epstein (2019), Range: How Generalists Triumph in a Specialist World, Penguin Random House (Reviewed March 2020)

To be a generalist in business also seems to matter. Founders and leaders with such profiles tend to win out over those who are relatively more specialized, often with the specialized strategies that they pursue. However, the editors wish to note that when it comes to business education, continuous learning, specialization can be used as a means to achieve a stronger generalist knowledge acquisition (1 + 1 = 3; in other words, multiple deep specializations can create a powerful generalist) and that there are clear benefits to being highly focused on a particular topic or course in the learning process itself.

David Epstein was previously a senior writer for *Sports Illustrated* and holds a master's degree in environmental science and journalism. His book performance improvement, that is, explores how to be more successful. Perhaps, surprising to many, the author convincingly concludes that essential is to embrace breath *and* to embark on a journey of experimentation. The author has convincingly documented that the power of breath is real, that experience matters, and that interdisciplinary experience is thus key. And this, together with experimentation driven by curiosity, must notably take place within organizations that increasingly seem to demand hyper-specialization.

Not surprisingly, the book starts out with a comparison of the careers of two successful sports legends: Tiger Woods and Roger Federer. Both became specialists in their disciplines, golf and tennis, respectively. While Tiger seems to have been focusing on golf, golf, golf exclusively, and from an early age, Roger, in contrast, seems to have initially been practicing a wide range of sports during his early years—skiing, soccer, badminton, …, until he eventually specialized in tennis. One might argue that this, at least in part, might be due to the different nature of the sports: golf being perhaps more routine-driven, thus representing a somewhat kinder learning environment, in contrast to the less predictable tennis, a more "wicked" learning environment. But beyond this, it seems clear that the more specialized Tiger hit the wall in his career much earlier than the more generalist Roger.

While an early specialized head start is clearly one answer to success, particularly when it comes to "wicked" areas of learning, a more generalist approach, combined with specialization later on, might be more appropriate. The two world-leading psychologists Gary Klein and Daniel Kahneman put diametrically opposite weight on the two dimensions. The reality seems to be that *both* specialization and generalization are needed!

How was this wicked world made, that is, where we have a world with relative weak repetitive patterns? We might expect relatively more cross-disciplinarity in these cases. To cope in such settings is certainly not easy. The so-called Flynn effect, for instance, seems to be documenting a steady rise in the quality of IQ in soldiers. But this may have to do with the fact that the gist of the questions for most IQ-tests tends to focus on more predictable issues. So, while people seem to get smarter and smarter over time, the reality is perhaps a steadier and more constant IQ pattern. The author thus focuses on the "wicked" world—with lack of predictability and regular, recognizable patterns. Cross-disciplinarity and a more generalist approach seems to be useful to effectively handle these settings.

The author then discusses how a more generalist background seems to matter to the field of music. His span of analysis goes from Vivaldi to Django Reinhart. New heights of difficulties in composing and/or playing appear again attainable, primarily for generalists.

Thinking "outside the box" as we commonly say seems to be closely related to "generalism" also. Among the many examples cited are perhaps the astronomical discoveries of Keppler the most noticeable. The free-wheeling thinking and reasoning here is in contrast to the so-called "inside view," a phrase coined by Tversky and Kahneman.

The ability to be able to decide when it might be time to quit, rather than to become trapped in decisions that could be leading us down a wrong path, seems crucial. Such entrapment is always hard to deal with. However, it is probably more easily handled by generalists. On a personal basis, one of the authors experienced this when it came to the sale of his shipping company. He was widely criticized for being very stupid, plainly "wrong" by many. However, it became apparent later that this decision seemed to be a good one! This co-author considers himself to be a generalist!

Mr. Epstein also analyzes career shifts and reports on several illuminaries' "winding" careers—critical when it comes to learning, testing, and becoming "fuller" generalists. This is thus not a "linear" career planning process. Leading artists such as Leonardo da Vinci, Paul Gaugin, or Vincent van Gogh are examples of this "winding" world career evolution.

Again, the nonspecialists win out with their ability to "see" things more clearly by having a stronger outsider's advantage! One story regarding this comes to mind in particular, which was told to one of the authors by his mathematics professor at Yale: The young undergraduate George Danzig was enrolled in a mathematics class at UCLA. The professor always started each session by writing down a problem for the students to solve at home before the next session. George Danzig came a few minutes late to one of the last classes (he had been caught in a typical Los Angeles traffic jam!) but just in time to copy down the problem that the professor had written down. He then went home and solved this the same evening. He has not heard that the professor had just said: "This problem has never been solved, and never will be!." The young Danzig, a generalist not a specialist, came up with the seminal proof of the theorem behind linear programming (the so-called Simplex algorithm)!

"Lateral" thinking is key to complement what we term "horizontal" thinking. We clearly need both "visionary birds"/generalists and "focused frogs"/linear specialists. But significant innovative contributions seem to be based more on lateral experiences. In contrast, when considering experts providing forecasts, they are almost always poor! Nonexperts, however, more curious and more actively open-minded, may often do better!

Familiar analytical tools, especially statistical ones, may lead statistics experts down non-sustainable paths. One should, of course, not ignore available data, but always keep in mind that there also probably are so-called missing data. There is a premium on generalist thinking in handling this.

The author sees that, while the funding levels in many areas of research have increased, in some cases dramatically, it is puzzling to register that the levels of research breakthroughs generally do not seem to have accrued as much as we perhaps might have hoped for. Is there too much narrow specialization in many research teams? The author thinks so! Perhaps, this is also illustrated by the wave of takeovers that large, established firms seem to be making, "gobbling up" smaller, more innovative firms! This is perhaps especially apparent in the pharmaceutical field. Larger firms seem largely to be built up around specialized departmental silos, in contrast to the cross-functionality that by necessity shall have to be the reality in smaller firms. It might perhaps not have been the intension, but more innovation and generalist focus in smaller firms seem to do better, in contrast to what we often find in larger firms, with perhaps more concentrated on departmentalization.

There is a renewed plea for a generalist view, based on breath and experimentation. Such experimentation must of course be done in a context that tolerates occasional setbacks, even failures. Without such an open culture, it may be difficult to see how the generalist's way might work. A willingness to adjust as you go is of course essential here, that is, with no defense of "old specialized departmental turfs!"

Patrick Flesner, (2021), Fastscaling, Self-Published (Reviewed September 2021)

This author makes the argument that while fastscaling is essential, thorough preparation, particularly up-front, when launching a new business is also important, perhaps above all to make subsequent fundraising easier. In contrast to dinosaur style or conservative growth strategies, or its opposite beast, blitzscaling, fastscaling allows for speed but in a more reasonable way. Taking the time to grow quickly, but not too much so, may make sense for many of our businesses.

This is written by a successful German growth capital investor and partner in Lead X Capital Partners, one of Europe's largest portfolios of B2B and B2C tech companies. It is primarily for entrepreneurs who are running start-ups or are planning to launch new firms. It could be equally valuable for investment portfolio managers, especially when investing in start-ups.

Dr. Flesner recommends that a venture should go through a preparatory stage before entering ultrahigh growth, in contrast to Hoffmann, who suggests Blitzscaling more or less from day one. According to Dr. Flesner, however, this may simply be too much of a gamble, too high a risk taking. We tend to agree with the Dr. Flesner.

The principal recommendation is to *first* to build a growth foundation, for *then* to go into fastscaling. So, it is not only a matter of top-line growth from the very start! At the early, preparatory stage, eclecticism and focus on several "lenses" of fit are discussed. And to burn cash in unnecessary ways should be avoided.

The harder one works, and the luckier one also might become. This is perhaps to "crawl, then walk, then run," that is, first do the necessary preparation before scaling up. As a venture grows, its main focus will tend to evolve from concentrating on a product to becoming relatively more distribution focused. Thus, the first groundwork preparation is to generate a good product/market fit. To find "must haves" for one's major customers is decisive here, that is, solving critical customer needs and getting high customer satisfaction. The author recommends extensive measuring, such as a net promoter score (NPS), which assesses the degree to which customers will recommend one's product, a customer health score (CHS), to spot whether there might be too much dissatisfaction and churn. How important might it be to continue with a product versus to stop? A good product/channel fit comes next. Stability of the channels chosen as well as solid predictability now seems to be paramount, and various measurement approaches are recommended here too.

To develop a healthy so-called unit economy comes next, that is, measuring the extent to which one might actually be making profits on a given product. A long-term view is recommended for measuring such customer lifetime value (CLV). The payback time for acquisition costs should be relatively short, however.

To develop a technology for one's business that is clearly also readily scalable is important. This might call for particular approaches to IT development, splitting separate costs of various aspects of one's business: sign ups, bookings, payments, and so on. Making use of the cloud and having good documentation are givens.

To go for large markets is crucial, especially if competition does not seem too hard. Again, the author recommends measurements, such as to try to determine one's total addressable market (TAM) as well as serviceable addressable market (SAM). Here, the following equation seems to universally apply: SAM < TAM.

So, with all five building blocks hopefully under control, one could be ready for the rapid growth phase, fastscaling. Again, to focus on the customer and on what makes him successful should be the point of departure. A major, personalized focus on target customers is <u>sine qua non</u>, involving a deep understanding, and the realization that customer preferences almost always evolve, calling for dynamic mindsets for entrepreneurs.

Ongoing assessments of how things are going are of course critical at this phase too, particularly to measure and predict sales (top-line growth) and cash flows. To grow efficiently therefore means a focus on both sales and on cash burn! Again, avoid extravagant spending!

Leading high growth organizations is central in this book. Execution, execution, execution is of course a must. The leader has to be impatient. It is necessary to lead by example and as is to communicate clearly. Only strong talent should be hired to join the growth organization, often easier said than done, of course! Assembling a group of "right" people, in contrast to "yes" people, is advised. Such persons typically expect proper salary compensations and also meaningful incentives. In-house search and hiring efforts may be more sustainable to be able to come up with realistic "fits."

Now to the board of directors. How might a board member be able to "help" the CEO? Trust seems to be central. Board members with relevant experience, as well as being well connected, also might be beneficial.

To raise additional capital to support rapid growth is indeed another primary task. A successful "pitch" should contain the various steps discussed so far, as well as a few more: the two issues of fit (product/market; product/channel), technology, unit economies, market size, competition, financial, timing, and planned exit. The valuation that is being proposed should be realistic, based on a long-term focus. Too often, a short-term focus might lead to a higher valuation. In the end, this might be damaging, in that investors may develop a sense of feeling "burnt!"

And, finally, more on the exit. There seem to be three alternatives:

– IPO
– Trade sale

– Sell to private equity firm

A founder may typically get a relatively lower price when selling to a private equity firm than through any of the other two options; therefore, to understand an acquirer's motive seems fundamental. To be open to an acquirer seems vital under any of these options. One should always have an updated "data room." And one's timing should be right, that is, to exit "when things go well." To bring in outside experts, such as M&A lawyers and bankers that specialize in exits might be advisable.

While several of the recommendations might come across as rather self-evident, a "handbook" dimension may be useful.

Reid Hoffman, June Cohen and Deron Triff, (2021), Masters of Scale, Penguin Random House (Reviewed October 2021)

To pursue strategies so as to be able to scale up quickly, thus making it hard (if not impossible) for others to follow, is the topic of this book, as well as the following two reviews. What we can take from this work is not only a reminder about the importance of looking at scalability in both our ventures and investments but also what is required to make a business scalable. Are we truly prepared for the commitment and requirements to scale? Is scalability an art or a science in your world?

This book is based on more than 100 interviews, most of them aired on Reid Hoffman's podcast *Masters of Scale*. Mr. Hoffman is widely viewed as one of Silicon Valley's most successful angel investors who sits on a number of technological corporations' boards in the area, including Microsoft. He is a partner of the leading venture firm Greylock Partners and is the author of several books on start-ups and scaling and co-founded LinkedIn. Any entrepreneur with start-up ambitions, as well as any serious venture investor, should study what can be found between the covers of this book.

To develop a working concept of scaling is at the core of the argument here, where scaling is more than a science, that is, a mindset, both in terms of a faith and a willingness to fail. Scaling requires knowledge about a specific business domain, insight regarding how a business might work, as well as inspiration and pure drive, even force.

Most entrepreneurs tend to receive primarily negative replies from potential investors. Patience is critical, however. Most "no's" in the end may lend inspiration to further improvements in given business models. Here are five types of rejections from investors:

- The "lazy" no—from ignorant, complacent investors. Nothing to learn here!
- The "squirmy" no—where investors might want to say "yes," and often say "yes, but," but end up saying "no" in the end. Here, there might be a lot to learn from such struggling, doubtful investors.
- The affirmative no—here an investor might have some clear principles, which, in turn, might lead to a no. Again, not much to be learnt.
- The honest no—this might be seen as a clear sign to stop and to try something else.
- The unhelpful no—an investor might simply be totally negative, and such individuals should be avoided.

The early phase of a project, that is, before any scaling attempts, should focus mostly on understanding passionate feedbacks from those few customers that typically might appreciate one's offering. These customers may often have a clue to scaling later on. Find them and ignore all the other customers!

To build trust is also essential. This typically requires hands-on responses to their suggestions and making specific improvements to what those few suggest. To forge a strong connection with these few customers is important And, once more, one should ignore the many others!

A "big" idea, the foundation for a new venture, almost never comes as an "aha" idea. Rather, it is typically something one would have actively looked for, testing it or them out on the network of people around the entrepreneur. And success is never evitable. It is thus critical to never give up! Note that a good "big" idea often tends to be relatively simple.

"Big" ideas typically come from entrepreneurs interacting with others, who might mount effective challenges all in the network setting. The cliché that a successful entrepreneur should be working on this in splendid isolation, alone, is mostly false. Good feedback might often also come from prospective investors. It is important to ask, "what is wrong with my idea," not merely "what do you think."

Good ideas may actually be nearby, virtually "hidden in the closet," being unsatisfied, regarding how a conventional approach might function. It is good to look for underlying patterns that might support an idea. Main trends might be noticed and built on. And such patterns might be "translated" into business ideas. Speed in doing this is paramount. It should always be kept in mind that a good idea might be hidden. What was perhaps initially considered to be a "bad" idea might, in the end, be "good." Successful entrepreneurs typically will have different "places" to "think big," in the car, in a café, on one's running machine, etc. What matters is to be intentional and to test these embryonic thoughts out on the critical members of one's network.

So, nos can often yield valuable insights for the development of a good idea. Early crises in new business might have such effects, likewise. And, once more, good business ideas typically do not have to be all that fundamental, but more frequently rather quite similar to common sense, that is, no need to search for "reinventing the wheel."

The culture in a new business venture is usually of critical importance, and the entrepreneur often provides significant impact here. The entrepreneur should avoid making a few common mistakes in this respect:

- Do not ignore the cultural dimension, but rather work on it from the start. It can then more easily be "molded" into the teams in the venture.
- Culture is always evolving, reflecting the people who work in the company. They define the firm's culture, not some more or less abstract dictum. Watch out for misplaced early hires and try to hire instead what Mr. Hoffman calls "co-founders."
- Thus, be cognizant to cultural impacts from hiring and try to avoid the inclusion of new members in the team that might have a "dysfunctional" culture.
- Always try to develop cognitive diversity, however, an eclectic culture.
- Try to build a culture that is able to evolve, always asking "what is best for the company."

Speed is essential when growing, always try to seize the initiative, so as to outgrow competition. This typically calls for making key decisions rapidly. What may be particularly important is to try to figure out how many resources and efforts to put "into" one's existing business, versus towards new products and/or new markets. It is always important to try to direct one's growth in a productive way, keeping in mind that "strategy means choice!"

There will always be problems, even mini crises. Mr. Hoffman is clear on how to handle such "fires"—try to ignore them for now! "Let fires burn!" At some point in time, of course, such mini crises will have to be dealt with, but only if there is a perceived probability of a disaster looming. And never panic!

To go for ultrarapid growth virtually always requires quite a lot of capital. There may be new opportunities coming up, in addition, that would then call for even more capital. The bottom line, therefore, should be that an entrepreneur might always attempt to raise more capital than the minimum he/she might actually need at the moment.

To try to identify venture capital firms that could actually add value in terms of helpful advice and not merely funding, might be critical. Most venture capitalists tend to say no. Only around 10% of venture capitalists might be ready to provide both money and value in the form of advice. There will typically also be need for more funds at later stages. To be able to secure backing from a venture capital firm that might indeed be comfortable with "going the full distance" could therefore be particularly critical. Such a venture capitalist will typically place much emphasis on an entrepreneur's personal abilities and track record.

Most ventures enter into unfamiliar territories—new approaches for serving the customers, new channels of distribution, unfamiliar territories, etc. Things might typically often not work out entirely as expected. Thus, to unlearn fast also becomes critical, even having to abandon much of what one might initially have known. We are all proud of our successes. To merely repeat what has worked in the past may typically not be too realistic. Conditions change frequently. So, for the entrepreneur to always ask "what to do better, and what to drop" is central. It is a constant race for new learning. We should "learn it all" not pretend to "know it all."

Experimentation is of course a key part of this in such a way that one's acknowledged speed is also critical, to be able to learn quickly, and consequently to be able to improve on product or service in a speedy way. To be embarrassed regarding what one might be in a position to offer customers at a particular stage generally does not work. One's offerings may become better. Thus, one should not be embarrassed about showing one's products and services at early stages. It is all about learning, so as to be able to move on from what one might have "just now." Experimentation is therefore critical. To have an open mind is essential—no vested interests!

Competitors are important and should be followed closely. They may, however, come up with various statements that they, in the end, do not follow. To try not to be confused by such potentially distracting statements is advisable. This may indeed also be so when it comes to one's customers.

To focus on a relatively small set of "trusted" customers, to treat them as scouts, might be particularly effective, trying to understand how to serve this relatively small group. What do they want? What does this subgroup do? And how might these consumers "cheat?"

To handle price increases is typically a particularly challenging issue, none-the-least so as to avoid negative reactions from consumers, that might feel that they may be treated in ways that they may think might be unfair and unjustified. This might mean to offer additional services, for instance, but with not much more of a higher price tag. One should try to avoid "pricing riots" or "mob reactions."

To be able to obtain relatively reliable customer data might be key, but may be hard. To test one's thoughts on the main customer may be good but should not lead to confusion. Be sensitive to key customers and respond early when necessary and with speed.

So-called "pivoting" is also important. This generally involves more dramatic changes of the product/service offering. Effective pivoting is also essential for enhancing speedy business growth, involving refocusing, so as to go after a new opportunity and to leave behind a now old, more or less useless idea. The entire management team should be behind such a pivot. The core team must then go for it. Again, strategy means choice. It is thus not realistic to both continue with the old direction and to embrace a pivot. One must abandon the old.

When should one pivot? Ideally, one should do this when one might see something exceptional coming, such as the emergence of the COVID-19 pandemic. To make fast changes in such situations is critical. One should try to avoid being forced to pivot only at such a late stage when available financial resources might be more or less depleted.

Mr. Hoffman points out that pivoting might at times lead to dysfunctional effects when it comes to some of the firm's employees. He points out, however, that while a "human" approach is always important, it is also to recognize that a healthy business, based on successful pivoting, may in the end tend to benefit even more the long-term well-being of the employees. Pivoting in a crisis might be difficult indeed but nevertheless best for most in the end. Effective leadership is indeed key to successful pivoting, "setting a constant drumbeat," as Mr. Hoffman says. When a company grows, a consistent focus by the leader on preserving the way for how a business is being operated is perhaps especially critical.

Debates, so-called Socratic thinking, are key. Some people tend to be more comfortable with this than others. Debating should thus be tailored to such realities. Constructive conflict is typically good, however.

Mr. Hoffman summarizes what he sees as particularly important leadership challenges as follows: Be an effective "drum major," compassionate, thankful, a good connector, among many people in one's network, a steady captain, to neutralize "pirates," instead develop one's people to become "stars!"

In reading the book's conclusions, a main issue raised is how to make good even better and thus, which walls to break down, that is, those based on prejudice, inequality, and lazy assumptions. It is important here to try to create changes that one would want to see. To align one's firms' mission with what might be a broadly shared motivation among many might be a precondition for successful crowdsourcing later and thus also for rapid scaling later on. Mr. Hoffman suggests that pivoting should always be made "for the good," including going for add-on focuses. It is all about providing a healthy entrepreneurial mindset.

Ro Khanna, (2022), Dignity in a Digital Age: Making Tech Work for All of Us, Simon & Schuster (Reviewed March 2022)

Technology, which now essentially means becoming increasingly virtual in all directions, opens up for the development of new types of cutting-edge firms in other areas from Silicon Valley on "I-95" and also internationally. The landscape for establishing this type of tech-driven firm might thus become "fairer." Here, our readers may glean ideas applicable to their own digital transformations or company evolution in this area. The essence is that digital transformation should be construed and executed for all, up and down, left and right, and within the organization.

This book discusses the dilemma of how to avoid too much regulation, nor too little regulation on the other hand, to better impact economic growth. In the United States, we see, for instance, that geographic areas such as Silicon Valley, Austin, Boston, and New York are growing but at the expense, perhaps, of what are coined "rust belt" regions. The author suggests that regulations in the best case might ameliorate this type of "skewed" development. He cites the legislature that Abraham Lincoln got through, more than a century ago, with the establishment of land-grant universities through the so-called Morrill Act.

Clearly, there seems to be an issue of finding a good balance here. But how do we best handle it? With the advent of the COVID-19 pandemic now more or less behind us, working from home via the internet has become a new reality. This may perhaps hold an important instrument for more evenly distributed technology-driven applications too. By the way, before proceeding, we seem to have very analogous issues all over the world such as regarding London versus North-Midlands, Berlin versus the Ruhr, and so on.

The author, Ro Khanna, represents Silicon Valley in the US Congress. He is a democrat. He studied at University of Chicago, where he obtained a BA in economics and also a law degree. He also served in the Obama administration. Mr. Khanna's book is full of creative proposals to address various unique challenges of the digital age. Mr. Khanna, the son of Indian immigrants, sees the solution to more widely distributed benefits of new technology to be so-called democratic patriotism, where democratic reasoning takes place through "governance by discussion," to quote John Stuart Mill.

This prompts us to make three brief general observations before delving into the specifics of the book. First, the current conflict between Russia and Ukraine seems to represent a stark contradiction to what the author proposes. Democracy represents the anti-thesis of aggression! Chapter 10, in particular, seems to deal with this issue. The dialog among the NATO partner countries, for instance, looks to have yielded remarkable unity, that is, in line with what the author suggests. Second, while Mr. Khanna proposes a number of social reforms, quite common for many US democrats, much of his thinking seems to be inspired by what we might find in "welfare states," such as in the Nordic countries. His reasoning, particularly as exemplified in Chapter 4, represents little to nothing new. Third, the digital age does represent a paradigm shift. And here lays the true strength of the book. Technology can now work for all of us, in this digital age. Mr. Khanna provides many important insights here.

Part one of the book deals with the twenty-first century economy. Part two shifts towards focusing on major citizenship challenges in this century. How might one expand technology-driven opportunities to people and places who have been left out of the first wave of the digital revolution? The challenge is to use technology effectively, so as to virtualize local economies, that is, "equity beyond geography," as Mr. Khanna writes. The internet is fundamental here, and our freedom on the internet must be protected. This is the anti-thesis of "hacking."

The virtual workplace is now a reality, and to enhance this further, the author proposes several main issues, including strengthening digital education and installing the internet even more broadly.

Racial and gender equality is perhaps becoming increasingly important now to enhance this development. Many technology companies need to be restructured, both when it comes to the way they are staffed and when it comes to the way they operate, for example, through more tech partnerships with institutions that serve communities of color. The author discusses several aspects of this, such as having access to capital ("opportunity hubs").

When it comes to the so-called progressive capitalism, the author identifies three key conditions, namely, to allow people to take risks without being penalized for failures, to permit people to "think big," and to not shun the unconventional, that is, to approve or encourage diversity and fresh ideas! Mr. Khanna points out that a well-developed educational system, good health care, adequate nutrition, and a reasonable level of pay are all critical to achieve this.

Moving now to the second part of the book, how to envision what might be the true essence of our citizenship in the twenty-first century, the author identifies our "internet bill of rights" with ten key issues:

- We as individuals must be offered the opportunity to give explicit consent.
- We must have full knowledge of data use (ref. the Cambridge Analytica scandal).
- We must have the right to delete personal data and abusive content.
- There must be adequate data security.
- Portability is important.
- Openness and accessibility are essential.
- No unnecessary data collecting!
- There should be multiple platform providers.
- Race, gender, age, and religion should not be sources of discrimination.
- Legal obligations must be adhered to, say, for banks managing money.

This might perhaps be summed up as taking strong stances against antidemocratic factors.

Censorship disinformation and digital deception, including dealing with fake news, accounts, and videos, are clear "no-nos." Protecting children from online addiction is part of this!

So, what is science in a democracy? To drop abstract scientific arguments and instead point out what might be done in specific practical cases is important, such as when developing a "greener" reality. Solar and wind energy are ready from a scientific point of view, and so is "clean tech," and are electric vehicles. And artificial intelligence is critical here too. But there are still challenges, such as how to cope with 5G mobile telephony, enhancing semiconductor manufacturing and safe biotech.

These issues are perhaps related to foreign policy. Mr. Khanna stresses that there must be universal democratic values to guide us here, in contrast to what we often see now, for example, with Russia's attack on Ukraine. Democratic patriotism may perhaps provide an "answer." The author stresses that diversity is a blessing when it comes to this. A spirit of civility is key. But a danger of dominance, nationalism, and isolationism should be guarded against ("America First").

The book spans widely, perhaps even covering too many different topics. However, our clocks need to be reset for the new digital age, an age that includes such broad areas. New paradigms are at work, for society, for politics, for business, and for individuals. This book copes impressively with many of these fundamental issues.

Shameen Prashantham, (2022), Gorillas Can Dance, Wiley (Reviewed March 2022)

This book focuses on how large firms might be able to link up with smaller start-ups, in the form of joint ventures, or to acquire them, so as to remain innovative and agile and to grow faster. It may stimulate our readers to lean further towards both intra- and entrepreneurialism. In other words, innovation is both inside and outside your firm.

The book reports on a 15-year research effort to explore how large corporations might effectively partner with much smaller start-ups, in order to tap into the originality and innovation drive that such start-ups may have thereby ensured, continuing innovation also in the large, established firm. The book addresses this critical issue from the vantage point of that bigger company. A corporation that has received the bulk of the researcher's attention is Microsoft, but many other large firms have also been examined including Unilever, IBM, Bosch, and BMW (for a list of the 47 firms examined, see the actual book's pp. 280–282). A main conclusion is that this type of cooperative venture can work, but it is usually difficult, demanding, or at least calling for long-term thinking and patience.

The author, Professor Shameen Prasantham, teaches at CEIBS business school in Shanghai, where he is also Associate Dean for the MBA program. He is a British national and received his doctorate at Strathclyde University, Glasgow, going on thereafter to teach at Glasgow University.

Paul Polman, the outgoing CEO of Unilever, clearly states the research issue that the book addresses is key: "It is imperative for large organizations to partner with more nimble start-ups, to help create a better world."

Let us now delve into this book's explanation on how this might effectively be done. In its introduction, a compelling case study of Microsoft is described. Three phases are identified: First is getting start-up partnership off the ground. The next phase calls for an extension of this engagement, by selecting various one-to-one partnering relationships to engage in. In the third and final phase, key lessons from the start-ups are to be adopted as part of the strategy of the established firm. A major element here is to focus on how core ideas from a start-up might be scaled up, now as part of the bigger firm's domain. The author calls this "scaleators."

The rest of the book then also falls into three parts. The first considers *why*, that is, why entrepreneurship matters to large corporations and why partnering with start-ups is typically not easy. Considering the first of these issues, the author highlights the different mindsets of managers usually found in large firms, versus the entrepreneurs typically driving innovative start-ups. The main point, according to the author, is to launch on a process, which often takes time, one that "merges" the best of each of these two sides, so that more of an entrepreneurial behavior might now be instilled among the managers of well-established, larger firms, while start-up entrepreneurs come to acknowledge the importance of scalability. Critical factors that might bring such an amalgamation along might include the fear of disruption when it comes to so-far established business models of the larger firm, as well as a growing sense of "win-win" for all parties.

So why is this process so difficult, despite the compelling arguments just given? The author identifies a so-called asymmetry between the two types of firms as critical here, and he discusses three types of these: goal asymmetry, as seen in the different planning in the two types; structure asymmetry, having to do with how the two types of firms are organized; and finally, attention asymmetry, which has to do with how a given strategy now to come out of a joint venture might be extended. Each of the three sources of asymmetry come about due to legitimacy issues (such as lack of confidence in the given start-up), learning (incompatibilities here) and incompatibilities within the wider ecosystem of the large firm, such as stringency of processes and criteria.

In the next part of the book, two sets of questions are addressed relating to *how*— first how to partner more systematically with start-ups and, second, how to build relevant capabilities to make such partnering work. The first issue, to come up with a more systematic way of partnering, seems to follow a sequence of six issues:

- Clarifying synergy: The author distinguishes between so-called *building block synergies* (incorporating a feature from the start-up to become part of the large company's offering, to extend the "power" of what is now being offered. This might result in joint marketing) and point synergies (the large firm "misses" a particular feature that a start-up could offer and buys this from the start-up).
- Forming a partnership.
- Creating interfaces, that is, areas where the two entities shall specifically interact. There may be so-called *cohort-based interfaces*, where a start-up might work with a number of managers cum interfaces at the level of the larger company, often involving mentoring and even coming up with

unforeseen innovation solutions. *Funnel-based interfaces*, on the other hand, would involve a much more specific focus, say, through a pilot project, often to "solve" a pain point.
- Given an evolution of the pattern of interface, the nature of the partnership itself may have to be "consolidated."
- Example of outcomes from a partnership would then, hopefully, come about.
- This, in turn, might call for another revision of the partnership, at times, perhaps even a takeover of the start-up by the established firm.

It may be important to deviate somewhat from the main focus of the book at this point and take the start-ups perspective instead. This might be seen as a shaping process evolving through the following stages: forming, consolidating, and extending.

The "smoothness" of such an evolution has a lot to do with the more established company's ability (and willingness) to build capabilities to partner with the start-ups. Capability shall typically be related to the acknowledgment of the fact that there shall be several phases of this building process: initiation, expansion, and systemization. There are different foci: purpose, people, and process. Thus, we have nine distinct capability building elements for the established firm. When it comes to the initiation stage, the involvement of entrepreneurial manager seems particularly critical—a "can do" perspective! When it comes to the expansion stage, the main point is to galvanize support. Internal champions and so-called opportunity generators are paramount and must be involved! The systemization phase has a lot to do with integration, for example, with the planning process of the larger firm, keeping in mind the corporate culture.

The final part of the book deals with *where*, that is, where to partner with start-ups around the world and where to find societally good synergies through such cooperation between start-ups and established firms. Regarding reaching a better understanding of the global reach issue, the author identifies three basic options:

- "Think global, act local." This is the most common way to think about the issue of venturing. To adapt the output of a venture to local circumstances is typically critical. Although the author does not seem to fully acknowledge the viewpoint that ventures with Indian or Chinese start-ups often tend to fall into this category.
- "Think local, act global." This is what we might find when start-ups located in what are typically highly innovative locations, such as Israel, come up

with truly breakthrough innovations that clearly might have much broader applications. Israel's drip irrigation system is, for instance, of great interest to established players in the fertilizer area. The author indicates that this type of venture could tap market hotspots.
- "Think global, act global." This would be the case when combining the two above options. Even though the author cites several examples of what he claims to represent this, this reasoning is perhaps not as evident to us. A company who aims to be global both in its way of planning as well as doing requires enormous resources, strong business intelligence and data, and a highly international network.

Partnering with start-ups as a force for good is the next theme covered in the book. Clearly, there is an element of "polyannaism" in this chapter. The basic messages are however important and highly relevant. Keys here are societal development goals (SDGs), societal synergy, and inclusive interfaces. The author also discusses so-called hybrids, as well as what are termed SDG goal coalitions (the African cocoa growers association with its links to major chocolate producers, for instance).

There is also an epilog. Here, the author discusses SDGs in the light of global crises, including the COVID pandemic. He rightfully points out that there are ample needs for cooperation, say, when it comes to manufacturing and distribution of COVID vaccinations for most of the developing world. The author claims that that complementary mindsets are called for—an entrepreneurial, a collaborative, and a global mindset, all three interacting with an individual actor in the middle. To harness all of this is, of course, crucial.

There is no doubt that this is an important book. It is very well researched and conceptually strong. As J. Woetzel, head of McKinsey's Global Institute says, "Shameen's insightful work on partnering between established corporations and start-ups, breaks new ground in identifying the why and how of effective alliance building." Growth is more important today than ever for established corporations. Their stock price often hinges on this, and so does cost of capital. A way to build up a strong defense against unfriendly takeovers is growth. But growth may no longer come easily. Innovations, to fuel growth, seem to be harder and harder to pull off. To look towards the sector of innovative start-ups might however be a plausible way out of this lack of innovation and growth dilemma for large, established firms. This book provides guidelines for this, in essence indicating how to revitalize large firms.

19

Executive Profiles of Business Leaders

Mirjam Staub-Bisang, Head of BlackRock Switzerland, (Interviewed November 2020)

Impact investing, particularly in the assets where the reduction of CO_2 is achieved and/or intended, constitutes a core area of Staub-Bisang's agenda. BlackRock is one of the world's leading investment firms with the purpose to help people experience financial well-being and advancing sustainable investing. Mirjam Staub-Bisang (MSB) has been head of BlackRock, Switzerland, since 2018. Previously, she was with Independent Capital Group, Commerzbank, and SwissLife among others. MSB raised several important issues in relation to sustainable investing. The present executive profile discusses where MSB sees risks and opportunities of sustainable investing. For most of our readers, sustainability is a central concern or commitment, and the transition towards a nature positive future can be achieved through the careful and complete analysis of options before making the choice.

CO_2. A task by many might be to trade in CO_2 "rights," but these seem to have relatively high price volatility. Such trading, however, is done rather than to focus on investing in assets with an intrinsic value. Common large emitters of CO_2: companies in sectors that "burn" or make use of high levels of CO_2, such as the following:

- Energy firms (e.g., electricity, generation of heat, transportation).
- Industrial processes, for example, cement, chemicals.
- Agriculture.

Impact investing, in general, seems to concentrate on financing solutions to the world's most pressing environmental and social problems, for example, financing of "green" infrastructure or private equity financing of technology companies. A key component of impact investing is also stewardship (large investors engage with top managements/boards in large companies regarding transparency of their sustainability risks, and in particular climate risks and their mitigation strategies).

BlackRock (BR), as a fiduciary, invests on clients' behalf to help clients meet their investment objectives. The investment approach is informed by three principles: client choice, performance, and research. BR applies the same approach to sustainability and the low-carbon transition. With its strong commitment to sustainable investing and focus climate as well as natural capital, it is perhaps the most vigilant player in this space. There are more than 1000 companies in BR's "climate focus universe," which primarily relate to the climate risk that a given firm is associated with. High carbon-emitting companies must provide transparency regarding their climate risks and the related mitigation strategies. In this context, BR encourages companies to use the framework developed by the Task Force on Climate-related Financial Disclosures (TCFD).

BR's Swiss business focus is the distribution of investment products and solutions across various asset classes for wealth managers/private banks and pension funds. BR also provides private market investments (infrastructure and private equity) with a global investment focus. BR's annual letter to a large sample of global CEOs emphasizes—among others—annually the importance of climate risk as an investment risk and the need for transparency when it comes to stewardship activities. BR's strategy in general focuses on commitments, follow-through, and delivering. Its approach is rigorous, with no compromises, no "green-washing!"

MSB is a driver regarding BR's sustainable and impact investing strategy and implementation. MSB also works on the strengthening of BR's distribution platform in Switzerland.

Now to Tesla and the other electric-driven automobiles in this car industry segment. There seem to be two competing assessments. On the one hand, some players seem to focus primarily on electricity as the propulsion, which is great! But others may lean on heavy pollution, specifically when it comes to the batteries for electric cars. To produce such batteries, mining is necessary, often open pit, damaging our nature, and using child labor. Thus, there is a dilemma associated with many industries, "good" or "bad." The so-called ESG ratings can differ depending on the relative weight being put on each side of the argument.

Ratings/certifications. MSCI is one of the dominant ESG rating providers. This company grew basically through acquisition and tries to include firms' future ESG-related development objectives in their ratings. Investors typically follow the ESG ratings of rating agencies, such as MSCI.

Key evolutionary steps. A great deal seems to be happening right now. The "big four" accounting firms are in agreement, in cooperation with the World Economic Forum, regarding aligning the sustainability reporting in their annual reports of their client companies. New Zealand is the first country to make it a law that sustainability reporting issues are to be reported in the firms' financial statements. New standards are indeed likely to come, but this is expected nevertheless to take time. It can be frustrating with the relatively slow progress, but one should fight pessimism! In general, public-sector regulation seems to play an increasingly key role. Yet there is not only regulation, but there are also other elements of critical evolution, such as investor behavior, the range of investment products available, and the technology.

The oil sector. Demand is apparently gradually slowing down driven by the lower economic activity due to COVID, but it is now back up at record heights! Prices are, however, likely to stay relatively low, long term. Oil supply, overproduction, and rising production of renewable energy appear to play important roles! The present value of most oil reserves is falling, leading to significant write-offs and reported losses. Also, investors might be regulated to gradually turn away from oil companies because of the falling stock prices that these firms now have. Impact on financing capabilities, that is, when cost of capital is foreseen to go up it shall be more expensive to borrow. This is a "demand spiral" as experienced by oil companies, for instance, and also applies to many coal and mining companies. Is there an "end point?" When valuations fall to low enough levels, and for a long period of time, then private equity companies and/or large private investors may try to purchase these companies, for then, perhaps, to split them up and resell various parts of the assets. An example of an oil company that has changed fundamentally its strategy is the Danish company, DONG. This used to be the largest player in the Danish offshore oil sector but has dramatically refocused itself to become the world's largest windmill owner/operator, for electricity generation. The company's stock price has skyrocketed!

Nuclear. The risks in this business are usually so big that they are uninsurable! Not surprisingly, therefore, governments are thus the usual major players. However, some debt tends to be sold to the public but with government guarantees. There are, however, also rare examples of private minority stock ownership in some governments such as majority owned nuclear plant firms. An example is, AREVA, where the French government owns 70%.

Large Swiss Banks. UBS is the biggest one and is the world's largest asset manager. Some 4 years ago, it launched a strategy with a strong commitment to sustainability and impact investing. Credit Suisse, Switzerland's second largest bank, puts investment banking as a large part of its strategic portfolio and now finds itself in a situation where it may "have" to underwrite the projects from sustainable firms. The "problem" is that the bank also has many so-called "brown" companies in its portfolio. They have therefore launched a "transition financing" program to support such "brown" companies in their efforts to develop more sustainable strategies. Goldman Sachs is also offering this, by the way.

All in all, there seems to be reason for optimism when it comes to sustainable investments. A new sense of urgency for sustainability appears to be present.

Oliver Blume, CEO Porsche AG (Interviewed December 2020)

Mr. Blume addresses several main strategic issues facing Porsche, particularly the major challenges of "going electric," as well as preparing to take his company through an IPO.

He discusses the evolution of his firm's strategy, now encompassing electric automobiles, being built in an all-new plant, while still maintaining the high standard corporate image.

Current main issues and challenges: The coronavirus crisis is a massive challenge for all of us. At Porsche, we are keeping a positive attitude. We have been resilient, and we are on a steady course. This is manifested by the positive results after the first 9 months of the year, which puts us among the performance leaders in our industry. The key to our success is our team. We've mastered the crisis together—with our safety measures, our business focuses, and our digital communications. We are also helped by the fact that we have invested in new products and innovations: for example, the new 911, the Cayenne Coupé or the Taycan. Significant changes to strategy and positioning: Managing the crisis systematically and responsibly and seeing it as an opportunity is important. Above all, you need to have an optimistic attitude, you need to look to the future, and you need to move ahead, again quickly, at top speed. We have not deviated from our strategy – not even by a millimeter: Porsche has consistently driven all its future projects forward. At most, we considered what could perhaps be delayed a little, in other words, changing some of the sequencing.

Investments in the future are also especially important to us at this time. We will certainly become even more digital in the way we present ourselves to the outside world: this year, we staged the world premieres for the 911 Turbo S and the 911 Targa online. Authentic, informative, and innovative. The insights gained are clearly positive—digital formats also work in sales. Of course, this lacks the certain sense of emotionality that you experience when driving a car. On the whole, my conclusion is positive, however; going digital makes life more flexible, but personal interactions continue to remain valuable, of course.

Future investments in electro-mobility: We are systematically driving our strategy and our future projects forward. We will invest around 15 billion euros in electric mobility and digitalization by 2025 and inaugurate a brand-new production facility for this.

Latest advances in autonomous driving, hybrid and electric: Many long-standing Porsche customers who drive the Taycan for the first time are completely enthusiastic about its driving dynamics. We have had very positive feedback about the car. With its exceptional driving dynamics and outstanding driving performance, the Taycan is 100% Porsche. We have be delivered around 20,000 Taycan cars to our customers in the model's first year already.

We are also particularly pleased that the Taycan was recently voted the most innovative car in the world by international experts. In addition to this accolade, the Taycan also won the Golden Steering Wheel award in the two categories "Best Sports Car" and "Most Beautiful Car." The current generation of hybrids is also packed with innovations. We have positioned the new generation of the Panamera Hybrid as even more powerful. For the plug-in hybrids, we have increased the electric range by up to 30%.

Autonomous driving is an interesting one for Porsche—not least because the Taycan is ready for autonomous driving. Nevertheless, driving without human intervention is certainly not the highest priority for Porsche customers. For us, the focus is on the sporty driving experience—and therefore on the active driver. Despite this, there are of course aspects of autonomous driving that are very helpful such as traffic jam assist or automatic parking, for example.

Shifts in strategy through SUV introductions versus sports-car market: First and foremost, all Porsche vehicles are sports cars. Even our Cayenne and Macan stand out due to the sportiness and performance typical for Porsche. At the same time, our cars are absolutely timeless. Certain styling trends have remained the same across our generations. As a general rule, it can be said that

Porsche is so successful because Porsche has always kept changing. Innovations are at the core of the brand and are the tradition for tomorrow. Our motto is: the right sports car for the right purpose. This is how Porsche will always remain Porsche. We are combining our strong tradition with groundbreaking future technologies.

Strengthening Porsche in the electric (and hybrid) car market: Electric mobility is a huge opportunity for us. Launching the Taycan was a tough task and required a lot of pioneering spirit. We set ourselves a great challenge, but we have also learnt a lot at the same time. It is tremendously motivating for our team to see how well the car has been received. Electric mobility is an extremely exciting and compelling technology. In the long term, we are aiming to sell half of all cars with a full or partial electric drive, already from 2025. Our fans can rely on the fact that we will launch only highly advanced vehicles with the Porsche DNA on the market in the future also. The Taycan, our first all-electric sports car, is such a true Porsche. With this electric vehicle, we have demonstrated that it is possible to transport our brand's traditional core values into the future.

Innovation: We have established a comprehensive toolbox in order to increase our access to innovations in a targeted way. This extends throughout all the divisions of the company. Our venture capital investments make an important contribution. We believe that we can become even more agile and innovative in many areas with targeted investments in start-up companies. We have developed a separate unit, Porsche Ventures, that deals exclusively with such investments and participations. Up to 150 million euros per year are available to invest in key topics for the future. Porsche Ventures has made more than 20 direct investments and is involved in a variety of funds in Europe, Israel, the United States, and China. Our strategic objective here is to identify trends, to obtain access to new technologies and business models, and to develop new relationships with a new generation of start-up entrepreneurs.

New mobility concepts: Porsche is continually expanding its flexible mobility offerings in response to changed customer requirements. Our premium rental service "Porsche Drive – Rental" provides rentals from a few hours and up to 28 days. This offering is currently available in Germany, France, Canada, Russia, Switzerland, and the United States. We offer the highly flexible car subscription service "Porsche Drive – Multi-Vehicle Subscription" in five cities in the United States and Canada. Customers can flexibly change their car via the app and choose from up to 20 models. This is an offer that meets the large demand and appeals to new customers: around 80% of Porsche Drive users have not owned a Porsche before. In the United States, the "Porsche

Drive – Single-Vehicle Subscription" offer is additionally available: users choose a particular Porsche model and subscribe to it as a new vehicle on a monthly basis. In Germany, this program is called "Porsche Drive Abo" and offers nearly new used cars.

Electric mobility, sustainable production, and digitalization are important future projects for Porsche. With them, we are sharpening the core of our brand and systematically aligning the company so that it is prepared for the mobility of the future. Porsche is pursuing a clear and consistent strategy: The transformation from a more traditional company into a sustainable technology corporation. For this reason, we are consistently driving our sustainability strategy forward—even the pandemic did not sway us from our course.

The start-up scene: Innovations are an integral part of the Porsche culture and are firmly anchored in our corporate strategy through the previously mentioned holistic toolbox. We have various touch points with the start-up scene. Our investment unit Porsche Ventures is always at the forefront, with offices in relevant trendsetting areas such as Berlin, Tel Aviv, Palo Alto, and Shanghai. Here, it is all about investments and joint ventures. Another example of our close links to the start-up scene is the partnership with the innovation platform, Startup Autobahn. This acts as an interface between industry-leading companies and technology start-ups in Stuttgart. The program enables corporate partners and start-ups to jointly develop prototypes to evaluate possible further collaborations between the two parties. Projects are generally set up to run for a period of 6 months. Porsche has benefitted with more than 70 projects through Startup Autobahn so far.

Market threats: As we all know, the world is changing radically at an extremely fast pace. It is therefore important to see the major challenges posed by transformation as an opportunity, at the same time providing orientation and support. Some key issues are the structural transformation in the car industry, climate change, new technologies such as electric mobility, changing markets, customer preferences, and our organization. These are also the focal points that we are aiming at with our Porsche Strategy 2030, thus establishing the foundation for the successful future of Porsche.

Supply chain management: Our supply chain is well positioned, with a 50:50 mix of national and international suppliers. Porsche is traditionally deeply rooted in Germany and Europe. However, the picture is made up of many different aspects. Our German suppliers also manufacture in other countries, for example. We have close ties with partners in Eastern and Southern Europe. Chinese suppliers account for a relatively smaller proportion, around 10%. They mainly supply electrical and electronic components. The pandemic has affected all of us, including our supply chain partners. We had to adapt to this situation in a very short space of time. We are therefore now concentrating on what is truly essential. For the supply chains, this means: Which routes are really necessary? How can we streamline the logistics? Porsche will ensure that it is positioned even more robustly in future. At the same time, we are also looking at the wider picture and asking ourselves: How sustainable is our supply chain? To answer these questions, we have developed a rating system for suppliers within our Group. This includes ecological and social components, all now parts of our order award process.

Porsche as a family business: Our people are what is most important. They are at the heart of what we do at Porsche. A good team can make everything happen. This is so, even in difficult situations, such as during the pandemic. Thanks to a great team effort, we succeeded in ramping up production at Porsche without negative effects. Despite the assistance provided by robots in production, machines will always be there only to help people. There will never be a factory that has no people, especially not at Porsche. This is what I stand for personally. The reason for this is that Porsche is made by people for people. Our special Porsche culture thrives because we meet up on-the-spot and because of our personal interactions. This creates a special spirit and rightly allows us to always speak about the Porsche "family."

Oliver Blume became CEO of Volkswagen in September 2022, while retaining his position at Porsche.

Jan Jenisch, CEO Holcim (Interviewed September 2020)

How might the world's largest cement producer and conventionally a huge CO_2 "emitter" develop a more progressive strategy, not only when it comes to CO_2 reduction but to also the inclusion of female executives. Diversity and inclusivity are central issues facing us today, across all sectors and markets. From forward-thinking companies, we can learn about the small and not so small steps required to make altruism in a general sense more a part of our strategies and cultures—whether towards the environment, our workforces or our customers—even as we forge forward with growth and innovation.

This interview took place on September 4, 2020, with Jan Jenisch, CEO of Lafarge Holcim, at the company's headquarters in Zug, Switzerland. In addition to inputs from this interview, there are also some inputs from a presentation that Mr. Jenisch made at IMD on June 29, 2022. Mr. Jenisch touched upon the following issues for Holcim and current challenges:

The CO_2 emission issue is key, also to develop new business elements to grow and further strengthen Holcim's stock price. The entry into roofing systems is an example.

To further reinforce the cost-efficiency side, as well as to enhance a flat and empowered leadership style, including completing a total restructuring after the merger between Lafarge and Holcim, which had taken place in 2014. For instance, two former headquarters, in Paris and in a suburb of Zurich, were closed down in 2018. Holcim established a new headquarters in rented facilities in Zug, Switzerland, more modern, with more light and open space. Headquarter space was reduced from more than 15,000 m² to around 2500 m²! To attract women in top leadership roles has been on Holcim's agenda for several years. Also, to further deleverage and strengthen Holcim's financial position has been instrumental to reducing net debt by more than CHF 5 billion in the past 2 years.

Holcim's stock price has fallen almost 30% in the last two and a half years. Principal reasons are that Holcim's revenues heavily depend on the level of construction activities. These fell around 40% during the first part of the pandemic. However, construction activities are more recently picking up again and surprisingly fast. Holcim's revenue for 2020 are not as high as the year before though. Holcim's image as a "polluter," especially when it comes to CO_2 emissions is also impacting the stock price. So is the firm's image as relatively low-tech. On top of this, Holcim has a fairly low growth.

Jan Jenisch (JJ) believes that a CEO should not be overly focused on the "flat" stock price but rather be motivated to improve it, through aiming for higher efficiency, as well as a further strengthening of the firm's financial structure, with less debt and more cash reserves. So far, however, these measures do not seem to have resulted in significantly higher stock price.

The CO_2 issue. Cement producers are traditionally high on emissions. There are at least four issues that might have an impact on this:

- The low price of cement. There is simply too little to no room for expensive CO_2 reduction measures. Thus, cement makers need further regulations and incentives to accelerate sustainability.
- Differences in legislation in various major geographic regions, such as Europe, where a political willingness, at least to some extent, seems to exist, to pay for the added costs from tighter legislation regarding CO_2 emissions; the United States, where it may not be realistic with tighter regulations on CO_2 emission, perhaps also largely due to an expected unwillingness to curtail oil production, and face the consequential employment layoffs and emerging price increases; India with no legislation; China, where around

20% of this country's cement capacity has been reduced through the closing down of older, more heavily polluting plants, thereby significantly reducing CO_2 emissions.
- Technological approaches, such as producing cement with lower temperature in the rotating kilns, and/or capturing emissions through scrubber-type filters. Such measures are technologically doable but are expensive, thus making them currently unrealistic ways forward.
- More use of "old" building materials, which have been ground down and then added into new cement. CO_2 emission is reduced, due to the decreased need to produce "new" cement, indeed an example of Holcim being part of the emerging circular economy. Holcim is one of the world's largest users of recirculated materials, and the leading country regarding this is Switzerland, with strict legislation in effect. 7% of Holcim's cement production output is recirculation-based.

Effects from the pandemic. There was a general travel ban until the end of 2020. This meant that web-based conferencing (i.e., zoom) was being used extensively and seemed to work well. Each cement plant was relatively autonomous and tended to operate largely within the local market (cement is expensive to transport!). Monitoring of operating performance from the headquarters was largely done virtually. It should be noted that there were more than 250 operating facilities, all over the world, in the Holcim group.

Jan Jenisch was comfortable with this way of working, especially because of significant time-saving due to the lower level of travel for him. He knew most of the various Holcim country managers personally, which was an important aspect that allows this remote controlling approach to work so smoothly. Jan Jenisch observed that if the pandemic had taken place 3 years earlier when he was new in the job and had not yet established a set of country manager relationships, then this no-travel approach might have been harder to pull off.

Innovations. The gist of the main manufacturing process at Holcim was the making of cement through grinding and re-using. There was also an effort to reduce emissions. Incidentally, new investments were needed for grinding mills for this. Other projects included to produce cement within lower temperatures in the rotating machinery and to capture CO_2 through filters and the use of "new" materials in the construction industry, such as carbon fibers, and/or glass, as well as coming up with construction of buildings with relatively more efficient use of cement/concrete. In general, advances in materials science were likely to play roles. The construction industry was conservative though.

Acquisitions. Holcim has adopted a bolt-on acquisition strategy, with various smaller deals each year, trying to be fast in integration and usually to gain higher synergies compared to larger, more complex, acquisitions. Holcim's entry into the roofing business has been through acquisitions.

Cultural issues. The merger between Lafarge and Holcim revealed that there were significant cultural hurdles when attempting to combine French and Swiss, as least initially. Thus, decisions were taken largely based on fulfilling the perspective of either Lafarge or Holcim, rather than on pragmatically addressing key issues critical to the success of the combined LH. The abandonment of both old headquarters and establishment of a "new" one, seen as neutral, seem to have contributed to a more unified Holcim culture. The company's name was changed from Lafarge Holcim to Holcim in 2022.

Executive development. Jan Jenisch is a strong believer in executive development and perceives it as instrumental to the development of a stronger Holcim. He has taken several programs at IMD and also co-developed customized executive programs for the Senior Managers of the company. He has also sponsored several in-company programs, at IMD as well as at other convenient locations in the Zurich region. He has made it a "rule" to attend each of these, say for half a day. The pandemic has brought all executive development activities to a halt. However, web-based trainings have now been restarted.

Reinvention. A main concept was that a successful company should try to re-invent itself. Holcim started out as a primarily Swiss company, family dominated, then became global, diversified (concrete, aggregates, building materials), then merged with Lafarge, then …

Old established corporate strengths should not stand in the way for evolutions of this type. There are many examples of reinvention failures. Thyssen-Krupp and Deutsche Bank come to mind. But what about the German automobile industry? Traditionally, this industry's success had been built on fossil fuel-based engine technologies and with a heavy concentration on optimizing production processes around this. However, it may be hard, with such an ingrained focus, to successfully shift to an electric engine-based reality. Time will tell!

The family business dimension. A properly functioning family business might have definite advantages, above all though allowing for more long-term thinking, as well as for a corporate culture, which directly reflects the core values of the owning family. This was, for instance, the case both for Holcim and for SIKA, Mr. Jenisch's previous employer. Holcim had benefitted from the dominant ownership as well as management involvement of the

Schmidheiny family for many years. The Schmidheinys had initially started Holcim.

Yet, when a family's financial/ownership position might become diluted, for example, when some family members from the next generation elect to sell out, then it may no longer be advantageous that a family continues to hold control through special voting rights. In line with this, in June 2019, Mr. Thomas Schmidheiny dropped his stake in LafargeHolcim to 7.2% from 10.9% to diversify his investment portfolio. And as per December 31, 2021, according to Lafarge Holcim's website, excluding the shares of the family members, he presently holds 8.44% of the shares.

Morten Hannesbo, Former CEO AMAG Group AG (Interviewed February 2019)

Hannesbo discusses how AMAG approaches its multi-brand strategies, by keeping the brands separate from each other, different stores for VW, Skoda, Audi, and SEAT, as well as different owners, presidents, and chairperson. There are times when consolidation and centralization of organizations or its departments and initiatives are advisable and times when creating distinct separators or distances can help to strengthen or grow a business. Important is to run your business through this filter—is force best achieved united or independent of the firm?

Morten Hannesbo was the outgoing CEO of AMAG Group AG (leaving at the end of 2021), a position he had occupied since 2009. Before joining AMAG in 2007, he held several positions at Nissan, Toyota, and Ford, including as the CEO of Ford Switzerland. AMAG is a privately held company owned by Martin Haefner and the Haefner family; it has more than 6500 employees and is Switzerland's leading importer and distributor of cars, including leading brands such as Audi, Volkswagen, Skoda, SEAT, Bentley, and Porsche. The annual turnover is approximately 4.7 bn CHF. The company has more than 80 dealerships and service facilities and a large number of partners across Switzerland. It also owns the Europcar franchise and a leasing company. AMAG is considered highly successful entity, holding nearly 30% of Switzerland's new-car market share despite the industry's fierce competition. So, what are some of the more prominent changes the automotive sector faces and how have manufacturers such as Volkswagen and major distributors such as AMAG adapted their strategies accordingly?

The automotive sector is subject to heavy cost pressures plus major technical and usage changes. For Mr. Hannesbo, a principal factor for driving major technological shifts in cars is the ability to take advantage of thus-far undeveloped potential factors, especially with respect to cars' power trains. For instance, the technologies behind traditional gasoline and diesel cars might not realistically be developed much further, and new emission rules will make internal combustion engines increasingly expensive. These technologies have been nurtured for more than 100 years and can now be considered mature. On the other hand, although invented over 100 years ago, electric cars are based on an emerging new technology. They have significant potential for further improvements and new developments over many years to come. The relatively low cost of electricity relative to traditional fuels, as well as lower operating costs, might also foster a shift towards electric cars—not to mention that electric cars definitely perform well, with breathtaking acceleration and comfortable driving! The so-called plug-in-hybrid (P-i-H) cars, however, are probably not going to become a widespread alternative in the long run, according to Mr. Hannesbo. Some advanced cars might be too complex and expensive for the mass market too, despite their excellent performance.

Another major technical change with broad implications for the automotive industry is the advance of driverless car technology. Here, again, we have seen many breakthrough innovations, likely to impact all segments of the automotive industry over the next years. But this technology might still be years—if not decades—away from mass adoption. Legal considerations are also holding it back, particularly regarding both safety and insurance.

With traffic congestion, especially in many larger cities, often also coupled with pollution problems, one might see the emergence of car sharing, rather than each customer owning their own car. This pool of shared cars might typically be electric and self-navigating and with much higher utilization rates than we see today for privately held cars, as these are often used less than 5% of time in a typical day.

Due to this abundance of technical changes, way-of-use and sheer cost-driven pressures on car manufacturers, the recent automotive structural changes across Europe should come as no surprise:

- Jaguar Land Rover: Record losses; downscaling.
- Honda: Closing UK plant; many uncertainties.
- Nissan: Not building its next-generation SUV in Sunderland.
- Ford: Reconsidering its strategy and footprint in Europe.

The Volkswagen Group's strategy. This group has developed a particularly effective product and brand strategy, with a clear positioning of each of the group's brands. Each particular brand might thus genuinely stand for the following:

- Audi: Cutting-edge technology and innovation.
- Volkswagen: Quality for all.
- Skoda: Value for the money.
- SEAT: Inexpensive but exciting cars that deliver.
- Bentley: Uncompromising, top quality.
- Porsche (partly owned): Timeless sports cars.

The Volkswagen Group thus seems to have gotten its product positioning more or less right and is exercising considerable influence over each of its operating units in preserving this brand positioning. While the technical platforms of the group's various car brands are often similar under the hood and thus yield considerable cost savings, the features that customers experience above all are different from model to model, from brand to brand. For instance, main design features in each car, such as the instrumentation and exterior design features, have been kept different from brand to brand but still more or less consistent over the years within each brand. The customer groups supporting a given brand can therefore remain as comfortable as possible with their preferred brand. This concept was first conceived by Mr. Ferdinand Piëch, Chairman of the Executive Board and later of the Supervisory Board of the Volkswagen Group from 1993 to 2015. Such brand loyalty is essential for the economic performance of any given brand. Note that this multi-brand strategy has many similarities to the one originally developed at General Motors by the legendary Alfred P. Sloan, in 1921.

In Mr. Hannesbo's eyes, some of Volkswagen's major competitors, such as Toyota, might actually be changing too many design features when introducing new models, thus potentially weakening brand loyalty and confusing customers as well. Still, Toyota cars are well known to have very high technical standards and quality, of course.

AMAG's strategy. AMAG is also trying to live up to the brand and product differentiation strategy. In support of it, the main brands each have their own distinctive dealerships and service organizations and complete brand separations. A customer can thus experience what a given brand stands for in a dealership specific to that brand, while perhaps being unaware that AMAG owns this, as well as various other brands. This strategy is better understood when seen in contrast to having many brands represented in the same store.

One of AMAG's main competitors follows this latter approach. A more opportunistic, bargain-hunting customer might perhaps find benefits in this approach at the expense of focusing more on a brand experience.

In the end, the customers' preferences dictate the strategy. AMAG therefore sees the task of continuously reinventing itself as essential, not the least to uphold its strong bond with its customers. Significant attention is therefore spent on what at first sight might seem "nitty-gritty" brand details. To strengthen this approach even further, the AMAG Innovation and Venture Lab was established in 2018, in which a team of more than 20 experts are continually trying to come up with new ways to help AMAG excite customers. This lab's ideas include: surprises (positive experiences); relevant innovations, as seen by the customers; and ways to increase the economic returns to the company and its customers, through financial performance, more sustainable and reliable cars, etc.

Formidable efforts have been made to keep customers loyal to AMAG's brands. The significance of this high focus on brand loyalty might be even better appreciated when one considers AMAG's low-profit margin when selling a new car.

To strengthen its efficiency further and offer even better service, AMAG's retail unit has introduced a so-called "hub and spoke" structure over the last years. There are now 14 regional hubs with several spokes connected to them. In this way, services are improved, with even the most complex repairs now handled within each region. This change allows for considerable cost savings and with more streamlined inventories. AMAG makes more of its annual profits through service than through the sale of new cars.

Mr. Hannesbo feels that it is rather risky to undertake major strategic and/or organizational changes without actually knowing very well beforehand where one might plan to go. Clarity regarding the intended direction is fundamental! To actually get there would thus be a matter of putting in as good an effort as possible, to "try to do things right but also do the right thing." Then, additional adjustments may have to be initiated as time passes by. Speed is crucial. Excessive risk-averseness will not do. This is an incremental approach—a "plan B" would not make much sense, none the least because of the capital-intensive nature of the business. In the end, it is evident that this approach does not always mean that one knows where one plans to go!

The management style at AMAG has become much less formal over the years, and various divisions have relatively high leeway along with clear financial, quantitative, and qualitative objectives. Also, the management teams of each division are clear about the fact that they must perform well, be on top of things! When things do not go as expected, they should try to understand why and initiate steps for improvement. Speed is also critical here and to never give up. The so-called 80-20 rule should apply: it is typically more than good enough to go with 80% knowledge instead of striving for absolute perfection or 100% analysis. To go for the last 20% tends to take up too many resources, be too expensive, and take too much time. It follows that occasional mistakes will be acceptable, if quickly corrected.

Mr. Hannesbo feels that his personal experience with endurance sports (marathon running; road cycling) is relevant also: again, never giving up, coping with pain, rationing one's resources, believing in self, walking tall, and being excited about the fact that the goal is nearer! In Mr. Hannesbo's view, working in a privately held company such as AMAG is closely linked to sustainability, robustness, and taking the long-term perspective. There are fewer short-term pressures! Furthermore, disruptions might be seen as leading to positive opportunities in the end, since the time horizon is longer!

20

Closing Remarks for the Part

We have now read and heard much about why strategy is so important for business. Vision, direction, clear goals that are vocalized, and the idea that strategy is a fluid process have been shared here. Strategy should create or improve business performance, but establishing, embracing, and communicating strategy is no easy feat. Strategic planning requires data, analysis, time, effort, and a constant assessment. Everything is impermanent. Accepting this can help us evolve, both professionally and personally as leaders. And, as we have seen, creativity and originality are at the center of this process. Each of the persons featured indicate how they have been able to "spot" something truly original, which has then become the "raison d'être" of the firms they lead. It is this uniqueness that makes the differences, but realism is also key here—there seems to be relatively little difference between success and failure. To push for positive limits seems to be key!

A major trade-off when it comes to strategic options is to decide on the degree of "asset lightness." On the one side and a typically traditional approach, a firm's leaders may settle on strong vertical integration, that is, to make most components, parts, etc. in house. While this clearly offers strong control over a firm's own value chain, there are also potential negatives: it takes serious capital to invest in all of these activities, and it may also imply a lack of flexibility, not being able to quickly respond to shifting customer preferences.

An alternative could be to outsource more, thereby also becoming less capital intensive. We might label this "asset light." Sub-suppliers are indeed becoming a sort of "partner." Such firms thus tend to develop relatively "flat," networked organizations. But control over one's value chain may now be weaker!

So, there is a dilemma here—strong control over one's value chain, through vertical integration and relatively heavy investments, that is, "asset heavy," versus less control over one's own value chain, relying more on subcontractors and adopting a flatter, networked organization, that is, "asset light."

Over several decades, until relatively recently, there has been a general trend to moving towards relatively asset light value chains, typically by transferring much of the manufacturing functions to low-cost countries, most notably China, or Bangladesh, Vietnam, Indonesia, and the Philippines. Over the more recent years, there seems to be a trend to reverse this. Manufacturing is increasingly moving back to traditionally more high-cost economies, such as the United States or Western Europe. Why? There appear to be at least three reasons:

1. Reliability. To re-establish a relatively high degree of control over one's own value chain may be important. Reliability increases, and exposure to supply disruptions due to, say, political instability in former sub-supplier countries typically decreases.
2. Cheaper automation. Increased automation of manufacturing in developed countries may make manufacturing of components relatively less expensive.
3. Customer sensitivity. To adapt to shifting customer preferences may indeed become easier when controlling one's own value chain. With modern IT-based manufacturing, such adaption may become easier. For example, a production line in a modern automobile plant—where every car on the line is individualized; different engines, colors are all different, and so on. Each car is customized to respond to a specific customer. Or, for example, with distributors of inexpensive fashion clothing, such as Zara, Mango, or H&M: Offerings are rapidly changed as a consequence of shifting customer preferences. We could go on and on! One solution is to control one's own value chain.

Part V

The Family Business: An Inspiring Source

Whenever we talk about the future, we look at it in terms of generations rather than quarters.
—Michael van der Post, sixth generation leader of his family business, Compaxo BV

The biggest reason that family businesses fall apart is that the family hasn't developed the kind of culture that supports keeping the family business in the family.
—Mitzi Perdue, family businesswoman and author

21

Practice Insights from Dennis Jaffe, Senior Research Fellow, BanyanGlobal Family Business Advisors

Family businesses, or as we now say, family enterprises (because business families usually own several shared assets rather than one single legacy business), are evolving and changing every day. Large societal demographic shifts take place alongside internal family generational change to form a fabric of continual change for every business family. The concepts of resilience and reinvention have become the central focus for continual family enterprise success. It has been many years since families faced a business and family environment that was predictable and consistent.

In every country, the commercial foundations are business families. Despite cultural and economic differences, we see some common trends facing these families, several of which are completely unprecedented. After a long period of optimism about global development and evolution, today, we emerge from a pandemic-traumatized world into further uncertainty and threat. Every family must deal with this new reality, but business families that want to remain productive, connected, and vital must "lean in" to actively respond to them.

I recently conducted a research project where I interviewed family members from two generations of 100 large, global business families that had succeeded as a business or financial enterprise and as a connected family for more than three generations (*Borrowed From Your Grandchildren: The Evolution of 100-Year Family Enterprises*). My interviews afforded me entry into the inner worlds of such families and enabled me to document how they evolved through multiple internal and external changes. In the five years since my study, such change has continued to accelerate.

Here are some of the most pervasive trends and changes I encountered:

From Legacy Business to Multiple, Diversified Enterprises.

After creating a successful legacy business, the family either harvests its wealth, sells the legacy business, or begins to evolve into a portfolio of enterprises and investments. If they are successful, they organize around a family office and other entities like a family foundation. The family cannot continue their business as usual but must set up a governance process to face change, continually evolve, move into different businesses, and redefine itself.

Longer Life Spans.

Since the older generation has control and ownership of resources, the fact that we have an active life span today that is a full generation longer means that family enterprises have an older generation that wants to be engaged and essential into their 80s and even 90s. A focus on wellness also means that elders are more active and energetic so that the whole concept of "retirement" has lost its original meaning. This means that there is not one but two or three generations waiting their turn, and families must find ways to invite and include members of multiple generations.

Educated, Inclusive Rising Generations.

The older generation has been successful in a different time, and the resource that allows the family enterprise to adapt and change is the rising generation of new family members. Their skills and commitment to the family create the future. Successful families with great wealth therefore invest in their children; they get the best education, they travel, they meet each other, and have a front-row seat to the world. (Though clearly many of them live in a self-created bubble and do not extend themselves.) Their life experience leads the rising generation to want to have a louder, more active, and impactful role in the family enterprise.

This takes several forms. First, rather than focusing on a single successor, young family members see themselves as part of a cohort or leaders, who all have a role in the enterprise, though often not as employees but as part of governance. Men and women see themselves as having equal roles, and all of this makes the younger cohort larger and more inclusive. As they look ahead to their lives, careers, and families, they want to know what the family enterprise offers and how they can play a role.

Social Agenda/Future Focus.

The rising generations of the family look ahead at social and environmental challenges, and they feel a personal connection. Their family is privileged;

they look ahead to the future and have concerns about the environment and community, and they want to use the family resources to make a difference—they have a social agenda that they want the family to enact. This leads families to have a values and social impact discussion not just about philanthropy but about their investment and business roles.

Nonfinancial Family Agenda.
The extended family shares a business, but what does that mean for them as a family? Families that share financial resources have increasingly begun to focus on who they are as a family and what is their wealth for. They make a choice to invest in their family and to build many forms of nonbusiness, nonfinancial wealth. To pursue this agenda, the family must meet, organize itself, allocate resources, and make a commitment to each other beyond being business partners. New activities, roles, and opportunities emerge that engage the family and give a reason for being connected.

Family Members to become Informed, Responsible Stewards.
With all these demands and open pathways, family members cannot allow themselves to remain passive or uninformed and delegate responsibility to advisors. There are not only opportunities but also responsibilities for acting in uncertain times. Each new generation must become more active, informed, and professional in having basic knowledge, skills, and level of engagement in the family enterprise. The new role of a "professional" family member is that of a steward—not necessarily an employee or operator of the business—but aware, informed, and ready to be engaged in making decisions at key points. The family members must organize, meet regularly, deal with differences, and make timely decisions about who they are and what they want to become.

These trends affect all families, but the largest and most successful are the most affected. If a family wants to success as a family and a shared enterprise across generations, it must work hard, remain engaged, and continually transform itself. Family enterprises that have been successful for one or more generations with a traditional format and legacy business find themselves faced with the above challenges. They cannot just do what they have always done. They must reinvent themselves. The rising generation will be the engine of change and renewal for the enduring family enterprise.

22

Introduction to Family Business: An Inspiring Source

To establish a long-term business focus is critical for any firm; hence, an approach taken from family businesses who are inherently good at this may be helpful. Many of the fundamental challenges facing business today call for such a longer-term focus. In privately held firms, there is often no need for short-term performance reporting. This Part focuses on the family-owned firm, usually privately held, and how it operates, invests, creates value, and generates wealth. The learning angle we wish to propose to all readers here, whether from family businesses or not, is to use experiences and information from entities in both related and unrelated businesses or sectors who excel at strategies based on future growth and horizons. In other words, let us avoid silo-thinking.

It should be noted that the two executive interviews at the end of this section are focused on the family business and where it is investing to grow and maximize value and wealth. These are ideal springboards to the Part that follows, which specifically deals with the topic of investing to maximize wealth. We wanted to include companies in this section that appear to have understood the true potential of value creation, wealth management, preservation, and growth.

The main factors for consideration for family businesses, or those nonfamily businesses open or keen to take inspiration from family firms, include balancing long-term focus with short-term agility, preparation for transitions and successions and what comes afterwards, and the ever-necessary digital evolution or transformation. Also, for family organizations, the themes of mentoring and coaching, legacy building/family branding, and giving back are particularly important. Many of the selected readings herein will cover these in some way.

So, what are the key takeaways that we can expect from this Part?:

- A long-term focus is key, not dependent on quarterly earnings and stock prices.
- Simple and portfolio: commitment to specific traditions and flexibility.
- The family/owners always to be informed.

23

Essential Books to Learn About the Family Business: An Inspiring Source

Roy Williams and Vic Pressier, (2010), Preparing Heirs, Robert Reed (Reviewed June 2019)

This relatively old book, though in many ways a classic, hones in above all on the critical importance of having a specific mission for one's family business, thus allowing various family members to be effectively informed, even those who are not necessarily participating actively in the management of the family firm, and also including those next-generation members who might be uninterested. A clear articulation of a mission may make it easier for some of those initially less interested to step into management roles later, as well as to facilitate a smoother wealth transition between generations.

Authors Williams and Pressier share a series of practical suggestions for how to successfully transmit family wealth and values through systematic preparation of family heirs. The authors developed a five-step model, calling first for the development of a family mission and then a transition plan, as well as the inclusion of all family members, effective coaching, and systematic post facto follow-up. The authors provide useful checklists for ensuring a successful transition of family wealth from one generation to another. Much of what is presented might appear rather self-evident. However, a key strength of the book is that it provides a set of comprehensive steps to check. Thus, it shall, of course, be up to each family itself to work through these checklists—that is, to put their own "meat on the bones."

Before further reviewing the central messages of the book, we shall point out what we see as a potentially major limitation, namely its implicit assumption that a family's assets typically consist of one business or perhaps a few.

Much of today's family-based asset preservation is not based on the transfer of such monolithic operating business entities but rather intended to contain a family's assets in a broader portfolio. Also, such a portfolio would typically lend itself more readily to be modified, say, through partial selloffs to compensate family members who might elect to exit. More importantly, such a carefully crafted portfolio typically allows for meaningful risk reduction when it comes to a wealth-transition process. Regrettably, the book does not discuss these issues and instead focuses solely on the transfer of a given business entity from one generation to the next.

In their introduction, Williams and Pressier point out the importance of relying on strong outside resources in this transition process. Effective coaching, research on various aspects of wealth transfers such as taxation issues, and family members' education are all crucial elements for success. The trigger to initiate a wealth-transfer process may often be the older generation's age or declining health. Another trigger could be the heirs' coming of age, having gained education, work experience, and competence, thus making them more ready to assume increased responsibility.

The authors identify several main considerations for achieving a successful wealth transfer: Is the family's mission sufficiently clear? Based on this family mission, does the family have a clear estate plan? Post facto monitoring and eventual modification of plans are fundamental.

The involvement of outside persons can be positive. These persons could come from academia or the psychology profession, or they may simply be experienced practitioners. The aim is to come up with an integrative process in which the entire family can be involved and through which trust can be built.

The model for the transition of wealth is discussed in detail. To start with, a family's mission and transition plan should be examined by everyone in the family with "fresh eyes." Governance and taxation are especially important issues. Through this process, required modifications might appear. Such a change should be the norm but many might find it too energy consuming, especially within larger families. A good coach might assuredly contribute in a constructive way here, provided he or she is trusted by all family members, of course. Carefully choosing the appropriate coach is crucial and can be challenging!

In addition to stimulating constructive changes mentioned above, another essential task for a strong coach is to prepare the family heirs with their diverse strengths and weaknesses. The coach must identify a role that leverages his or her strengths for each heir. Various aspects of philanthropy might be particularly well suited for such role delineations. However, the actual running of the family business is, of course, the most critical task. If none of the next-generation family members are qualified and ready for this, outside professionals should be brought in. The coach would be key to safeguard realism here!

In the end, nothing may work better than various next-generation family members' self-preparation when it comes to shouldering responsibility. However, many potential challenges arise, including how to bring on board more-or-less uninformed owners, how to activate nonparticipating heirs, and how to welcome uninterested next-generation members.

A systematic wealth-transition process from one generation to the next would typically benefit from following guidelines such as those they have outlined. Wealth-transition failures might be avoided this way! Yet the challenges can often be formidable!

Joachim Schwass and Anne-Catrin Glemser, (2016), Wise Family Business, Springer (February 2017)

To develop a strong brand for one's family business is seen as important, drawing not only on insights from the former German chancellor, Dr. Angela Merkel, but also on the classical model of Taiguri and Wells, the goal being to build a brand integrating the family, ownership, and business. Fifteen successful case studies are provided as examples, spanning a wide range from, to name but a few, LEGO (scalability), Lundin Energy (entrepreneurship), Firmenich (vision), or Ayala (ability to learn from mistakes).

Let us start with a background observation by Angela Merkel, who states that:

> Family Businesses typically seem to be: More long-term; taking responsibility in society; and are often socially engaged. In sum, family business tends to represent both freedom and responsibility!

Let us now review three key take-home implications for business, according to Schwass and Glemser: It is key to develop one's own Family Business Brands whenever possible. Typically, these give large economic advantage to society! And how does one build such family business brands? Building family brands seems to be based on the overlap between three different factors (Fig. 23.1):

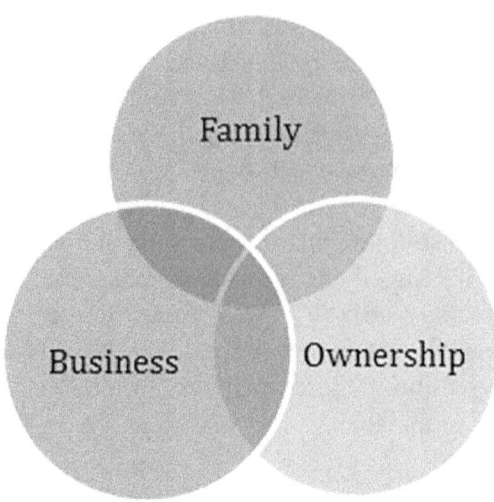

Fig. 23.1 Intersection between family, ownership, and business (from the seminal article by Tagiuri and Davis, 1996)

There will often be centrifugal forces that might contribute to pull brands owned by family business apart. A strong, evolving family business brand can constitute a centripetal force, a counterbalancing force, and might then eventually even hold a family business together.

Case Study Insights: The 15 case studies encompassing family business brands are Lego (Denmark), Odebrecht (Brazil), Patek-Philippe (Switzerland), Lundin (Sweden), Ayala (Philippines), Bata (Canada), Lee Kum Kee (China), Henkel (Germany), Bonnier (Sweden), Bavaria (Netherlands), Firmenich (Switzerland), Zegna (Italy), J.M. Huber (USA), Royal Selangor (Malaysia), and Puig (Spain). These reveal that there seem to be several rather common key features that might be important for developing strong family business brands: scalability of the basic business concept that underpins a family business brand (Lego), entrepreneurialism (Lundin), vision (Firmenich), and ability to learn from mistakes (Ayala).

Dynamic development is part of it all. Each family generation should attempt to add its own innovative feature to the business and hence also ensure the dynamic development of the family brand! A challenge, when it comes to continuous development in family business contexts, might be that there typically are many paradoxes in play, such as lack of stability and dynamism and overabundance of tradition and innovation.

It seems important that the family opens up to innovation even though family business is often a mainstay of more traditional values.

Tom McCullough & Keith Whitaker (2018), Wealth of Wisdom: The Top 50 Questions Wealthy Families Ask, Wiley (Reviewed April 2019)

McCullough and Whitaker spent more than a year questioning wealthy individuals about their major concerns; as a result, they identified 50 main issues. They then commissioned a different specialist for each of the 50 points to address how each issue might affect wealth and family business management. These contributors are largely North American. They include consultants, family business office managers, and researchers.

Here are nine areas that have been addressed:

- To think about what matters, such as legacies and inherited values. Family histories and storytelling can also shed light on this, often differentiating family business from regular business. It can provide the former with a distinct competitive advantage.
- Planning thoughtfully. Entailing more thoughtful decision-making, road maps, and conversations about sustaining wealth between parents and their children, even planning for the continued use of a family vacation home!
- Investing wisely, paying special attention to the goals, risks, and choices related to their investments. A key question centers on a family's goals, realistic returns expectations, and the risks that a family is willing to bear. A scheme is given for dividing overall portfolios into specific areas of interest.
- Preparing the rising generation. The editors argue for the use of the term "rising generation" in place of "next generation" to signal a sense of evolution and continuity rather than any possible degradation after the first or older generation. The development of independence and self-worth is key, entailing of education embracing, a nondominant leadership style, and assigning meaningful tasks.
- Making shared decisions, i.e., family governance. This might be interpreted as referring to the study of how people make shared decisions. A primary advice here is the need to share financial information, transparency. Initiatives such as a family constitution, a regular family assembly, an established board of directors, and a family owners' council might all be used. Open, nondominant styles are crucial.
- Combining family and business. No family business lasts unless the members of subsequent generations are motivated to continue it. As a result, the alignment of family and business goals is crucial. However, this prioritization does more than just motivate the rising generation; it also helps

develop strong future leaders, ensures that the family stays together, and so on.
- Giving is a central concern for many wealthy families. This includes charity, philanthropy, and impact investing.
- Seeking sound advice. This section addresses the best ways to find good advisors. None the least, given the increasing complexity in this world, most people need advisors, trustworthy, credible, and reliable. An advisor should also be good at discussing relevant issues when needed and have few or no potential conflicts of interest. Such objectiveness is not always easy to find; thus, it may also make sense for investors and business owners to join together in communities and associations to discuss major issues with each other.
- Facing the future. It is essential to learn from history and to resist the temptation to extrapolate too much from current trends, i.e., think that events might proceed differently in the future than in the past.

Paul Hokemeyer, (2019), Fragile Power, Hazelden (Reviewed March 2020)

This book is written by a leading US-based psychologist and provides cases based on many of his clients from family business owners' circles. Celebrity-related issues are seen as a major potential problem. Behavioral style issues, such as being guarded, defensive, even arrogant, likewise! Dominance by some family members or others often represents a major dysfunctionality.

The focus of this work is on treating the wealthy and famous, written by one of the world's leading psychoanalysts, expert on celebrity identities and marriage counseling. It aims to shed light on the conundrum of why "having everything" never seems to be enough! Various conditions signifying mental imbalances might indeed represent significant value-destroying risks.

A basis for the rest of the book is a profound respect for all human beings and acknowledgment of their unique individualities. It turns out that wealth and power are often relatively uncorrelated with mental happiness.

Individuals' insecurities and thought distortions might cause dysfunctionalities. Their roots can often be found in the so-called imposter syndrome, implying that many believe they are not adequate despite the successes they may have. As a result, people become guarded, defensive, and even arrogant.

Vanity, lack of self-worth, vulnerability, and narcissism stem from the pervasive phenomenon of shame-based fear of being ordinary and thus of never feeling extraordinary enough to be noticed. There seems to be a virtual tsunami of narcissism, perhaps stemming from widely distributed smartphones, social media profiles, and "likes." This feeling of inferiority with overdependence on external acclaim often originates early in life and might perhaps be the single most destructive factor facing the rich and famous.

Dominance. Several leading companies, such as Uber, have been known to encourage particularly dominant male behavior when it comes to interactions with women. The rich and famous tend to employ escorts to a larger degree and engage in marital infidelity more often. Both sexes seem to be represented when it comes to these practices, including prostitution, objectification, fetishism, and other transactional relationships.

To better understand the resolve of partners to stay in a marriage/relationship even though abuses have occurred or continue to come from the other partner, it is pointed out that divorce often leads to condemnation—in one's family or in society. This may contribute to people resolving to stay. "How dare you leave!" Many are capable of keeping a spouse after committing marital infidelity as a means to preserve power and/or position. Even if abuse is clear, the betrayed partner may elect to "eat the shit."

Beauty. Human beauty can activate one's primitive or basic instinct and drive. Beauty, thus, should be clearly acknowledged, and this principle holds equally true for the rich and wealthy. Are some employees taking advantage of their own beauty? To recognize beauty is always an issue of who perceives it! Many of us may have nonidentical views on beauty.

Opulence, particularly with regard to luxury rehabilitation facilities and the dynamics of mental health treatment, is discussed. Efforts to make treatment approaches more scalable cannot get around the basic fact that luxury implies uniqueness.

Connectedness. The development of a new standard for healing seems to focus on the links between therapists and patients, as well as between therapists who support each other. It is recommended to selectively ask questions, selective and nonaggressive, to help the therapist gain more clarity regarding the nature of an issue. This approach may also demonstrate to a patient that a therapist might be seen as intellectually engaged, not merely aloof. It should all lead to a commonly developed plan for treatment to be bought into by both patient and therapist.

To explicitly recognize dysfunctional psychological factors among the rich and wealthy, family, business members, and independent investors may provide another answer to effectively dealing with value destruction when it comes to at least some members of our target group.

Philippe J. Weil, (2019), Woes of the Rich, Self-published (Reviewed April 2020)

Even though there may typically be many positive aspects with family business activities, there are, regrettably, also woes that family business owners might have: misjudging a business outlook; excessive spending, including borrowing; too much "confrontation" among family members, even lawsuits, all-consuming the family's energy.

Sadly, the emergence of such negative issues might often be associated with what is termed the "third-generation syndrome." Establishing a strong family office may ameliorate some of these problems—for example, for dysfunctional generational transitions, a focus on philosophy, say, may be a remedy for those who are relatively less inclined to concentrate on the family business, and so on.

In his book, Philippe Weil discusses how successful families deal with financial and nonfinancial challenges to preserve family wealth and to pass it from generation to generation. Weil was born in Zurich and worked for many years at Julius Bär. In 1996, he emigrated to Israel, where he started a family office in Tel Aviv.

Weil has worked with many wealthy families in Switzerland, a "capital" of old-world money and traditional family fortunes, and in Israel, a more entrepreneurial setting. Yet despite the apparent differences between old and new wealth, Weil writes that the reason for losing wealth is often the same:

- Investing disproportionate capital in one business, which may then fail.
- Misjudging business outlooks, i.e., not taking proper action in business cycle positioning.
- Family members simply spending too much on things like houses, aircraft, yachts, and lavish parties.
- Borrowing too much at a high rate, making it increasingly difficult to pay back the debt.
- Spending too much of the family's "energy" on confrontation.
- Lawsuits that drain the family, both emotionally and monetarily, including through "expensive" settlement fees.

Weil makes the point that emotions, unfortunately, tend to play a role when it comes to all of these causes. Such emotionality can make it difficult for families to avoid "throwing good money after the bad"!

Conclusively, the author stresses that it is a matter of family members "connecting" with money and, at the same time, living a comfortable lifestyle. Be comfortable with talking about money and wealth, without showing off! A common generational sequence pattern is observed. The first generation is hardworking and innovative. Their personal spending is typically modest. The second generation improves on the business that the previous generation has established. They are more sophisticated and look towards expansion and substantial wealth creation. The third generation often has a loss of focus. Their rate of additional wealth creation often tends to flatten out.

This sequence of generational prototypes represents a "best case." Often wealth can end up being lost, with the advent of less capable new family members. A family office might play a crucial role in liaising with and supporting the owner(s), the family, and management, especially when it comes to wealth/asset management. Here, a family office may take an approach more tailored to the performance of a specific family, as opposed to what a typical portfolio manager might be able to do. A family office may suggest more non-traditional types of assets to focus on and also adopting a longer time horizon; preparing reports and tax returns; supporting family members with ongoing lifestyle management tasks, including handling of payments, studies, cars, insurance, etc.; philanthropy and social impact investing; and supporting an orderly transition from one generation to the next.

The execution of these tasks depends a lot on a family's philosophy on wealth. Weil makes a useful distinction between a stewardship approach, which primarily focuses on preserving wealth to be handed over from one generation to the next, versus an ownership approach, where the owner decides, say, to donate considerable amounts to charities. Clearly, a family office will be taking on its tasks differently, depending on whether the main focus is on stewardship or on ownership.

Weil also recommends that the family write a, what he terms, Family Constitution to regulate future decision-making in such ways that family disagreements can be kept to a minimum. Here too, a family constitution will usually differ greatly depending on whether there is a stewardship focus or an ownership focus. In the former case, a family constitution may often make a lot of sense, and considerable care should be put into drafting and discussing such a document. Where there is an ownership focus, in contrast, the owner will basically decide anyway, and there is probably little need for a family constitution.

Clearly there is a need for proper strategizing and planning for all firms, whether family firms or not, so as to ensure a business' potential for solid future earnings. There seem to be three types of planning here:

- Financial planning—How can financial assets be passed on from generation to generation from a stewardship perspective? Taxes, currencies, inheritance fees, etc. play a role. The ownership perspective also requires financial planning. In what ways and how many funds can be allocated to philanthropic activities?
- Physical asset planning—Analogous arguments given above apply.
- Planning for heirs—This is clearly primarily applicable when it comes to stewardship cases. An appropriate analog may be with constitutional monarchies, which indeed might represent a good example of stewardship. The key in this case is when the old boss steps down as a "monarch," to allow the next generation the benefit of running things, while the old "monarch" may act as a mentor.

Melissa Mitchell-Blitch (2020), In the Company of Family: How to Thrive when Business Is Personal, Eredita Consulting LLC (Reviewed April 2021)

Running a family business can at times be challenging. And running a nonfamily business clearly too, yet often for different reasons. What can we learn from family businesses about balance, unity, culture, and values? How should we look at both the differences and similarities we share with family members or fellow executives? What are the roles we have or should play? Enhancing the relationships is essential for success, all while maintaining our own well-being and vitality.

This book covers how a family business and a family can function together in a balanced way so that the two sides not only flourish but even create a substantial positive synergy between the two. The author, who is an accomplished consultant to family businesses with backgrounds in psychology and finance, introduces the concept of boundaries as a strong element for how to handle this challenge. The author likens a boundary to a fence or a hedge with a gate.

One boundary would surround the family, and the other, the family business, i.e., analogous to two circles, with clarities in roles and foci for the various family members who would be inside one or both circles. Further, the "gates" in the circles allow members to be "invited" into the other circle, or intentionally kept out, both based on specific decisions by the person who is, or persons who are, in charge of a given circle. In this way, positive additional contributions might be built, i.e., synergies.

This short book also contains many useful examples, all disguised of course, as well as questions to consider at the end of each chapter. As owners of family businesses, with clear ambitions also to "safeguard" the harmony within our families, we find this book to be very helpful. It is a useful reminder that differences, if handled well, can be constructive rather than divisive.

Josh Baron & Rob Lachenauer, (2021), Family Business Handbook, Harvard Business Review Press (Reviewed February 2022)

There are many different aspects of how a privately held, family-owned firm is managed, and this book covers many of these. It provides a "how to do it" when it comes to addressing most key issues facing family businesses. An appendix, with materials from BanyanGlobal Family Advisors (www.banyan.global) further elaborates on the philosophy of family businesses as well as on the major issues facing such firms. This handbook's authors, Baron and Lachenauer, are highly qualified and respected individuals within the field of family business. Both authors are cofounders and partners at BanyanGlobal, a management consulting firm specializing in serving family businesses. Dr. Baron teaches family business courses at Colombia Business School in the school's MBA, EMBA, and Executive Education programs. Mr. Lachenauer, the CEO of BanyanGlobal, has worked closely with scores of family businesses throughout the world, helping them sort out the dilemmas they face as owners while also strengthening family relationships.

Now to a brief summary of the handbook, which falls into three parts ("Cracking the Code of Your Family Business," "The Five Rights of Family Business Owners," and "Challenges You Will Face"), more or less corresponding with three traits that most successful family businesses often seem to have: Curiosity: Living with the challenge of lifelong learning, Teamwork: Keeping a family business "on track" requires constant effort in team building and teamwork, and Adaptability: Embracing challenges and being open to meet these.

Understanding the main individuals in a family firm is generally important, i.e., the interconnectedness among such key individuals, as well as the systems that may shape critical behaviors in family firms. It should be noted here that in family firms, the leaders will often broadly influence not only the business itself but the family as well, in contrast to publicly traded companies, where a market focus tends to dictate nearly all decisions. However, this may not always be a positive force, rather can also at times be destructive. The power to sustain a family business seems intertwined with a willingness to explicitly invest in developing the next generation—to making them better prepared! To understand what this form of ownership implies seems critical for the successful continuation of a family business. To a certain degree, this means looking at the owner's responsibility as stewardship.

There may be five fundamental "rights" of family business owners. A starting point is perhaps to delineate explicitly the type of family business ownership type that has been determined (sole owner, partnership, all decedents take over, a subset of decedents shall have control). Decision-making then may take place within a "four-room model" (owner, board, management, family). Significant processes shall then have to be put in place to ensure integration across the "rooms" (decision processes with formal connections between "rooms," conflict resolution procedures, shareholder agreements, etc.).

To create a strategy which is both good for the family firm and in line with the interests of the family owners is paramount. This has to do with how interrelated factors such as growth, liquidity, dividends, debt, and control are to be coped with. An owner strategy might often be grappling to find a realistic tradeoff between liquidity, growth, and control.

To strive for realistic ways to inform is important. This has to do with building trust. There are several groups in such a network for information dissemination: owners, next gen, spouses, employers, community, etc. Information might be shared when it comes to design issues (ownership of a family firm), decision-making issues (roles, representatives), values (financial performance, …), transfer (how the family firm changes hands), and so on. The communication may be characterized as "open," "metered," or "not at all"!

How are the main family firm values transferred? Explicit considerations of what might be the best for the firm, combined with a focus on what might be seen as fair, seem critical here. If a broadly accepted way to deal with both of these two factors together is not found, then conflicts, even court cases, might emerge. It is critical to not overstructure a transition. This might lead to conflicts, even court cases, and in turn to a breakup of family portfolio firms.

There are also other challenges managers of family firms might typically face. This may partly have to do with how to cope with "disruption," such as a death in the business family, new employees entering the business family, growing senses of inequality, dealing with behavioral health issues among some family members, and so on.

To be able to work effectively in a family business is another fundamental issue. To be prepared for "a life under the microscope" is something that should be of central concern. This might perhaps be especially difficult for in-laws joining the business. All of this leads to developing more explicit employment policies in the family firm, particularly when it comes to embracing career plans for key individuals, as well as allowing for fair compensation. A realistic family employment policy might also contain rules for family members' entry into the firm, feedback mechanisms to enhance further development of weaknesses of these, as well as exits.

How to protect family business wealth is commonly another central topic. The authors provide several recommendations when it comes to this. Paramount here is "to survive," to ensure profitability in the firm, and to grow, while keeping debt low. Above all, to develop a portfolio must of course also fit the owner's interests. What is important is to exit from one particular business so as to diversify into such a portfolio instead. To articulate a realistic dividend policy, to prepare for responsibility, and to avoid favoritism seem significant.

There may regrettably still be conflicts within an owning family, perhaps calling for a seven-point "conflict spiral" when it comes to dealing with this. To escape such typically devastating family feuds, it seems important to put all options on the table. For instance, a possible buy-out of some family members should be based on full transparency and trust.

For some families, a way forward might be to create a Family Office to manage the investments for a family. In addition, family offices could provide various forms of support to family members ("make life easier for them") and enhance effective governance within the various parts of a family's holdings. The two most common types of family offices are the single-family office (SFO) and the multifamily office (MFO). A common source of resistance to the creation of a family office might have to do with the realization that this shall typically lead to additional expenses for the owners. Also, what should owners spend their time and energy on when professionals in the family office take over management?

There may be several associated "warning signs" associated with the loss of family control and wealth reduction: when dividends never change; when Board meetings have become a formality; when information is either too much or too little; when a CEO is considered irreplaceable; when family members are shut out of the business, as a policy. To cope with "red light" factors such as these, it seems fundamental to bring the family back in control—reapproach the design of the family firm, revisit the governance structure, reaffirm one's owner strategy for the company, and readdress the implications of ownership transfer to the next generation.

Amy Hart Clyne and Dennis Jaffe, (2021), Finding Her Voice and Creating Legacy, Pitcairn (Reviewed January 2022)

This book discusses the main roles of female family business leaders, both those who are new to wealth, typically having started and built their own businesses, as well as those who are inheritors of wealth, where they may be stepping into an already established family business after taking over from a deceased or absent family member. The authors have interviewed some 34 leaders, half approximately who are new to wealth and the other half who are inheritors of wealth.

Their methodology is focused on lengthy conversations with each other, and thus with no analysis based on numerical data. Rather, the authors try to understand how each of these women came to wealth, their roles in their families, the major obstacles they had to overcome, and how they prepared the next generation.

Women are now increasingly finding their rightful roles in business. We have, for instance, seen a welcome increase of women pursuing higher level education (now more or less 50/50 with male counterparts in the USA). We have equally observed female political leaders becoming more and more prominent worldwide. Still, in business leadership functions today there are relatively few women leaders. But progress is being made here too. A sense of perspective must be kept when it comes to this, however. After all, the Equal Credit Opportunity Act came about in 1976 only, i.e., relatively late. Only then were women in the US given the right to obtain credit without the consent of their husbands. In many parts of the world, restrictions such as these, and others, still exist.

Amy Hart Clyne is the Chief Knowledge and Learning Officer at Pitcairn, a US-based venture firm, and a leading expert on how to support wealthy families with relevant education. Dennis T. Jaffe is an emeritus professor of family business, organizational systems, and psychology at Saybrook University, San Francisco, and a leading consultant on family business. He is also a world-recognized author of books on family wealth.

What are the key issues to consider facing women leaders who are new to wealth. Most of the women in this category had husbands who were leading entrepreneurs in their own right. The spouses found their role to support this, i.e., partnerships with their husbands. Strong determination and inner drive were key characteristics of these women, and they shared these values with their husbands.

Women leaders were seen to play key supporting, complementing roles, critically important for allowing a family enterprise to succeed. Three such alternatives were identified: a complementary one, such as supporting a wine-making husband with finance and marketing functions; working behind the scenes, being an essential confidante; and pursuing an independent business career, such as being an "as needed" partner-in-charge after the death of her husband.

This group of women leaders thus typically held two critical roles, namely that of raising children as well as being involved in businesses spearheaded by their husbands. This amazing duality often called for a lot of energy to be able to "do it all"! Above all, to impact the children to respect good governance, guiding the next generation in one or more of the following five ways seems quite important: developing the children to better recognize family relationships, raising the children to be ready to become active in business, instilling a strong sense of gratitude in the children for having such access to wealth, introducing illustrations regarding how one's family might be governed, and encouraging the children to be creative—no limits!

When husbands died, the wives typically had to step out of the shadows and assume much greater leadership responsibilities. Many of these women leaders might have different leadership styles than their late husbands, but to cement a legacy, so that the next generation could eventually take over would be central. At times, parts of a business might however be transferred to now-distant relatives.

Remarriage may of course also represent a challenge. To connect with stepchildren, and even with the former wife, can be difficult indeed. New wives might not be able to shift the tenor of a family, to build/sustain family connections, and even act as mentors to the "new children."

As a way of summarizing the various roles of the new to wealth, first-generation women leaders, the following archetypes are identified: to be an essential business partner and contributor, to act as a catalyst to foster multi-generational family business success, to stimulate business creativity at the next generational level, and to instill "sound" family values, especially when it comes to coping with wealth.

The authors were, however, also cognizant of the need to conduct more research to "fill in" several more or less "open" areas for how to delineate what might constitute a successful woman leader new to wealth, such as What might be key dimensions of proper preparation? The inner drive and confidence: what may be healthy versus dysfunctional? The husband: what is proactive support from him? The female leader may essentially be "alone." But how might she handle this so as not to be "lonely"? To build awareness when it comes to effective leadership would be critical. But how? How might a successful woman leader be able to identify what could be essential business "gaps," and then fill them? The husband versus the rest of his family. How to be an effective mediator? How might children's development be driven as efficiently as possible?

Let us now move to focusing on women leaders who were *Inheritors of Wealth*. Most of these women, while taking on leaderships of often considerable sources of wealth, often ran into preconceptions that made their leadership tasks more difficult. Above all, there were often biases that perhaps made male family members be considered better equipped to lead. There might also be trustees with such biases along the way. There were typically few role models in the past, if any, for such female leaders to be effective. Still, there are more and more examples of female leaders stepping up to the task of leading established family businesses, often having to challenge traditional standards.

Many leaders who were inheritors of wealth saw their central task to be "serving as family diplomats" to enhance transitions to new generations of family members in one or more of the following ways: to ensure the continuation of a positive impact for the future; to spearhead new women leader role models in families of established and more conventional business ownership; and to impact the traditional family dynamics when it comes to leading family businesses, perhaps especially by impacting a lessening of traditional male dominance.

There were thus several traditional cultural dimensions that successful female leaders would have to cope with: How to fit in when it comes to well-defined family cultures? How to ensure frugality, i.e., be at the center of the preservation of wealth, how to work with traditional "hierarchical" family setups, dealing with secrecy regarding one family's wealth, handling "hidden" alliances that may have been formed among some family members, how to remain relatively independent of a family's growing pool of wealth, and coping with marriage. Can this enhance a women leader's "power" or "weaken" it?

The authors identify several stages that successful women leaders cum inheritors of wealth tend to go through:

- Making the choice to challenge some of their families' established core cultures. This might include dealing with strong bonds with other family members, perhaps most often with their fathers, integrating their own

sense of self (above all, idiosyncratic interests), and views regarding formal education, often seen as effective vehicles to challenge established family cultures.
- Entering the family enterprise. This might be linked to handling particular challenges, such as finding ways to coexist with other siblings, including perhaps having to buy them out, and so on.
- Balancing business and family relationships. Transforming one's family culture and norms represents perhaps a significant aspect of this.
- Moving into leadership. To take over the CEO role from a father, or a mother, might be necessary in order to take one's place in a forthright way.

To attempt to impact strong family governance so as to enhance family harmony and unity could perhaps often be a significant task for women leaders who are inheritors of wealth. This may include developing practices for shared decision-making within a family. Also, it could comprise instilling shared educational activities within a given family. Good family governance might imply:

- To focus on governance that is "creative" in nature so as to stimulate self-discovery and self-realization, in contrast to governing procedures that could be overly focused on control, or to "maintain the status quo."
- To find a leadership style, reflecting the way a family governance process is implemented, that might be seen as truly unique for a given family.
- To assure that family and work are complementary, equally important, aspects of a family's governance. Thus, a female leader cum inheritor of wealth might need to be prepared to handle both business and family.
- To nurture openness and opportunity-seeking occasions when it comes to effective family governance approaches.

There are some big lessons here. The main point for effective women leaders of wealthy families, whether new to such wealth or inheritors of wealth, seems to be explicit and clear regarding how to split the focus between work and the home (raising children in particular). This should not be seen as a dilemma to be avoided or delayed, however. There are several factors for successful women leaders to deal with this conundrum:

- Encourage self-discovery, concentrating on finding new ways of achieving a good work/home balance, rather than seeing this as a major problem.

- Refresh and model values. This seems to have a lot to do with impacting family members to embrace the ways to balance the work/home balance conundrum.
- Teach a stewardship mindset; How to pass on values to the next generations, rather than on "owning" as such, might ameliorate many sources of resistance from various other family members.
- Maintain an entrepreneurial spirit, and a successful woman leader must embody this fully.
- Stay together as a family, if possible, thus calling for moderating a female leader's business approaches if so needed.
- Play a key mentoring role. The successful female leader might have a main task when it comes to this, illustrating what it might take to adjust to specific work/family tradeoffs.
- "When in doubt, do the right thing," to quote General Schwarzkopf's famous slogan. The successful woman leader might wish to highlight "right" decisions when it comes to dealing with core work/family dilemmas.

Mitzi Perdue, (2021), The Frank Perdue Way: Simple Steps. Super Success, Tremendous (Reviewed December 2021)

This review discusses what made Mr. Frank Purdue so successful, building the world's largest poultry growing and producing businesses, privately held, of course! A strong sense of focus, keeping things as simple as possible, is seen as a primary success factor. Frugality is a part of this, an insight that some family business leaders seem to have forgotten!

This book chronicles what Frank Perdue did, which made him so successful! While there are many books on successful business leaders, this book is unique in that it is written by Mr. Perdue's widow, thus providing us with an exceptionally close view of what kind of person Mr. Perdue seemed to have been. Mr. Perdue built what became the world's largest chicken processing firm, privately owned. Today, the firm that he built has sales in more than 50 countries and employs more than 20,000 people.

The author, Mitzi Perdue, is a well-known professional writer and TV host, with particular interests in environmental issues as well as in family business.

Frank Perdue used several approaches to achieve success, and effectively, taken together they seem to have worked.

- Listen well. It takes a certain humility to be a good listener. It is essential to be open-minded and flexible so as to be able to make fast adjustments where improvements might be made. By being a good listener, one might also be able to build loyalty amongst team members so that more talented executives might stay on in the organization.
- Build a solid organizational culture. This should largely be founded on "human"" values such as supporting one's people, celebrating with the team, paying attention to names, and so on.
- Strong leadership so that the team might see critical issues the same way as the leader. Critical issues in this respect might be manifested by giving people credit when deserved, to encourage broad "ownership" of ideas. Again, a good leader should be flexible and open to change when merited. Or, as Mr. Perdue apparently said, "a business that doesn't change, is a business that is going to die."
- Create and develop a sturdy network. To make contacts with people is particularly important. These contacts should be as powerful as possible and be seen as meaningful. And, when promising something, then always follow up. When in meetings, one should try to interact with as many different people as possible. Networking is a vital skill, as Mitzi Perdue says.
- Learn, learn, learn… Learning is another effective way to become inspired to get good ideas. All ways of learning will do—reading, listening, attending lectures, and so on. It is important to actively try to obtain helpful information relating to a particular project that one might be working on. It costs nothing to ask! Specialists, suppliers, and customers are typically good sources for this type of learning. But even competitors might at times be willing to share key information. The task of learning should have a broad focus. Seemingly irrelevant issues might prove to be useful in some future settings or at least be an inspiration for creative thinking. One should do whatever it takes to make one's aptitude for learning as strong as possible—read a lot, scan newsletters, have a good coach for mentoring, and so on.
- Be frugal. To keep a low profile is recommended. There should be no spending to show off. One should live relatively modestly, not be excessive when it comes to the choice of one's car, use public transportation where possible, fly economy class, and so on. It comes down to the dictum of spending less than one earns. It is important to have "free" liquidity that might be drawn on when opportunities arise, a critical part of running any business, including family firms, as well as when it comes to managing one's personal economy. This is a good way to take advantage of opportunities!

The book now concludes with a discussion of how to put together what might be labeled one's "ethical will," not only to leave a legacy but also so as to guide future generations and perhaps even be a source for future strategizing within the family firm. According to the author, the inspiration for Frank Perdue to put together his ethical will came from the observation that wealth without values tends to lead to unhappiness. So, an ethical will should reflect the principal values of the person who is putting it all together. And the process of creating such an ethical will might serve as a good way to clarify one's core values.

For an ethical will to be effective, it should also be relatively simple, say, containing maximum ten points or so. Mitzi Perdue reports how Frank Perdue started out with a much broader draft, around 50 issues! But "strategy means choice," so after hard deliberations, Mr. Perdue ended up with a final ethical will with only ten primary points.

It is perhaps above all an issue of being inspired. Such inspiration might lead to clearer direction and increased energy. It is never too late to be inspired to become better and better! This might be a fitting way of summarizing Frank Perdue!

A good strategy is indeed equal to a cohesive set of principles. This is reminiscent of another successful entrepreneur cum leader of a family business, namely Ingvar Kamprad, the founder of IKEA. Principles such as those outlined are what can be equated with business success, much more than the typical principles that we might find in most textbooks on strategy, the five forces model, SWOT analysis, dominant market share, and so on.

Tom A. Rüsen, Heiko Kleve & Arist von Schlippe, (2021), Managing Business Family Dynasties, Springer (Reviewed December 2021)

This book analyzes what seems to be highly critical for the long-term success of family business dynasties (the authors label them dynastic business families) and has analyzed more than 50 German-based business families. It seems to come down to several forms of caring, both for the family and for the business: caring for family members, prudent dividend payouts, and liberal but realistic views on reinvesting in the business. Proper governance processes, including information sharing and even IT-based processes to make it easy for all to assess the state of the business, play a significant role.

This book reports on research carried out by three members of the staff of the Witten Institute of Family Business, Witten/Heidecke University, Germany. The primary aim of this research project was to come up with a business model for how so-called "dynasty" business families are managed. A dynastic business family is defined as one with at least 50 family business owners. As of today, according to the researchers, there might be relatively few such dynastic business families, but still more than 30 in Germany alone! There are also examples of dynastic business families that are reported to be much larger than the 50-member minimum cutoff. The authors cite the French de Wendel family, with more than 1000 members, and the Belgian Solvay family, with more than 2300 members. In Germany itself, the Henkel Group is owned by more than 450 family members.

Tom A. Rüsen is the managing director of the Witten Institute for Family Business (WIFU) and an honorary professor at Witten/Heidecke University. Heiko Kleve is a sociologist and the holder of an endowed professorial chair at the Witten/Heidecke University. Arist von Schlippe, an experienced psychotherapist and professor of leadership and dynamics of family enterprise, is also at Witten/Heidecke University.

The study that is reported took place between 2017 and 2019, when 13 persons from seven dynastic families agreed to be interviewed, and with a narrative sociology methodology.

The authors make useful distinctions between three types of family firms: nuclear families, classified as (1.0), which relates to the founding families of a privately held business, typically relatively small when it comes to the numbers; formally organized families (2.0), which relates to the owners of a now slightly larger, mostly older family business. Various formal governance structures are typically implemented in such firms and the number of family members on the ownership side tends to be larger; dynastic business families (3.0), where the owning family counts at least 50 people, and where various forms of network-like approaches prevail when it comes to regulating relationships among the owners.

There seem to be three separate "logics" that can be observed when it comes to how dynastic family businesses operate: social cohesion, i.e., how a dynastic family holds together; the formal organizational structure that might have been put in place to regulate relationships among members of a dynastic family; and networks, typically widely ramified, for holding together a dynastic family.

Underlying the fact that these three ways of keeping dynastic families together might also be a strong will to hold a family business together, often widely shared, i.e., based on a broad belief that main assets are to be handed over from one generation to the next.

To "stick together" is seen as important by many, in the sense that this might lead to significant business opportunities, not available for smaller family businesses. Some challenges regarding this are: to come up with an "inclusive" committee structure that provides an opening for widely shared participation; a well-developed approach to internal communication; the development of relevant business competences for those members of the family that might be selected to serve in management—and/or in various committee positions; dividend policies, but so that differentiations might be made depending on size of ownership, as well as degree of active input in the running of the given family business; how to resolve specific conflicts. A seemingly quite common paradox here often seems to be that, while "troublemakers" often tend to own a relatively small share of a given family business only, they tend to "consume" a lot of time and attention; to pick up main impulses from society, when it comes to changes in heritage rules, gender and race legislation in taxation, and so on.

To develop effective committee structures that also open up for wide participation, so as to improve practice good governance in dynastic families, is seen as critical. "Competence-driven" selection for selectively involving individuals where they might have the most positive impact seems to be quite typical.

Communication is a basic ingredient in social life. For well-functioning dynastic business families, the quality of communication must obviously be good. Also, however, "the more the better, as much as possible" seems to be a mantra here. Communication among generations may be particularly essential. To be open to communication in a widely understood language is also critical. It is, of course, both a business consideration and a way to maintain widely shared family values that make effective communication so key, but equally hard to achieve.

When it comes to competence development and assignment of qualified individuals to various tasks, there are useful discussions of requirement profiles for positions to be filled, with factual, social, and "time" dimensions of competences; distinguishing between various types of personal commitments—career, private life, role as a shareholder; various forms of motivation—sense of duty; purpose; money; specific criteria for selection—business logic; family logic; political logic, as well as assessment of personality traits—rationality/cognition; emotional profile/empathy; performance/action orientation.

There may also be major challenges when it comes to the distribution of assets (dividends). There tends to be several areas of tension in wealth management of many dynastic business families. It all comes down to balancing several forms of caring: restrictive: taking care of various family members, who, as quid pro quos, are expected to be loyal to the family; moral: the calls for individuals to be prudent, with relatively modest lifestyles. Dividend payouts might thus be relatively moderate, more like a trustee mentality; liberal: for shareholders to get access to an abundance of wealth, and thus with relatively large dividend payouts, more of an investor mentality.

To cope with conflicts in dynastic business families is fundamental. Here are several specific causes of conflict:

- The overall economic situation, i.e., how to deal with "business crises."
- Transition to the next generation.
- Selection of individuals for management and/or committee positions.
- "Troublemakers"—how to handle them.
- Adjustment in share ownership ratios.
- Conflicts between various sides of a dynastic family.
- So-called tribal conflicts. This cause of conflict seems to be quite similar to what has been discussed immediately above.

Then in the concluding chapter, the authors provide an overall synthesis for how to create a viable strategy for a dynastic business family. Perhaps most important here is to devise a way to counteract centrifugal dynamics so that the family might continue to dominate the family business. Bonding and motivation are of utmost importance, and all within a large family network. The authors specifically raise seven (again!) strategic challenges:

- To develop a design for how to effectively manage a dynastic family as a network.
- To delineate forms of communication that keep the focus on major business decisions.
- To select and motivate qualified family members, also so that these are motivated.
- To construct a way to make new types of investments for the dynastic business family, i.e., to encourage a move towards a portfolio business strategy. Special committees to assess and implement such diversification might be established.
- To develop a differentiated logic for including a growing variety of family archetypes to preserve family cohesion.

- To establish proper IT and data processes to make it easier for family members to track the "state" of the family business.

A test to determine whether a dynastic family strategy is working might be to "look at the large group as a whole, but at the same time keep an eye on each individual member…".

24

Executive Profiles of Business Leaders

Carole Hübscher, President Caran d'Ache (Interviewed April 2020)

Carol Hübscher is the chairperson of one of the world's leading art materials and writing instrument companies, with around 50% of its business from the artist sector and the rest from retail (office and private). The importance of quality and innovation are highlighted, both typical, it seems, for Swiss-based firms.

Caran d'Ache was founded in 1915 in Geneva and has been majority owned by the Schweizer family since 1924. The company is now directed by Carole Hubscher, representing the 4th generation of the family and involved at the top level of the firm's decision-making since the 1930s. The name Caran d'Ache is the translation of "pencil" in Russian! The company's business falls into two parts: writing instruments, ranging from classic ball pens such as the 849 or unique luxury pieces, and Beaux-Arts or colors, which covers coloring-related items for artists, as well as for hobbyists and amateurs. The company employs 300 people in Geneva, representing around 90 different know-hows.

The company is a stock-based entity, with the President of Caran d'Ache, Carole Hübscher. Her sisters, cousins, and another family are among the shareholders. Ms. Hübscher has been President of Caran d'Ache since 2012. She was educated at a Swiss hotel management school and then worked for a while for Caran d'Ache USA, the distributor of Caran d'Ache in the USA, and a corporation independent from its parent. She went on to further education at Harvard, for then to return to Switzerland, where she first worked for Mr. Hayek, the Swatch Group, in its joint venture with Calvin Klein in the watch business segment. Ms. Hübscher felt that her experience in the watch business was particularly helpful for a better understanding of branding. After four years she started then her own consulting company, with a focus on branding and retailing. Then she joined Caran d'Ache, first as a board member and, as noted, as President from 2012 onwards.

The philosophy of Caran d'Ache is based on a long-term vision. This implies that all manufacturing, except for a small leather good business for making covers for writing instruments, is based in Geneva, with nothing located in the so-called low-cost countries. The company's wide variety of products are all made in-house. Thus, Caran d'Ache controls all manufacturing know-hows that are critical for the company. Other aspects regarding the firm's long-term philosophy can be seen when it comes to the company's choice of only top-quality raw materials, as well as for its emphasis on sustainability. This is all part of Caran d'Ache's unwritten contract with the consumers: top quality, sustainability, and superb functionality.

The focus on reuse and recycling is thus a principal feature in Caran d'Ache's long-term philosophy. This takes many forms. For instance, through a joint venture with Nespresso, the company makes use of recycled aluminum from coffee capsules, making these for the casings of its upper-scale ballpoint pens. To use wood waste and dust from its pencil manufacturing operations for heating is another example.

Ms. Hübscher spends a good part of her time in interacting with consumers. She feels that this helps her to better understand their needs and changing preferences. Four classes of main issues seem to be emerging from this, above all:

- Changes in distribution seem to be particularly critical. And, while Caran d'Ache started its own online shop already eight years ago, and virtual distribution is going well, this move is, perhaps, particularly significant these days with the pandemic threat issues being an issue. It should be noted here that the company's products in general are well known, as well as relatively compact in size and easy to understand. Thus, there is, for instance, little to no need for the consumer to try the products out at home, for then to potentially return some of these. In short, virtual shopping seems to be well suited for Caran d'Ache's offerings.
- To communicate with consumers in actual purchase settings, in-stores are important. Traditionally Caran d'Ache has worked largely through distributors. Most of the store outlets are upper-end department stores, as well as book or paper stores, art stores, and specialty stores for writing instruments. The shop-in-shop concept is also well developed. Caran d'Ache has also

always had its own shops, however. Today we count two in downtown Geneva, and one at each of the following locations: Geneva Airport, Zurich, Tokyo, Berlin, and Lausanne. These are locations where Caran d'Ache can further strengthen direct communication with the consumer. They do not only serve as product outlets, where customers can interact with the firm, but also as educational entities for art education. Artists are coming to these stores and often discuss their experiences when it comes to the use of various Caran d'Ache products. Incidentally, Carand d'Ache now also offers virtual courses in response to the pandemic.

- The Caran d'Ache website. Although it has been there for a long time, the website has been redesigned around one year ago and gives the management of the company relevant insights about emerging consumer preference shifts and needs. According to Ms. Hübscher, this has inspired the company to come up with several new direct innovative product ideas.
- There is a rapid advent of emerging IT technology, such as laptops, email, and mobile phones—and this could have had a negative impact on writing. But reality tells us a different story! There is no doubt that mankind's mode of communication is changing dramatically, with more email interactions on iPads, mobile phones, etc. perhaps resulting in less conventional writing. Still, the act of writing remains a strong reality! There will now be a more exclusive activity, which underscores that the sender is actually taking care and spending sufficient time! On top of this, everyone would own a pencil anyhow and/or a ballpoint pen. And most people still know how to write! Writing is partly becoming an act of exclusivity, partly an act of writing short daily notes.

As noted, the company's business can be broadly divided into two parts, more or less equal in size: fine arts/colors and writing instruments. Thus, the company's range of products is indeed broad! And, as noted, all of these products are made at the plant in Geneva. There is a wide base of know-how residing in the company in order to make it a reality to produce this wide array of quality products.

There is also a strong focus on in-house training to maintain this array of knowledge. Caran d'Ache is one of the few remaining producers of pencils in Europe, with in-house training being the only option when it comes to remaining on top of relevant technologies.

To maintain efficiency is, of course, also key. Employees are themselves also strongly encouraged to come up with better ways with the dictum being "good can often be made even better."

Caran d'Ache has become an integral part of Geneva and Switzerland. There are at least three corollaries here:

- All manufacturing is done in Switzerland, as noted, and in line with the company's focus on the upper end of the prestige and quality scale.
- The company image is thus one of exclusivity, consistent with the image of Switzerland as a high-quality producer. As noted, only the best raw materials are used. There are many similarities between Caran d'Ache and other luxury brands. Still, the company has resisted any attempts to broaden its product line into other areas through building on its strong brand. Focus on its high-quality niche is seen as central!
- The firm's staff of 300 represent a stable part of the company, with the average employment tenure being more than twelve years. This is part of Caran d'Ache's top-quality/exclusive profile.

A strong focus on innovation is critical to most Swiss-based firms to stay competitive, so also for Caran d'Ache. Here is how:

- There are two Research and Development groups, one for the Fine Arts business and one for writing instruments. Both groups are closely linked to their customer bases.
- There is thus close contact with the exceptionally loyal customer base.
- The employees' ongoing efforts to always improve are also fundamental. The long tenure for employees does not seem to hamper the employees' ability to stay open-minded and to adapt. The workforce sees this as essential!

There are six or more members from the next generation of family members, who all might potentially have future leadership roles in the company. But these persons are still young! The Chairperson is adamant that any of these who might want to enter the firm in the future must both wish it and want it, and they must be good! They must be interested and also prove that they deserve it! A leadership position is never just simply granted. These issues are openly discussed among the family stakeholders.

It should be noted that the CEO is a nonfamily member. He previously worked for the surveillance firm SGS and for the security ink company SICPA.

Caran d'Ache seems to be successful primarily for the following reasons: strong family values; with a long-term focus, as well as a committed leadership team; total focus on high-quality products; customer-driven initiatives for improvements appear a priority! Use of the best raw materials only; and to reuse/recycle whenever possible; a strong brand and image, and a great team of employees behind this; innovation, not only in products but also in distribution, so as to maintain the highest quality and relevance; and finally, a stable workforce.

Carl Elsener, CEO of Victorinox (Interviewed May 2019)

This family-owned Swiss company with its iconic, world-famous Swiss Army pocketknives, is also active when it comes to kitchen knives, luggage, watches, and fragrances. It successfully combines top-quality manufacturing (Swiss made) in Schwyz, Switzerland, with global marketing.

Carl Elsener is the fourth-generation leader of the family firm Victorinox, a world leader in producing the iconic Swiss Army knife (35% of sales), cutlery and travel gear (each close to 25% of sales), watches (15% of sales) and fragrances (3% of sales). Selling in over 120 countries through 14 subsidiaries and with 2,100 employees worldwide, the Victorinox group generated a turnover nearing 500 million Swiss francs in 2018. The company was founded in 1884 by Carl Elsener's great-grandfather, with the same name. The first soldier's knife was delivered to the Swiss Army in 1891, and the company's relationship with this long-standing customer remains strong to this day.

Carl Elsener joined the company at the age of 20 and became the CEO at 49. He is the second oldest of 11 siblings. In 2000, all of his family members transferred their shares in the company to the company foundation that controls 90% of the company. 18 family members currently work in the company. The identity of Elsener's successor remains to be determined, but it will probably be a family member, as long as he/she is fully motivated; has the necessary talents to run a large, complex, multinational corporation; shares the family's values and long-term focus, especially regarding a strong team orientation; maintains family unity; and is genuine and modest. Only family members who work in the company receive financial compensation (i.e., salaries). The executive board consists of five family members and six nonfamily members.

The key milestones of Victorinox's century-long history include:

- 1909: The world-famous "cross and shield" emblem was patented.
- 1921: The name Victorinox was adopted.
- 1989: The firm entered the watch business.

- 1999: The company entered the travel gear business.
- 2000: The family foundation was established. 90% of all shares in the company are owned by this foundation, which is controlled by the Elsener family. 10% of the shares are held in a charitable foundation.
- 2001: Sales of the Swiss Army knife dropped by 30% in the aftermath of the 9/11 terrorist attacks. Diversification gained momentum.
- 2005: Victorinox acquired its main competitor, Wenger (Delemont), and entered through this acquisition also into the fragrance business.
- 2017: The firm discontinued the fashion business to focus on its other core categories.
- 2020: Opening of the new European distribution center.

When asked about Victorinox's success factors, Mr. Elsener pointed out the following:

- Employees. Employment at Victorinox is on a long-term basis. Employees are encouraged to speak up, seek continuous improvement, and stay innovative. Training is emphasized.
- Customers. The key here is to be customer-oriented and to bring them products they consider having superior value. It is essential to build upon the positive perception of Swiss design and quality.
- Products. Since its inception, Victorinox has continuously focused on always innovating and pushing for improvements. The brand's value is thus based on superior quality, functionality, innovation, and iconic design. Sustainability is another central part of the products and the firm's production processes.
- Brand. The Swiss Army knife clearly seems to be a driver of the firm's brand. For instance, it has won several awards and is even used in NASA's space missions.
- Corporate values. The organization as a whole feels committed to its values: "honesty, trust, gratitude, respect, modesty, courage and responsibility." Mr. Elsener added that "serving our fellow human beings around the world with practical, functional and competitively priced quality products gives our lives a deeper meaning and enjoyment and is at the heart of Victorinox's job satisfaction."

Mr. Elsener emphasizes the key importance of learning from experience, especially regarding the firm's internal workings. He points out the critical importance of improving internal best practices. His father played a primary role here, with a strong focus on "how to make good even better." But adapting to market changes entrepreneurially is perhaps equally important. Inputs from global customers are critical too, another main source of learning. It is a matter of balanced learning!

As noted, a long-term financial perspective underpins Victorinox's core values. A related aspect of this long-term focus is to invest relatively heavily during recessions while perhaps holding back on investments during economic booms. This approach has manifested itself in several ways, such as to make do with spending more versus spending less on various factors, as a consequence of the specific stages of economic cycles.

For instance, when Victorinox's own business activities dipped after the 9/11 terrorist attacks, some employees were outsourced to other companies that were fortunate enough to have good order backlogs. However, the employees were still being provided salaries from Victorinox, which in turn billed these other companies for this "service." The results were not only to secure job stability for Victorinox but also to improve employee motivation and loyalty as well as to benefit from learning from other firms.

While countercyclical investments were routinely made by Victorinox, at the same time, there were strong sentiments against taking too high of a risk (i.e., always try to avoid overinvesting). Such financial overextension by Victorinox's competitor Wenger was perhaps the main reason why Victorinox was able to take it over in 2005.

Victorinox's strong long-term focus was also demonstrated when the company took over its US "partner" (originally in Shelton, CT, and now in Monroe, CT). When this partner company went public in 1980 and subsequently abandoned its obligations to Victorinox—the partner cited short-term profit motives—Victorinox started purchasing available shares. After having acquired around 30% of its shares, Victorinox made the decision to acquire the rest of this company. General economic conditions also blew in the Swiss company's favor. This entity has since become Victorinox's wholly owned subsidiary. Long-term economic thinking prevailed at Victorinox!

Mr. Elsener also cites many banks as not in effect supporting a countercyclical strategy. Rather, they often seem keen to provide funds during good times but are perhaps not equally committed to stand by clients during difficult times. Accordingly, Victorinox is very restrictive when it comes to drawing on bank loans.

The firm's location in Ibach, a relatively small community in central Switzerland, is seen as a stabilizing factor. This valley, surrounded by high mountains, seems to create a positive outlook among the firm's working population. However, as noted, it is also important to maintain an open mind so as to spot global shifts and new trends. Once again, balance is essential, i.e., to stay grounded but be open-minded! This attitude is perhaps reflected in what is sometimes labeled "the Swiss way" of hard work, strong discipline, and a modest character.

Mr. Elsener emphasizes two factors as particularly important in becoming a good leader: Being a role model (modesty, open-mindedness, fairness, etc.). Above all, this is perhaps a function of the fact that a good leader must like people and also be authentic! Above all, how can this trait help innovation in a family business? Authentically gauging, meeting, and exceeding the customers' expectations is essential, by discovering new things in new cultures and interacting with new groups of young people!

Victorinox has developed a business model that, in many ways, might be seen to reflect the best of family-owned firms: a long-term focus; countercyclical behavior; strong teams ("we, we, we"!); the "family is all" in contrast to the "me, me, me" attitude; and strong focus on quality in design, production, and marketing.

25

Closing Remarks for the Part

So, what are the main insights a family business may provide other family-owned or family-run businesses? Is it to maintain a sense of core values? Focus on the long term? Is it to do good, give back? And can these insights be useful to nonfamily businesses, regardless of size, geography, culture, and sector? We think so. Lessons are everywhere. What is important is to stay curious, look for inspiration at every corner, and use the experiences and perspectives of others when running and growing our own organizations.

Perhaps the most critical for us is the absence of having to satisfy the investor community through the generation of steady quarterly earnings. This not only opens up for the issues raised above but importantly allows for pursuing strategies with payoffs some time further into the future.

It is worthwhile observing that there seems to be a growing agreement regarding the main benefits of being (or going) private! This category of firms has indeed become relatively much more prominent over the last few years. And this has called for the advent of another group of successful managers. The success formula is shifting!

Family businesses are not only very common but are also often claimed to be quite successful, even when comparing such firms to publicly traded firms. Family businesses often outperform public firms. Why? The main reason is the long-term horizon that characterizes the family firms, relatively free from short-term pressures. Let us highlight these such areas.

There is no need to adhere to short-term financial pressure. There is simply no call for the delivery of quarterly earnings to impact a firm's stock price. Since family businesses are privately owned, with their shares traded privately and typically less frequently, this link to the financial markets is nonexistent, or at least much weaker. Family businesses are thus in a position to treat their financial side as long term.

Management also tends to be more stable. Family businesses are typically run by family members or by the executives nominated by the owning family. A sense of stability, valued and respected, is thus often found at the top.

A social focus may also prevail. Many family firms are closely associated with the local communities from where they operate. Social concerns are often apparent. Stability characterizes the relationship between such a firm and the society in which it operates. And here too, family firms are in it for the long term!

There is indeed another side to this too, however. It may be relatively harder for family businesses to downscale their workforce or even to close down and relocate their operations.

Part VI

Investing to Maximize Wealth: Value Creation and Growth

Wealth is created from creating value.
—Randy Gage, author and public speaker

Rule No 1: never lose money. Rule No 2: never forget rule No 1.
—Warren Buffett, investor, business leader and philanthropist

26

Practice Insights from Anders Endreson and Peter Lorange

How can we invest to maximize wealth? This is an important question for businesses as well as investor executives. Let us take a look at a few strategies and approaches gleaned from some investment experts. Their concepts and input can also help organizations and their leaders better assure long-term wealth maximization.

Francisco Paramés is widely considered one of the world's leading value investors. From 1994 to 2014 he had an average return on investment of 16%, which is more than double the return of the Madrid Stock Exchange of 7.8% in the same time frame. Paramés is often compared to Warren Buffett, while The Financial Times named Paramés the most successful fund manager in Spain.

To get to this success, Paramés followed a specific investment strategy focused on value investing. We have outlined Paramés investment approach below and provided some of our own observations on how to become a good investor.

Paramés' three dimensions of value investing:

- Apply the Austrian School of Economics approach to investments: this is a people-centric approach, with a particular focus on the individual creative entrepreneur and on rivalry among entrepreneurs.
- Invest in real assets with a long-term view—real estate, shares in companies, commodities, etc.
- Meaningfully incorporate risk in investment decisions.

To add to the three dimensions to value investing, Paramés also draws heavily on investment gurus such as Warren Buffett and Peter Lynch.

The Austrian School of Economics' relevance for successful value investing

The two most famous scholars of the Austrian School of Economics are certainly Ludwig von Mises and, the 1974 Economics Nobel Prize laureate, Friedrich Hayek. Other famous members of this group include Joseph Schumpeter, Fritz Machup, Gottfried von Harberler, and Eugene Böhm von Bawerk.

A central element in the Austrian School of Economics is the theory of human action, which gave rise to behavioral finance. The theory of human action can be broken down into nine main ideas specifically applicable to the investment process:

- The market works and is reliable. If needed, there is always the choice to exit.
- The market is never in an equilibrium, thus allowing the investor to invest when the market is low and exit when the market is high.
- Economic growth is financed by savings. It is best to invest in markets where the rate of savings is high.
- A short-term sacrifice must be made in order to achieve greater economic value in the future. Having a long-term horizon is crucial.
- The control of interest rates by the central bank impacts the nation's currency. Stay away from investing in markets where growth is primarily a result of artificially low interest rates.
- Deflation will occur when there is no artificial injection of the amount of money in circulation. Investing in housing assets, with little to no debt, is a good investment strategy in deflationary situations.
- A currency will permanently depreciate in relation to real assets. Accordingly, always invest in real assets.
- Product price determines cost. First, calculate demand, then the costs necessary to meet the demand.
- Production cost is subjective. Do not take cost as a given.

Real assets reflect ownership. Equity offers both greater returns and less long-term risk. Exposure to stocks, on the other hand, is attained either through passive management (via Index Funds or Exchange-Traded Funds) or through active management.

- Successful passive management depends on:
- Selection of low-cost funds.
- Wise choice of advisors (and they are typically expensive!).

- A thorough analysis of a fund and, especially, of its performance.
- Avoid the advice of guru investors.

Successful active management depends on the valuation of assets; for example, by applying the Capital Pricing Asset Model. When investing in funds, can an active manager do better than a passive manager? Active managers follow several key principles that enhance their success. However, in the end, Paramés believes that the best option is a combination of index funds, the investment choices of active managers, and stock picks to "keep us on our toes!"

Rules of thumb from some of the most accomplished active investors

Benjamin Graham: Buy shares in companies where the stock price is lower than the company's liquidation value/intrinsic value.

Phil Fisher: Invest in stocks with a long-term growth projection, robust competition advantages (moat), and the capacity of sustainable growth over time. The price you pay is not that important; if the company performs well, it will be able to sustain a high multiple.

Joe Greenblatt: Look for quality shares at a favorable price. These will always outperform other stocks. Quality is key!

Warren Buffett (and Charles Munger): Invest in stocks as if buying the whole company with the ideal holding period being indefinite.

Buffett's strategy prefers buying in the markets rather than via IPOs. He invests in stable businesses, where there is a relatively low chance of major changes in market conditions. For this reason, he has typically stayed away from tech firms. Buffett generally focuses on quality businesses, i.e., companies with a high return on capital employed (ROE).

Buffett believes that there should be an appropriate separation between shareholders and management, with a clear delegation of responsibilities. Moreover, directors should own significant amounts of stock in the company where they serve on the board. Thus, incentivizing their remuneration through the company's performance rather than receiving large fixed remuneration in their capacity as board members.

Buffett does not put much emphasis on growth plans. He also warns against making acquisitions for the sake of growth. He warns to watch out for managers who overpay simply to gain mass. What matters is the quality of the eventual acquisitions.

As noted, Buffett's focus is on the long-term; as a result, he typically does not have an exit plan. In line with this, he sees it as an advantage when there is a stable shareholder base.

Companies to avoid:

Paramés identifies nine factors that make companies less attractive:

- An excessive growth-focus
- Companies that are constantly acquiring other companies
- IPOs
- Businesses still in their infancy
- Questionable accounting (and poor governance)
- Overdependence on one or a few key employees
- Heavily indebted companies
- Stagnating or falling sales in a firm's business
- Overly expensive stocks

Factors to focus on when determining a good investment opportunity:

Ultimately, the only thing that matters is "earnings, earnings, earnings," as Peter Lynch said. Paramés recommends the following criteria when assessing investment opportunities:

- Careful analysis of a firm's financial statements.
- Cash flow analysis.
- Credibility of the income statement.
- The balance sheet.
- Careful estimation of a firm's normalized earnings.
- Where are we in the economic cycle for this firm?
- Has there been a disruption to supply or demand, or is there a risk of this?
- Is the firm still in its infancy?

Above all, one should focus on the inherent quality of a stock and have a long-term time horizon and a stable, predictable context within which to operate.

The concept of risk:

Warren Buffett defines risk as the possible loss of long-term purchasing power. To avoid this, he advocates analyzing:

- A business's long-term characteristics (customer, suppliers, competitors, technology, etc.)

- Management's ability to optimize the business and its ability to effectively reinvest earned profits as well as to remunerate shareholders.
- The purchasing price.
- Inflation and tax levels.

In Buffett's opinion, these four factors determine risk, and not the share price volatility.

Accordingly, an investment's risk is the possibility of a permanent loss of purchasing power as the result of making an error of judgment.

Final pieces of advice from Paramés:

- Look where others are not looking. Go beyond the superficial and commonplace.
- It is better to own assets than be a creditor.
- Invest in what you know and know your limits.
- Have patience and think long term. Often it is best to do nothing. Stick with your strategy and do not let noise disturb you.
- Focus on the quality of the business. Invest in companies you can hold for twenty years.
- Study the companies and not the stock market. Buying a share should be like buying the whole company.
- Prefer established businesses with a long, successful track record.
- Speculators, volatility, and/or liquidity shortages often lead to good purchasing opportunities and good value.
- Buy what nobody else is buying.
- Favor companies that are partly family owned. A majority of the companies Paramés invests in are family owned. Family-owned businesses think for generations. They are long term, and they focus on long-term value creation.
- When you find a company you like, you can start with a small investment. As your confidence for the company grows and you begin to trust the management, the company strategy, and the financial growth and development, you can slowly begin to increase your investment.

Lastly, a final piece of advice: Invest all your savings that are not needed in the immediate future in shares.

With several decades of demonstrated performance to show for it, Paramés is credible in his advice. Experience counts!

In addition to what we have reviewed above, we also would like to turn your attention to some other aspects of investing that are important to becoming a good investor:

On noise. In the world of today, with unlimited flow of information, it is easy to "be taken for a ride" and be influenced by the last piece of news read in the newspaper. Try not to be influenced by such noise. Store it and consider it together with all the other information you have gathered and digested.

On portfolio construction, it is important to construct a portfolio that suits you and your family's situation for the short term and long term. The less need you have for short-term dividend, the more long-term shares you can have in your investment portfolio.

On index funds. The authors of this article do not follow Paramés in his advice on index funds. Index funds are bound to invest in all shares in the index, even the most expensive and overbought shares. To give you an up-to-date example: would you be willing to invest heavily in TESLA shares at their current value? We guess not. However, if you were to invest in index funds, you would have to.

On following the herd. Don't be influenced by what everyone else is doing. Make up your own conclusions after having studied the alternatives. Trust figures, especially historic figures. Most often figures don't lie.

On moats. Historically, companies with good moats have had them for many years. But in today's world, the moats do not last as long as before. For this reason, it is important that you focus on the company's future strategy, the quality of its management, the company's ability to reach its goals, and your own expectations for the company. Is the company likely to do well long term and develop new moats?

On costs. Pay attention to the cost that your asset manager is charging. By paying too much for asset management services, you will lose return on your portfolio and, as the years pass by, the monetary loss will be considerable due to the compounded interest principle.

As a final remark, allow us to share our best advice on investing: That is to read. Read a lot. Read every day. Reading is one of the best investments you can do for yourself. As Charlie Munger put it: "Spend each day trying to be a little wiser than when you woke up."

27

Introduction to Investing to Maximize Wealth: Value Creation and Growth

We have looked closely at a few family businesses and family business topics and can now move towards the vast and exciting discussion of investing to maximize wealth, clearly of importance to all categories of firms, including, as we saw in the previous chapter, also for family firms. Although an enormous topic and, at times, very subjective, there are certain investment strategies that appear to be more successful than others. Issues such as risk propensity and appetite for this, choice of different investment vehicles, picking investment advisors, and so on, are all important elements of the overall investment decisions you could face. Understanding the complex world of investing is critical in order to achieve growth.

Thus, it goes without saying that investing, so as to allow for the pursuance of particular projects, is at the very core of strategy implementation. Making commitments is important. The fact that such decisions, with these types of commitments, often are irreversible adds to this challenge!

The business factors we identified that are tied into this Part are finance (including management systems, treasury, foreign exchange, blockchain, cryptocurrencies, bitcoin, digital banking, handling, and tracking) and impact investment. Also, long-term focus and speed come up here as critical elements. The readings selected all treat or include mentions of these issues in some way or reference.

Here are some takeaways that you can expect from this section:

- Cycle management: in/out, timing, exits, nos.

- Risk-taking, based on thorough analysis: what can we impact? Expert teams, close to the action.
- New geographies, such as expansion in Asia/Africa. This entails impact investing.

28

Essential Books to Learn About Investing to Maximize Wealth: Value Creation and Growth

Max Gunther, (1985), The Zürich Axioms, Harriman Classics (Reviewed January 2022)

This book discusses how leading bankers seem to deal with issues such as risk and chaos. A total of twelve axioms are provided for how these leading bankers appear to operate. Positivism and optimism are seen as especially important.

The author has identified eleven so-called "principles" for how Swiss bankers might tend to invest. These so-called axioms are, in part at least, based on observations from the author's father who was head of the US branch of Schweizische Bankverein, then Switzerland's second largest bank (now part of UBS). The author was a leading US business journalist who worked for several leading US publications and had written several best-selling books and scores of feature articles. He passed away in 1998.

One shall, of course, have to take some risks in order to make money to place some bets if one expects to do well over time. But to do this in an orderly way is paramount! The eleven axioms are all about having a good, thorough process for investing.

To worry about outcomes when taking risks is normal. Worrying might indeed be seen as a sort of enjoyment! A good investor is driven by a sense of adventure! To place meaningful bets is crucial, but no small "listening posts," not too much diversification. Focus is needed in order to build relevant competences and to learn. It is fundamental to find a good degree of balance between focus and diversification.

Another main principle is to take profit when one can, say, without waiting too long when a market is rising, thus risking to "tip over" and ending up falling into the other steep valley on the other side. "The market tolerates bull and bears, but not pigs." So, taking profit when one can is critical, not being driven by greed. To set some approximate targets for when to exit from an investment might be good. One should exit without any hesitation, "jump" whenever an investment might develop negatively, in comparison with what one might have planned for. While hesitation and procrastination might perhaps often be the more comfortable, it is usually better to cut losses sooner rather than later. So, no hesitations, no delays! To counteract feelings of regret, to be ready to abandon, and indeed admit that one might have made a mistake are important for being able to jump ship resolutely.

Be skeptical to forecasts! In reality, somewhat more akin to chaos is to be expected. Do not assume that things are orderly. It can be dangerous indeed to believe in too orderly patterns. One should avoid thinking that history repeats itself. To draw curves, graphs, and charts can add to false feelings of orderly patterns. The same might be the case when looking for correlations. A sound skepticism when it comes to believing in the power of various lead indicators is probably merited.

To have solid instincts is indeed good. Yet do not confuse an instinct with a hope. Steer away from wishful thinking! Do not expect miracles! While some degree of superstition might be accepted, this must never be allowed to take over. In the end one should stick to one's own thinking, reasoning, and instincts. Optimism is needed, but it is not enough. Confidence is also recommended. Constructive use of pessimism might however be called for to build confidence. To always have an exit is important, however.

To go with the majority shall typically be dysfunctional, i.e., no "flock-mentality." Disregard majority opinions. "Cogito, ergo sum," as Descartes said ("I think, therefore I am"). Stay away from speculative feels. Instead, attempt to look for relatively immediate positive outcomes or forget it! We know from discounting approaches that the value of positive money streams would be far less if it comes through only sometime in the distant future than sooner. So, an expectation of a relatively immediate payout is key!

Long-range planning should be considered with a healthy degree of skepticism. The power of long-term planning is to stimulate critical thinking, nothing more! As such, long-term plan outputs should not be taken as anything more than another mere set of inputs. What matters is the process applied in coming up with the plan documents.

These axioms are indeed quite firm recommendations regarding what to do and what not to do. Although all in all, these should never be interpreted as more than recommendations are meant to, namely as inputs for thinking, issues that it normally might make sense to think about before investing.

David F. Svensen (2005), Unconventional Success: A Fundamental Approach, Simon & Schuster (Reviewed September 2021)

Davis Svensen, the legendary head of Yale University's endowments and with an extraordinarily strong track record as an investor, points out the main attractiveness of going for equity investments (such as start-ups), the importance of paying attention to a properly diversified portfolio with several different asset classes (including real estate), and being cognizant of tax issues along with utilizing tax advantages. Svensen's approach seems to be quite analogous to what Dr. Lorange recommends, i.e., family portfolio businesses.

The author, David Svensen, was the chief investment officer at Yale University for more than three decades, where he generated an annual return on Yale's endowment of more than 16% per annum, having thereby gained the reputation as perhaps the most pre-eminent chief investment officer of not-for-profit institutional endowments.

Mr. Svensen's principal advice is to create an investment portfolio that is more broadly diversified; typically, passively managed, drawing on top-notch professional investment managers within the various classes of investments that are being pursued; trying to build an equity-minded portfolio; utilizing, where possible, good seeking managers, comfortable with working in the not-for-profit sector; and finally, to pay close attention to tax considerations.

The fallacy, in his view, of actively managed portfolios for most individual investors is critical, perhaps above all so when it comes to relatively smaller portfolios. And mutual funds may typically be biased in favor of large investors here. There are simply not enough good investment choices available to most investors. Truly attractive deals typically get funneled towards the largest investors, including big institutional ones. Also, Mr. Svensen points out that there tends to be a quite common extrapolatory tendency, a flock mentality, indicating that "good is expecting to continue virtually forever," or vice versa when it comes to downward trends. Thus, many independent investors end up getting in at the high end, for then to sell at the low end.

Mr. Svensen points out that developing an effective investment portfolio will have to be based on the following three principles: the importance of equity ownership, the efficacy of portfolio diversification, and the significance of tax sensitivity.

He highlights that one's basic portfolio should ideally be relatively stable and that high transaction costs might make it expensive to make changes in a fundamental portfolio. Dividends are always key for stocks, bonds, and the timing of the sale of assets. Most investors depend on a certain amount of such current cash flows, though.

There seem to be three fundamental sources for generating a value-enhancing investment portfolio:

- Asset allocation.
- Timing. To come up with long-term charter parties in shipping, for instance, rather than going short, i.e., asset play, is a common consideration when managing many asset classes.
- Security selection, i.e., valuation, so as to buy low, sell high, with a good likelihood of value appreciation.

Among the various classes of equities, Mr. Svensen seems to prefer high-yield equities such as particular stocks and real estate. He appears generally skeptical when it comes to bonds.

When discussing how to come up with which core asset classes to invest in, Mr. Svensen stresses that such assets must be able to produce basic differentiable characteristics, i.e., as uncorrelated as possible! And such assets should fundamentally be driven by market characteristics and not by having to put in a high degree of managerial efforts to create value from an asset. The availability of a well-functioning market is thus key! Many real estate deals, for instance, may involve too much work, indicating that fully effective market conditions might not be there! Also, it always seems to be advisable that a promoter of a particular "deal" might be an active investor in this given deal him/herself, i.e., to have "skin in the game."

Mr. Svensen highlights that to develop one's own investment portfolio might not only involve "science," i.e., applying relatively objective criteria for an asset's attractiveness, but also "art," i.e., reflecting an investor's preferences. The overall "risk" imbedded in a portfolio might tend to diminish as one's time horizon is shortened. It should be noted here that one might combine what now tends to be denoted risk versus uncertainty, i.e., the picking of undervalued assets (good risk propensities) and with relatively high upside potential (good uncertainty prospects). Various asset classes in a given portfolio shall, of course, tend to have different expected returns.

There seems to be skepticism when it comes to the so-called leveraged buy-outs. The risk relative to the returns in many such situations would not be meritable. Also, fees often tend to be too high. And, as promoters typically tend to launch larger and larger rounds of new projects, accelerating fee structures may now become unreasonable. One may also be on guard when it comes to too much venture capital.

Rebalancing a portfolio might often be difficult, even at times "painful," calling for the needs to act against the crowd. Tax consequences must of course be central when it comes to coping with such changes. Too "active" thinking by individual investors might not work too well. To go for carefully selected mutual funds may therefore be viable. If you can't beat them, join them, as the saying goes! So, to work with the so-called low-profit market funds such as Vanguard, Fidelity, or State Street might be the way to go. It should be noted that the above mutual funds should not be seen as nonprofit in the strict sense, but that they are not primarily going for profit maximization, rather simply covering their costs plus a reasonable margin. Most mutual market funds seem to basically fail, however, because of lack of consideration regarding tax, outrageous fees, excessive funding leading to earning too high commission on each trade, overvalued assets when it comes to assessing such firm's safety margins, kickbacks, and irresponsible redistribution of capital.

Alternative guidelines for how to work with mutual funds, i.e., all mutual funds, not only not-for-profit ones:

- Have a clear long-term strategy.
- Follow a relatively concentrated portfolio, and do not let a mutual fund invest in areas outside one's portfolio.
- Keep stability in the client base, i.e., which mutual fund to work with.
- Negotiate fair fees.
- "Insist" on substantial coinvestors by the mutual funds themselves, i.e., "skin in the game."
- Limit the size of each deal.
- Demand good communication.

Mohnish Pabrai (2007), The Dhandho Investor, Wiley (Reviewed September 2021)

This successful investor stresses the importance of picking firms that have a "defendable" advantage. The so-called Dhandho principle that he proposes includes going for stocks that represent low risk (i.e., defendable positions) but with high returns. However, it may be hard to find stocks that fit this prescription, but to undertake a one-at-a-time, in-depth analysis of stocks is advisable. It is all about learning!

How individuals can make better investments, particularly in stocks, is once more the key topic, particularly through the so-called value-based stock picking. The author is the managing partner of Pabrai Investment Funds, which has delivered exceptional returns to its investors for many years.

A mantra that seems to be practiced in investing in quite a similar style to gambling is: "Heads, I win; tails, I don't lose much." It is still a matter of picking investments when cycles are down. Those investments should be relatively "safe" and not involve the spending of too much cash. This implies low risk, and while the uncertainty might be high, there should still be clear limits to what one might lose.

Investments should be concentrated, not spread out so as to have basically a good understanding. To be disciplined regarding one's cash is also crucial, above all to reinvest most free cash as one grows, so as to minimize dilution. To try and assess an asset's future potential is important! This is hard enough when it comes to most stocks; hence, stick to relatively "simple" stocks.

The author points out that it is important with a defendable advantage; he labels this a "moot"! But such moots tend to disappear over time.

Investing might seem to be more or less like gambling. Thus, make only a few bets; when the odds are good, the stock value is down, but make these bets high and accept that such betting situations will typically only take place infrequently. One particularly attractive investment option for investors is to look for the so-called arbitrage advantages. Again, such advantages shall typically last for only a short time. Traditional commodity arbitrage typically comes to mind, but the author also discusses three other types, namely, correlated stocks, mergers, and the so-called Dhando spreads. For all these Dhando investments (low risk/high returns), there is a notion of a high margin of safety. The author points out that this, of course, is contrary to the commonly accepted dictum that high risk and high returns typically go together. The attractiveness of this Dhando approach is exactly that this common convention does not always hold!

So, how is this done? How are such Dhando investment opportunities found? The author is not very clear on this, except for looking for undervalued stocks or other opportunities and unloading some of this when the market/the valuation hopefully goes up, so that some of these investments can be off-loaded, i.e., a "free ticket," for the remaining holding. One should thus go for low risk when investing and accept that uncertainty may be high, i.e., when and whether the market might go up or not. One must not mix these two concepts: risk has to do with whether there is a "safety cushion," while uncertainty has to do with *future* accruals in the value of the object that one has invested in. And, as said, go for low risk and high uncertainty.

To invest in good concepts, i.e., cloning, rather than in innovations often seems to be associated with the above dictum. To scale good concepts more regularly seems to meet the Dhando criteria, i.e., ignore too much innovation! To look at businesses that have been hit hard, for one reason or another, might be good. And there should be relatively small executive teams of executives doing all of this. So-called "Polish Parliaments" and "discussion/debate clubs" may typically lead to inaction.

The exiting stage. Clear plans for this may ideally have been made already at the time of investing. And one should not despair in case of an immediate, latent potential loss. There tends to be an element of truth to the concept of keeping an asset over some time: it almost always comes back in value! If you have good alternative investments on hand, you may of course sell earlier to free up cash. But the general rule is "wait and see," not sell at a loss!

The author points out that to have a relatively good knowledge regarding the underlying facts of one's various investments shall typically be good, i.e., to know a lot about what one owns. To own more than five to ten value stocks, for instance, may be difficult.

To follow some sense of indexing might not be it. Instead, one could try to identify fund managers who might have a good track record in picking value stocks, so that indeed good stock picking takes place.

Here are two additional recommendations:

- Fixate solely on analyzing one singular investment at a time. Most investors fail here in that they might look at several investments in parallel, thus perhaps becoming too "shallow." As the author has pointed out, to only invest in relatively "simple," well-understood businesses is paramount!
- Do not be afraid to aggressively leverage a particular business that might fit the Dhando criteria. Go as heavily as possible into relatively few investments.

To look for undervalued assets that might have a reasonable upside potential looks to be critical. To emphasize the "degree of safety" associated with such assets, such as for instance, abilities to spin off parts of these stock holdings may also be worth serious consideration.

Joel Greenblatt (2010), The Little Book that Still Beats the Market, Wiley (Reviewed October 2021)

Mr. Greenblatt, a highly successful Wall Street stockbroker and indeed a legend when it comes to stock-picking, presents specific tips for finding "good buys" to invest in. For example, go for fairly cheap stocks, undervalued, and also from relatively well-managed firms. Another strong suggestion is to keep one's stock portfolio as focused as possible, say, with a maximum of 30 stocks.

The formula for successful stock market investing is to seek out good stocks when they are available at bargain prices, i.e., above-average quality company stocks at below-average prices, i.e., value stocks, or value investing. Key principles of value investing are delineated in a simple, straightforward way.

The first edition of this book was published in 2005. The principles for investing that the author came up with then remain the same in this new edition, but the author has written a new introduction as well as an afterword.

This way of investing for creating successful stock portfolios, based on the purchasing of undervalued, high-quality stocks, compliments very well the thesis for investing laid out by Pabrai (The Dhandho Investor, 2007), which focuses on finding "safety cushions" that might be sold off during adverse times, as well as Svensen's Unconventional Success (2005), which concentrates on developing a wider range of asset classes as a basis for growing a value-based portfolio of investments.

The aim is to "only buy shares in good businesses, ones with high return on capital, and only when these are available at bargain prices (priced to give us a high earnings yield)." This method requires discipline and calls for a long-term time horizon.

The importance of getting one's money to work is also stressed. The riskier one engages, the higher the returns one might expect, such as relatively higher returns on riskier loans. Self-evident! And when it comes to the valuation of stocks, this a clearly a function of future earnings. Again, the riskier the expected income stream from a given stock, the higher valuation, in contrast to more or less risk-free government bonds, which tend to yield zero interest or close to zero at best.

To figure out what a business is worth is not easy, the author admits. Yet while the value of most companies tends to remain relatively stable, say, over a year, the prices of most stocks tend to move around frequently—market expectations are at work! One should try to buy particular stocks when its market price is down, so as to establish a comfortable margin of safety. Attractive companies also tend to be able to reinvest often, thus mostly having a higher return on capital than most "average" companies.

An ultimate goal might perhaps be to buy shares in companies that happen to be priced at net liquidation value, so-called bargain issues, or net current assets stocks. But for such a magic formula to work, one must maintain a long-term investment horizon. In contrast, we know that to purchase the so-called short-term indexed-priced stocks has largely been in vogue for the last few years, say, until recently, in contrast to value stock-picking/value investing. Thus, long-term commitment to the author's principle seems to be "in" again. For companies that earn high returns, i.e., generally "attractive," one might reinvest dividends rather than to "pocket" these.

To choose stocks without being explicitly clear about what we might be looking for might be highly risky. A clear value investment strategy would be needed. To make such investment decisions on one's own on a long-term basis might typically be difficult, often next to impossible. The amount of time it takes, entailing heavy work and a great deal of hassle, might indicate that one might be better off working through a good fund manager, who may be good at value investing. In theory, however, there would be nothing to stop individual investors to make the required assessments needed and, thus, to do the investing themselves—it is all a matter of ability to put in the hard work! Well-managed index funds seem to be acceptable, however, but it should be kept in mind that to search for good deals must be central for the way such a fund is managed, in contrast to more or less mechanically following a given index. To avoid excessive trading might also typically be dysfunctional, in the sense that one may not get an effect similar to earning compounded interest, in addition to also having to pay a great deal of trading fees.

Here are some step-by-step suggestions. To identify "good buys," he suggests visiting an available screening tool. Alternatively, one might use ROA as a screening criterion. The author suggests a minimum ROA of 25%. From this group of stocks, one should screen for those with the lowest P/E ratio. However, utilities, financial stocks (mutual funds, banks, insurance), and non-US stocks should generally be excluded. Special attention might be given to stocks that simply have a too low P/E ratio, say 5 or less. To be on the safe side, these type of stocks might be eliminated too. There may simply be hidden risks of something fundamentally wrong in such cases. Finally, firms that have recently announced earnings results might also be eliminated from the list.

An investor could aim at building up a portfolio of, as an example, 30 stocks. To find all these stocks at once may be totally unrealistic, however. Instead, one might aim at developing one's portfolio over time, say, by purchasing a few stocks per month (5–7). And every stock holding should, in turn, be sold, for instance, after one year. New stocks should then be purchased, again, following the same selection principles as before. In this way, an actively managed stock portfolio is created and maintained, built on sound value-investing principles. It is all about following a disciplined strategy in looking for a strong, positive yield from one's portfolio.

Guy Spier, (2014), The Education of a Value Investor, MacMillan Education (Reviewed October 2018)

Zurich-based investor and fund manager Guy Spier discusses how to become a more successful value investor. If you are expecting a technical approach to investing—with metrics and the like—you are looking in the wrong place. This is not value investing. What is useful is to absorb the solid tips he provides, underlining, in particular, the importance of doing one's homework and due diligence, practicing concentration, and maintaining a certain degree of skepticism. The ability to pick assets that are possibly undervalued seems to be critical. To hold on to such assets as long as it takes for them to significantly appreciate appears equally key. Transparency is a major factor characterizing many of the organizations in which Mr. Spier's Aquamarine Fund invests.

Being an investor is, in many ways, like being the hero of one's life story: full of ups and downs, difficulties, challenges, and possibilities to prove oneself and one's character. There might be a rather simple, mechanistic prescription for investing. This art is best expressed through long-term value investing by searching for outstanding companies with transparent, robust business propositions. When stocks are undervalued relative to their intrinsic value, one might hold them until they reach a fair valuation.

Here is some additional advice:

- Stop checking stock prices all the time. This typically leads to buying/selling out of order. Only buy a stock if you are more than willing to keep it for several years.
- Be wary if someone is trying to sell something. Watch out for hidden agendas!
- Do not talk to management. They tend to be overly optimistic and smooth/persuasive but do try to find out as much as possible about the management.
- Do your research in the right order: first, the fundamentals—growth, profits, cash positions, then the "gossip."
- Discuss investment ideas only with those you trust and have a network of such people to pool your thoughts with. Being part of a trusted network is a way of systematizing such exchanges of ideas instead of one-offs only.
- Do not follow the emotional roller coaster of the stock market. Buy/sell when it makes sense to you.
- Talk as little as possible about your investments, except to those trusted friends.

- The entire business ecosystem must be considered when investing. For instance, if the firm is introducing a new product, what will be the switching costs for the customers?
- Watch how "distant" changes in the value chain might negatively affect a business. For instance, how does the financial health of the American consumer influence the German automotive industry?
- Focus on stocks that are not only cheap and have good cash flow but also on the fit with your personal values. For instance, do you invest in companies that do not comply with certain environmental and governance standards?
- Respect the perils of debt, and be patient, i.e., embrace conservatism in the best sense! Remember, stock-listed firms have leverage already. There is no need to leverage your own stock portfolio.
- As an investor, and as a person, one should follow one's "inner scorecard" to judge how well one is doing. This is a very liberating insight.
- Learn, learn, learn. Be a learning machine! If you keep learning all the time, you have a wonderful advantage.

Jacob Goldstein, (2021), Money: From Bronze to Bitcoin, Atlantic (Reviewed July 2022)

Will Bitcoin still exist, say, in 20 years, for instance? In order to try to gain a deeper comprehension of these complex issues, it is helpful to have a better idea of how the evolution of cash seems to have taken place. This book covers the history of money, providing us with a deep understanding of its evolution, and also perhaps the right "lens" in which to look at "new" forms of money, namely bitcoin and other "additions" to the world of finance. As in all things that change over time, a conscious, attentive look at how today's reality has come to be can bring greater knowledge as well as appreciation for what it is and how to use it: its role as a medium of economic exchange, unit of account and a symbol of value.

Jacob Goldstein is the host of a well-known podcast *Planet Money*, and an established writer and journalist. He previously worked for the Wall Street Journal, but there, his area of focus was mostly on health and medicine. Thus, a true eclectic, he seems to have been successful in discussing cutting-edge financial matters in fundamentally nontechnical ways. The book discusses the origin of money, as well as educated speculations about the future.

The first part of the book focuses on how money came about, first various sorts of objects, such as clay, stones, even cattle, and then coins, invented by the Hydans of ancient Greece. It was all about dealing with specialization stemming from trade. But coins were heavy and at times cumbersome to handle. With the invention of paper as well as of printing, paper money emerged. China was the first. Governments shifted towards collecting taxes in coins and money. While money was initially based on tributes, i.e., backed up by physical assets held in typically tribal societies, markets, and modern money stimulated not only the development of cities but also prompted economic growth in general.

Nevertheless, China's use of money came to an end with the Mongolian invasions.

It was not until the 1600s that money reappeared, this time in Europe. Goldsmiths took deposits from clients, which were then lent out to others. As money reemerged, so did the development of banks, the way we have come to know them today. The book's second part discusses this early advancement of capitalism, again largely driven by how the concept of money took form. The UK was in the lead, but money was not standardized. Each bank, large or small, issued their own funds. It was all a mess. It was the French, during the reign of the Duke of Orleans, who came up with a unified concept of money through the establishment of the forerunner of a central bank. This entity had various monopolies, including on trade with the West Indies, and was thus able to back up the paper money it issued with these real assets.

This evolution gradually led to the concept of money we know today. However, each bank would still issue its own money. In the USA, for instance, there were several thousand different currencies. Gradually, this evolved into state-based currencies, perhaps quite similar to the situation we had in Europe with many independent national currencies before the advent of the Euro.

Gradually, a single currency emerged, the dollar, being linked to gold; one ounce of gold equated to $20.67. Whenever there was economic uncertainty, citizens would typically wish to exchange their paper money for gold. Banks would customarily not be able to meet all such demands, and an economic crisis would emerge.

A way that was latched onto by the then central banks to cope with this was to raise interest rates and to limit the free flow of money. Yet this led to a further worsening of the economic crises, such as accentuating the financial calamities of 1929 and the Great Depression. Walter Bagehot's advice was never adhered to, "Lend freely into a panic" (Me. Bagehot was the famous editor of The Economist in the 1870s). Perhaps the main reason for the reluctance to increasing the amount of money in the free flow might be a fear of not having large enough gold deposits in the banks to be able to pay gold to the public that was called for.

Gradually, however, a modern concept of money emerged, initially still linked to gold (the gold standard). This evolution was driven by a combination of financial crises, major political shifts, and some new technology. We saw the progression from paper money backed by gold to paper money backed by nothing, to today's numbers on a computer! But before we get to this latter evolutionary stage, let us first spend some more time on modern money, the fourth section of the book.

A central theme here was the combined backing of the gold standard, typically spearheaded by central banks. Again, a significant event was the crisis that began in 1929. Central banks did not increase the flow of money, and raised interest rates, both factors being devastating. Important empirical work by Friedman and Schwartz, more than any others, has manifested the disastrous negative effects from these fallacies. Modern economists such as Fischer and Keynes were critical to maintaining the gold standard. The gold standard locked countries in a terrible economic cycle. However, the gold standard was nothing more than the choice people had made. So gradually the gold standard was abandoned.

The final section of the book deals with what seems to be some of the major monetary issues that have been at the center of attention after the gold standard was abandoned. The emergence of banks which spearheaded transactions in bonds that were largely stemming from real estate assets was a milestone. When the value of such bonds diminished, often becoming worthless, we saw the financial crisis of 2008. Financial institutions such as Bear Stearns and Lehman Brothers went into bankruptcy. In the end, massive infusions of funds from the Federal Reserve saved the day.

Yet this sparked the emergence of the Euro. A single currency was created for 12 countries, with vastly different economies. Admittedly there were limits imposed on what any country might go into the red in a given year—a 2% budget deficit was all that was allowed. But some countries, notably Greece and Portugal, were unable to live with this. The European Central Bank had to "bail out" these nations. This, in the end, was indeed a successful operation. Mr. Draghi, the then head of the European Central Bank, made a promise that people generally believed, namely that the ECB would do "whatever it takes" to save the Euro. Such statements hold water only when they are widely believed, however, which was indeed the case.

The radical dream of digital cash became more and more accumulated. The era of Bitcoin had emerged! The emergence of vast improvements in the speed of communication and in computing power separated two parallel developments when it came to creating digital currency. Giant corporations would spend millions of dollars to create proprietary digital cash, spurred by such giants as Citicorp, but individuals would also work on this challenge, for free. In the end, the latter group came out ahead. The early forerunner to Bitcoin was DigiCash, which went bankrupt in 1997. Bitcoin was developed (including others) by Satoshi Nahamoto, a fake name; we simply do not know who the individual(s) is (are) behind this name. The key was to come up with a ledger maintained by everyone.

There seem to be five salient features with Bitcoin:

- Every new transaction gets maintained by everyone.
- All computers in the network record a given transaction at the same time.
- The first computer to be able to acknowledge a given transaction acknowledges this on the ledger as a block.
- All computers check that the ledger is correct.
- Each block is linked to the blocks that came before, i.e., "chains of blocks."
- This cannot be changed or manipulated.

Is Bitcoin safe? Are they facilitating illegal practices such as paying for drugs? While there are undoubtedly examples of this, there are naturally also many legitimate uses. Payments and deposits can generally be done more easily and without the influence of "big brother," i.e., central banks.

What about the future of money? The author speculates that there might be a few major developments: The first would be a world without cash. We already see how payment of various sorts may be taking over the use of cash. Countries such as Sweden and Norway are in the lead here. Paper money of large denotations, above all, may be eliminated. Small transactions may still be conducted through cash coins or paper money. The possibilities for criminal actions may be decreased, and transactional expenses could be dramatically decreasing.

A world without banks may also be coming. There may instead be a full-reserve bank that backs up loans and facilitates money deposits and payments. Cash would be provided, as needed, through cash machines (ATMs) and mutual funds would take over the rest.

This brings us to what might perhaps be an ultimate evolutionary stage, namely that money is freely printed for anyone who may want a job. Why should governments need to tax citizens, so as to spend money? Why not simply print it as needed? This is Modern Monetary Theory. This might perhaps not be as far off as we think!

William Green, (2021), Richer, Wiser, Happier, Simon & Schuster (Reviewed July 2021)

This author, a successful Wall Street investor, is a strong proponent of investing in the so-called "value stocks," i.e., in well-established, well-run, typically quite conventional firms, that also tend to provide solid dividends in contrast to "growth stocks" where one would count on an increase in a stock's value as the company grows. Eight sources to increase the likelihood of success are given. The secrets to successful stock investing seem to be valid, indeed!

This accomplished New York-based independent business writer interviewed more than 40 successful investors for this book, finding that most of them appeared to have significantly broader life interests than simply succeeding in investing and amassing financial wealth. The author points towards eclectic realities, such as "take risks by playing games, but be cognizant of the risks," "be particularly careful when the market goes up," and "go for a few solid, but relatively cheap stocks." And, when a rally is all over, the learning gained is the consequential!

What might one see as broad essentials for such success? One is to be disciplined, move slowly, and be patient. Inspired by successful investors such as Warren Buffett, stocks might be seen as reflections of the firms they represent, similar to as if one might want to take over the given firm itself; buy only when relatively cheap, avoid firms with too much leveraging; invest only when the price is relatively low, and so on. These are all "principles" for the so-called value investing that are set forward by the likes of Buffett. Perhaps one might add: trust the CEO of the firm where one is investing and try to work only with people that one considers stronger than oneself and, therefore, from whom one truly can learn.

To be different from the majority of other investors is also seen by many to be of utmost importance. This implies that successful investors shall often have to accept a sense of loneliness. Be aware of emotions, including the danger of becoming overoptimistic when things are going well, or, on the converse side, avoiding the danger of becoming over-pessimistic when things are not going as hoped. Other aspects of managing one's emotions may include always seek data and facts, to be patient, to study failures in a general sense (as opposed to, in too much detail), to find out more about the why and whether there might be a likelihood of recovery. The legendary John Templeton seems to have been following these "rules."

Everything appears to be changing in this world. Dynamism is aplenty. Perhaps the most important conclusion from this is that it is impossible to accurately predict the future. Yet we know that there will typically be cycles! It seems crucial to try to take advantage of this, with a counter-cyclical focus! A precondition for this is probably a certain degree of humility, prudence, and skepticism. One would also need to be open-minded, indeed, so as to not become trapped in false beliefs regarding stages of cycles.

To build enduring wealth seems to be highly correlated with following a value investing approach, to always try to go for good and inexpensive firms to invest in, i.e., only at a favorable price. To try to build in some measure of safety here seems important also to minimize the risk that one is taking. Is the price truly fair? Is the quality of the firm that is issuing a given stock solid? To further reduce uncertainty, one should limit the taking on of debt to a minimum. Realism is paramount. Overconfidence should be avoided, including avoiding too much short-termed thinking. It all comes back to having a reasonable margin of safety.

To go for simplicity seems to be fundamental to meaningfully be able to practice the above. This might increase one's ability to make realistic evaluations and thereby to avoid major disasters. A corollary of this (i.e., to go for simplicity) would be to resist any sense of gratification from success. Maintain one's ego "under control"! Again, keeping a long-term time horizon might help here. And being honest with oneself is primary!

Is it possible for an investor to develop habits that might actually lead to high performance? Warren Buffett for one seems to believe in the importance of sticking to a relatively small set of "good" habits, such as to invest only in assets that one might understand relatively well, and always try to learn more when it comes to this. Discipline and hard work are recommended! And a long-term view is indispensable, to try to find stocks that might be yielding dividends on an ongoing basis, so-called *compounding machines*. Companies such as Nestlé, Novartis, or Roche come to mind!

The final rule of thumb for successful investors is to try to systematically ameliorate stupidity, typically easier said than done, of course. Charlie Munger, Warren Buffett's senior partner in Berkshire Hathaway, is known for this. To analyze one's own mistakes seems paramount here: "Why might I be wrong?" And to not repeat these types of mistakes again may hopefully be a result of this. Munger labels this *inversion*.

Having identified these guidelines for successful investing; to borrow other people's best ideas; to act independently; to acknowledge that there are cycles that one might take advantage of; to go for value investing; to strive for simplicity; to avoid being trapped by one's own ego; to develop good habits and to stick to these; to try to learn from mistakes to avoid doing these again. It is now concluded that successful investors typically also have additional personal traits, hobbies of various sorts, an openness to support others, i.e., a willingness to share, to "give," i.e., a realization that to be a successful "rich" investor implies a commitment to intellectually discover new things in life, interest in art and music, and so on. But such an open-mindedness commonly may also mean that a successful investor may have an "exceptional ability to take pain"! There seems to be a duality here, i.e., both being broad-minded and at the same time being comfortable as a loner.

By being able to "buy on the cheap and sell on the high," successfully managing according to cycles seems to be the answer above all, however. And this requires adherence to the various personal traits that have been identified, above all being able to "go for it" alone, with discipline, and to learn with a long-term horizon in mind!

Peter Lorange, (2021), Reinventing the Family Firm, IMD (Reviewed December 2021)

This book and its review argue for the establishment and pursuance of a family-owned business portfolio, in contrast to the classic family-owned heritage business, the latter often focused on a single-family business. A portfolio approach allows for more flexibility in adapting to emerging business challenges, it is argued, by not having "all eggs in one basket."

A family business can be defined as a family owning a significant share and the ability to influence important decisions, such as the selection of a chairperson as well as the CEO, important business investment and/or exit decisions, debt policies, as well as decisions regarding the hiring promotion or termination of key dividends.

Family firms are by far the most dominant form of corporation in the world. They are prevalent especially in countries where the law allows for private ownership. It is estimated that 70% to 90% of all firms worldwide are family firms. The contribution of these firms to GNP is estimated to be as high as 60% in many advanced economies, including the United States and Switzerland. The percentage of employment provided by family firms within national economies also tends to be high. Further, family firms represent more than 85% of the world's companies. In the UK alone, more than half of those employed in the private sector (Clark, 2021) come from the family business sector.

The term "business families" is used for families of heritage firms, while families who own portfolio businesses are labeled "families in business." There are at least two overriding challenges facing owning families who wish to maintain sustained business success: achieving strong business performance and ensuring family harmony.

There are many reasons for declining performance, even business failures in family enterprises. These include family conflicts over matters such as roles, salaries, and succession. There may be fundamental differences of view over risk appetite and entrepreneurial endeavors and so on. For example: How much might be reinvested in the established firm, and how much in new ventures? Establishing and maintaining strong family values is closely linked to such strategic decisions. They provide the underlying guide, while formal governance procedures are helpful to create the forums necessary for difficult decisions where there may be genuine and sincerely held strong differences of opinion. This may especially be the case when the number of family owners grows, and small informal decision-making groups become unrepresentative and inappropriate. Such formal entities might include a family assembly, a family council, and so on. Family offices could be established to undertake some of the administrative chores as a family grows.

Family-owned businesses represent the backbone in many economies. The role of the family is always central, and the family may represent a main resource for particular inputs. For example, there may be competences and/or industries where members of a family have particular expertise—manufacturing, finance, medical, shipping, real estate, and so on. In turn, the enterprises can create employment opportunities for family members, enhancing the links between the owning family and its businesses. In the case of a portfolio of businesses, there is typically a more diverse array of such career options.

The role of an owner is significant in its own right and comes with many commitments and responsibilities. Family members may feel that they are custodians, which has a completely different scale and time horizon to being a salaried executive, or a stockholder in a publicly listed firm, where the interests are typically more short term.

Where a family or families hold ownership control over a company in question, the family decides on the composition of the firm's board of directors, as well as the appointment of the firm's management, including the CEO. The CEO, as well as other members of senior management, will often come from the owning family. The owning family controls the firm's strategy, including levels of investing as well as dividend payouts.

Many of today's cutting-edge management practices in family businesses are impressive. The field does indeed seem to have advanced dramatically. There seems to be a strong relationship between family-owned business portfolios and portfolio entrepreneurs. There are several aspects of the portfolio business–portfolio entrepreneur relationship:

- A portfolio entrepreneur is defined as a manager who holds ownership of multiple businesses. Wealth creation seems to be an essential driver for many portfolio entrepreneurs, above all to develop profitable new businesses. A second driver might be to try out a new business concept, inspired by creative impulse or simply by intellectual curiosity.
- We might also label a portfolio entrepreneur a "serial entrepreneur" to underscore the fact that enduring entrepreneurship is the key, based on the drivers discussed above. As such, there are no differences between the various labels, "portfolio entrepreneur," "serial entrepreneur," or simply "entrepreneur."
- A strategic commitment can result in the long-term building of family-owned portfolios over many years, even over generations. Maintaining the required level of entrepreneurship over the generations requires active commitment. Strong involvement in business activities in the portfolio seems critical, including the ability to grow businesses, as well as diversify, wind businesses down, or exit certain sectors. New businesses might be developed using, at least in part, the "recycled" resources that are generated or released from exits or sales of other businesses. Entrepreneurial drive is thus critical when it comes to a business portfolio's evolution, equally so when it comes to expansion, construction, and repeat actions and learning.
- The portfolio itself might be diverse. Geographic locations might influence strategic decisions and provide focus to a portfolio. Size differences between the various businesses might be an alternative way of focusing a portfolio, for example, if there is a strategic choice to go for scale. Choice of currencies (including Bitcoin) might be another distinguishing factor and so on.
- Starting a portfolio may not only be driven by financial considerations, manifested as profits, cash flow, risk, and so on. There may be personal motives too, say, to do with career fulfillment or certain interests and passions.
- Let us now finally discuss "decline," or the closing down of a portfolio. How does a business family manage a portfolio's decline? How might the portfolio's sustainability be enhanced? Freeing up resources for new investments when exiting a business might be seen as more of an entrepreneurial activity rather than as a dysfunctionality, scaling back. Family offices may often be dealing with these issues.
- Raising more capital—for example, for mergers or acquisitions—is also primarily a family concern. These decisions will likely impact the

concentration of ownership: Is the owning family comfortable with the potential dilution created by such a move? Alternatively, acquisitions might be financed through taking on more debt, implying a higher degree of risk for the firm, with no dilution of ownership other than by "paying" with shares in the company held by the owning family. This is also an issue of control, which may often have more of an impact than the decision about whether to merge/acquire or not. There could also be situations, of course, where the acquiring firm uses cash reserves to make purchases and is in many ways an ideal scenario, implying a relatively small increase in risk exposure and no dilution. Such situations tend to be rare, however. Family offices are again often central when it comes to these decisions.

Business environments seem to be more and more volatile, with increasingly rapid changes. This is often described by the acronym VUCA, which stands for Volatile, Uncertain, Complex, and Ambiguous. Product life cycles are tending to become shorter, with rapid changes in customers' preferences and with significant technological shifts as well. So, anticipating change and demonstrating great agility in pursuing new opportunities will be more important than ever: the ability to adapt quickly, reinvent oneself, and show strong resilience, vision, and responsibility.

A common pattern tends to be for the family initially to have owned a particular business enterprise—such as a manufacturing plant, a store, a building, or a fleet of ships. Let us label this the "heritage" or "legacy" business, and for the family to then later on to diversify, perhaps in the light of an increasingly turbulent and unpredictable VUCA environment.

A heritage firm is what we may classify as a family's traditional core business, and these vary greatly. Often, we find that it is in such types of heritage firms where many business families start out and thus where the bulk of their wealth might have been accumulated. This initial investment may later be sold, with the family then going on to make a series of new investments, thus creating a family business portfolio.

When a business-owning family diversifies and creates a portfolio firm, it typically uses proceeds from the sale of the legacy firm to finance the investment for such a transformation. Some families who sell their legacy businesses and, now finding themselves with ample cash in hand, might fall into the trap of rushing into a number of new investments far too quickly, at times also with too great a financial commitment per investment. Due diligence may be also lacking when reinvesting such a windfall.

In addition, families in such a position may lack the competences necessary, and, in the end, may struggle to manage their new portfolio business. On the other hand, it may also be that a portfolio opens up opportunities that suit a broader set of talents and interests from within the wider family. Managing a 100%-owned heritage firm typically requires specific skills and experience relating to a particular type of business. In contrast, a portfolio business can offer a wider set of career options. Family members' involvement might entail roles on subsidiaries' boards and/or being advisors. These family members may often have no specific line management responsibility and little need for specialized functional skills. Therefore, it may be relatively easy for the next generation of family members to become involved in meaningful ways. A more realistic context for long-term family involvement might thereby have been created.

Experience-building and learning seem to be especially critical for family business portfolio firms. How can such a firm's portfolio strategy be improved? Below are some key pieces of advice:

- Avoid becoming "trapped" in too many capital-intensive businesses. For example, the very capital-intensive shipping business requires substantial investment in new ship assets. An excessively asset-heavy business will often call for larger investments in capital than the owning family might be comfortable with.
- Build on the specific competences of the members of the owning family.
- Diversify into a range of different fields and learn from early successes and mistakes. And the lessons from outside the silo may prove to be transferable to other investments.
- Invest in the development of family members' education and skills and especially in the commitment to continue education and skill building regularly and over the long term.
- Learn from the best practice of venture firms. Family businesses should approach their ventures in a dynamic way, similar to public venture firms.

For many family business portfolios, having a value-based culture is therefore key. Values directly influence investment strategy. Perhaps the most important aspect of this is that as large a proportion as possible of the funds generated from the various entities within the firm's portfolio should be reinvested by the firm, with only a relatively small fraction of the firm's economic result being paid out as dividends. Dennis Jaffe, in his research on successful family firms, has identified the importance of stewardship, i.e., such firms reinvesting the bulk of what is being earned, this being perhaps the most critical success factor for family businesses in the long run. It should be pointed out, however, that Jaffe's research did not seem to make a distinction between various types of family firms, i.e., between those focused on one or a few typically related entities (heritage businesses) versus family business portfolios. What is unique about a family business portfolio in this context, however, is that while some parts of a portfolio might be relatively easily "milked" and generate reliable cash flows, others might be more suited for reinvestment. The owning family thereby will benefit from a much greater degree of flexibility when it comes to the withdrawal of cash from the business portfolio type of firm.

Family businesses tend to do well in crises, as has been seen during the recent pandemic. They also tend to have lower insolvency rates than their counterparts. Their longer-term focus and greater resilience work in their favor. They also tend to be more frugal and less inclined to undertake "flashy" acquisitions. They are often more community-minded and more innovative, with more patents and new products per dollar spent on R&D than their public counterparts.

One way of viewing a portfolio might be according to its degree of risk, say, than falling into these parts: Moonshot—very risky investments, typically found in start-ups, and with significant payoffs when successful; core wealth creation—family-owned and actively managed businesses; steady income generation—to support a family's living expenses, for example, through rental incomes from real estate; and hurricane—to support family members in case of a crisis, say, by holding gold (physical rather than certificates) in various locations. Holding cryptocurrencies may represent another way to achieve this.

Another way to look at the configuration of one's portfolio might be geographic: for instance, investments in the Americas versus Europe versus Asia. If in the Americas, how much is invested and where? If in Europe, how much in the Germanic part versus the Latin part? How much in Scandinavia? How much in Switzerland? In the case of Asia, how much is invested in China? Ensuring that businesses are located in sufficiently high growth as well as politically safe areas is paramount.

A portfolio might also be assessed according to which currencies the portfolio investments are exposed to such as USD, GBP, EUR, CHF, and NOK. Still other "cuts" might focus on the service sector versus manufacturing, on subscription businesses versus not, and so on.

A final way of looking at what might be a good portfolio for a family firm is through the lens of the particular human competences in the firm. A business portfolio might be built based on the core capabilities that exist in a company. This is in contrast to an often industry-based portfolio delineation or a geography-based portfolio delineation. What is essential for the leader, then, is to empower the people in their organization to actually take advantage of what they seem to know best, typically in a bottom-up process. The leader's willingness to listen might be particularly key in such an approach. One can add to this too the importance of allowing people to do what they love, namely, to recognize that performance excellence is often also linked to passion.

So, we can see that a portfolio can be viewed through several lenses. It is important to undertake these various assessments of one's portfolio to come up with what one might consider a good mix when it comes to risk exposure relative to return. Thus, it is also important to operationally manage a portfolio in such a way that it allows for investment decisions to be made by drawing on accumulated know-how in each of the areas of the portfolio. Periodically and in a disciplined manner, assessing the quality of this portfolio according to currency mix, geographic focus, and so on, is also critical.

A note on risk-taking may be appropriate here. Taking some risks is crucial. The proviso must, of course, be made that prudence be shown when it comes to such risk-taking: both when it comes to not taking excessive risks (family firms are commonly rather conservative) and to not taking higher risks than necessary. Still, it seems to be the case that the lack of some risk-taking tends to correlate with periods of stagnation of organizations, rather than development. For a manager of a family business portfolio, the following question might be raised when considering a new investment: "Am I … risking enough for this project?" And risk is not only financial but also reputational for both manager and family. The manager's job might even be at stake.

Selling one's legacy business is never easy. A decision to sell commonly requires a robust mind. A decision-maker should be mentally prepared to be more or less "alone" when it comes to making such decisions. To outperform the market, one should be willing to think independently, with all that this entails, including receiving blunt preliminary criticism from many. But still, to exit from a legacy business might be tough!

Here are a few additional, hopefully relevant, factors when it comes to a decision to sell the legacy business:

- The predominant philosophy within many family firms seems to be that they should be set up to run forever, i.e., as if the ideal time horizons of their existence may be "for eternity." However, actual managerial time horizon tends to be much shorter. A particular generation of owners/managers, for instance, might only be in charge for a relatively short time period, say, for 15–20 years. The ability to assess the extent to which members of the

next generation are suited to successfully running a specialized firm becomes an important consideration. In the long run, it might be more appropriate for the next generation to manage a more diversified portfolio of activities.
- Having "all one's eggs in one basket" might not be desirable for an owning family, especially when the value of their assets concentrated in one sector might fluctuate wildly—for example, owing to developments in the freight markets facing shipping firms. Having all the family's assets tied up in one highly capital-intensive business may also create difficulties: The bulk of the free cash flow might have to be needed to be virtually continually reinvested in the legacy business, with little or no free capital to be used at the discretion of family members. There may be little to no discretion for the owners when it comes to the payout of dividends, causing frustration even though family owners are not necessarily inclined to be reliant on dividend income. Such restrictions might be reinforced by clauses to limit the distribution of dividends, typically imposed by financial institutions as a condition for having provided loan financing. In many cases, it would be unlikely that a family could come up with all the capital needed to make the reinvestments required to keep a capital-intensive legacy business going.
- There might also be emerging industry trends that call for exiting a particular business. The emission of CO_2 in our atmosphere resulting from the burning of oil and other fossil fuels, for instance, has led to a significant scaling down of offshore oil exploration. Therefore, the offshore supply ship business has become much less attractive. Health considerations and governmental regulations on cigarette smoking have had a similar effect on the attractiveness of tobacco firms, and so on. It should be noted, however, that the author did not foresee the negative development in the offshore supply ship segment due to increasing concerns regarding CO_2 emissions from oil. In general, it can be hard to pinpoint such negative macro-developments in many industries' attractiveness.

Example: S. Ugelstad Invest

As already alluded to, selling one's legacy family business, which is frequently an emotionally difficult process, might be made somewhat easier by considering the following three-step sequence:

- Step 1: Sell the "hardware," such as one's fleet of ships or factory.
- Step 2: Sell the "software," i.e., the organization, including operating procedures and files, as well as organizing job transfers for the people employed by the firm. It is particularly critical that all, or at least most, of the key

managers agree to continue in their positions after the sale. However, many of these managers may have developed particular loyalties to the owning family on the seller side and therefore might prefer to leave. In these circumstances, it can be difficult to sell an organization with most of its key people in place, allowing the organization to continue to function in a practical way.
- Step 3: Sell the legacy company's name—which, by the way, often incorporates the name of the owning family, making this a particularly emotional step!

In the case of the sale of S. Ugelstad's legacy ship-owning assets, we sold the "hardware" and the "software" (steps 1 and 2) but not the name (step 3). This facilitated the repositioning of the firm to eventually become the family business portfolio firm SUI.

There may be many important considerations playing roles when it comes to decisions that eventually could lead to a portfolio structure:

- A desire to spread the risk has been central. In consultation with the family, the decision was taken to retain approximately half the assets as "next-generation money," i.e., at relatively low risk, to be more easily preserved for generations to come.
- A need to secure a positive cash flow, so as to be able to more easily support the author and his family's personal needs, has also been a priority. It was seen as vital always to have some free cash available in order to be able to capitalize on emerging investment opportunities, particularly in family businesses where the original owners of a prospective investment might be short of cash.
- A decision on whether or not to borrow against the assets in the portfolio largely related to risk exposure versus growth.
- An aim to try to build as much as possible on one's own competences and network, as well as on the core skills of several members in a family (entrepreneurship, finance, etc.).
- A wish to immerse family members in the latest thinking in investment theory and to attempt to implement this in practice.
- A decision to use scenario planning as a central tool when developing the investment strategy.
- A desire to continuously reassess investment processes and investor psychology to try to continuously improve capabilities as investors and to learn more about this new craft or art.

- A drive to make use of the latest available technology when possible. A key objective here would be to attempt to take advantage of scalable opportunities.
- A preference for backing managers in the various business entities of the portfolio who showed strong commercial capabilities. Our philosophy has been to emphasize a desire for continuity and stability and to not create disruption unless strictly necessary. Further, we felt that to become too heavily involved in the management of operating businesses might be seen as undesirable and could easily "burn up" too much of our time. Consequently, it was preferable to invest in well-managed funds rather than investing directly in new ventures. There are, of course, exceptions to this rule. Investing in search funds is seen as an attractive way to save time. Time is the scarcest resource for many family members.

One final consideration needs to be raised when it comes to arriving at a good strategy for a family portfolio firm. An important determinant for continuing business success is the ability to be flexible. What are the keys to such flexibility? While there may be many important factors, the author believes that the concept of "listening posts" is particularly relevant for family firms. Although "strategy means choice" for most large established commercial firms, relatively small family firms might actually benefit from not following this dictum. Instead, investing in a relatively large number of listening posts might allow them to better identify what seems to work. This can best be done through investing in well-managed funds, which allows the firm greater flexibility in its approach: By testing out a relatively large set of options, they can exit quickly when things do not turn out as hoped. More substantial follow-on investments might then be relatively easier to make in that they might have been able to try things out at a lower level of investment initially. This flexibility, through trial and error and gradual, incremental levels of commitment, could be seen as the DNA of many family business portfolios.

Family offices have been established at a high rate in the past few decades in order to strengthen the management of family-owned portfolios. These tend to be of two types:

- Single-family office, which manages the assets of a single family.
- Multifamily office, which manages the assets of several families. This type of organization might be seen as quite similar to the way in which many venture funds are organized. A multifamily office will commonly have more resources at its disposal and thus also be able to employ a larger cadre of professionals than the typical single-family office.

Family offices are often seen in instances when families have disposed of their legacy business and moved towards portfolio diversification. But there are exceptions. Some families may set up a family office while continuing to own and run their heritage business. In some of these cases, they might also have a considerable number of additional diversified assets.

29

Executive Profiles of Business Leaders

Martin Stadler, CEO of Altoo (Interviewed May 2020)

Martin Stadler's interview unveils the importance of involving banks in constructive ways when it comes to investing successfully. For business-to-business, the players include investment bankers, in contrast to business-to-consumer, whereby we speak of banks that provide portfolio transparency, something typically offered by most commercial retail banks. It is a matter of being actively involved as a partner with specific resource persons acting as counterparts in both of these types of banking institutions.

Altoo stands for "all together," which gives a good indication of what this start-up founded to support investors in tracking their businesses firm is all about, namely, the assets of independent investors are faring, including contracts, cash flows, new calls for capital, and so on. Making use of advanced technology, the company is able to address all of this. And total secrecy and discretion are a hallmark. The company's clients are the focus, and the firm's key philosophy is to make it easier for the client by employing the latest technology.

Altoo initially started in December 2017 as a distressed technology buy-out from Switzerland's first fintech bank FLYNT. This bank was targeting entrepreneurial families and received its banking license from the Swiss banking regulator FINMA in July 2017 but ceased its activities shortly afterwards due to funding challenges.

Martin Stadler, Altoo's CEO, was hired by FLYNT in 2016 to build up the business development, took the opportunity together with the core team of

FLYNT employees, buying out the core technology and the hardware for private cloud services at a distressed asset price from FLYNT. This transaction was financed by two Swiss entrepreneur families who had been using FLYNT's services already. Today, Altoo has 24 employees, all also being shareholders in Altoo, with stock holdings that they actually paid for, i.e., "skin in the game."

Altoo was trying to take advantage of the strong tradition of Swiss wealth management banking. While the cost of running a business such as Altoo in Switzerland is relatively high (high salaries, etc.), the company is attempting to sell itself through "Swissness," i.e., a guarantee of premium service and the relatively safe data storage in Switzerland would be of value to its clients. Altoo is the only company providing this unique combination of service and technology and with 100% commitment to Switzerland. The company seems to attract about four to five new customers per month, mostly family businesses, including many from outside Switzerland. The typical annual cost for a client might be within the range of CHF 25,000–30,000.

Altoo's founder and CEO Mr. Martin Stadler started out working at UBS when he was 16 years old, working initially at the bank's branches in St. Gallen and in his home village, Toggenburg. In parallel, he studied economics at the Fachhochschule in Eastern Switzerland, earning a degree in economics. He is thus an example of the highly successful Swiss way of studying (20% of the time) and working (80% of the time).

At the age of 26, he was sent by UBS to Singapore and given the responsibility to serve wealthy German-speaking investors there. After three years, his career took him back to UBS, now in Zurich, where he continued to work as a client advisor for entrepreneurs and single-family offices. In 1996, after 20 years with UBS, he left for the endeavor with FLYNT.

The Swiss banking sector is strong, in Mr. Stadler's view, as it has been for a long time. But, for the banking sector, the challenge would, of course, be the same as in most other businesses sectors with a past history of success: How to make good even better? Here, there might perhaps be several opportunities for future strengthening:

- How might a client's specific needs be more realistically put at the center when it comes to the work of banks' client advisors, in contrast to a "push" to "sell" the bank's own products?
- How can a bank's call for formal internal procedures (often imposed by FINMA) be modified in such a way that requires less time, so a client manager can spend at least some of this freed-up time with his/her client?
- Publicly traded banks are, of course, under pressure to come up with relatively sturdy bottom-line results on an ongoing basis, i.e., "to deliver every

quarter." This is in contradiction with the long-term nature of a client relationship, which is necessary so to build trust between the parties private banking.
- The remuneration of senior bankers, including account managers, is commonly high and largely a function of achieving the abovementioned bottom-line stability. How can remuneration and incentives be modified to become more in line with that of supporting customers' needs, being based on achieving longer-term performance targets.
- How can more openness regarding clients be achieved, in the sense of acknowledging what are a bank's main areas of competence? Are all proposed "solutions" "honest"? Non-listed banks may perhaps have an advantage when it comes to this.
- Senior management might often find its role to be primarily "controlling" that expected revenue streams indeed might be coming. How can this group, instead, be "empowered" with rethinking parts of their bank's future strategy so as to implement anticipated changes proactively?
- The size of some of the leading public banks may represent a challenge in the sense that investing for such banks in new assets within their wealth management offering may "crowd the market," rather than being opportunistic.

The above challenges, or dilemmas, perhaps facing many leading banks today, may, of course, make it difficult to "make good even better." Perhaps a way forward for some of these large traditional banks could be to try to build their own "new" banks with more reasonable cost levels and with a stronger customer focus, i.e., a call to "reinvent" themselves!

So, what is the way forward for the typical family firm, with its own unique portfolio, when it comes to seeking support from the banking sector? Perhaps the following needs might give signals regarding such a direction:

- Choose a reputable bank to handle one's daily needs, including cash flow management.
- Choose another bank to support the family business when it comes to handling investments. A non-listed bank might be ideal.
- Choose an independent organization, such as Altoo, for instance, to support the family, regarding its portfolio, i.e., with maintaining a firm oversight over the portfolio.

A way to accentuate the difference between the second and the third issue in the above is to think about them in terms of "b2b" or "b2c," as follows:

- b2b: This is the second of the above issues and is for investment bankers.
- b2c: This is for providers of portfolio transparency, above all, to cope with the increasing complexity that typically often takes place. Total wealth aggregation might be advisable here, and it must allow for secure interactions. This is the third issue on the above list.

Two examples might serve to illustrate how a company such as Altoo might add value, especially during extraordinary periods such as the one with the Corona crisis:

- The stock market may fall dramatically now and then, say, dropping as much as 10% on an overall basis. Many adverse issues might have come together in one day! To have the necessary information in order to cope with all of this might be key. Action may have to be taken quickly in order to minimize economic losses! The overall structure provided by Altoo might be of great help.
- A successful family-owned conglomerate was de facto managed by the father (mostly), in his role as the paterfamilias. The children were only involved on a partial basis. When the father suddenly died, the issue came up of whether an important part of the information, the "corporate memory" of the father, has been lost. It did not take long, however, before the rest of the family was able to reassess the inherited portfolio, for then to make three key changes: Learn more from the data; restructure the group; and reassess the overall risk, implied by the totality of holdings in the portfolio deemed to be too high.

Alisée de Tonnac, Cofounder and Managing Partner, Seedstars Group (Interviewed October 2019)

Seedstars is an unusual investment fund focusing on impact investing in developing countries, with sub-Sahara Africa representing its major area of activity. A central part of Seedstars' success is its emphasis on educating local talents to help them to become better entrepreneurial businesspersons/leaders. These trained persons, in turn, are running the various entities where Seedstars invests. To provide additional business support, when needed, is another central part of Seedstars activities. So far, Seedstars' performance has been excellent. Speed and focus on local initiatives, while still emphasizing Swiss quality, are central parts of this inspirational success story.

Seedstars is an investment holding fund founded in 2012 in Switzerland and focused on impact investment. Its mission is to impact people's lives in emerging markets through technology and entrepreneurship. The company was launched by a group of four, including Alisée de Tonnac, born in France and having spent several years abroad in countries such as Singapore, the USA, and Nigeria.

Currently, the company consists of over 80 team members from over 20 nationalities located all across the world, with some teams based in each of the 12 Seedspaces, the Seedstars coworking hubs for entrepreneurs. "We are proud of the diversity and gender balance within our organisation as we believe it is one of the main business drivers for success," states Alisée de Tonnac.

She adds, "With a global and fully remote team, autonomy and independence are extremely valued. That is why we have a flat organizational structure where everyone is the "owner" of their own projects, accountable for their actions and decisions. We see that this not only motivates our teams but also gives room for flexibility and agility, even more so during these uncertain times."

Thanks to the limitless extent of the organization, Seedstars is able to recruit the most sought-for talent around the globe and expand to new markets with great ease. In fact, in 2020, Seedstars was present in over 91 countries with local representatives, partners, and alumni, amounting to a global community of 150,000 members.

Seedstars activities fall into two main areas:

Seedstars Community is part of the business that supports entrepreneurs in their personal and business growth as well as preparation for fundraising. The flagship project that encompasses these aspects is the Seedstars World Competition, a start-up pitch contest that has been running since 2013 and the winner of which is able to win up to USD 500,000 in equity investment. The project started off with a world tour in over 20 emerging markets led by Alisée de Tonnac and Pierre-Alain Maisson, cofounder of Seedstars. Today, the competition covers over 90 countries and gathers more than 7000 entrepreneurs each year, also bringing together a network of more than 700 active mentors as well as more than 1200 active investors. Additionally, Seedstars has developed more than 130 training programs to educate entrepreneurs on topics ranging from growth and revenue, fundraising, and international expansion to talent and management development. To date, Seedstars has trained over 4000 entrepreneurs.

Seedstars International is an emerging market VC fund focused on impactful seed-stage tech start-up companies. The fund has invested in 59 entities in 28 countries, covering key sectors such as financial services, health, education, and agriculture. The team invests in batches of 10–15 ventures that are supported through an intense three-month program focused on growth and fundraising. 54% of portfolio companies have already gone on to raise follow-on capital from later-stage investors, including Omidyar, Sequoia, and YCombinator. Seedstars is to continue to strengthen this positioning to support more high-growth ventures that drive economic, social, and environmental change with collaborations with other regional funds and in the process of putting in place Seedstars Global Fund 2. To date, the investors that have participated in the first investments include HNWIs, family offices, and business angel communities. But for the larger funds, Seedstars attracts more institutional investors such as Development Financing Institutions, Impact funds, and Corporates.

Seedstars largely functions based on a set of primary values that hold its team and community tight together and are used as the reference point for both strategy and day-to-day operations. But unlike other enterprises, Seedstars is very blunt about their values and truly holds all their people, management included, accountable to those, especially when it comes to their biannual staff assessment, or as they call them "tribe councils." Moreover, individuals who excelled at specific values are featured in the monthly internal newsletter as a public praise for their achievements in mastering the company values. These are:

- Get Sh*t Done, which reflects the importance of creating an impact, moving the needle, and being able to prioritize.
- In Experiments We Trust, which encourages taking data-driven decisions, trying out new things that no one has ever done before, and learning new things.
- Independently Together, which means being able to take initiative with a greater common goal in mind as well as being able to give tough feedback.
- Out of the Comfort Zone, which challenges the status quo and pushes people to take risks and do great things.
- Follow the Money, which symbolizes profit with purpose and the importance of understanding the financial impact of decisions.
- Hack the System, which is about having a growth mindset and finding new ways of doing things better and faster.
- Keep it Swiss, which stands for delivering high-quality work, paying attention to details, and being professional.

- No Excuses, which keeps people accountable for their tasks and at the same time encourages them to ask for support when needed.

To engage in the so-called angel investing in start-ups with a high potential for growth was seen as fundamental. And to assess a prospective venture's scalability was seen as particularly key. But to maintain a common focus among a growing population of employees, a consequence of the growth in the businesses, was seen as hard. Another difficulty might be for the various entrepreneurs of the chosen businesses to maintain their energy intact and at full "drive" throughout longer periods of growth. A third problem would now and then be found at the governmental level, including at times introductions of restricting regulations, often with short-term focus, and often also to support particular political agendas. Scaling might thus become hard.

The mission of Seedstars is to create a positive impact in people's lives through entrepreneurship and technology. They are doing so by investing in ventures that might make a true difference in the world. "By investing in socially responsible businesses with a high-growth potential, Seedstars is able to accelerate and scale the positive impact created by these businesses not only in their initial local markets but also by expanding them internationally and introducing them to new potential partners and investors," mentions Charlie Graham-Brown, Chief Investment Officer at Seedstars.

Seedstars is an expert when it comes to attracting the most promising start-ups. As well as in managing its deal flow. With its wide range of educational programs run throughout the year with its private and public partners, founders might be significantly able to grow their businesses faster, expand their international networks and visibility, receive actionable feedback on their performance, and be much more likely to qualify to receive follow-on investment.

For this reason, Seedstars runs its own so-called Growth Program, a three-month post-acceleration program designed to help start-ups build a growth team and implement a growth methodology in order to support scaling up the venture and raise more funds. Selected start-ups are entitled to an investment of USD 50,000, a USD 100,000 worth pack of in-kind services and perks provided by Microsoft, Intel, Hubspot, Amazon, and others, as well as a USD 500,000 follow-on investment from Seedstars and its global investor network.

Seedstars' operating model is rather complex yet complementary in its actions and completely in line with its mission to impact people's lives in emerging markets. For the sake of simplicity, it can be split into these parts: start-up selection, cash flow management, team building and acquiring talent, branding, training and experimentation, and finally decentralized management.

One of the key aspects of Seedstars' operational model is to find the most promising tech start-ups from various emerging markets and, most importantly, to try to find out whether these start-ups have the potential to grow and to scale. Do the founders of these start-ups have what it takes to be successful entrepreneurs?

Over the past years, Seedstars has been refining its secret formula to help the selection process, developing an investment Readiness Score. This is an algorithm based on the scalability of the start-up, team fit, and team experience that creates an analytical model to review the potential of each given venture to succeed.

"The Investment Readiness Score can provide a rather solid judgement regarding the start-up's potential and can influence our decision to invest in a business, however, our Investments Team makes the final call. There are simply also some factors that need to be brought up case by case, given the diversity of solutions and scenarios existing in each country we operate in," says Alisée de Tonnac as a reflection of the methodology.

Some of the most common reasons for failure include misjudgment of the entrepreneur. At times, they might simply not have what it takes, which is incredible resilience and willingness to persist over lengthy periods of time. Other reasons may be related to an inability to actually achieve anticipated scaling effects, say, due to a business' nonviable planning, the introduction of new legislation or regulation that might make scaling more difficult, or simply unrealistic cash-flow estimates.

One of the most difficult aspects of managing a start-up might be to come up with a realistic forecast regarding future cash flow. It goes without saying that it is generally not optimal to attempt to raise more cash when a business' current cash flow is already stretched and/or low due to unrealistic ways of running this business until now.

Another key aspect of the success of a business is its people. Hiring and managing talent that will take ownership in their assignments and will have a proper cultural fit is a great challenge for any start-up, and perhaps particularly so when facing rapid growth and added complexity. For this reason, Seedstars has optimized its recruitment processes to approach this as a collaborative decision-making method, in which various team members are consulted at different stages of the hiring process to make the best assessment possible.

Branding is critical for any start-up since this is the statement of the firm's positioning of its products and/or services, as well as the driver of its external image. Besides building a distinctive brand identity through a unique logo and brand name, Seedstars has also invested heavily in its online and offline presence in its major markets by vigorously spreading its brand message and amplifying it through Seedstars Ambassadors, active supporters, and enablers of entrepreneurial ecosystems and widely influential figures who also believe in the power of entrepreneurship.

Training and experimentation are an integral part of Seedstars' approach. Staying up to date with the latest trends, building on good practices from other start-ups, having a data-driven approach, and discussing the learnings are all part of the development of both the Seedstars team and its portfolio companies.

In order to achieve an effective experimentation mindset, people must be given the freedom to try out new ways of doing things better and faster. Only then can the best talents be attracted to the Seedstars network and be kept in it! This entices a flexible approach and the ability to go out of one's comfort zone while also keeping the eyes on the prize. This is a perfect symbiosis between the "In Experiments We Trust" and the "Follow the Money," two values previously described.

"At the end of the day, it's the organizational health that carries the day. Good executives are comfortable with some ambiguity and with giving more than one takes" mentions Alisée de Tonnac in a comment on how to keep the balance between experimentation and maintaining focus.

Seedstars has thoughtfully been developing decentralized management processes with the goal of enabling each team member to take their own decisions and also be able to be accountable for them while never hesitating to ask for support. It is not the traditional hierarchical top-down system where decisions are imposed by the top management, but a group approach in which every squad, be it in marketing, finance or tech, makes the best call as the experts in their field. This type of management policy encourages people to be the leaders of themselves and avoids bottlenecks related to the decision-making processes. It keeps business operations fluid.

Seedstars considers it critical to cope with several critical dilemmas and strives to find a reasonable balance when it comes to these main challenges.

- Idealistic purpose and business profits, i.e., need to create value, but with a clear integrity driving this, so that good business growth and reasonable societal impact are combined.
- Business focus to serve one's customers and to raise capital is also seen as critical and to take place in parallel and not as sequential "on-offs."

- Learning through experimentation and building on good examples of business practice.
- Getting the job done and being appreciated in the community is essential to entrepreneurs who want to be robust enough to be ready to be "disliked," as they promote sound business practices. It is "for entrepreneurs by entrepreneurs."
- Pursue formal analysis and exercise behavioral judgment. But analysis can substitute good face-to-face interactions.
- Balance growth and focus. When Seedstars was in its start-up phase, it had to live with a relatively high level of complexity to ameliorate a too high-risk of exposure. But after having grown, it was able to simplify its operations by focusing more on clusters with relatively similar investments in specific countries and regions.

Seedstars is indeed a good example of a successful organization that pursues impact investing. It has also demonstrated that systematic investments in the developing world can indeed be profitable. There does *not* have to be a conflict between a social purpose and making money, profitable idealism!

Brigitte Baumann, Founder and co-CEO of GoBeyond Investing (Interviewed June 2020)

This investment fund aims its attention exclusively on participation in ventures that are at the early stage, termed "Angel Investing." The fund has been highly successful so far. When it comes to investing at a firm's very beginning stage, there is a strong focus on assuring this firm's vision and its management team, particularly its likely ability to avoid being too compartmentalized and too hierarchical in thinking. Later on, when new rounds of investment might be called for, to develop a "mind map" for what it might take for this given firm to succeed, including also being specific regarding potential exits—when, to which new owner, future role(s) of the existing management, and so on.

Ms. Brigitte Baumann, the founder of GoBeyond, a community for Early-Stage Investing, has 17 years' experience as an angel investor and was named European Angel Investor in 2015. Before GoBeyond she was with American Express, where she led intrapreneurial teams. One innovation led to the creation of Expedia.com. This is where she got the entrepreneurial "bug," and over time became a business angel. She started the first learning by founding

GoBeyond group in 2008 to encourage individuals to support start-ups, so-called angel investing. Primarily, it is focused on the Swiss and EU markets.

Brigitte Baumann has a portfolio of 41 investments and has "lived through" 76 financing rounds. She is often a keynote speaker, trainer, and consultant and focuses on designing educational content for investors, Board members, entrepreneurs, and corporations. In May 2015, Brigitte received the European Investor of the Year award from EBAN. In 2017, Brigitte was also selected to EY's European Winning Women Entrepreneur program. In November 2016, 2017, and 2018, Brigitte was listed as one of Europe's Top 50 Most Influential Women in the start-up and venture capital space and Top Women in FinTech. Brigitte is President Emeritus of EBAN, the European trade association for Business Angels and Seed Funds, and is Chair of the Global Deal Network at Young Presidents Organization (YPO), which currently consists of 28,000 CEO's. She also works for the World Bank as expert trainer designing and delivers an investment readiness program in Georgia.

GoBeyond offers access to angel investing in both a fun and professional way. Its approach to angel investing as an asset class. It curates connections between like-minded investors and entrepreneurs. It is key that these are at the forefront of innovation, with talent, drive, and determination to succeed. Most GoBeyond members are also entrepreneurs. GoBeyond aims to provide constructive support by sharing valuable resources, facts, figures, insight, and expertise, i.e., comprehensive start-up building, with managing and exit process in place. GoBeyond equips investors with intelligent analytics and also provides comprehensive training programs.

As of early 2020, the following facts apply:

- 884 early-stage investors that come from 45 different countries and represent 48 nationalities.
- Invested a total of EUR 24.1m (CHF 27.3m) in cash.
- 88% of investors who have invested at least once have had breakeven or positive returns based on actual exit values and Net Asset Value.

As of now, Ms. Baumann foresees a typical 3-stage finance support process for entrepreneurial start-ups:

- Key first round for an emerging start-up. The vision and the team are particularly important at this early stage. An entrepreneur raising financing should understand at what stage her/his company is in the way that investors think about development and what they are ready for. Lay out what they want in terms of money, terms, support, and valuation now as well as

forward-thinking to the next rounds. It is useful to develop a matrix that includes the different types of financing that could fit each financing round. 2–3 types of financing can happen at the same time.
- Second stage: Additional funding is conditioned on positive testing of the basic business concept—does it seem to be viable or not? From an investment portfolio point of view, follow-on financing rounds are then very important. 10 years of angel investor data that GoBeyond has collected shows that investing or not in follow-on rounds is a strong driver of returns, in contrast to merely the static attractiveness of a given project at the first round. So, the secret is to assess the attractiveness of strings of investments for a given project, having used the first round to "test the water."
- The third and possibly fourth, and typically final rounds that involve bringing in considerable additional financing. For these rounds Ms. Baumann, as a business angel develops a "mind-map" including who might be the potential acquirers of this start-up? From whom do these usually hear about the start-up? Are some of those investors who may be interested to come in already present? GoBeyond members often coinvest with other investors. Recommendations are important! So, to focus on investors that are likely to bring in others is critical—the power of recommendations.

Ms. Baumann strongly believes in meaningful diversification of investments, both when it comes to her own holdings as well as when it comes to the asset mixes of other investors in GoBeyond, i.e., a portfolio of investments. She emphasizes that diversification can help to get rid of biases. Keeping humility in the process is also critical. So, taking a portfolio approach to angel investing is key. Ms. Baumann applies several approaches to assess and manage her angel investment portfolio:

- Published real (rather than self-reported) data, say, from other GoBeyond member portfolios.
- Careful listening to investors' experiences.
- Ms. Baumann already prefers to rely on her own network of experts, whom she can trust.
- Curiosity, open-mindedness, willingness to learn, and ability to deal with new challenges are key features of successful members of this investor community, whose principles rely on co-sharing and peer-to-peer intervention.

The pandemic represented a wake-up call. Having previously been through several crises, Ms. Baumann felt:

- Investors generally seem to feel that they must always let their money work, i.e., continue to invest, whether there is a pandemic or not!
- More thinking about which ways key developments might take the world will not necessarily add up to much.
- To adapt fast is more key than ever, i.e., maintain speed!
- Be agile! Show leadership, "agility muscle." During crisis is the time to use this muscle!

So, entrepreneurship seems to matter more during times of crisis than usual (a mindset). Early-stage investments will not disappear, even during times of pandemics!

It is not only the CEO who should be responsible for keeping the burn rate under control, but the entire team, typically consisting of two to three people near or at the top. And learning is paramount. Some learn faster than others how to latch onto a more realistic burn rate.

There are above all four factors that seem to impact decisions regarding burn rate:

- The strategy: how fast to grow (often with a high burn rate, when growing fast)
- The cash position ("How much reserves in the bank?")
- Exit strategy (understanding how important or not it will be to have the burn rate under control when attempting to exit)
- The founder and his/her team, as well as other shareholders (what can they accept?)

There seem to be two other platforms comparable to GoBeyond: BAS (Business Angels Schweiz) and SICTIC. Ms. Baumann considers both of these as excellent. GoBeyond collaborates with both of them. It is good for business angels to have choice in angel communities they might join. Many join more than one.

To better understand GoBeyond's uniqueness, it is perhaps useful to look more clearly into Ms. Brigitte Baumann's unique background and investor philosophy:

- Ms. Baumann was an angel investor for a number of years, from 2003 onwards, before creating the first GoBeyond angel group in 2008.
- Angel investing is an asset class and should be approached as such rather than viewed as a charitable activity.

- An angel investor is not necessarily an exited entrepreneur or very wealthy individual with excessive business experience, time, and money, but rather, can also be an individual who is willing to learn how to invest. This said, individual can advance from novice investor to lead investor, and at a later stage, to investor group coach as well as a venture partner.
- Do not think too local! Ms. Baumann does not.
- The service providers to angel investors are critical to an angel investor's journey and success.
- Besides, doing "good" is of course great to do truly well. Angels can indeed make money too!

A number of GoBeyond's members are also shareholders in GoBeyond! They do buy into GoBeyond's philosophy of learning, investing, and networking, of course.

Diversity is important, particularly to include women and next generation! GoBeyond has had close to 50% women as members since its infancy, ten times the industry average. It also offers Next Gen programs with its legacy mix of learning, investing, and networking, i.e., education, while investing with others. The learning is not just via webinars and videos but also through working with experienced angel investors and investor group coaches. This, above all, seems to differentiate GoBeyond from BAS and SICTIC. These latter two are perhaps somewhat less hands-on, according to Ms. Baumann.

Training now seems to have become a business on its own, virtual and global!

Ms. Baumann set up Efino to "fill the start-up financing gap." She feels that although entrepreneurial ecosystems have blossomed globally, their developments are hindered for several reasons:

- Investors often lack early-stage investing training to more fully understand the journey upon which they are embarking.
- Entrepreneurs may not always know how to properly prepare or run financing rounds, and they may also commonly struggle to develop diverse teams for continued innovation.

Efino's mission is to fill the start-up financing gap by accompanying the entrepreneurs, educating them, enlightening and coaching them, and enabling the following participants:

- Angel investors: to have a more successful personal journey and investment portfolio.

- Entrepreneurs: to prepare, plan, execute, close, and leverage the next financing rounds.
- Start-up board members: to prepare new and experienced board members to handle situations associated with being on a start-up board.
- Ecosystem players: to design, create, and sustain ecosystem building initiatives.

In collaboration with key local partners and stakeholders, Efino's trainers are specialized in analyzing entrepreneurial ecosystems and identifying where support is needed, ensuring that local players acquire relevant tools and knowledge to support and scale up their early-stage financing ecosystems, and helping them acquire more independence in the process. As such, Efino's expertise is thus in financing, training, and coaching future Deal Leaders, Group Coaches, Business Angels Networks Managers, and Start-up Board Members.

GoBeyond, Efino, and former Lorange Network (now part of IMD) seem to have a lot in common. All three are focused on stimulating better investments, and they have "matching mechanisms" between investors and entrepreneurs. All are focusing on learning as a key way to better investments as well as learning to be sharper by doing. And learning is not only about formal training but also about building gut experiences! Finally, each sees networking as central to success, being part of communities that enriches, diversifies, tests, challenges, and evolves, both a person and his/her project or idea, the person and the company.

Thomas Dübendorfer, President, SICTIC (Interviewed December 2020)

Mr. Thomas Dübendorfer made his first start-up investment in 2010. In the last ten years he has directly invested in 28 start-ups, out of which he has exited 4 so far. He is currently actively involved in about ten start-up companies. He holds a Ph.D. in Computer Science from ETH Zurich and is cofounder and president of SICTIC. He has worked in Silicon Valley and at Google as a tech lead and security software engineer. He is an angel investor himself, cofounder and board member in several Swiss tech start-ups, and has had several successful start-up exits. He was among the "Top 100 Digital Shapers of Switzerland" and featured as one of the "Top 200 Most Prominent Personalities" in the 2019 edition of "Who Is Who in Zurich."

He spends around one day per week on SICTIC-related activities. This is the second association for which he has been president. His first one was for information security professionals, and he has more than doubled the membership base, to sustainably more than 1000 members. Growing it in the French-speaking part was a particularly big challenge.

Is Mr. Dübendorfer trying to get himself into the "best" deals? In reality, however, this does not seem to be an issue. On the contrary, there may be investment projects where a given proposer might not actually prefer a relatively large set of angel investors to participate but might prefer only one or two investors. In such situations, where SICTIC's pool of angel investors is thus not a realistic financing alternative, Mr. Dübendorfer has, however, at times decided to participate in order that such specific projects might also "get off the ground." Furthermore, he gets a large number of high-quality start-up deals that are not a fit for him personally. Thus, he merely encourages the entrepreneurs to apply to SICTIC.

SICTIC is a Swiss Investment Club. This nonprofit organization aspires to fulfill two major functions. Partly, it attempts to identify attractive business candidates for early investing. Closeness to Zurich's world-renowned university ETH as well as to the equally strong EPFL in Lausanne, seem to be central here. Both top institutions, by the way, comprise the Swiss Federal Institutes of Technology. Adding a perspective of what this firm's market might be, as well as how to reach these customers, seems to be particularly critical. Also, SCTIC attempts to line up investors as part owners in these angel investment candidates, partly through the commitment of relatively modest fees from a large number of individuals who might have contributed to SICTIC. Also, partly through Zürcher Kantonalbank (ZKB), who may coinvest. Similarly, various independent angel investment funds might coinvest (SEEDX; Wigham Ventures; Alpha Ventures; Tomahawk Venture Capital; …). Sustainability is seen as particularly important, and the capital need shall not be larger than 2M CHF before exiting.

Swiss ICT Investor Club (SICTIC) is an angel investor club, a matchmaker between founders of high-tech innovative start-ups and angel investors, who often tend to be different from usual investors. It is a nonprofit association with the mission of matching smart money investors with the best early-stage tech start-ups in Switzerland. Investors tend to invest relatively small sums in each given start-up; at SICTIC, the minimum is CHF 20,000 per investor per investment, but all are free to not invest at all. Each individual investor pays a small annual fee to get access to the online deal flow database and pitching events. Each of these angel investors must also, however, sign an agreement that binds an investor to confidentiality in investor deals, fair and ethical behavior towards other investors and the start-up, and also stipulates that an investor must be ready to support SICTIC when it comes to the running of its various governance functions.

Some family firms have also joined SICTIC's investor community. The fee is significantly larger, however, for so-called "preferred co-investors," which include certain banks (currently just Zürcher Kantonalbank) as well as venture funds (SEED X Liechtenstein, Wingman Ventures, Alpana Ventures, Tomahawk.vc, and two more). This group of currently seven staff are all also professional investors. They have invested between CHF 200,000 and about CHF 1,500,000 in particular start-ups alongside angel investors. There are around 340 angel investors that are a part of the SICTIC investor club—large and small!

It goes without saying that most of the angel investors are indeed also undertaking other activities, such as running a company or a large company division and/or also attending to their own investment portfolios and attending to various private investments. Angel investing is perhaps more like a leisure activity to many of them. And, as noted, these angel investors have also agreed to help the start-ups they invest in, or in different other ways, say, by giving access to their business networks, coaching the founders, making introductions to potential customers, or joining an advisory board.

This nonprofit network was founded in 2014. It charges no transaction fee of any sort, nor does it go for any overall profits or carried interest. Legally, as noted, it is an association., with its own board, with twelve members, an operations team with around 3.5 full-time job equivalents (seven persons) and a start-up jury that acts as a projects evaluation committee which can be expanded/exchanged to a total of around 20 persons. This includes savvy angel investors, financial, legal, and technical experts, and so on.

SICTIC might be seen as very highly focused, perhaps in contrast to most other such "matchmaking" organizations, which often tend to be broader in scope. Specifically, its focus is on:

- Technology-based companies exclusively, and of the kind of technology where one might often have to build a "demonstration" product first and hence most start-ups typically have no cash flow for at least, say, the first two years or so.
- Star-ups tend to be in the so-called "seed stage" or "early stage."
- They must be scalable.
- There must be a balanced team in its leadership.
- It shall need a maximum of 2M CHF in financing.

SICTIC is not a good fit for life science start-ups, consultancy firms, real estate investments, or companies with their domicile outside Switzerland.

As of today, SICTIC is screening around 400 start-ups per annum. The jury rejects many of these. Only around 100 end up being deemed strong enough to be pitched at one of SICTIC's Investor Days, where many angel investors are present. In the end, only between 40 and 50 of these end up being qualified to receive funding from the SICTIC network of angel investors. Prominent "meeting places" between angel investors and fintech start-ups are the two annual Swiss Fintech Investor Days, where, say, 12 or so Fintech start-ups "pitch" to more than 200 investors.

Many of the proposed start-ups have their origins in Switzerland's technical universities, above all ETH (Zurich) or EPFL (Lausanne). While a lot of good research is done, by faculty and students, academic institutions such as these may have something lacking in their capabilities to commercialize good research ideas. This may be partly due to a perhaps natural resistance to build on government-funded research for later commercial efforts. And it may partly simply also be that such institutions in general may not have very good access to broader investor bases. There are, of course, dedicated technology transfer offices in most such academic institutions, but these might, in general, not be large and effective enough to be able to fully cope with the challenge of finding sufficiently many good investors. These are thus perhaps not as effective as one might have hoped when it comes to stimulating effective commercialization.

SICTIC has two offices as of present: Zurich and Lausanne. The plan is to soon open a third office in the Italian-speaking part of Switzerland in order to stimulate more effective "matchmaking" there too.

What are the formal steps that a start-up proposer shall have to go through? First, each project proposer must send in an actual application with a 90-second video pitch, a 2–3 page fact sheet, and a short pitch slide deck. As noted, there are around 400 such applications per year. These proposed projects should be based on an innovative, scalable, technological business idea. It is often found, however, that while many of these products may be built around a basically strong idea, many of these may be lacking in one or more other dimension, the most common being the following three:

- A project's organization may have an uneven competence mix in its team. A clear leader, for instance, might be often missing. Business development and financial competence are also often absent.
- The marketing strategy may be lacking in realism. Many of the proposers are, perhaps, overly technical. And some may not even have considered in

earnest who their customers might be! They may simply not have put much thought into this!
- Legal and ethical aspects. Often, these typically relatively young and unexperienced individual proposers might not even be aware of the fact that there might potentially be illegal sides with their proposals, such as, for instance, a need to have a license from FINMA (the Swiss regulator of financial institutions).

The start-up applications are judged through a formalized panel with typically eight jury members. This panel might, however, at times be larger, in that specialist judges as well as other alternates might be drawn from a total group of around 20 judges, as noted. They all work pro bono. But they are of course benefitting from a flow of diverse learning inputs, from each of the many submissions, as well as from interacting with fellow jurors. Thus, jurors are indeed learners too! Approximately half of the panel of jurors, about four, tend to come from the pool of SICTIC board members. The other half is coming from the members of angel investors and preferred coinvestors.

Each project is rated by each juror according to the following rating criteria:

- Factor 1: People. Is the project team able to deliver and appropriately put together?
- Factor 2: How promising is the business potential?
- Factor 3: How innovative is the project?
- Factor 4: How well is it all presented, i.e., the quality of the proposal documents that have been submitted?

Throughout this evaluation process each juror is also being encouraged to look out for "red flags" in any given proposal. It is clear that this evaluation process is both time- and energy-consuming for each juror. The contrast between SICTIC and a typical angel investor indicates that each person must indeed be prepared to invest both money and time in activities such as this. Angel investors thus benefit from the pro bono work the jury is doing.

There are also "matchmaking" meetings between angel investors and those founders that have passed the screening by the panel of jurors. Most prominent among these is the so-called Swiss Fintech Investor Day. As noted, there are two large annual conferences, each with around 200 or more angel investors participating. There are also another 12, or so, additional events annually, as well as more than 40 luncheons, apéros, seminars, and so on per year. There is a common principle for all of these events, however: A large majority must be angel investors, with the aim being at least around 90%.

A survey among the around 340 angel investors members was sent out in connection with how each of these might consider the recent pandemic threat. This revealed the following:

Investment profile:

- A majority, around 80%, will modify their investment strategy only moderately or not at all due to impact from the pandemic.
- Around 40% intend to invest less than before but shall focus more on the quality of each start-up instead.
- Only a small fraction, around 6%, said to have stopped investing.
- In contrast, a very small group of members plan to invest more than before in new start-ups.

The Swiss Economy:

- Around 89% of the angel investors foresaw a significant slowdown in the Swiss economy as a consequence of the pandemic.
- Thereof, around 10% even expected even a depression.
- Only around 11% foresaw a mild impact on the Swiss economy.
- 44% of the respondents expected that we shall be back to normal economic activity in Switzerland from before mid-2021.
- 37%, however, expected a return to normality only after the end of next year, 2021.
- In general, there seemed to be considerable pessimism among the angel investors in light of the pandemic crisis.

Project Valuation:

- There appears to be around a 25% decrease in the valuation of typical start-ups. This implies that the start-up founder's ownership parts may tend to go down, while in contrast angel investors might tend to end up with the same or higher ownership share as before!
- Rounds for funding tend to be smaller.
- The start-up managements had to be able to cope with less abundance of funds than before and, further, had to be more prudent in "burn rate" management!

As noted, SICTIC charges no finder's fee to start-ups, neither before nor after actual funding, nor any exit fee when a start-up is sold. The financing of SICTIC is thus largely financed through the annual fees from the angel investors as well as from the preferred coinvestors. In addition, there is also financial support from several corporate partners.

SICTIC is indeed highly successful, as might perhaps be evidenced by its growth of angel investors and the high number of start-up investments done. As of end-2015 there were only around 24 angel investors, while at the end of 2019 there were more than 330! Key contributing factors might be:

- SICTIC has proven itself to be an effective matchmaker between angel investors and technology start-up founders.
- Clear focus: Swiss, technology innovation (but not med tech!), scalable, with plausible business rationale, and realistic organizational capabilities.
- Effective in matchmaking conferences and other events; Two flagship events (Swiss Fintech Investor Day, Swiss Blockchain Investor Day), about 12 smaller events, more than 40 unique investor workshops and lunches, etc.
- Panel of strong expert judges, with a formalized approach to the screening and ranking of projects.
- No finders fee nor any exit fees. SICTIC is financed exclusively through membership fees and from corporate partners, i.e., with no conflict of interest.
- A clear and simple governance structure and a very lean organization.

Urs Wietlisbach, Cofounder of Partners Group (Interviewed April 2019)

Partners Group (PG) Impact Investing, run by Urs Wietlisbach, is making investments in entities that satisfy the criterion of being able to deliver "impact at scale." This is close to what we call "deep" impact, which attempts to open up opportunities for investors to create positive environmental value, i.e., to stimulate such businesses. This is indeed relatively near to charity and philanthropy, but with a clear business angle to it. Impact investing is becoming increasingly significant, and this may represent a good way for general and positive future societal growth.

Urs Wietlisbach cofounded Partners Group in 1996 and PG Impact Investments in 2015. He is a member of Partners Group's board of directors and chairman of its markets committee, based in Zug. He has 29 years of industry experience. Prior to founding Partners Group, he worked at Goldman Sachs & Co. and Credit Suisse. He holds a master's degree in business administration from the University of St. Gallen (HSG), Switzerland. Nowadays,

Wietlisbach spends around 70% of his time on Partners Group business and management issues. In addition, he is heavily committed to impact investing and was instrumental in establishing PG Impact Investments as a separate company from Partners Group. Wietlisbach is also interested in sports; he is involved in Swiss Ski and Sport Life, as well as in higher education and research, through his involvement in HSG. Additionally, he is an advisory board member of the Swiss Startup Factory. Recently he also invested in a hotel in Arosa.

Urs Wietlisbach is one of the three founders of Partners Group, a global private market investment manager headquartered in Zug, Switzerland. This highly successful firm was founded in 1996 and now has 20 offices worldwide and more than USD 83 billion in assets under management, with a market cap of 285 billion dollars.

Wietlisbach has a unique interest in impact investing and was instrumental in establishing PG Impact Investments, an independent impact investment firm fully owned by the nonprofit PG Impact Investments Foundation. Though independent, PG Impact Investments has access to the global investment platform, infrastructure, and specialist resources of Partners Group. Being so closely aligned with Partners Group's people, professionalism, know-how, and governance, an efficient and performance-driven approach to impact investing seems inevitable for PG Impact Investments.

PG Impact Investments is currently investing its first fund. It had raised USD 210 million from a mix of private individuals and institutions. It has a team of fourteen full-time staff led by Urs Baumann, a former serial entrepreneur who now enjoys "giving back" to society through his role as CEO of PG Impact Investments.

PG Impact Investments' mission is to improve the lives of underserved people by investing in companies that provide access to basic products and services, including those in the following sectors: financial inclusion, energy, health care, education, food, agriculture, and affordable housing.

For first-time investors looking at the world of charitable or impact investing, it is important to understand the full spectrum of options available. These range from purely charitable donations to the support of specific causes or projects to investments seeking a mainstream financial return (alongside impact) at the other. The spectrum of impact investment options might run as follows:

- Charity entails personal donations to support specific causes or projects with no expectation of financial return. It is worth noting that although the "charity industry" is considered many large charities, they might not

necessarily be very well run. They may have heavy overheads, excessive bureaucracy, and even questionable governance.
- Philanthropy often involves supporting particular causes or projects with no expectation of returns, i.e., quite similar to charity. However, philanthropy is often more strategic and long term in nature than charity; investments are usually made in philanthropic foundations that are attached to a company or a family (office). For example, in addition to his activities at Partners Group and PG Impact Investments, Urs Wietlisbach manages his own philanthropic foundation, which has a particular focus on supporting education, sports, and socially disadvantaged people in Switzerland as well as an international focus on education and human rights.
- Deep impact is a traditional form of impact investment management in which capital is raised from investors and invested on their behalf by professional and regulated investment managers, such as PG Impact Investments, with the ambition of generating positive social (and/or environmental) impact for an underserved population alongside an attractive financial return. The strategy and approach of impact investing tends to be similar to that in private equity in that investments are made from dedicated funds and recipient companies are generally private. Typical impact investments are relatively small in scale and also typically focused on emerging markets.
- Impact-at-scale is a term for mainstream private equity funds that also have a mandate to generate social or environmental impact. These funds, which are offered by several of the largest private equity managers, including Partners Group, are typically much larger in size than deep impact investment funds. They tend to operate on a larger scale and to have a longer track record, which can also be a requirement or preference of large institutional investors.

GoodLife—Founded in Nairobi in 2014 and is an example of how PG Impact Investments is investing. GoodLife matches trusted pharmaceuticals to customers across East Africa, where almost a third of pharmaceuticals sold are believed to be counterfeit. By establishing stores in convenient locations that typically have a lot of traffic, such as shopping malls and/or near gas stations, non-counterfeit drugs can be distributed to a broad set of the local population. The project demonstrates that it is possible to both "do something good" and turn a profit. Eventually, this project may be sold to a strategic buyer, which, as a key exit plan, is essential for any project of this type.

Shared-X produces specialty and organic high-yield crops, sold directly to farmers at premium prices. Under the shared prosperity model, Shared-X is providing 1000 independent smallholder farmers in Latin America with farming know-how and market access, resulting in three to five times more income for these farmers.

Most deep impact investment funds focus on emerging markets and make investments in several countries. In addition to the usual risk of the private equity of investments failing to make their expected return targets (in a worst-case outcome, an investor would not get any money back at all), two other types of principal risk surround traditional (deep) impact investments:

- Currency risk is a difficult and challenging area, particularly for equity investments in which cash flows cannot be accurately predicted and hedged.
- Political risk cannot be influenced by an investor. The only way to manage political risk is through a high degree of diversification, e.g., through investing in a fund that makes impact investments in several countries and geographic regions.

Impact investing is indeed now a reality that both contributes to good causes and can secure a reasonable return on investments. Urs Wietlisbach has contributed significantly to the growth of this industry with the founding of PG Impact Investments.

30

Closing Remarks for the Part

Investing is complex, yes, but can be made simpler by pushing hard to stay focused and linked to your investment strategy and goals. We have seen the importance of diversification, constant reviewing of the portfolio, and continuous learning. Investment mistakes to not make—trying to time the market, fallacies of staying too narrow, paying too high fees, not choosing the right employees or talents to back up one's investments, pitfalls regarding over- as well as under-investing, "dragging one's feet" and thus not exiting at the right time—were all key.

There are, perhaps, several biggest mistakes when investing. It is perhaps a matter of balance, attempted harmony. One should thus try to be realistic regarding this upside/downside balance. If in doubt, wait! There will always be new opportunities. There is no stigma to saying "no." But when saying "yes," avoid underestimating one's financing needs. Be more realistic regarding most ventures' potential financing needs. Also, assess the financial solidity of any coinvestors. To be able to look at established businesses, with actual sales and customers, real cash flows, shall always be an advantage. Never forget to consider the quality of a key project promoter, especially regarding realism and ethics. To stay clear of fund managers in banks, promotion of own in-house products offered by given banks almost always tends to yield disappointment.

To invest so as to maximize wealth thus has to do with modifying a firm's portfolio of activities by means of deliberate investments. The intention is, of course, to improve performance, to maximize wealth! There are at least three approaches when it comes to this.

To invest relatively more in "new" activity areas, such as high tech, bio-medical technology/medical sciences, and/or IT. The Swedish Wallenberg industrial group has created a wholly owned subsidiary, Patricia Industries, for instance, to pursue medical science investments, now an increasingly important part of the group's portfolio.

To shift investments towards particularly attractive geographic areas, such as those characterized by relatively high growth, a high degree of economic and political stability, and a positive attitude towards business, with, say, less regulations, favorable tax regimes, etc. Countries such as China, SE Asia, Singapore, and parts of the USA (Silicon Valley) come to mind.

To invest in senior executives who might have a strong track record when it comes to being able to "deliver." The business search firm, NCA (Novastone Capital Advisors), comes to mind, where successful executives are being backed by investors so as to be able to go after specific firms that these leaders deem to be attractive. Or consider the Singapore-based firm Antler, where the approach is to identify executives with exceptional business acumen and to "invest" in these people.

It is interesting to notice that investing to maximize wealth typically involves much more than emphasizing freestanding projects that might feature high ROIs. Effective wealth accumulation involves deliberate business repositioning, getting into more attractive business areas, focusing on attractive geographies, and backing successful business leaders. To focus exclusively on picking projects with high ROI is not enough!

Part VII

Leading the Organization: Towards Fulfilling the Mission

The first responsibility of a leader is to define reality. The last is to say thank you. In between the two, the leader must become a servant and a debtor.
—Max De Pree, businessman, author

Competence, caring, and conviction combine to form a fundamental element — shaping the fighting spirit of your troops. Leadership means reaching the souls of your troops, instilling a sense of commitment and purpose in the face of challenges so severe that they cannot be put into words.
—General James Mattis, Former Secretary of Defense

31

Practice Insights from Mitzi Perdue, Entrepreneur & Author

When it comes to running a business, my late father and my late husband followed a technique for success that can work for you. Who were they and what is this technique?

Father was the cofounder and president of the Sheraton Hotel chain, and Frank Perdue brought his chicken company from no employees to 20,000 at the time of his death. Both were advocates of the notion that "One good idea can change your life." To get these good ideas, they took courses, attended lectures, read books, studied magazines, hung out with thought leaders, talked with their competitors, attended trade conferences, traveled, and generally did everything possible to enhance the knowledge-related skills they could bring to running and growing their businesses.

I have a word that summarizes both men. They were extreme *informavores*. That is a made-up word. Just as a carnivore consumes meat, an informavore consumes information. By endlessly accumulating knowledge on amazingly different subjects, they were able to see connections that were invisible to others. With so much information under their belts, they were able to see both the big picture and the details. To me, one of the magic keys to success is becoming an informavore.

32

Introduction to Leading the Organization: Towards Fulfilling the Mission

The persons who actually run the business are obviously utterly important. We often speak of "top-down" management and, in some cases, even "bottom-up." The main point is that people matter, whether they are at the top of an organization or further down. Leaders especially play a major role in the way a firm at hand is driven. Their business-self matters, as does their personal-self! This latter point shall be covered in this next chapter.

All top leaders are different. For this reason, every business will be different than any other. Leaders' strengths and weaknesses and aspirations and inspirations have sharp impacts on their entire firms. A component of executive education and lifelong learning, therefore, is evidently top management leadership. This involves pragmatic analysis of self, taking a real look in the mirror, but also opening oneself up to feedback from employees, peers, superiors, customers, investors, and business partners. So, also how do we all become better leaders and better people?

The business world has been sensitized to the off-balance representation of women and men. Educational institutions are not spared by the fairly weak, but fortunately, growing number of women in business, especially in leadership positions. Many business schools still report the numbers of female students to be relatively low, say, between 25 and 40%. Very few have managed to equalize this to an even 50% split. There is hope however, as well as progress. Each year, we do witness higher amounts of female students at business schools, as well as more female professors and staff. Significantly, the fraction of women leaders in business is indeed increasing, although more advancement into top management and board positions is still called for.

Many women can bring what is often labeled the "female element" to business or the classroom, a label that regrettably at times is considered sexist itself. With the risk of oversimplifying or stereotyping what this element is, our conversations with key players, both women and men, have indicated that women in business are often characterized as being more "humane" and more "caring" than their male counterparts. For this reason they are increasingly being called for to work in executive suites, actively shaping many decisions.

Also, executives that sign up for executive development programs at business schools may typically now expect that this side of learning—a certain "bringing the heart into business"—is adequately covered. We see more courses offered in today's leading management education institutions in topics such as listening, negotiation, how to reach compromises, mindfulness, compassionate leadership, diversity and inclusivity, leading in teams, and mentoring. This calls for adding new faculty members, often women, and provides a benefit to traditional business curricula where perhaps many of these topics were formerly not adequately covered nor prioritized. The days of the more one-sided "rational" professors are thus probably numbered. In our educational institutions, we can play a role in accelerating this trend. Top management business has changed!

We shall read how about how leadership of organizations is one of the most fundamental variables to success. Very few businesses can survive over time with bad leaders or weak leadership. Ultimately, "what goes around comes around"—karma. However, there are different types of good leadership or principles we can strive for as leaders, and these vary greatly. And they are culture, generation, market, geography, product/service, etc. dependent. There are no rules.

What is shared commonly though across the multiple ways one can be a strong leader or practice solid leadership is a huge focus on trust, knowledge, vision, altruism, management, and communication skills. In our next section, we shall also examine the leader as self. Who are you really? Strengths and weaknesses—the *real* you—not just how you position your reputation or how you operate in your business—are important to understand.

Business factors we have identified for this Part comprise the dysfunctionality of silos and how the silo phenomena influence leaders of organizations, open-mindedness and listening as critical skills, and the "über" importance of talent management. The readings herein raise some interesting questions about cross-functionality as a way to break down biases and silos within an organization, how quality decisions may be achieved through more open attitudes and a whole lot of listening and dialogue, and how to recognize and develop diverse talent throughout the organization.

Now, the three major takeaways that you can expect from this Part are as follows:

- Clear vision, inspiring, compelling, big moves, do not show off.
- Always have the best people, in teams, dismiss underperformers.
- Stimulate openness, regarding new approaches. Example: AI.

33

Essential Books to Learn About Leading the Organization: Towards Fulfilling the Mission

Daniel James Brown, (2013), The Boys in the Boat, Penguin Random House (Reviewed November 2019)

This book chronicles the famous win by the US "eight rowing" boat in the 1936 Olympics in Berlin, a foot or so ahead of the German boat and another foot ahead of the Italian, after having completed a distance of 2000 meters, with Hitler himself in the stands. It seems to be a matter of six key issues: focus on "me" *and* on the team; a shared culture, the coach's instrumental importance; the ability to sustain tough periods; to stand up for each other; and confidence in a strong social network of support.

The Boys in the Boat chronicles the highly challenging journey of the eight-person US rowing team that won a closely fought Olympic gold in Berlin, 1936 with a mere 0.6-second win over Italy's crew and a 1.0-second win over Germany's. It deals with perhaps the most difficult dilemma facing most modern organizations, corporations, sports teams, and even families: how to create a dual culture focusing on the team, "we, we, we," and on the team's individual performers, "me, me, me." In many modern organizations, high-performing individuals work largely driven by their own interests, and the organization's overall performance is thus far from guaranteed. Similarly, focusing on the team alone may result in unhappy individuals, and thus also an unsatisfactory performance. Organizational cultures that combine these perspectives, however, can lead to improved performance!

In The Boys in the Boat we can learn a great deal about the fundamental dilemmas facing many top executives, based on how the team of US oarsmen handled this to achieve their top performance.

The US rowing team came from the University of Washington on the West Coast. All the crewmembers came from working-class backgrounds and were marked by the Great Depression, which had just ended in 1936. The legendary Al Ulbrickson, of Danish descent, coached the team. The book describes how this group of eight gradually melded to form a superb rowing team that gradually mastered a combination of physical strength and technical superiority. It took a lot of training, discipline, and strong commitment. A series of tough races lay ahead, culminating with winning the US qualifier at Poughkeepsie (ahead of the favorites from the University of Pennsylvania) and the introductory round at the 1936 Olympics (surprisingly ahead of the UK team). Finally, their ultimate triumph was winning the Olympic gold medal, on August 13, 1936, at Grünau Lake in Berlin.

Why is reaching a balance when it comes to handling this dilemma, "me, me, me" versus "we, we, we" so difficult to achieve? What might we learn from the US rowing team's experience? At least five critical success factors seem to emerge:

- A broadly shared common culture. The rowing crew's members all had blue-collar backgrounds, a very tightly knit group. The particular socioeconomic class where team members come from may perhaps not be critical as long as they share a vision. Today, we rightly strive for diverse teams, but we must not forget the unifying force of a shared corporate culture, vision, and mission.
- The coach. Good coaches matter! Al Ulbrickson did not just teach his team members the various technicalities of rowing—he also inspired them to handle setbacks, to "do best when it matters." He was always available when it mattered, and he played a major role in orchestrating all key aspects of his team's preparations and performance. We see that the coach's top-down emphasis allowed the rowers to achieve ambitious performance goals. A productive coach can clearly instill strong team performance, none the least through being a seasoned "psychologist."
- Tough periods. The team confronted and worked through various severe problems, even crises; for instance, the difficult economic realities facing the eights rowing team with expensive travel and being away from work. Most of today's leading top performers, executives, and athletes do not face these issues, of course. Paradoxically, overabundant funding might at times negatively affect teams. Easy funding may hamper creativity or induce

sloppiness, for instance. The US eight rowing crew of 1936 certainly did not have to deal with this issue; all the team members were facing the same challenging economic parameters. These hard times seem to have resulted in toughness, a fighting spirit! Tough rowing competitions helped further "harden" the team spirit. Such competitions included being backed by superb coaching. We see this in business too.

- Standing up for each other. Reading about how close the team members were is remarkable. They stood up for each other as in a family. Furthermore, when the stroke Don Hume suffered a respiratory ailment during the Olympic competition in Berlin, teammate Joe Rantz was ready to step in. An eight rowing team consists of a coach—the equivalent of a Chairman of the board in a corporation—and on the boat, the cox is like the CEO and issues orders from the helm. The stroke is second from the helm and acts as the President, implementing the orders, with the crew following the lead of the stroke. Hume was ultimately able to row, but he became so exhausted that he collapsed after the Olympic semifinal and almost blacked out during the final. Again, another team member was ready to take over.
- Social network. All the crew members found meaningful career opportunities after the team's Olympic achievement. There was broad societal support and appreciation for the team, not only in the Seattle area but across the entire USA. The team members must have felt this support, and a sense of security undoubtedly resulted. No one seemed to worry about what would come next! In a business context too, it seems vital that no-one in major roles has to worry about the potential dysfunctional personal consequences of being left out, displaced, or even sacked.

As businesspeople, we can learn from the extraordinary journey of these nine working-class youths who "gave" it all that they had, literally sweat and tears, to achieve ultimate glory. This can teach us several lessons on dealing with the "me, me, me" vs. "we, we, we" dilemma in top teams and on leading a productive balance between these two forces, which is the only way to ensure top performance!

Yvon Chouinard, (2016), Let My People Go Surfing, Penguin Random House (Reviewed May 2019)

The author is the founder and CEO of Patagonia, the well-known brand in sports garments and mountaineering equipment. A non-compromising, environmentally friendly way of doing business dominates this privately held firm when it comes to functional design, production based on top quality raw materials, distribution with service, marketing without senseless advertising companies, conservative financing, people that are committed to the "Patagonia way," and above all, a steady environment-friendly policy. This company represents a good prototype for sustainability!

Striving for quarterly profits and short-term performance may at times come in conflict with environmental and social aspirations, such as reducing the use of fossil fuels, discouraging product design extravaganzas, and minimizing the number of layoffs in times of crisis. In this light, the approach of sportswear and mountaineering equipment manufacturer Patagonia is particularly refreshing. Mr. Yvon Chouinard, the founder, owner, and CEO of the 2000-employee California-based company, explains his company's meteoric rise and delineates how his company has been able to cope successfully with core environmental and social issues while also successfully pursuing business priorities.

There seem to be eight elements in the firm's strategy to achieve this:

Product design. For Patagonia, product design and social mission seem to go hand in hand. It appears crucial to make the best product possible. He further articulates the implications of such an imperative for his company: Is the product functional? multifunctional?; "Why buy two pieces of gear when one does the work of both?"; is the product durable? This incorporates a focus on "reparability," in contrast to the "throw away when broken" focus characteristic of many of today's products. And can it easily be cared for and cleaned?; fit with Patagonia's customer profile? Rather than simply responding to mere fashion trends, the product should be designed not to "chase" fashion but rather to meet the needs of Patagonia's core customers; as simple as possible, and does it enhance a simple product line?; an innovation? Here, the author stresses that he often gets inspiration from and "steal(s) with pride" innovations spearheaded by others; a global design, and also authentic, even beautiful?; does it cause any unnecessary harm?

thus emphasizing the use of organic cotton and other natural fabrics with wool, hemp, and linen, and avoiding dyes and synthetics.

Production. There is an emphasis on flexibility and adaptability involving the designers with the production people, to develop stable relationships with key suppliers and contractors, who, in turn, should be evaluated on whether they have a healthy relationship with their employees. Quality should be prioritized over cost-optimization. Again, to "borrow with pride" from others might lead to better practices!

Distribution. The company's growth, at least in part, relies on several forms of distribution: wholesale, mail order, and e-commerce, as well as retail outlets that may fit the core values of the company, often occupying older, restored buildings. Patagonia has a very explicit philosophy regarding architecture! E-commerce allows the firm to react more quickly to the needs of the market and its customers.

Marketing. The key here is to "tell people who we are!" to build upon Patagonia's image: based on passion for outdoor pursuits as well as sustainability, core values shared by the firm's founder and its employees. To "tell the entire story" of the brand and educate and inspire is more essential than spending money on expensive marketing campaigns to attempt to force buying. Traditional advertising is thus kept to a minimum.

Finance. A 2014 Patagonia commercial stated: "Fundamentally, businesses are responsible to their resource base. Without a healthy environment, there are no shareholders, no customers, and no business!" Thus, making a short-term profit should not be a goal in itself. The firm's famous advert in several sports magazines ("Don't buy this jacket!") underscores this ethos.

Human resources. With regard to human resources, the company focuses heavily on attracting and keeping employees who fundamentally share the firm's basic cultural values, i.e., an appreciation and passion for quality, the environment, and the outdoors. Employee remuneration, incentives, and benefits reflect this imperative. Employees have access to good daycare centers, underscoring the importance of managing and making HR decisions that are consistent with the company's philosophy and basic principles.

Environmental philosophy. Mr. Chouinard articulated a clear environmental philosophy, which is embodied by a set of practical ideas: Avoid massive growth for the sake of itself, to see the firm as a social movement. Regarding growth, stay true to the company's goals and principles and take a clear stance against global warming.

The CEO has also pronounced a set of principles that he tries to follow for himself and for his company: Live a modest life; clean up one's act; penance levying a tax on itself—1% on sales or 10.5% on net profits, whichever is the highest; and an attempt to influence other companies.

Are these management principles applicable to other businesses? Perhaps this is a perfect example of how family businesses can delineate themselves from publicly owned businesses. The firm's owners have no intention to "dress up the company for an exit" nor to maximize the quarterly profits. Thus, their latitude to pursue a set of environmental goals is relatively high. The company has indeed succeeded in becoming something more than a brand. This prudent focus on environmental issues may indeed be paying off for business too!

Ray Dalio, (2017), Principles, Simon & Schuster (Reviewed November 2017)

The author is the founder and head of one of the world's largest hedge funds, Bridgewater Associates, based in NYC. There seem to be four key principles behind both his and Bridgewater's success. The process of decision-making is what truly matters—always go through all process steps—analyze/due diligence, review, discuss, decide, follow-up, and with no shortcuts. Try to involve only the smartest people, and do not tolerate mediocrity—let average people go. Honesty is critical, also meaning that one must at times imply that the boss's own ideas may not always be the best ones! Disagreements are fine as a starting position but should be resolved so that all main people are on board when it comes to a given decision. If this would turn out to be impossible, then do not go ahead with that deal.

Ray Dalio is one of the most successful investors of our time. His firm, Bridgewater Associates, is the largest hedge fund in the world, with over 150 billion USD under management. Bridgewater has made more money for its investors than any other hedge fund in history. Dalio's firm has had a 12% per annum net return performance for over 40 years, with only three years of losses. Bridgewater has been a pioneer in quantitative trading, risk parity approaches to investing and all-weather strategies for global macro investing. The book covers the author's management principles. This set of principles, considered to represent the backbone of Bridgewater's success, falls into four: life principles, developing a good organizational culture, the people in the firm, and finally, how to build and evolve a successful money-making approach.

Here are some major threads behind the author's thinking: Meritocracy, based on a few factors. It is the process of decision-making that truly matters;

involve the smartest people that you might be able to identify; and be brutally honest and realize that one's own ideas are not necessarily the only ones. Freshness, enjoying disagreements, is vital; get beyond such disagreements, however, and be ready to move on with speed! Respect the results of voting.

The author believes that to develop, systematize, and test are instrumental. This systematic approach may be a good way to move forward with speed, avoiding reinventing the wheel, constantly learning and improving. To believe in the fundamental power of teams, particularly when it comes to debating cutting-edge dilemmas. This may perhaps be a rather "brutal" setting to work in, with no winners or losers, no stigmatization in being wrong, but with a strong expectation that all should learn from their mistakes. "Tough love" means to be both brutally honest and realistic. To attract teams of executives that can actually work this way, with frankness, willingness to take and give, de-emphasizing the ego, and with open-mindedness, is critical. Attracting the "right" people is a central premise behind his success. To match individual strengths to tasks where they might fit and to pay close attention to a person's individual track record.

To confront problems head-on seems to be another reason for Bridgewater's success, emphasizing their importance, their analysis, to come up with a better understanding. Having control processes in place in order to be able to assess and measure progress and not being "cheated" by "dishonest" employees. This is leadership wisdom indeed!

Satya Nadella, (2017), Hit Refresh, Harper Business (Reviewed March 2018)

Nadella had previously been heading up several smaller divisions at Microsoft, including Cloud computing, before he became CEO. Back then, Microsoft seemed to have put relatively too heavy emphasis on its Windows technology. What had traditionally been the company's key strength may have been held onto for too long! Cloud computing in contrast to Windows, called for new capabilities. However, the firm appears to have been too complacent and was thus not allowing for technology shifts in time. It seemed to have had a rather self-centered culture, always knowing best, not cooperating with others.

When the author took over as CEO, he asked all of Microsoft's 120,000 employees what would happen if Microsoft would disappear. At the time, the firm suffered from some unpopularity with many consumers, and out of this came the realization that it would have to move from making products that people may need to making products that customers could want!

As one step in this direction, Microsoft bought LinkedIn for ca. 26 billion USD in 2016. Nadella felt that this would allow Microsoft to bring its content technology into LinkedIn's network and thus create a better way to serve B2B customers. Microsoft's culture had become relatively more open, thus "allowing" for the LinkedIn acquisition.

Let us consider what the author may see as major aspects of good leadership:

- To instill energy and enthusiasm in the firm
- To have a supportive style
- To be able to have multiple perspectives (i.e., eclecticism)
- To listen a lot
- To create a culture more open and partnership focused
- To combine cloud/quantum computing, mixed realities, and Artificial Intelligence (AI)

A principal learning here is to expand quickly within the new business area (Cloud) by adding resources and capacity and to not allow for slowdowns due to potential overfocus on problems and traditions (Windows). A new mission for Microsoft is thereafter momentum, "full speed ahead," when it comes to:

- Reinventing productivity and business processes
- Building an intelligent Cloud system
- Moving Windows users to become creators of their own personal computing

This focus was indeed a cultural renaissance: The emerging culture would focus on learning, as opposed to "knowing." Several main points would be:

- Listening
- Letting others speak
- Existing as <u>one</u> company (unity of purpose), but eclectic, with no "silos"

A natural next step in such business transformation was to focus on building partnerships, perhaps even before one may fully need them. Interestingly, there had been a close cooperation between Microsoft and LinkedIn even before the takeover. Thus, in advance, a key condition for successful integration had been set.

A discussion of the Cloud might include these three major shifts:

- Mixed reality: not only the more obvious virtual reality but, in addition, various classes of mixed physical and digital "realities." (Nadella used Microsoft's HoloLens to be "transported" to the surface of Mars, and he was able to walk on its surface and inspect rocks. This was based on a feed from NASA's Mars rover, Curiosity).
- AI, or machine's ability to "learn to learn" will influence the Cloud and be further enabled by the Cloud.
- Quantum computing. This topic is often overlooked, but recent advances in theoretical physics and materials science will profoundly influence electrical engineering, app-developments and the Cloud.

How might we normal citizens develop trust in this emerging technology? The author stresses that central timeless values in the digital age remain; privacy, security, and free speech; the latter, particularly relevant today. Strong trust, over time, the author argues, is perhaps above all a function of empathy, shared values, and a sense of safety/reliability.

So, what is the future of humans and machines? Perhaps the most pressing issue discussed is a framework for ethical AI design based on four issues: empathy (again—this is a recurring theme), education, creativity, and judgment/accountability. However, there may still be a long way to go before we reach some sort of agreement regarding how to handle this important dilemma.

How do we restart economic growth in the world? This is a difficult and cutting-edge dilemma! In his typical style as an engineer, the author offers a formula for economic growth: the sum of education and innovation multiplied with the intensity of technological use. But the "tech" side, through innovations, education, and intensity of technological adaptation, still drives it all.

What would constitute effective management practices? These might include:

- Strong focus on empathy. It is people who make value, and they must be supported! Eclecticism is fundamental.
- Innovations are essential! Technology is a vital driver.
- Culture must encompass growth and renewal through openness, listening, and learning.
- Speed is paramount!
- A long-term commitment must be there, but with action now!

Sam Zell, (2017), Am I Being too Subtle? Straight Talk from a Business Rebel, Portfolio (Reviewed April 2018)

The author, a self-made Chicago-based billionaire, has forged success in the real estate business and other entrepreneurial ventures. He emphasizes that education is essential in order to become a more effective entrepreneur. Philanthropy is also good, but this should be directed. This book outlines several key business principles, primarily from the real estate sector, and also details some of the author's business dealings.

Here are his three major business philosophies:

Strategic outlook. Be contrarian, "if everyone is going left, look right!", i.e., find such opportunities, also in relatively unglamorous industries. Be long-term!

Values. Urgency is key. Also, be transparent. Base your business on fast expansion with credible partners (win-win). Safeguard your own reputation and integrity. Develop strong negotiating skills, even toughness, but without negotiating for "nickels and dimes," as this so often creates win-lose dynamics.

Be an entrepreneur. Focus on opportunities with good potential upside! How to achieve sales is key, and liquidity equally so. To also accept key risks and potential for downside is a part of the entrepreneurial experience. To manage the risk is as well a priority. Critical thinking is the trademark of an entrepreneur!

A key learning from being an entrepreneur is someone who does not just see problems but also sees solutions, opportunities! A successful entrepreneur would go for any business opportunities that are found to be attractive, irrespectively of industry. The entrepreneur might typically, however, be able to draw on relevant experiences and insights from other involvements, often from other industries. Perhaps this is in contrast to what many family offices and individual investors may preach, namely that one should focus exclusively on one or a few industries, to build up a relevant in-depth knowledge there. In contrast, the author states that for a true entrepreneur, it is the specific business opportunity that matters, not the industry! And there are no boundaries between work and fun. Hard work is fun, so be driven by being truly "hungry"!

The author also emphasizes the critical importance of philanthropy as well as entrepreneurial education:

- Charitable giving might be both natural and important. Such philanthropy might be linked to causes that the donor(s) is/are deeply passionate about.
- The author has been very active in entrepreneurial business education activities. This means supporting several original approaches. The author feels that typical Israeli graduate students may perhaps often be more driven and more motivated than their US counterparts. Active involvement in the Israeli armed forces may have a positive impact here.

This book provides great take-home value and practical insights, coming from a highly successful entrepreneur, with valuable "how to's."

Steven Johnson, (2018), Farsighted: How We Make the Decisions That Matter the Most, Hodder & Stoughton (Reviewed August 2019)

Greater diversity appears to support better decisions: a mix of genders, nationalities, age, and experience differences, …. Good future-orientated decisions should attempt to identify and assess as many main factors as possible that may have a long-term learning: technical, economic climate, political and trade factors, possible shifts in consumer propensities, and so on. The author recommends several approaches for this, such as the use of maps, models, or graphs; cost–benefit analysis, decision trees, and the degree to which a particular project might allow itself to be further modified, "improved on" in the future.

The author argues that greater diversity tends to support better decisions. Top management teams that consist exclusively of middle-aged white males with common political beliefs thus may not be ideal for good decision-making. He notes that good decision-makers do not rely entirely on their gut instincts but instead have a creative, future-oriented approach that involves considering as many options as possible. Good decision-makers draw heavily on analysis, but in the end, experience and intuition also play important roles. The author tends to largely base his reasoning on dealing with the relatively slow, analytical approach to decision-making considering a number of variables as well as pressures from reality.

The use of maps, models, and influence diagrams may represent a useful first step when considering complex decisions. Divergent views can lead to new ideas, another plea for diversity. In a crisis, leaders are typically responsible for making a multitude of difficult decisions, and it is, as they say, often lonely at the top.

The next step might be predicting. Scientists are gradually starting to understand how the brain works in this situation. Today, the available tools for improving predictive power in decision-making include simulations, war games, and scenario planning.

In the end, of course, decisions shall have to be made. Procrastinating is rarely helpful, even with the best maps, predictions, or simulations. There may be several approaches to support good decision-making:

- Cost–benefit analysis—asking if the yields of an activity are high enough or examining if the risks are too high in relation to the possible rewards.
- Linear value modeling, which—similar to decision-tree analysis—involves giving weights, Bayesian probabilities, to each option.
- Improving on decisions post facto, i.e., after the initial decision is made.
- Brainstorming to come up with new perspectives.

Some of the most far-reaching and complex decisions involve the development of approaches for dealing with possible life coming from other planets or galaxies, e.g., the measurement of extraterrestrial intelligence, as well as those dealing with changes to the Earth's climate, such as global warming. Supercomputers are essential tools for improving analysis in these areas. Typically, it is necessary to apply several axioms in making complex decisions. Perhaps the biggest challenge involves determining how to anticipate emergent problems. Unfortunately, we see a trend towards more homogeneity and populism among decision-makers in politics today—groups of all white males or polarization between Democrats vs. Republicans, for instance. Prudent, globally driven decision-making is thus becoming increasingly difficult to achieve.

Why is decision-making not taught more in schools, and at all levels? The author thinks that this might have to do with:

- Educators simply not having enough information to justify a full-fledged program on decision-making.
- Realistically, a wide variety of disciplines must be cited to do justice to this topic, which makes it difficult to track, and also might jeopardize borders between disciplines.

- The pedagogy of decision-making is simply not yet very well-developed, and doing so is not only challenging but might take time.

Clearly, Steven Johnson's *Farsighted: How We Make the Decisions That Matter the Most* is a relevant book. Yet despite the author's notable ambitions, it is hard not to be left somewhat disappointed upon reading it. Specifically, Johnson fails to highlight even more clearly how best to make difficult and important decisions. As practicing business executives, we wish that Johnson's book contained clearer answers to this question. Still, there is a lot of value in farsightedness, particularly in that people can better prepare themselves for good decision-making, perhaps gradually less of an art, even though it probably will never become a science.

Stephen A. Schwarzman, (2019), What It Takes, Simon & Schuster (Reviewed November 2019)

The author is cofounder and CEO of Blackstone, one of the largest and most successful investment firms in the world. He has identified seven main principles that seem to guide him in running his firm and guiding business activities. To follow a clear process when investing seems particularly critical, including proper analysis, a focus on what might be identified as the true essentials, and a stress test of all contemplated investments, including deliberately slowing down for a moment before finally deciding. To build a strong executive team, entrepreneurial, with top talents and to be able to practice a healthy corporate culture (open-minded, consensus-driven, and with no backbiting) are part of "what it takes." Mr. Schwarzman has pursued many investments in China and shares how openness and trust-building seem to be paying off.

Stephen A. Schwarzman is Chairman, CEO, cofounder, and largest shareholder of Blackstone, the large, highly successful NYC-based investment firm; Blackstone, with the author in charge, seems to have built its success on several main lessons:

Entrepreneurship. The author sees three tests to identify good entrepreneurs:

- Their business idea must be big enough to be worth it (i.e., it must have a sufficient upside).

- The business idea must be truly unique. In particular, the potential customers must wholeheartedly declare, "I need this!"
- The timing must be right—neither too early nor too late.

Entrepreneurs also need to put in an extraordinary amount of work, "blood, sweat and tears"! They may perhaps also need to be somewhat paranoid! To find such good people to join one's team is critical because it increases the likelihood that the firm can grow from a scrappy start-up to a well-managed growth firm.

On Investing through Ups and Downs. Understanding the relevant business cycle underlying a specific business is important. A successful investment will greatly depend upon where the business is in this business cycle, as it will impact when to invest (get in) and when to exit (get out). In that regard, the author provides a few simple rules for recognizing the tops and bottoms of cycles. When approaching the top of a cycle, many actors tend to become overconfident; a lot of capital is normally available, typically cheaply; and many people tend to get rich relatively fast.

Identifying the bottom of a cycle can be relatively harder. The author's approach is to invest only when an asset's value has somewhat recovered from its trough, such as, say, with a 10% appreciation. But when it comes to getting in, a flock mentality must be resisted—if such a groundswell movement to invest is taking place, then it may be too late!

Develop an Investment Process. The trivial idea is to never lose money. The author's way of operationalizing this is to pay attention to the following:
Create a framework to assess the key risks.
Ensure that all members of Blackstone's investment committee actively participate in assessing every project. Junior and senior committee members have equal say!
Make certain that all investment committee members act as if they are owners of the firm about to be invested in.
Align the incentives among all members of the investment committee—in the case of success, all get a fair share.
Encourage committee members to learn and accumulate experience when it comes to assessing projects.

Finding New Talents: Interviewing. To attract highly motivated talents, Schwarzman highly emphasizes an orderly interview process and evaluates interviewees on their success: punctual, authentic, prepared, candid, confident, cautious, and finally not discussing potentially divisive issues (politics, values, etc.) unless asked, and mentioning people the interviewee knows and respects only if he or she likes them. This might actually reveal the candidate's tastes. Selective name-dropping may be acceptable!

A Healthy Corporate Culture. The corporate culture in many high-performing Wall Street firms is regrettably rather egocentric; while everyone on board is often expected to fully contribute to a firm's success, they may get away with being highly self-serving when it comes to this and work primarily to enhance their own ways. The author warns that this tendency must not be allowed to be taken too far. A corporate culture must have a team aspect—a "we, we, we" dimension, as we see in Blackstone's investment committee's operations. Here are four principles for dampening "me, me, me" tendencies:

No backbiting or bullying.

Avoid excessive individual greed. Schwarzman alleges that greed had become a dominant driving factor at Lehman Brothers and eventually contributed to his departure from the firm.

Be willing to change behavior in light of new information. Prestige should be avoided; open-mindedness should be encouraged.

It is okay to ask for help! What matters in the end is a clear commitment to push for excellence and to have the integrity to try to make this happen. Asking for help is not a weakness.

Stress Management. Deal-making typically causes a lot of stress for the principal actors. The author's recommendations for handling stress are to practice slow breathing, lower your shoulders, and slow down.

Focus on the True Essentials. A leader and his/her team might have many factors on which to focus, but only a few factors may turn out to be truly critical. These are the "make or break" factors, and a good leader should have the ability to identify and primarily focus on these. Such a leader should try to avoid the "fine print" in a pile of paperwork associated with any given deal and be able to concentrate instead on what is truly essential. A less experienced leader might work just as hard as an experienced one but look at too many nonessential factors. This may sometimes be due to more than a lack of competence or experience, i.e., also a lack of leadership talent, or even due to escapism.

Eric Schmidt, Jonathan Rosenburg and Alan Eagle, (2020), Trillion Dollar Coach, Hodder & Stoughton (Reviewed June 2019)

This book is about a famous management philosopher, Mr. Bill Campbell, who acted as a coach to the top management and boards of several successful Silicon Valley companies. This coach seemed to have identified several key principles, all having to do with "giving" power to critical people to be trusted to lead, not merely to manage. While strong performance should always be pushed for, this nevertheless calls for being humane. Learning is central to all of this.

Trillion Dollar Coach by Eric Schmidt, Johnathan Rosenburg, and Alan Eagle deals with the managerial philosophy of Bill Campbell, a management thinker, guru, and coach. Although perhaps not a household name, Campbell helped to build some of Silicon Valley's greatest companies, including Apple, Google, and others, before passing away in 2016 at the age of 75. He began his remarkable career as a football player and coach and was captain of Columbia University's varsity football team, with Columbia winning the Ivy League title in 1961. He later went on to be a successful football coach until he went into business, rising to several major positions, first at Kodak and later in Silicon Valley. In 1994, he became CEO of Intuit, and gradually he also joined the boards of directors of several of the leading firms in the "Valley," including Apple's. Perhaps even more importantly, he developed a trusted role as a senior advisor to many of Silicon Valley's leading executives, including the late Steve Jobs. Campbell was also a trusted advisor to Eric Schmidt, the coauthor of this book, who was Google's CEO/chairman from 2001 to 2011 and executive chairman from 2011 until 2015.

This unique book thus reports on how a particular individual was able to impact the success of several large multinationals. Here are some of Campbell's "dos and don'ts":

Be a leader of teams, don't be merely a manager. It is the people in an organization who make the difference, and these work best as members of effective teams. Decisiveness matters greatly. One shall have to accept that highly talented but perhaps somewhat difficult individuals are often part of such successful teams. Another main leadership consideration concerns the important role of the board of directors: It is the CEO and not the board that should manage. Nevertheless, the board too might actually contribute to advancing the entire organization by offering counseling and advice.

Trust people. One should only attempt to provide advice where there is trust (i.e., "only coach the coachable"). He put particular emphasis on four traits to determine the extent to which someone might be coachable: honesty, humility, willingness to work hard, and openness to learning.

There are some additional critical guidelines: listen; tell the truth; and tell employees what goals to reach, but do not indicate how to reach these goals.

Prioritize the team. The importance of teamwork is <u>sine quo non</u>. This perspective can be summarized as promoting a "we, we, we" culture, in contrast to the so common "me, me, me" outlook: The leader's essential role in making the teams work more effectively, the leader to demonstrate loyalty and commitment to the team. There might be a willingness for self-sacrifice and to demonstrate decisiveness to a team as well.

Be humane. Give praise when it is due. Those people who belong to strongly knit communities are more able to jointly take pride in individual peers' accomplishments. Leaders should practice their humanity when giving praise.

Make performance-enhancing decisions. Ultimately, an organization is measured through its performance. Having strong leaders, who get things done through teams based on trust and humanity, is not enough if improved performance does not result from such efforts. Performance-enhancing actions might be:

Be creative
Do not be a dilettante, a "light weight"
Focus on people who have vitality
Build on what each person might be particularly good at
Do not waste time worrying about the future, just "do it," now!

It is always interesting to read about factors that are proven crucial for strong performance in leading companies. In much management literature, top executives share various perspectives of what drives success. Yet to some degree, these seem to converge around factors that we can find in many places in this book and elsewhere:

- Learning, being open-minded towards knowledge
- Role of people, who are also "teachers/coaches"
- Dynamic, non-bureaucratic teams
- Speed and adaptability

- "Human" approach: genuineness, honesty, and trust

There seems to be a clear link between high performance in sports and high performance in business. A coaching role seems to be central when attempting to go for the top!

Dorie Clark, (2021), The Long Game, Harvard Business Review Press (Reviewed November 2021)

This book, which pushes for more effective long-term thinking, falls into three parts. First, "white space"—how to bring one's agenda under control, not allowing for ad hoc arrangements. Secondly, focus where it counts—concentrated effort provides a series of heuristics for clearing out one's calendar. The implication for all of us is that we too should try to establish such a set of principles. Finally, keep the faith—clearly there are always short-term pressures, and to say no may often be difficult. It is paramount to remind oneself about the costs of giving in—physical, emotional, and, of course, opportunity-wise. A strong commitment is always asked for. Try to never always say yes, nor to feel bad if doing so.

This book deals with what has become one of the most important dilemmas facing most leading managers today, namely, how to be a long-term thinker in a so-called short-term world. Ms. Clark is a well-known coach. Her book provides many real-life examples, reflecting the author's ground-breaking research on the topic.

In White Space she shares how to control our agendas, saying no more often, so as to perceive that the reality we live in may be driven more by a true sense of what might be critical for one's business. Then Focus Where It Counts is about how to actually successfully clear our diaries, including an in-depth discussion of how effective networking might actually support us in becoming more long-term. Keeping the faith then deals with how we might actually go about" cementing" our focus on long-term thinking.

There is a crucial difference between failure and experimentation. To successfully experiment, we need to allow ourselves more "white space" in our diaries to explore what this type of life might mean to us. We have to get smarter and selective about what we focus on and be clearer regarding what we truly want. How to say "no" to nonessentials is thus paramount. The author offers us an important solution, namely, to "delay" what might be relatively less important. And never write so-called "to-do" lists, as these may have the opposite effect of creating white space, actually filling up one's agenda further.

The author suggests that politeness is always essential when saying "no," and that good ways to reach at a "no" might be to request more information, then even more, and so on. And many presenters of requests may simply fail to follow up. When evaluating such requests where additional information is to be provided, there are four questions to be answered: the commitment, the opportunity cost, physical and emotional costs, the "feeling bad" effect from saying "no."

Moving on to Focus Where It Counts, i.e., where to concentrate our limited time and energy for the best results, to start is to set clear goals, to "optimize" for meaning and interest, reconnecting with what motivated one in the past.

Exploring new ways is central. While we should always "play things safe," we should also take some more risks "in the small," be a little bit bolder! We need to carve out time for interesting opportunities: Get support where needed; get a coach? (The author is a coach); set clear deadlines; learn, learn, learn; turn setbacks into things that can be salvaged; and always be a long-term thinker.

More effective long-term thinking calls for what the author has labeled "thinking in waves": first learning, then creating (sharing what you have learned), then connecting with others, so as to learn from them, and finally reaping (enjoy!). To create the so-called strategic leverage is important, i.e., how to do something, say, only once but hope that this will make it count ten times? This fundamentally different archetype for leveraging is built on: leverage one's key relationships; leveraging for the life one may want, i.e., conducting work and personal life in better ways; leverage for professional goals; and the currency we have, i.e., connections, podcasts, memberships, …

Networking is crucial but avoid being seen as opportunistic when asking for things from others. Research has shown that networking may at times and by some feel "dirty"! Even contemplating networking might lead to this. This might be particularly so when we are dealing with the so-called short-term networking. Some persons that have been mobilized for this type of networking shall probably never be willing to help out again. The author has introduced a good heuristic here, namely, to wait a year before asking for any "new" favors. This leads us to longer-term network building. Effective networking is essentially long-term! One should keep in mind that every relationship shall have to be reciprocated.

Keeping the faith refers to making one's long-term focus last. Patience seems to be particularly important. Clarity of goals is probably critical for achieving patience! This strategic patience has to do with seeking exceptional growth, including observing how others approach key challenges, and also being open to advice from experts — again, practicing patience! Thus, to stay connected with one's strategy is of long-term importance. The author discusses several failures in this respect. To follow the so-called lean start-up methodology, namely, to test before you fully invest, treating everything as an experiment in the early days. To come up with multiple paths, "plan B," and finally, to put clear dates for when to switch, even abandon, or, hopefully, when to scale up.

To Reap the Rewards is another useful concept introduced, namely, the "distance to empty," the time that one's organization may be able to run without the manager, i.e., you! To succeed in creating "distance to empty" is an indicator of relative success in implementing disciplined long-term thinking. Here are three "habits of mind" that might support this more effective long-term thinking: independence (stay true to oneself); curiosity; resilience, openness to new things, and experimentation.

Oleg Konovalov, (2021), The Vision Code: How to Create and Execute a Compelling Vision, Wiley (Reviewed October 2021)

A clear vision for one's firm seems critical for enhancing long-term success. And such a vision should be widely shared. The so-called CAVIAR process tells us how to set an effective vision: Clarity in creating a vision; Ability to make it a reality; Viability; Influence; Active participation and support; Revitalizing—a good vision evolves in sync with the evolution of the firm itself.

This book deals with vision creation, making vision strong, execution of vision, and visionary you. The author was born and raised in a small town on the Kola Peninsula, northern Russia, and is a well-known business educator, consultant, and coach, indeed one of the top global thinkers when it comes to leadership, vision, and culture.

Creation of vision. Perhaps the most central proposition is his assertion that a good vision looks at the present from the future's perspective. The author identifies several so-called "defining purposes" here, among which curiosity. Specifically, curiosity regarding how we can do something better so as to find compelling reasons to change ourselves, to strengthen our vision by putting our minds into the future, trying to imagine it, for then to try to look back to the present, in order to better figure out how to get there. A focus on the past, on the other hand, might tend to distract. To maintain a simplistic focus would be particularly important; it is a common temptation to make things too complex. Simplicity, focus, and clarity also inspire people to become supportive! And this might add an additional sense of purpose to those involved, steering them away from negativity and even hopelessness. Critical energy is thereby released, and day-to-day boredom largely avoided. Yet, regrettably, too many people seem to live in the past!

As George Bernard Shaw said, "imagination is the beginning of creation." So, how do these "a-ha moments" come about? How does one create a reality that might change the future? Hard work is, of course, paramount, perhaps already with years of focused thinking. Listening so as to learn more effectively is also critical. Boldness in thinking is "it"! And there are of course risks that shall have to be accepted.

One's own ego must not be allowed to interfere. The author identifies several additional potentially negative factors that might "derail" a visionary process: lack of confidence, detachment from reality, as well as simply being too comfortable with the status quo, even laziness. So, becoming a realistic visionary takes courage, humility, and discipline. Excellence thus becomes key. Anything less than a clear commitment to excellence could lead to an acceptance of mediocracy!

The author recommends the development of a "knowledge bank" for fighting anti-visionary tendencies. He proposes a so-called CLICK checklist for this: Courage, Learning, Inner excellence, and Confidence/Credibility. And the content in such knowledge banks should be updated and shared by the team. Visioning tends to be a process with a lot of top-down flavor, carried out more or less alone by the leader. Team involvement, in contrast, is fundamentally bottom-up! But any top-down-driven vision should also be understood in the bottom-up context by one's team.

How does one make one's vision stronger? A clear structure seems important here, with six criteria for structured visionary:

- A strong stimulus, so that people might enjoy being involved! They must be stimulated to do this. Bonus systems, for instance, may be delivered.
- Scale, i.e., to come up with a vision that has sufficient breadth and depth, so that its impact might be ever-growing.
- Responsibility to develop a vision that is also relevant among a broader set of stakeholders, particularly the next generation.

- Continuous scanning may be necessary in order to "see" what other people do not. To have a good imagination when it comes to reading major changes; To firmly identify opportunities! A good vision points towards such opportunities.
- Simplicity is important.
- Excitement and passion, typically linked to "pushing" for a vision's upside potentials. Emotional drive is key!

Clear communication comes into the picture now. It goes without saying that this must be in a simple language, further contributing to the opening of minds and hearts of people.

What are some of the key features of such an effective communication process? Listening! Setting the tone for more realistic sharing with the rest of the team. While visioning is fundamentally a top-down process, a humble attitude, with a lot of listening, rather than being arrogant, may set an effective scene for the sharing of a vision more broadly. But, frequently, people are afraid to share. Why? People often think that good ideas may be "stolen"! The reality is typically different, however. Open debate often leads to a further improvement of ideas! Such broad sharing might also lead to the creation of a wide network, with many "ambassadors," all promoting the vision. "No force is stronger than people united by a common vision."

Execution is about how to align effective action and vision. Strong leadership seems important here, with a focus on empowering people, rather than on controlling them. These leaders connect people to go for results that can be shared broadly. The culture is focused on the people in the organization rather than solely on the leader. Broadly, people should feel the benefits of a clear vision. An effective leader must of course have a strong will to be able to push for all of this. Clarity, commitment, and coaching are key, as is quality. "Quality efforts" should be part of the implementation of a vision, including to develop appropriate metrics to gauge progress and to help identify what can be done better.

A clear growth element of a vision also seems critical. This implies coping with uncertainty, accepting or taking it as a given. A clear roadmap for change may alleviate common misperceptions or even discomfort when it comes to such uncertainty. However, one must be ready to make decisions that contribute to a vision's implementation. Indecisiveness might be a problem. The author points out that many organizations, particularly those with overly complex formal structures, may be weak when it comes to such decisiveness. Some leaders are uncomfortable "sticking out their neck." To enable effective decision-making is, however, essential and must be based on discipline, imply freedom to act, and allow for an openness in order to find new opportunities of choice.

The author suggests a six-step model for checking that a good vision is in place, the so-called CAVIAR process:

- Clarity in the creation of the vision, based on what might be perceived as a clear view of the future as seen now in the present context.
- Ability to make it a reality.
- Viability of a vision. This draws on the scheme of stimulus, scale, spotlight, scanning, simplicity, and excitement/passion.
- Influence. This focuses on adopting a clear, common language for communicating the vision.
- Action. This is a matter of demonstrating strong leadership, through culture, strong will, and clear communication, to strive towards high quality, enabling unconstrained decision-making with no procrastination!
- Revitalizing. A vision dies if it does not grow. Thus, growth is needed!

The author recommends that a CAVIAR type of reassessment of one's vision should be undertaken regularly. This vision represents an implied tension between "today for today" and "today for the future." Critical!

The vision and you delineate a set of "commandments" for visionaries. In particular, to talk solutions, not problems, i.e., with optimism and positive thinking; charisma; courage; humility; simplicity; and open-mindedness are all key. And visionaries are realistic, "todayists," different from futurists, the latter group making forecasts regarding aspects of the future and are virtually always wrong! This seems to be the essence of healthy visions, reflecting how we might want to position ourselves for the future, today. To articulate such a clear vision also ties to our responsibilities to future generations. It all perhaps comes down to what Harry S. Truman said, "it is amazing what you can accomplish if you do not care who gets the credit."

Jim Mattis & Bing West, (2021), Call Sign Chaos, Penguin Random House (Reviewed October 2019)

Three forms of leadership are identified: direct, executive, and strategic. Direct leadership typically entails enhancing the coordination within relatively small organizational teams, including avoiding frustration when it comes to conflicting messages from above. Executive leadership, in larger organizations with several organizational layers, implies setting clear priorities and getting things done, in contrast to becoming "discussion orientated, but with no action." Leadership issues at the top, strategic, has much to do with maintaining morals. Members of a top management team with different agendas, in the extreme, disloyal ones, should be asked to leave the top team. To maintain momentum is necessary! Direct, hands-on leadership is part of being strategic, but one should walk away from overcontrolling! Four-Star General Jim Mattis, who retired from military service in 2013, narrated his more-than-40-year military career as well as his two-year tenure as secretary of defense in this book.

The first section of the book is on direct leadership—that is, how to lead in relatively smaller organizational entities. This situation contrasts with more indirect leadership situations as they occur in larger organizations. In such a closely knit setting, direct team coordination is vital. The authors raise the issue that conflicting messages from higher-up in the organization can frustrate the leadership efforts of those at the lower levels.

The authors then discuss executive leadership—that is, leading in larger organizational entities, typically with multiple organizational layers. General Mattis draws heavily on lessons he learned from leading the 1991 military campaign in Iraq. A key insight is to keep pace with issues and maintain responsiveness! To maintain the speed, one should be action-oriented, "just do it!" The general warns us here about placing too much focus on processes, which might often be embedded in excessive bureaucracy or at least lead to it. Orders from higher organizational levels might often contradict speed-driven actions taken in the field. At times, higher-level objectives, perhaps with a broader focus than the narrower scope of a given project, may cause conflict, which can be a source of frustration and difficulty.

Finally, the authors discuss strategic leadership, key military–political interactions, and the reconciliation of such higher-level objectives in conflicts. There are thus leadership issues at the very top level. Several issues are highlighted:

- Set clear priorities and stick to them, above all in order to keep speed.
- Try to fight loss of morale.
- Try to be clear on who is with you versus who is not. Allies are instrumental!
- Dismiss people who do not seem to be fully committed, however uncomfortable this decision may be.

The book does not deal with General Mattis' years as Secretary of Defense. After two years, he left his post to protest against what he saw as a unilateral decision to withdraw US troops from Syria, conflicting with one of Mattis' basic leadership principles, dialogue, and deliberations at the top.

The book reports on how carefree young talents may join the disciplined US Marines, with their three "C-pillars" of values: competence, caring, and conviction. Recruiting and selection are always essential in successful organizations, in this case, with a focus on recruiting for attitude and then training for skills. Having the right team in place keeps the momentum to be able to go full speed.

With larger organizations, even more indirect leadership is needed, and the same principles remain applicable. The authors do, however, point out two caveats: Watch out for overcontrolling, and appreciate the relevance of advisory-focused staff, with another set of roles.

To work together in teams is a must. However, the authors warn that bureaucratic in the team might tend to slow things down, sometimes even stop, specific initiatives. Even temporary slowdowns might have grave dysfunctional consequences. Failing to move when one has a unique window of opportunity can be very expensive.

All of the above leadership insights relate primarily to situations in which the meaning of the lead task might be directly related to a particular strategic initiative. An often-overlooked additional point is to prepare well and avoid "traffic jams," again so that top speed can be maintained.

When considering an entire organizational unit (such as a division), General Mattis' mantra is to "improve, adapt and overcome." These principles entail changing those members of a division's key management who might be hesitant regarding a chosen strategy and may thus be relatively less committed. Also, when progress is being made, one should not celebrate success but take success in very measured ways. Furthermore, since momentum is crucial, those higher-up in an organization need a high degree of consensus regarding the chosen strategy, so as not to later jeopardize its momentum.

Poor leadership decisions can unfortunately be made at the top of any organization. Such decisions often lead to dysfunctional pressures between a speed-driven strategic propensity of a given division and a hold-driven strategic propensity from the top. At times, the clarity of strategic intentions may be even more obscure, intentionally or not. Divisional "guerrilla warfare" may be the result of such a case. Here, a division's leaders should, above all, ensure that these main issues are covered:

- Train (and bring along) executives at lower levels within a division, so as to ensure maximum effectiveness.

- Coordinate more explicitly with other divisions—effective guerilla tactics are synonymous with good coordination.
- Involve stakeholders on the ground, i.e., civilians.

The top level should, of course, ideally back such a guerilla strategy, although perhaps most often only covertly.

Mattis offers additional thoughts on how to render a guerilla strategy particularly effective. Strategic planning is often counter-functional; it can foster complacency and generate slowness to act. Rather, Mattis calls his readers to "act," "seize the day," and "just do it!" Overly bureaucratic organizational entities and individuals should ideally be isolated and, if possible, even replaced.

At the highest level of an organization, Mattis finds that several main priorities should be clearly held:

- Support the organization's division managers.
- Secure political friends and strategic allies.
- Prepare eventual strategic contingency options.

The authors further suggest that interaction at the top can be sorted into these categories: Housekeeping, such as dealing with strategic inventory resources; decision-making and ensuring that things run smoothly; and alarms.

Diminishing strategic support might have clear risks. Unilateral withdrawal may be seized upon by an enemy, for instance, who might attempt to take advantage of it. Thus, withdrawal is typically risky, even though there may be overriding political (or corporate) reasons. Specifically, the authors add, in closing:

- An effective organization requires an emphasis on recruiting, training, educating (and learning), equipping, and promoting. The acid test is to prove that such effective organizations are not exceptional.
- Speed is key, and decentralization is fundamental to guaranteeing speed.
- Spirited leadership is equally valuable to achieve speed. Open dialogue that leads to specific conclusions regarding given strategic debates is a must.

The strategic insights offered by one of the most successful leaders of what is perhaps the largest modern organization in the world deserve to be taken with great consideration. Many of these insights can apply equally to modern business leaders as well.

Carolyn Dewar, Scott Keller, Vikram Malhotra, (2022), CEO Excellence, Simon & Schuster (May 2022)

This book reports on interviews with 72 leaders covering what constitutes effective leadership. Six core responsibilities of an effective leader are identified. These responsibilities become perhaps more evident when discriminating between excellent and not-so-excellent top leader performance, *after* the conventional steps of strategy formulation and implementation have been properly adhered to. These are direction setting, organizational alignment, mobilizing the organization, teams to "help" the business, dealing with boards, handling shareholders, and finally, the CEO's personal effectiveness. Recognizing that bottom-up leadership matters (listen, share, strive for consensus, …) but also that a top-down leadership approach is important (speed, decide, avoid procrastination, …). It is a healthy balance between the two that makes the difference!

This book, written by three senior partners at McKinsey & Company, is about the mindsets that seem to differentiate what are deemed to be 200 truly high-performing senior leaders from "the rest." There are useful introductions and summaries also including many anecdotes.

There are no statistics, but the book still offers a very obvious framework when it comes to analyzing the empirical materials, i.e., 72 interviews of senior executives as well as anecdotes. This is an effective way to provide a sense out of an otherwise overly complex set of materials. The results that were given portray mostly successful senior leaders, but at times also occasional failures.

The days of so-called strategic analysis based on various more or less deterministic models do now seem to be complemented by what we might label *strategic culture*. Strategy no longer exclusively consists of applying well-documented approaches such as the five forces from Porter, the BCG matrix in various versions, market share/growth analysis, and/or SWAT analysis. Strategic culture is indeed a necessity and often is indescribable with neat and handy business models; without corporate strength when it comes to this, there may be relatively little benefits from strategic positioning and modeling. Strategic culture does matter!

Carolyn Dewar, Canadian, went to St. Andrews University in Scotland and is the coleader of McKinsey's CEO Excellence Service practice. Scott Keller was born and raised on the US West Coast, with an eclectic set of nonbusiness interests such as social enterprising and music, and Vikram Malhotra, Indian born, educated at Wharton. Mr. Malhotra was earlier on the board of McKinsey, also formerly head of the firm's US business practice, and is currently chairing McKinsey's Professional Standards Committee.

Are there perhaps some critical questions that might be raised? In our opinion there are possibly three: First, why these six factors? Why not others, such as a CEO's attitude towards speed? The authors do not give a good explanation of how they ended up with this set of six critical factors, except by saying that their own long and direct experiences interacting with senior executives have provided them with the guiding light to focus on these. There might, of course, be other key factors less obvious, which could determine strategic culture.

Second, when conducting the interviews with the various senior executives, did the researchers bring up issues that perhaps did not fit into their framework so neatly?

Our third potential question has to do with the fact that the authors in their capacities as senior partners of McKinsey might perhaps have shied away from being critical about some specific firms, perhaps clients or former clients of McKinsey. If not, they may undoubtedly be on the firm's list of perspective clients.

Here are the six core responsibilities of a CEO: Direction setting and vision: Reframe the "game." The most successful CEOs do not just raise aspirational levels. They change the definition of success! They reframe their approach to the running of their firms. To find so-called intersections would typically be important: Needs/competences/passion/making money! But it is normally about more than money. Profit comes after achieving one's vision. Financial outcomes follow. A way to make this happen is to look back in order to look forward. Established levels of ambitions can be manifested through looking back. But good CEOs usually always try to boost levels of ambition, now looking forward. Many people get involved in this. They support what they help create. To find ways to include key employees is thus essential. A simple vision, i.e., a straightforward articulation of one's "North Star," is critical to redefine success, to influence decisions, and to provide incentives, so that they all act in desired ways.

Good strategic practice must entail making big moves early, and often. Five strategic movements seem to characterize such boldness: buy and sell, invest, improve productivity, differentiate, and allocate.

To be an exceptional futurist is relevant for addressing each of these factors, including keeping track of major technological shifts, changes in customer preferences, new competitors, and threats over the horizon. To keep an eye on the downside is also part of this. This should not imply endorsing recklessness, instead involve thinking and acting like an owner. To regularly apply one's so-called "heart paddles" is fundamental for going forward, implying changing all the time. To create a series of performance-enhancing curves may, for instance, be it! In short, it seems critical to make big moves early, and to back them up with sufficient investments. This seems indispensable to setting the firm onto a progressive path.

Resource allocation is thus paramount, with capital allocation being a main lever for growth. To free up some resources in order to have sufficient discretionary resources to go after new, exceptional opportunities is also vital. This implies starting with a "zero base" so as to come up with a portfolio of businesses that has a substantial fraction of new "entries" every year. The next would be to "solve the whole," i.e., to move resources around so that the overall benefits to the entire firm might be maximized. Progress is then monitored by meeting milestones, different from meeting annual budgets. Finally, one should get rid of what no longer adequately yields within a firm's strategic portfolio, allowing for a balance with new initiatives to be added, "kill as much as you create."

Organizational alignment is also fundamental. It seems particularly important to treat so-called "soft" issues as if they were "hard" ones. Emotions and culture are also key! To reshape the work environment is central here. The most successful CEOs seem to try to do this! Their role models are perhaps particularly meaningful.

This brings focus on trying to make it personal for the CEO, for example, when it comes to demonstrating his/her own interest in learning, perhaps as a juxtaposition to blaming others when things do not work out exactly as hoped. To make it personal is therefore indeed relevant, such as asking for improvement suggestions from the staff, even way down, on a regular basis. And to measure progress is also important, also when it comes to attempting to assess shifts in so-called culture change issues, which may otherwise easily be perceived as too vague. To concentrate primarily on one or a few measurable factors and to try to get this/these "right" are perhaps particularly important.

The concept of "stagility" is indeed a hybrid, entailing the elaboration of a hybrid framework, i.e., organizational design practices. Flexibility is central here and also a sense of stability, i.e., stability plus agility. It seems to be a matter of achieving both, not a trade-off.

A first approach to this might be to "stop the pendulum quote," to avoid leaning too much one way, with a typical reaction tilting too much the other way. ABB under Percy Barnevik might be an example of "overtilting," by first dividing ABB into five thousand profit centers, for then later to centralize his company's focus into merely five major groups.

But accountability remains important also, of course. To have clear decision-making authority goes with this. A so-called "Helix organization" might be advocated, in contrast to the more typical matrix organizations. This implies no dotted lines and clear responsibilities and capabilities for each manager, i.e., clarity rather than ambiguity.

To mobilize one's organization, teams must be engaged. In the end, nothing can substitute the making of smart choices. To focus on the best talents in one's organization is a necessity. Being smart is not the only expectation one might have for one's best talents. To have a resolute mind, i.e., to never give up, is another major feature of smartness. To define core roles where talents might be able to contribute the most value seems especially critical. Successful CEOs are likely to be good at this: defining clear roles with precise tasks and assigning one's best people to these jobs.

To have a purported "left tackle" individual at senior level who might relieve the CEO from having to face-off stakeholder groups everywhere can be helpful. An effective CFO, for instance, might be able to do wonders relative to the financial analyst as well as the investor communities.

To identify the "best" candidate to take over the top job when it comes to a CEO's success is also pivotal. It is never automatic that a next-in-line executive is the best choice. What is perhaps more important for a CEO is to bring in good new talents whenever possible. Organizational challenge is, in summary, a matter of focusing on one, or very few, cultural practices where the CEO can make a personal difference, to organize the company in such a way that "*stagility*" is achieved, and to always concentrate on attracting the best talents and putting them to work where they might make the most good.

The top team is particularly central, of course, and this team must be able to work together! However, cooperation among group members is seldom and automatic. It may therefore be necessary for the CEO to make staffing changes so as to end up with key people with more cooperative aptitudes as well as attitude. For each member of a top team to have both aptitude and attitude seems particularly vital. When a good CEO has to make occasional interventions, he/she should be quick but fair. For team members to know what may be expected of them, as well as to understand the consequences of not falling into the expected mold, is decisive.

To stay connected while also keeping "distance" is a reality many good CEOs might find it hard challenging. A strong CEO has not entered into a popularity contest. They may never wish to become too close to the rest of the organization, although do not want to be seen as aloof either. To build a network of particularly trusted advisors, a so-called "kitchen cabinet" might be useful. In the end, the team should be the star, not the individual. It is a matter of "we, we, we," not "me, me, me." What are the core "we, we, we" norms for such teams? What are the main role dimensions for each member of such a team? How can decision-making speed be achieved and maintained when teams are working at their best, in contrast to solo decision-making?

For all to have a relatively good understanding of how major decisions should be made seems crucial. Good CEOs set their expectations clearly. Discipline is an important part of it. While meetings are needed, they must be focused ones and not allowed to drag out. To evaluate how well such meeting practices are followed may be especially useful for a CEO. In the end, it may be a matter of finding a good rhythm for the top management team, i.e., setting the tempo for how an organization is run, whereby the CEO acts a bit like a conductor of a symphony orchestra. This also implies that the CEO cum conductor shall have the right to request discipline. The various members of a high-performing symphony orchestra are all connected in an evident, disciplined way, each with definite roles, quite similar to what one might expect to find in a well-performing organization. So, it is a matter for the CEO to mobilize the senior leaders by ensuring that the composition of the leading members in this orchestra are truly the best ones, to make this orchestra the star, and, finally, to maintain the proper rhythm in his/her role as the conductor.

To deal effectively with one's board, and to help directors to support the business is also key. As a pre-ample, it should be clearly stated that the job of a board chair (or lead independent director) is to run the board. The job of the CEO, in contrast, is to run the organization. Thus, the key is to "help" the board chair run the board, so that its directors can also help the CEO run the business, but not to create "disruption," unnecessarily "meddling," or "friction." It would be essential to "invite" the board members to be involved in a constructive way. For this, there should be strong relationships between board members and the CEO, reflecting the unique capabilities of various board members and also attempting to enhance board meeting effectiveness.

The first condition is to build a foundation of trust, with wide transparency and direct links to management. To tap the individual wisdoms of board members is crucial. Roles of board members and management should be carefully delineated. And the board should also attempt to more or less continuously renew itself, including through rotation of membership, education, and retreats.

To instill a clear focus on the future may be the most critical of all. For individual board members to also be members of other companies' boards can be good in this respect, as long as there is no conflict of interest, of course. To tap the wisdom of elders, particularly regarding how they see future challenges and opportunities, can be truly beneficial.

In summary:

- "When in doubt, share"!
- A close relationship between the Chairperson and the CEO is advisable, again one built on trust.

  - As each individual director of a board counts, the trust needs to be established with each!
  - To always focus and be consistently prepared is perhaps the best advice to give a CEO in order to establish such trust.
  - Another trust-building action is for the CEO to always let board members have access to other members of the organization. To allow them to "dig down" signals that the CEO has trust in his/her board members. This fosters more transparency regarding what is "good" as well as "bad," even "ugly," and what is working and not.
  - To be able to delineate the main roles of the board more explicitly would be good. What docs the CEO expect here? How might new board members be identified who might have desired profile? In the end, it may primarily be a question of what it shall take to drive a business forward in a successful manner. And there may perhaps be educational remedies. To attend courses, above all, to get a better perception of cutting-edge managerial practices, as well as outside trends, might be recommendable.
  - To exchange experiences with the members of other boards can prove valuable.
  - To be exposed to the norms for the functioning of good boards may be equally beneficial.
  - Some degree of renewal of a board is almost always good. Board members' performances might be evaluated, yet how can such evaluations be objective? It is typically always sensitive, often hard, to remove individuals from a board. A problem here is often that such individuals seldom "see" their dysfunctional sides themselves.
  - A strong CEO might find support in well-defined board meeting practices. How can all board members contribute to a focus on the future, i.e., a forward-looking agenda? Fiduciary grilling is of course not enough. Strategy, organizational health, and honing in on talents are perhaps even more crucial!

Dealing with diverse sets of shareholders remains essential for a CEO. He/she needs to build trust with them all, not only with main customers but also with employees, suppliers, investors, the government, and so on. Perhaps a good starting point could be to try to find a clear sense of purpose for one's organization. Why are we here? And then, is the core of how a business interacts with its key stakeholders aligned with such a purpose? There are certainly risks here, based on adverse developments from environmental, social, and governmental factors, so-called ESG risks, and a CEO may do well in closely monitoring such ESG risks. But he should be ready to speak up when called for and take a stand in those (hopefully) few instances when he/she might feel that things might be getting out of control, even becoming totally unreasonable.

There are valuable heuristics that might guide a CEO when it comes to dealing with outside stakeholders, such as allowing him/herself to only spend a certain fraction of his/her time on such matters, and always in focused, efficient ways. Additionally, to try to better understand why various stakeholders may think in particular ways may be helpful. New ideas might even emerge from outside stakeholders. In the end, it seems fundamental to aim to always be open, honest, and consistent.

A good CEO should be able to bring in revenue. A close relationship with one's major customers is thus an absolute must to truly understand the customer base! To be able to react quickly when it comes to potential "derailments" here is thus also fundamental, which may entail creating command centers, doing stress-testing, and so on.

Personal effectiveness sums up what a good CEO might be all about. What might be some parts of a personal effectiveness mindset of a strong CEO? It is perhaps a matter of: being both physically and psychologically fit, discipline, priority setting is central, to think about this reaching a good work–life balance is perhaps not an optimal approach to this challenge. To imply that there is a trade-off may not be it either since both work and private life must be successfully and harmoniously dealt with.

To keep a "tight" and "loose" calendar is recommended, i.e., to control it but always be open to address new challenges that might unexpectedly emerge, above all unforeseen opportunities. This is opportunism, not a compartmentalization, nor classical time management.

For a good CEO to be able to infuse energy in the organization is paramount, and for him/her to constantly become re-energized is useful as well. The second law of thermodynamics applies here, i.e., to build the so-called entropy. To collect art, for instance, might provide such energy infusion for a CEO. There are of course other ways too: piano playing, mountain biking, walking long tours, etc.

To have a strong office staff is strategic too. Personal assistants are essential for supporting busy, successful CEOs in many ways. To rotate up-and-coming talents into such personal assistant roles might be a good solution. The CEO may not only gain more insights regarding a given person's potential but could actually be able to receive perspectives on key organizational issues as well as to offer valuable input.

A CEO's leadership style should be adapted to evolutionary forces regarding the firm's needs, and also reflect the CEO's own intellectual growth. Perhaps particularly important is that the CEO should always aspire to act in ways that inspire his/her organization to remain optimistic, with good hope for the future. Even negative feedback should be cast in ways that might offer some "light" at the end of the tunnel; in other words, constructive criticism for improvement is the way to go, the aim being to make good even better! To always stay humble is advisable, letting no pride or arrogance getting in the way. Any self-centered focus should clearly be tempered. To have a servant's attitude seems critical, as is to stay grounded and to always listen. To display a sense of gratitude, hopefully genuinely felt, should be explicitly acknowledged. All of these "musts" would probably contribute towards creating energy in others.

Not surprisingly, there do not seem to be many overriding generalizations to make when it comes to what constitutes truly effective CEOs. Three overriding conclusions, however, are stated: starting and finishing strong, prioritizing well, and being insightfully futuristic. To this reviewer, these generalizations almost sound like "platitudes." Final advice that the researchers provide for the exceptionally effective CEOs are: ethically accountable, diverse (in gender, race, ethnicity, and class), resistant, and impactful.

There is however probably no way to "crack" the secret of what makes a truly effective CEO in a matter of a few simple principles. This is a truly complex issue and this fact, in itself, may perhaps be the most fundamental conclusion.

There are two final "bonuses" in this book. First, there are 67 brief biographies of successful senior executives, as previously referred to. The second extra benefit are three separate worksheets for leaders to utilize, regarding "the reader's mandate," say as CEO or as a senior executive.

To be an effective CEO in any of the world's largest companies is perhaps among the most challenging roles in business today. The researchers have found "pearls of wisdom … a must read for everyone in the works of ideas and enterprises" as Mukesh Ambani, Chairman of India's Reliance Industries states.

David Gergen, (2022), Hearts Touched with Fire: How Great Leaders are Made, Simon & Schuster (Reviewed July 2022)

The author, David Gergen, served as White House advisor to four US Presidents (Nixon, Ford, Reagan, and Clinton) and now teaches at Harvard's Kennedy School. Few, if any, may be more qualified than the author to discuss how modern leaders are shaped, and how such leaders can be both moral, see a clear "True North" and get things done! A new generation seems to be transforming the practice of leadership. It is no longer a matter of seeing a good leader as a phenomenon of being a single great person, but to see him/her as leader of a team. The author thus has a "concern for establishing and guiding the next generation" and is clear: much of the future rests on the "infusion of fresh blood into civil life."

While the author's experience seems to be primarily within public sector leadership, most of the principles he puts forward may be equally applicable to the private sector, and he also draws extensively on experts that have studied this sector, such as Bennis, Collins, and Hackman. Good leadership appears to be universal, with little difference between settings or sectors. A trend towards more collaborative leadership seems to be emerging, including having strong focus on courage, compassion, and character, all embedded in such a team approach. Again, it is a matter of "we, we, we," in contrast to "me, me, me."

The author sees a total of seven common factors that characterize them as strong leaders. Further, he suggests five factors that seem to be particularly significant when it comes to self-awareness, and another two that focus on strengths and relentlessly improving performance (p. 49).

Not to rush things, but to prepare oneself systematically over time seems essential. To draw on effective coaches and sponsors are important. A central outcome might be a clearer perception of one's "True North," one's core values.

Having sufficient inner strengths to survive setbacks. Perhaps it might all be summarized as having a "sunny temperament," being highly adaptable, although with hardiness and stoicism, i.e., no rash emotions.

The leader's outer journey. "Leading up" is how to cope with one's boss, but it is a matter of "leading sideways" as well, drawing on friends, such as how George H. W. Bush drew on his friendship with James Baker, Chief of White House Staff. And above all, leading a team is central indeed. This includes getting the right people to join one's team, and in the most meaningful capacities, as well as asking dysfunctional personalities to leave. Good group-centered leadership is then a reality!

The leader needs to be an effective persuader. Effective presentations and inspiring public speeches are crucial, focusing on three key elements: ethos (building on the speaker's/presenter's credibility), logos (the argument(s) the speaker/presenter is advancing), and pathos (appealing to the audience's emotions). It is indeed increasingly important to successfully make effective presentations in a digital world.

Leadership in action also includes having a "Plan B," in case things do not work out as initially planned. A leader might indeed lose his/her way.

To lead through a crisis, a so-called VUCA (volatility, uncertainty, complexity, ambiguity), perhaps the most critical, however, is to always attempt to be prepared for the worst. By not doing this, former President Trump mishandled the COVID-19 crisis, for instance. This probably significantly lessened his chances for re-election.

Heuristics, such as careful documentation of decisions, practicing ardent reading, and always trying to be upbeat, maintaining good humor. It is critical too to exercise strict discipline when it comes to how a leader spends his/her time, i.e., balancing priorities.

The author also offers a 20-item executive summary. The following 14 are perhaps especially meaningful when it comes to leading in the private sector:

- Leadership seems to have become harder and harder.
- Leadership starts from within.
- Articulate three key objectives early.
- Find your "True North" / purpose.
- Focus on your strengths.
- Extend your leadership journey outside yourself.
- Remember that you are never too young to lead.
- Secure your finances.
- Learn to manage your boss.
- Mobilize others through persuasion.
- Consider that your greatest enemy might be you.
- Seek guidance from the past and present.
- Friends, and networks, still matter.
- Maintain a celestial spark.

Gideon Rachman, (2022), The Age of the Strongman: How the Cult of the Leader Threatens Democracy Around the World, Bodley Head (Reviewed July 2022)

This book provides 11 biographies of more or less dictatorial leaders, including Putin, Xi, Bolsonaro, Erdogan, and Orbán, as well as analyses of former strongmen such as Boris Johnson, Trump, and Netanyahu. All of these are ably done. There are also chapters on how more democratic leaders such as Biden, Merkel, and Macron are or have been attempting to counteract actions from these strongmen. Finally, the author offers his own insights regarding why this age of the strongman seems to be more profound than ever, starting with its inception in the early part of this century, with the fraction of democratically run countries falling steadily over the last 15 years. The author also discusses the counterpoints between Soros versus Bannon to further highlight this battle between autocracies and democracies. The author, Gideon Rachman, chief foreign affairs columnist for The Financial Times since 2006, and previously with The Economist, was educated at Cambridge, and is uniquely qualified to write a book such as this, brilliant, succinct, and original!

What seems to characterize strongmen? Typically, they are nationalists, cultural conservatives, often with strong stances against immigration, often tending to stand up against the (liberal) elites typically found in capitals (major cities), but rather building on support from their nations' countryside. And they tend to have strong personality traits. Also, they are often prone to committing to restore their countries to what they consider to be past glory. Law and institutions seem to be less respected than in typical democracies, to the point that acknowledgements of election losses might be disputed, even rejected.

The author tries to address the following five questions through his biographical analysis:

- First, why did this strongman tendency take hold? Answer: Putin took office at the beginning of this century, and the bulk of his thought disciplines cover the ensuing 10–15 years.
- Second, what are its main characteristics? Answer: we have already attended to this, but it might perhaps be added that many of these strongmen typically play up their own importance. As Trump said: "Only I can save the US."
- Third, why did it happen? Clearly this had a lot to do with what many saw as the "downfall" of the formerly predominant system, often manifested by

the financial crisis of 2008 (but there was no such crisis in China!), and perhaps too much perceived arrogance, even elitism, now and then found within the then ruling circles. The relatively ineffective handling of the COVID-19 pandemic in several Western countries may also have contributed (800,000 deaths in the USA versus the officially reported 5000 deaths in China; many deaths in several European countries, as well as in countries such as Brazil, Mexico, and so on).

- Fourth, what is strongman policy? Answer: The importance of the singling out of a specific (group of) enemy(ies), and not to hesitate in "smearing" such enemy(ies), often with excessive, even often with totally incorrect arguments. Manipulation of facts and denial of truths seem to be common ways of operation for the strongman.
- Fifth, why is the strongman phenomenon on the rise? Since many strongmen seem to be hanging onto their positions for long periods of time (longer than their opponents, democratically elected officials), often initially perceived as relatively liberal reform-orientated leaders, but then over time, typically becoming more and more authoritarian. Regrettably, the number of strongmen tends to rise, and their abusive profiles frequently become more dominant over time.

It should be pointed out that while some strongmen are, in effect, installed without credible election processes (Xi, Putin, …), others might initially have come to power through relatively democratic elections (Orbán, Modi, Bolsonaro, …). Further, others have been voted out of office (Trump, Johnson, …). Some readers may argue that it may perhaps be a little bit too farfetched to classify relatively democratic leaders such as Trump or Johnson in the same category as Putin or Xi. All the so-called strongmen leaders seem to be characterized by a number of common nationalistically inspired factors, however.

There is indeed a crisis in liberalism, economic, social, technological, and geographical:

- Putin: Speed of consolidating power.
- Erdogan: Imprisonment of "dangerous" opponents.
- Xi: Personality cult.
- Modi: Make Hindus great again.
- Orbán: Zero tolerance against immigrants.
- Johnson: Take back control (Brexit).
- Trump: Endorse big lies!

- Mohamed bin Salman (MBS): Growing intolerance for opposition and dissent.
- Bolsonaro: Shocking rhetoric, to make himself stand out.
- Ahmed (Ethiopia): From liberal hero to despotic strongman.

There is also often a reaction against the strongman, between nationalism and globalism, exemplified perhaps by leaders such as Merkel, Macron, or Trudeau. They, and others, tend to see globalism as an opportunity, in contrast to the more nationalistic traits of strongmen. This might perhaps also be seen as a battle of ideas, contrasting the successful investor, George Soros, with his concept of open society, with Steve Bannon, with extreme nationalism and more than implied criticism of globalism.

How might Biden handle this increasingly long list of strongmen? His position with Putin and Xi looks to be non-compromising. However, with other strongmen, such as Erdogan or MBS, he appears to have been more willing to accept certain compromises. The prospect of Biden's term in office being only relatively short, four years, seems to be real, with the emergence of someone with strongman leaning after the next presidential election.

We seem to be in a democratic recession. The strongman epoch is likely to continue for quite some time. It is therefore paramount to know more about these strongmen since they definitely will be playing central roles in shaping this world's political picture for many years.

34

Executive Profiles of Business Leaders

Joël Mesot, President, ETH Zürich (Interviewed March 2020 and June 2023)

ETH, one of the highest-ranked engineering universities worldwide, has a clear strategy, and ETH's leadership helps them to remain in this top tier. Entrepreneurship is key, attempting to create business opportunities from its many cutting-edge areas. To maintain its preeminent multidimensional focus is fundamental. A high degree of cooperation also seems to be at the center of ETH's strategy, with industry, for example, in Switzerland's world-famous pharma sector. This goes both ways. Cooperating with competing schools is also seen as mutually beneficial. In total, an open approach is driving its strategy, which is also manifested by ETH's truly international staff and student body.

Since mid-March 2020, with the pandemic raging, ETH Zurich had been operating in emergency mode, like the rest of the country. Overnight, ETH had to switch its classroom teaching to online teaching and was forced to reduce its laboratory research to a minimum, with the exception of research on the coronavirus. The entire administrative staff, including the Executive Board, was asked to stay at home to work from home offices. ETH Zurich, together with other universities, was involved in various initiatives and platforms to support the needs of hospitals and other healthcare institutions. ETH students launched an online marketplace to refer students to hospitals and pharmacies. There were many more initiatives that came about as a consequence of the pandemic.

ETH Zurich—the Swiss Federal Institute of Technology in Zürich—currently ranks seventh worldwide in the prestigious QS World University Rankings, making it the best university in continental Europe. "The result shows the university's strong standing thanks to a broad foundation of scientific excellence," says Dr. Joël Mesot, President of ETH Zurich. "The ranking also reflected the exceptional reputation that Switzerland enjoys as a research hub." ETH has two campuses in Zurich—an original one in the city center as well as a modern facility in Hönggerberg on the outskirts of the city. In Basel, near the university hospital and major pharmaceutical industry companies, it hosts its Department of Biosystems Science and Engineering, and in the canton of Ticino, the Swiss National Supercomputing Centre. Furthermore, ETH operates a research hub in Singapore focused on future sustainable cities, resilience, and health technologies. There are over 10,000 undergraduate students (bachelor's), 13,300 graduate students (master's and doctoral), 524 professors, and 6700 scientific staff, in the ETH community. The institution's annual budget is around 1.8 billion CHF, of which 30% comes from third-party funding. ETH Zurich and its sister institution EPFL, in Lausanne, are the only Federal universities in Switzerland. All other universities in Switzerland are financed and administered under the auspices of cantonal authorities.

The Federal Council elected Dr. Joël Mesot as President of ETH Zurich in 2019. Previously, he had been the Director of the Paul Scherrer Institute (PSI) for ten years, the largest publicly funded research institute in Switzerland. PSI is a world leader in the field of lasers. Dr. Mesot, a physicist by education, earned his doctorate from ETH Zurich. He had also attended IMD in Lausanne.

ETH Zurich is one of the world's leading research and advanced teaching institutions in the field of science and technology. A key part of ETH's strategic process is therefore to focus on what might be key critical success factors in the future for a top-quality academic institution such as ETH to maintain its commitment to excellence and lead in research and teaching. In light of the increased political and societal expectations as well as technological changes, traditional universities such as ETH must find ways to embrace change. This is why the President launched an initiative called "rETHink." Its purpose is to enable ETH Zurich to:

- Further strengthen individual responsibility throughout—professorships, academic departments, Executive Board, and central administrative units.
- Establish adequate professional structures within the university for student support and personnel leadership.

- Strengthen strategic and operational leadership at all levels.
- Foster and further develop the collaboration and core values that promote a strong sense of belonging among all members of the ETH community.

As part of the rETHink project, two new members joined the Executive Board as vice presidents: one for Personnel Development and Leadership, the other for Knowledge Transfer and Corporate Relations. This project includes six "work streams" with operative work packages with well-defined content. The work streams would allow for the strengthening of important connections and interrelations. The first five work streams focused on the institutional structure of the organization: the professorships, the academic departments, the Executive Board and central administrative units, university bodies, and the institution as a whole. To promote a sense of belonging in the ETH community, as well as further develop cooperation and core values, an overarching work stream was devoted to cultural development. Dr. Mesot saw this as perhaps the most critical of all the six parts of the rETHink program.

The implementation of the rETHink project ensured close cooperation among professors, academic departments, and relevant participating bodies. With a project structure that consisted of external support and an Executive Board representative in each of the work streams, the design anticipated an efficient and carefully targeted implementation.

For a growing number of students, starting a company had become a valuable alternative to industry employment. This strong entrepreneurial mentality was the result of a new culture that had taken hold over the past 20 years at ETH. This manifested itself in various programs and initiatives to foster entrepreneurship:

- Pioneer Fellows: The Pioneer Fellowship program, launched in 2011, has enabled master's and doctoral students to apply for financial support of up to 150'000 Swiss francs in order to develop a prototype within an 18-month period. Coaching and professional guidance is offered through the "Innovation & Entrepreneurship Lab." Since the inception of the program, Pioneer Fellows have founded no less than 80 start-up companies.
- Spin-off support and venture capital: Every year, ETH students and researchers found some 25 new spin-off companies. There has also been an impressive development in terms of venture capital. ETH start-ups were responsible for more than half of the total venture capital raised in the canton of Zurich in 2019, amounting to 1.2 billion Swiss Francs.
- Project and research-oriented education: There is a long tradition of involving students in research projects from an early stage in their studies. One

such program, the "Focus projects competition," affords student teams at the end of their bachelor studies the opportunity to develop a fully functioning prototype from scratch. ETH Zurich recently opened a student project house to facilitate the testing of ideas.
- Critical Thinking and ETH Week: As part of the Critical Thinking initiative at ETH, student teams across all 16 departments work on highly relevant global issues such as nutrition, health, or mobility. Within just one week, students rise to the challenge of framing a problem and coming up with a solution.

"Scientific breakthroughs often happen at the interface of different disciplines" underlined Dr. Mesot. This is why he sees a multidisciplinary approach to research as necessary, while, as noted, also maintaining ETH Zurich's strong departmental orientation. The latter is the instrument to being able to "go deep" to truly undertake fundamental scientific research. However, the university makes a strong case for working on cross-disciplinary projects also. It is important that students learn to work beyond their own field of expertise early on in their academic studies and develop cross-disciplinary communication skills. In the special programs, student teams build, for example, electric cars or quantum computers. Allowing students to test how things work without too much professorial involvement (i.e., bottom-up driven projects) is great for learning how to address big issues that carry strong social implications.

ETH Zurich plays a vital role in the Swiss innovation ecosystem. Many of the big IT companies such as Google, Microsoft, IBM, and Disney have located research activities in Zurich and opened labs in close cooperation with the university. There is a strong recognition that ETH Zurich and its alumni act as catalysts to bring high-tech firms from all over the world to the Zurich area. Here are just a few examples:

- IBM's Research lab in Rüschlikon was founded some 60 years ago. In 2011, IBM and ETH Zurich deepened their partnership by opening the Binnig and Rohrer Nanotechnology Center.
- Google operates its largest research facility outside the USA in Zurich with 4000 employees. In choosing Zurich as a research site, ETH alumnus Urs Hölzle proved instrumental.
- Disney Research Studios in Zurich, led by ETH Zurich Computer Science professor, Markus Gross, has made numerous contributions to Disney movie productions and has even won two Tech Oscars for its technological innovations.

Zurich is a place where academia meets industry, creating a highly desirable "talent ecosystem" that fosters an understanding of the needs of society, enables researchers to address such needs, and facilitates relevant knowledge transfer. Such an ecosystem perpetuates a positive feedback loop that attracts even more top students to professors and top industries.

The other leading technical university in Switzerland, also an entity of the Swiss Federal Government, is the École Polytechnique Fédérale de Lausanne, in short EPFL. The dynamism and excellence of this "younger sister institution" continuously inspire ETH Zurich to improve, a positive effect of a competitive dynamic. The Swiss ETH Domain consists of the two technical universities, ETH Zurich and EPFL, and four research agencies, among them the Paul Scherrer Institute (PSI). ETH Zurich relies on a global network with more than 9000 research contacts and a close cooperation with Swiss institutions, including, for example, the University of Zurich, the Zurich's University Hospital in Medicine, as well as with leading pharmaceutical firms such as Roche or Novartis in the field of biology. In addition, Dr. Mesot keeps a network of contacts with top administrations in around 20 or so of the world's leading academic institutions.

As buildings and research infrastructure represent a long-term investment, ETH strives to construct buildings of high quality. In recent years, sustainability and the decarbonization of the campus have become a key criterion for the university's whole real estate portfolio. The Anergy Grid, an underground storage system, was developed at ETH's Science City campus in Hönggerberg. Since the Anergy Grid began operating in 2013, it has continued to expand. In constructing the Anergy Grid, ETH Zurich is building a dynamic system aiming to reduce CO_2 emissions from heating and cooling to meet the goal of an 80% reduction by 2040. In 2019, the system consisted of three underground storage units and five substations that supply 14 building clusters with heat and cooling.

While there are large auditoria, most of the undergraduate teaching of basic disciplinary foundations primarily takes place in smaller rooms, typically heavily discussion driven. Concepts such as flipped classrooms have been introduced at ETH, and online teaching tools have become an integral part of the school's teaching endeavors.

ETH Zurich and EPFL are indeed "elite" academic institutions, both among the best in the world. They both receive the bulk of their funding from the Swiss Federal government. Yet, an increasing part of the budget comes from third-party contributions, in fact close to 30% in the case of ETH. Although the two Federal universities differ in a number of aspects from the rest of the Swiss Higher Education system, their funding is negotiated every four years within the Dispatch on the Promotion of Education, Research and Innovation (ERI Dispatch).

There has been a tendency for governments as well as for other institutions, such as the European Union (EU), to provide support to specific research projects. This might have unintended consequences by making it more difficult for basic research to obtain funding. It is however essential for world-leading institutions such as ETH to be able to carry out such strong fundamental research. To secure reliable funding and full access to the European and global science networks remain top priorities for ETH Zurich's leadership.

There are 26 cantons in Switzerland, all with their own educational systems. While some cantons may be stronger than other cantons, say, when it comes to teaching "the basics," ETH Zurich accepts every student who has earned a Swiss "Maturität." Unlike many universities in the world, ETH Zurich does not have an entrance exam. Such an open access to higher education tends to lead to quite a large attrition rate at the end of the first year however, as much as 50%! Students who fail in the first year are afforded a second chance to pass their first-year exams. While some 85% of the students seeking a bachelor's degree have a Swiss educational background (with instruction offered only in German at the undergraduate level), one-third of the student body at the master's level (with instruction primarily in English) comes from abroad. At the doctoral level, over 70% of students are foreign nationals.

While ETH Zurich's students are highly valued for their scientific expertise, the institution has put more emphasis on promoting social and communication skills in the last years. Therefore, new courses and interdisciplinary project work, such as the aforementioned ETH Week, have been de-signed to improve the overall competencies of ETH students.

Established in 2010, the Singapore-ETH Center is ETH Zurich's only research center outside of Switzerland. The center strengthens the research capacity of ETH Zurich, by developing sustainable solutions to global challenges in Switzerland and in the world. Set in southeast Asia, in a rapidly growing urban region, the Singapore-ETH Center aims to provide practical solutions to some of the most pressing challenges regarding future urban sustainability, notably smart cities, resilient systems, and future health technologies. Breaking down disciplinary "silos" by establishing thematic-oriented research objectives ensures a strong focus on teamwork that might serve as a model for the university's main activities in Zurich.

Alfred Escher, whose 200th birthday was celebrated in 2019, was instrumental in the foundation of ETH Zurich or, as it was called in 1855, the

"Polytechnical School." Mr. Escher was a man of many talents. He is well known for his work in initiating the construction of the Gotthard tunnel that connects the north and the south of Switzerland. Escher had a long-term, strategic perspective and thought "big." He was aware of the fact that for young Switzerland to become an industrialized nation, the country needed engineers, money, and a way to manage risks. From these needs, he formulated the creation of ETH Zurich, the Schweizerische Kreditanstalt (that became Credit Suisse before being taken over by Switzerland's UBS in 2023), and the Rentenanstalt (today: Swiss Life). In all of these enterprises, Escher played a crucial role.

Perhaps fewer barriers stood in the way of launching far-reaching complex projects in higher education, banking, and insurance during Escher's time. Today's society has become more complex, regulated, and controlled in many matters. Still in terms of innovation and technology, Switzerland is poised to the standards. Access to big data, artificial intelligence, and powerful algorithmic computing power have created novel possibilities for society. ETH Zurich is at the forefront!

Laurent Freixe, EVP Nestlé, CEO Zone Americas; Global Youth Initiative Program (Interviewed March 2019)

Three main pillars seem to characterize Nestlé and its strategy, Nestlé being by far the world's largest food company and a highly successful multinational. These pillars create shared values for Nestlé and for society. First, a strong social responsibility commitment is sought. Second, the company invests in innovation, now with a main focus on introducing healthier food, also for "fragile" human groups, such as the elderly, the very young, and those with certain illnesses. Pet food innovation is also part of this. The third pillar is to invest in people, particularly young talent worldwide. A successful traineeship program has been developed under the leadership of Mr. Freixe. This has impacted Nestlé's corporate culture, enhancing social responsibility and consolidating the firm's global footprint.

Born in Paris, France, Laurent Freixe joined Nestlé in 1986. Laurent plays a leading role in promoting youth employment and employability across the company. Starting in Europe, Laurent launched the Nestlé youth initiative, Nestlé Needs YOUth, in 2013 and has been successfully driving this global initiative that aims at providing a wide range of employment opportunities for young people under 30 and strengthening their capabilities and professional skills to raise their employability. Additionally, on May 23, 2018, Laurent was named International Youth Ambassador by the International Youth Organization for Ibero-America.

When the global financial crisis started in 2007, Mr. Freixe was in charge of Nestlé Iberia. Until that time, much of the economic growth in Spain had come from the real estate sector, fueled in part by relatively low interest rates and by demand coming primarily from a constant flow of immigration from Latin America, Eastern Europe, and North Africa, as well as from investors coming from further north (above all from Germany, the UK, and Scandinavia) and partly by more speculation. However, it all collapsed in 2008, and a social crisis emerged. The younger generation of Spanish society was hit quite hard, suffering an exceptionally high rate of unemployment. Outside of Spain, youth unemployment also grew. It was time for Nestlé to act.

Mr. Freixe realized that the task of creating new jobs should primarily be the responsibility of the business sector. Further, such opportunities were generally scarce in the public sector. However, there seemed to be a dilemma here: many companies generally prefer to hire workers with experience, and youths generally do not have the type of experience that businesses typically might look for. Furthermore, in the context of crisis, more attention would be placed on cutting jobs rather than on investing for the future.

So, when Mr. Freixe became Head of Zone Europe, he launched a youth program for apprenticeship and traineeship throughout its facilities (i.e., the head office, factories and distribution centers, and across all European markets). This program gradually came to be called The Nestlé Global Youth Initiative and was to be driven entirely by Nestlé's line organization instead of by staff groups such as HR or PR. The basic underlying premise was to create value for each youth involved. The program also indirectly benefitted society through better youth integration in the community in the following ways:

- Job opportunities.
- Education and on-the-job training.
- Readiness for wider work activities, through participants' acquisitions of relevant skills (e.g., CV clinics and preparation for job interviews).

The aim was thus to raise the employability of young people. Launched in Europe, the program was further expanded into the Americas (Mr. Freixe was promoted to EVP and CEO Zone Americas in 2014), and Zone Asia/Middle East/Africa also eventually became involved.

At the inception of the program, Mr. Freixe estimated that Nestlé could create opportunities for at least 20,000 young persons. Additionally, Nestlé asked its suppliers and business partners to participate, and 15 quickly responded with enthusiasm to create the Alliance for Youth (All 4 YOUth). They were able to offer another 80,000 job opportunities/internships so that the program came to encompass more than 100,000 young persons. The program's success has been spectacular for its impact on Nestlé and on society. This case has shown that 1 CHF invested would return benefits multiple times to society.

Three often-asked questions, or possible objections, should be discussed:

- How can this internship program be implemented without causing major disruptions to Nestlé's internal operations and its ongoing drive to be efficient? The answer seems to rest on the fact that in each location (factory or distribution center) only a few interns would be employed, and they would not create a "disturbance," but rather be a source of pride and inspiration when it came to local transfer of knowledge.
- What happens with those youths who are not offered permanent jobs at Nestlé at the end of their internship periods? The very fact that these youths have been trained at Nestlé would significantly improve their chances of obtaining subsequent employment elsewhere.
- How can Nestlé simultaneously restructure when required and engage in such a program? There may actually be no issue here, understanding that Nestlé could downsize structures as business required, even while investing for the future in talent development and acquisition.

Nestlé's traditional culture might have been characterized as rather discrete and understated. Some might even have described it as "shy"! The youth employment program, widely shared early on in the financial crisis, came to be seen as a manifestation of Nestlé's human and social responsibility. Importantly, this program was not met with suspicion from society; it seemed to be generally noncontroversial, perhaps in contrast to sometimes-raised criticism from societal activists. The program became widely visible within the Nestlé organization and a source of inspiration, even pride. As such, the program seemed to contribute to Nestlé's drive towards an even stronger symbiosis with society.

Today, civil strife has created large groups of relatively young, displaced persons and former civil war combatants in several parts of the world. These vulnerable and/or traumatized persons are often in acute need of reintegration into "normal" society after the end of given military conflicts (e.g., in

Columbia and Syria). Even in the USA, specific challenges remain in reintegrating veterans into civilian society. Most experts agree on the need to involve these groups of youths in youth employment programs. It should be noted that Nestlé's global footprint represents a definite advantage here.

The youth employment program seemed to have led to easier ways for Nestlé to dialog with the public sector, also on other issues such as regulation or health and safety. Moreover, it was particularly interesting to observe how this "training on the job" approach seemed to resonate well with the Swiss or German public, none the least because of their long traditions of using this type of apprenticeship approach in these countries.

Nestlé and its traditional suppliers might be seen as representing the more conservative side of a productive society. To broaden the program's reach from mostly blue-collar employment to so-called "new economy" positions, Nestlé widened the scope of the Youth Initiative to also encompass digitalization. Companies such as Google, Facebook, and Microsoft became partners. E&Y also became involved to measure more precisely the impact of this program (i.e., value to society and value to Nestlé).

Nestlé is committed to this program for the long term and has defined ambitions until at least 2030. Nestlé's CEO, Mr. Mark Schneider, is fully behind the program, and so are Nestlé's three zone heads (Europe, Middle East, North Africa, the Americas, and Asia/Oceania/Sub-Saharan Africa). The next major challenge is to further strengthen the program, which has been in existence for more than 6 years and seems to be thriving more than ever!

Interestingly, Mr. Freixe wisely perceived youth unemployment as a global issue, with similarities and also differences across regions. The youth unemployment rate is globally two to three times higher than the adult population rate. These differences come from the dynamics in the economic sector and demographic development across regions, combined with the fact that informal employment is prevailing in emerging markets. A key success factor for Nestlé is its global footprint, as well as its focus on investment to drive growth, which in turn then also creates job opportunities. People employed in the program are below 30 years of age, with no discrimination in terms of gender or educational background. And Nestlé provides opportunities across and deeply in its entire operations. In the USA, the company is not allowed to discriminate by age group, calling the project "Project Opportunity" and mainly including apprenticeships.

These success factors are probably applicable for other organizations too. After all, the most direct contribution of a business to society and to the communities is through providing formal jobs. The global nature of the Alliance and the commitment of its members is the best guarantee of the sustainability of the program.

Peter Brabeck-Letmathe, Chairman Emeritus Nestlé (Interviewed February 2019)

A desire to develop healthier food is central to Mr. Brabeck's business philosophy. This includes focusing on drinking water, an essential element of human health. Nestlé is the largest drinking water producer in the world, by the way. When it comes to research and development, particularly in larger companies such as Nestlé, there is often a concern that new approaches may actually cannibalize various existing businesses, an example being perhaps the more recent Nespresso line versus the established "cash cow" Nescafé. And the opening up of online direct sales has allowed Nestlé to establish an even better direct contact with main customers, in effect bypassing the retail sector. To meet concerns to create a better environment, Mr. Brabeck envisions a relatively stronger focus on entire value chains, say, with farmers, ingredient providers, manufacturers, and retail chains all working together.

In April 2017, Peter Brabeck-Letmathe became Chairman Emeritus of Nestlé SA. He had been CEO of the Nestlé Group from 1997 to 2008 and then held the dual positions of CEO and Chairman from 2005 to 2008. After this, he remained as Chairman.

Mr. Brabeck was born in 1944 in Austria and graduated from Vienna's University of Economics and Business with a degree in trade and economics. After joining the Nestlé Group in 1968, he spent a significant amount of his career in Latin America before being transferred to Nestlé's international headquarters in Vevey, Switzerland, first as Senior Vice President and then as Executive Vice President and a Member of the Executive Board. He was in charge of Nestlé's strategic business units, marketing and sales, and corporate communications during this time.

Mr. Brabeck also served as vice chairman of the Board of the World Economic Forum and as president of the Foundation Board of the Verbier Music Festival. He was an independent director of Delta Topco (Formula 1) and served as a board member of Hoffman and Roche, Credit Suisse, L'Oréal, and Exxon Mobil Corporation. He was also chairman of the 2030 Water Resources Group, a public/private partnership that he founded in 2008. He received an honorary doctoral degree from the University of Alberta for his work on the responsible stewardship of water resources and has received numerous awards and accolades throughout his leadership career.

Being no longer an active member of Nestlé's organization, Mr. Brabeck stressed that his interview comments express only his opinions and that they do not necessarily reflect Nestlé's official positions. Starting with his thoughts on healthy food. Mr. Brabeck thought back to the history of mankind, where a major concern had always been the issue of availability of food, so as for people to get sufficient amounts of calories. We humans were able to figure out how to improve our own food by having access to fire, thus making food safer and in general better quality. Now, there is generally enough food per capita and enough calories, especially in the more developed part of the world. The concern today has gradually shifted to assessing the quality of our food, especially its impact on health and wellness. Paradoxically, the focus is now increasingly shifting towards reducing the calorie content! An evolution is taking place, from a scarcity of food to having enough food to now having healthier food.

Science has played a major role in the evolution of food. The so-called industrialization of food started some 150 years ago and came to focus primarily on three factors:

- To increase agriculture's yield (mechanization, use of man-made fertilizers, hybrid technologies, good-quality development,. ..).
- To ensure that safer food was being produced.
- To conserve food more safely, above all so that it might be more easily transported and stored (Pasteur, for instance, came up with a way to treat red wine from Bordeaux so that it might be transported without becoming vinegar pasteurization).

Thus, as of the 1990s, a general realization came about, namely that fewer calories may be preferable. Nestlé pioneered this development during Mr. Brabeck's tenure as CEO. Indeed, many of the changes and priorities that were made back then have also had fundamental effects on the entire food industry. The industry went from being what we might call a food business to now being a nutrition and health business. And life sciences increasingly came to play a central role. Nestlé's slogan became "Good Food, Good Life." Consumers were seeking fewer calories, less salt, and fewer carbohydrates combined with relatively more proteins and vitamins.

The interest towards healthier food was relatively new in the marketplace, coming about over time. It became clear that core businesses such as coffee, ice cream, and chocolate would still remain core pillars, even after the nutritional upgrading. However, coffee, for instance, became significantly modified, with more antioxidants, chocolate became darker, etc. Nestlé was the first food company within the industry to see this paradigm shift and to go for it in full. Among its competitors, Danone also jumped on this almost immediately. Others, such as Pepsico, Unilever, and Coca Cola, became early adopters. Gradually, the whole industry followed. Most experts estimate that Nestlé gained a four-to-five-year advantage over the competitors, thanks to being the first!

Mr. Brabeck's predecessor as CEO of Nestlé, Mr. Helmut Maucher, led the establishment of Nestlé as a world-leading water bottler. He saw a potential long-term lack of clean water. Under his leadership, leading brands such as Vittel, Perrier, and Poland Springs were acquired and developed. Then, under Mr. Brabeck's time, the company created Nestlé Pure Life, the world's most important water brand today, and made many more acquisitions, including San Pellegrino.

Let us now discuss the so-called 2030 Water Resources Group. A report was prepared by McKinsey & Co. in 2009, "Charting our Water Future." The report pointed out that, on a global basis, there seemed to be around 20% more water consumed than what was added back in a natural way. The deficit was ameliorated by various unsustainable means such as tapping aquifers (until they were ultimately becoming dried up) and emptying lakes (Aral) or rivers (Rio Grande) or melting glaciers (Greenland). The report further pointed out that this problem was likely to become significantly more severe relatively soon, with 40% over-usage in 2030, unless something was done to ameliorate the situation. The findings showed that solutions to these problems would tend to be local, not necessarily national. And the water challenges would definitely not be global, i.e., not analogous to the challenge of limiting CO_2 emissions. Local governments got involved, and initiatives such as the Sustainable Water Initiative and the Hydro-Economic Analytics framework followed. As of 2019, there seems to be a consensus that the 2030 Water Resources Group has had a significant impact.

In general, Mr. Brabeck feels that the common way of life tends to be far too resource intensive. Humans take from our Earth much more than what we are able to channel back! We are definitely not in a sustainable circular economy. This seems, in particular, to be the case regarding resources such as water, arable land (for farming to support suboptimal food consumption), and mining (especially of rare types of materials such as lithium for the batteries used in electric cars). However, more resource-friendly business firms are developing more sustainable business models such as Airbnb or various car-sharing solutions. However, Mr. Brabeck does not want to oversimplify.

For instance, the advent of the electric car might paradoxically bring with it a particularly serious new challenge, namely the scrapping of lithium batteries (exceptionally heavy, with around a 5-year life span only).

It is a myth that start-ups are more innovative than large companies. We know that many start-ups fail; it is said that, out of 10 start-ups, eight typically fail, one barely reaches its breakeven, and only one becomes a big success. This one big success tends to be the one we hear about. Many of these successful smaller companies are ultimately acquired by larger firms; however, this contributes to the myth of smaller firms generally being more entrepreneurial than larger ones. Yet large companies keep their eyes on disruptive, fresh entrepreneurial initiatives which can be added to their portfolios or holdings in order to jump-start or diversify their own directions in key areas.

That said, there are of course also challenges when it comes to the agility of larger companies. The risk is real that new innovative approaches might threaten existing established business activities. Thus, the risk is relatively higher that existing revenue might be jeopardized. Nespresso, for instance, was to a certain degree held back at Nestlé for ten years due to concern regarding potential dysfunctional effects on Nescafé sales—the latter being a main business for Nestlé. One of the first things Mr. Brabeck did as CEO of Nestlé was to allow Nespresso machines at the Nestlé headquarter! In retrospect, we see how unwarranted the fear was; we should only have started earlier.

Often, innovations that involve new processes might meet somewhat less resistance in the sense that there might be fewer cannibalization concerns. For instance, Nestlé launched the corporate-wide GLOBE IT system. With comparable types of information regarding sales, margins, volumes, production, purchasing, etc., it gained a vastly better overview and transparency throughout. Nobody could "hide" their own unique information, which might have been applicable to their own markets only! Again, today everyone takes the GLOBE system for granted, but back then, it was sometimes a struggle to get it done.

Closeness to the consumer is probably more critical today than ever. Up until some ten years ago, food producers such as Nestlé would find retail chains and distributors to be positioned between themselves and the customers, many of them powerful and with significant resources. Over the last decade or so, the emergence of internet sales and marketing has allowed producers such as Nestlé to establish direct contact with the consumer.

We also see a move towards a "bundling" of services where the traditional products may be only a small part. To be able to put together service/product offerings that the consumers would need and want is likely to become increasingly important! What gives value to the consumer beyond the product?

Perhaps being able to order a tasty Asian dinner online or a good-tasting low-calorie diet (to counterbalance overeating at lunch) rather than simply buying a Maggi bouillon cube is the answer!

Let us keep in mind that organizations typically are "flatter" and less hierarchical today than before. This means that organizational structure, in effect, now represents a more networked reality than before! Effective leadership skills will become even more key in such contexts.

Second, good leadership is built on being able to interpret the future in a reasonable way. Some call this strong analytics-based intuition! But, to do this, the leader must have a good sense of where he/she is coming from, i.e., a solid understanding of the past; historical insight. Only then might he/she have a reasonably good idea of where one's industry might be likely to go, and where it might be in, say, ten years.

Third, a strong leader must already have thought through the overall vision before a problem occurs. Be prepared to act, not be surprised or hesitant.

Gillian Tett, Senior Editor, US, Financial Times (Interviewed November 2022)

In her latest book, *Anthrovision: A New Way to See in Business and Life (2021)*, Gillian Tett writes about the behaviors of organizations, individuals, and markets, by "looking through an anthropological lens." In this interview, the focus is on the role of anthropology in decision-making, drawing in part on her book.

We note that a common misperception may be that anthropology is still predominantly focused on exploring the functioning of relatively primitive societies, following the tradition of anthropological pioneers such as Margaret Meade. As we learn in this interview, this no longer seems to be the case. Today, the focus appears to have increasingly shifted towards exploring phenomena in our modern world. Leading academic centers in this respect seem to be Stanford and NYU.

To start, for the benefit of business readers, what is "anthrovision"? Ms. Tett asserts that for much of the typical reasoning around key issues in the many diverse fields of inquiry (including forecasting in business and economics, predictive reasoning in political science, and so on), the common approach is to base one's reasoning on various underlying models, typically developed from the second half of the twentieth century and onwards. However, such models for forecasting are built on specific assumptions. Thus, the insights that we might depend on, the degree to which the assumptions that we have specified, are reasonable or not. Assumptions are functions of a given physical context as well as social context. Culture matters! Thus, different people might come up with radically different "solutions." Anthrovision is thus a manifestation of the fact that people may think in different ways, and that a range of different outcomes might thus be valid. It is thus a matter of recognizing that outcomes may be different for various organizations, businesses, or persons.

It is perhaps useful to embark on a "three-part journey" to come up with one's specific position:

- First, try to envision what might be a reasonable end result.
- Second, try to look back in one's mind regarding why these specific results have come about. What seem to be particularly critical assumptions?
- Third, try to balance the various assumptions. Are we coming up with a more multifaceted set of outcomes compared with where we started from?

Perhaps a good way to think about this process might be to consider it as going from a more internal focus, to reach a more outside focus.

The anthropological "lens" in its ideal form might be applied by business leaders. For good business leaders to be on top of decision-making, he/she should attempt to reflect on the extent to which a given decision might "belong" in a given contextual department, quite similar to examining the anatomy of a fish in a fishbowl. Might this given decision be part of a different context? Perhaps analogous to observing a fish swim from one side of the fishbowl to another. Or consider a totally different, alternative way! Perhaps analogous to the fish jumping out of the bowl.

Why are many business leaders not thinking this way, not considering broader arrays of assumptions? It could be that a particular business leader might see him/herself to be too busy, and/or "trapped" in his/her own so far relatively successful track record, and/or that there is some fear to focus on alternatives. It might perhaps be useful to review how many of the major decision-makers handled the recent COVID-19 pandemic. In general, many of us could tend to be blinded! (Journalists included!)

We have seen how the "three-part set of principles of the anthropologist's mindset" (making the strange familiar, making the familiar strange, and listening to social science) could apply. However, there may be additional issues of importance, such as some which have come up, say, in the Ukraine/Russia conflict. Specifically, much of the thinking of "Western" leaders seemed to assume that Putin was putting high priority on factors of economics, when in reality he apparently had less of a focus on this, and rather on more nationalistic factors to "re-establish" the Russian empire! Also, however, what might be seen as a "dominant cultural view" at a given point in time could be moving. For instance, rather than annexing the entire Ukraine, the culture seems to have shifted to later focusing on securing a land-bridge from Russia to Crimea. While the outcomes of Russia's war efforts definitely seemed to have played a role in this change in position or culture, it could also, to some extent, be a realization that the Ukrainians may be difficult to reign!

Shifting focus to China, it appears clear that the country has become increasingly totalitarian, none-the-least with the recent consolidation of central "power" by Xi Jinping. But do we understand how these factors are "accepted" at the grassroot level? Perhaps a more multifaceted interpretation of what culture entails could be called for!

Ms. Tett encourages curiosity, listening, and observation for business leaders—adopting a "beginners mind." Why is this often lacking in today's business world? This might perhaps have to do with the extreme interconnectedness among most of the world's economies. (While it is true that there may be relatively less focus on open-world trade today than before, the interconnectedness is still there!) Business leaders may thus do well by considering what might be "shocks." We saw this when it came to COVID-19, spreading from China. And another "shock" stemming from the pandemic might be that it now seems acceptable to reconsider how we work—why should we go to the office every day? Shifts in technology can also "induce" shocks!

So, what could be the biggest advice to business leaders today, as Ms. Tett sees it? "Test" what one is seeing! For instance, can one be blinded by one's own success? Explore openly, talk with different people, try to understand different cultures, dialogue with people from all types, and yes, also the young.

It does not seem clear whether executive education/business schools could be up to the task to play key roles in improving our mindsets along the lines that are outlines. Perhaps relatively too much focus may often be given to exploring disciplinary fields, say when it comes to finance, accounting, manufacturing, or strategy. Classical "models" of the twentieth century still seem to dominate much of what is going on. Perhaps typical departmental structure and/or even offices assigned to various disciplinary faculty groups might add to such silo-thinking. Instead, students should be "taught" how to look around more, i.e., get ready for the unexpected!

Conclusion

In the author's opinion, a more anthropological focus can add to how one might come to research various economic phenomena, in contrast to more common axiomatic foci, perhaps more sociological! This higher degree of openness, stemming from this dual approach, also seems to have benefitted the business performance that she "delivered."

The author has valued her own readings in the area of business anthropology, recognizing too that social sciences such as sociology, psychology, and anthropology each contribute immensely to insights into human behavior and business organizations. Clearly, observation and learning enrich the anthropological review process and can help business leaders to understand interaction and societies, consumer behavior, marketing, and management.

Annika Falkengren, Managing Partner, Lombard Odier Group (Interviewed January 2022)

Long-Term Focus

During my years of experience in different leadership positions in financial services, the most important thing that I have learned is that staying focused long term is fundamental.

Adopting such a long-term approach requires vision, patience, persistence, a practical understanding of sustainability, and an agility to adapt tactically to headwinds. Markets fluctuate, forecasts change, and opportunities come and go—staying disciplined yet open, flexible but firm, opportunistic and simultaneously systematic, reasonable and rational—this all counts in achieving success both for clients and the firm.

People Focus and Clear Values

Essential in any leadership position is having a strong focus on people. As an example, successful relationships between clients and their bankers in a wealth management context rely heavily on trust on both sides—being clear on expectations and ensuring that clients' needs and demands are met and that they continue to be met over time.

Being passionate about what you do and why you do it is important in creating such long-term, trust-based relationships. As a leader, it is important to create this passion throughout the organization as a whole and this is done through having a strong set of unifying values based around a common purpose. This passion and common purpose ultimately are what drive the DNA or culture of the firm and allow people (staff and clients) to thrive and succeed day to day.

Knowledge Bases

Being a successful leader requires an understanding of how to use different sources of knowledge in the right way. The amount of knowledge and experience existing within organizations should not be underestimated—the key is to allow this knowledge to emerge and, when necessary, to constructively challenge it either with objective facts and data or with external support.

Creating this culture of using knowledge and experience from within is a critical aspect of a leader's role, and there are two specific aspects to achieving this:

1. Creating team spirit and collaboration—it is increasingly important in a world where flexible working/working from home have become much more common, that a firm does not lose the team spirit and effective collaboration which comes from physically spending time together. To do this, the physical office environment needs to represent a "pull factor"—somewhere where staff want to come to thrive, create, find solutions, and learn together.
2. Learning from mistakes—in complex business environments where not everything is predictable, having a willingness to accept that you cannot get it right all of the time is critical. Creating such a culture of accepting that mistakes happen but always using them as a learning opportunity requires maturity, patience, an ability to listen, and also humility.

Sustainability

The need for a long-term vision is something that is also relevant in ensuring a business is sustainable. It is increasingly important for organizations to think beyond pure short-term bottom-line performance. What counts more than ever is having business models and strategies that support a wider purpose. Environmental, social, and community factors are all topics on the agendas of leaders across all industries—delivering on these topics alongside the day-to-day business requires this long-term focus as well as an enduring passion for people and being creative around how to find solutions to what are some of the biggest challenges leaders have ever faced. Companies who achieve all of this are the companies who will ultimately remain highly investable and outperform their competitors.

35

Closing Remarks for the Part

An effective leader is able to find a good balance between top-down and bottom-up aspects of leadership, i.e., between top-down actions closely associated with the leader him/herself, and bottom-up actions coming from the leader's organization, typically stimulated by the leader. Let us discuss what is implied in each of these two sides of leadership.

Top-down involves at least four different aspects of leadership, all embedded by actions taken directly by the leader him/herself.

- Vision. This must be spelled out by the leader and provide clarity on the direction in which the firm intends to go. The CEO of ABB, Mr. Björn Rosengren, for instance, has spelled out a clear vision for his firm, i.e., to focus on various aspects of electricity—products as well as systems and services—as grouped into some 21 autonomous divisions. Each of these divisions is number one or two in their field. Or Nestlé's CEO, Mr. Mark Schneider, who indicated that his firm's focus shall be primarily on coffee, pet food, and baby nutrition. All other business activities, which do not fit this vision, have been/will be sold off, such as water and chocolate.
- Experience. For a leader should have sufficient credibility when articulating his/her vision, and it is important to be able to point to a strong prior track record. Mr. Rosengren, for instance, had previously led Sandvik, and played a major role in leading Atlas Corp. Mr. Schneider was the former leader of Fresenius.
- Inspiration. A leader must be an inspiration, in the sense of being hands-on, interacting with many members of his/her organization, and traveling globally. He/she must not appear to be a reclusive boss! His/her behavior,

emotional intelligence, and empathy also have an impact on the level of inspiration.
- Integrity. Speed and action are critical. But these realities can come about only when the leader at the top has integrity. A good leader must be a role model. He/she must not be excessive, not mix up personal motives with the job, and in no way be "corrupt." A former leader who has failed here was the leader of Telefonica, Mr. César Alierta, who left Madrid and moved to Florida where his girlfriend was living.

Bottom-up involves activities coming from the organization, typically inspired by the leader. There are perhaps at least three such dimensions:

- Allowing people in the organization to provide inputs, by being able to listen at the top, and create an organizational culture of "no fear," where no idea is a bad one.
- Giving "space" to creative actions and initiatives, coming bottom-up. Here, it is crucial that an effective leader does not fall into the trap of feeling that he/she must in essence take care of all main actions him/herself. The good leader must thus not become a "bottleneck," and equally ensure that there are no bottlenecks in staff functions within the organization. Such bureaucracy can be highly demotivational, by insisting on delaying, often pedestrian procedures. Much of this might have to do with "building" positions of importance for various staff functions and a corresponding "protecting one's turf." A good leader should seek to improve all such issues!
- Being impartial and not personal when giving feedback, as well as when deciding on incentives, promotions, etc.

Part VIII

Leadership and Self: Now to You

Before you are a leader, success is all about growing yourself. When you become a leader, success is all about growing others.
—Jack Welch, business leader, chemical engineer and writer

Mastering others is strength; mastering oneself is true power.
—Lao Tzu, Chinese philosopher and military leader

36

Practice Insights from Peter Brabeck-Letmathe, Chairman Emeritus, Nestlé Group

Let me first elaborate on what I see as a fundamental motivation for me as a leader and individual, indeed a passion that has driven me in the past and still continues to inspire me to learn every day. And this learning should focus *on* the future, stimulate one's thinking *about* the future, and help *anticipate* the future. In contrast, learning should not dwell on the past nor on mastering what is already established as known phenomena.

This "future-focused" learning should lead to actions that help shape the future. With inaction, in contrast, not much can happen, or things just happen "to us," so to speak. So "doing it" implies intentionally creating something new, hopefully positive. Thus, this type of learning requires commitment so as to anticipate what is coming and then to take those actions that might be appropriate in light of this.

My work at GESDA, the Geneva Science and Diplomacy Anticipation Foundation, where I am Chairman, is perhaps an example when it comes to this. Here, a group of scientists from all over the world, "The Scientific Forum," have identified a set of science trends over five, ten, and twenty-five years. Together with a selected group of high-ranking politicians and diplomats, "The Diplomatic Forum," they identify what potential actions to take at each stage, and which debates to address.

I initially asked the scientists these critical questions:

- *What does it mean to be a human being?* Key factors that might impact how to address this issue might be AI, chips implanted in humans, artificial hearts, etc.

- *How are we going to live together in the future?* In coping with our way of living in our society, the world of relatively small minorities seems to prevail, as well as fairly isolated entities.
- *How might we be able to find a new healthy equilibrium between humankind and planet Earth?* Here, I see the latter as expected to fundamentally take care of itself, as it always has done. The call for change is probably more with us humans.

GESDA has come up with an annual report, called *Science Breakthrough Radar*, which focuses on relevant trends for better understanding the three questions that I posed, followed by suggestions for actions and debates, for then to conclude with delineating opportunities coming through proactively handling my questions.

Perhaps the statement by Kirkegaard might summarize this challenge in a succinct way: "To live implies forwardly focused, and backwardly understanding." In other words, one shall have to "live" things, not trying to understand them now. Do things first and think so as to try to gain understanding later.

Perhaps a reflection on the climate crisis and the related CO_2 emission issue may be appropriate here. As of today, I believe we do not know for sure if, typically, deterministic statements made in climate reports are correct. There are often a lot of opinions involved. The reality is that we are talking about degrees of probabilities. Yet we make decisions that are based exclusively on the greenhouse gas emissions effect but which are extremely harmful for the health of our planet Earth and its natural resources, water being the most precious one!

We may be back to one of the issues discussed in the GESDA report, namely for better understanding the difference between molecules and electrons. While the conventional wisdom seems to be that there shall be electrons that will save the world, this requires more debate. Perhaps the larger molecules, with their ability to carry energy (the second law of thermodynamics), may be more of a solution when it comes to dealing with climate change.

Consistency should also be called for. For instance, when purchasing an electric car, many governments offer cash stipends, with their intention being to stimulate the switch to electric cars. New owners of electric cars then typically have to install charging equipment in their homes, where the bulk of the electricity drawn takes place during the night. Here comes the inconsistency shown by public decision-makers. There is now a general call for trying to save electric energy. To lower temperatures in dwellings, even to limit the use of electric Christmas lights, comes to mind. But it is exactly during the night that electricity consumption is up, from charging. This is where we might need electricity to keep temperatures at comfortable levels in our homes. Yet the latter is not allowed. So, we have a combination of more use of electricity from car charging and less use of electricity energy to moderate our heating.

Regarding the need to see one's career as not only being focused on the upside, i.e., how to succeed, but also to prepare to handle what might happen afterwards, the downside, is an important element within the concept of leadership and self. I have spent considerable time climbing mountains. It is a fact that most accidents happen when going down and not when one is attempting to ascend to the top. This is perhaps largely psychological – loss of concentration, less adrenaline, overoptimism, and so on, although clearly physical fatigue also plays a role. Many executives experience this in analogous ways. They may focus on how to be successful in their leadership roles but not on understanding and preparing for who may take their place afterwards, when they are "back in the valley," so to speak, or in quieter and less exciting business moments.

Many CEOs are focused more or less unilaterally on maximizing financial results. And it is amazing how often many of these CEOs simply fade away after they step down. They have typically not prepared themselves for life afterwards. Having other interests—political, cultural, and hobbies—tends not to be the norm for this profile group. Open-mindedness, listening, and interacting with others appear often nonexistent skills here, or at least quite underdeveloped at the top. The prevalent style tends to be "I know best, I don't need to listen to or interact with others." A contrast may be one where a retiring CEO can still be a source of good input for successors. At Nestlé, I tended to invite my predecessor, Helmut Maucher, to lunch several times a year. I picked his brain and got free advice. There was no obligation from my side to actually follow such advice, however.

Business schools, as well as headhunters, may do well in emphasizing how to prepare for or look for the post-CEO phase. Eclecticism in what is being taught is central, not only finance and leadership, for instance. Many business schools may find inspiration in the curriculum often found in US arts colleges, for instance. At Harvard, Yale, and other such high caliber schools, we see a need to take courses in science, social science, and liberal arts. Thus, broadening or diversifying knowledge, scope, and interests can eventually serve to help "prepare" the senior executive for life after the buzz or beyond the company.

Most leaders develop into effective leaders through their job assignments. Few or none are born good leaders. Good leaders tend to evolve over time, becoming stronger as they gain experiences. An example of a leader who seems to have grown with the task is the President of Ukraine.

Institutions are important. Good leaders tend to be institution builders. Their legacies thus tend to last beyond their lives. Such robust institutions continue to manifest what the effective leader stood for. A case in point could be Egon Zehnder, who built an entire global organization that indeed outlasts him.

The World Economic Forum (WEF) is also a good example. Incidentally, I am Vice Chairman of WEF. Two major changes have transformed WEF in the last few years, indeed strengthening, first, WEF as an institution. WEF has been transformed into an international organization with its own board and adequate corporate governance rules. Previously, it was a Foundation controlled by Mr. Klaus Schwab and his family. Now, WEF is positioned to continue as a significant entity even *sans* Mr. Schwab. Second, the world-famous annual meeting in Davos is no longer the only place to convene, to meet, to be seen. Several *impact fora* have been established. These now constitute the bulk of the Davos programs. Participants at Davos have to put in work on the *fora* where they tend to engage throughout the year. There *fora* are now labeled *activity platforms*, and they are dynamic, indeed active.

Allow me to also share a critical experience I have had since leaving Nestlé. I have become chairman of two relatively small companies. Both are highly successful, and they are growing quickly—between 25% and 50% last year. While many of the managerial challenges tend to be similar to what can be found in larger companies, there is definitely less complexity. This allows for a strong entrepreneurial drive. Focus is clearer. Even I, in my role as chairman, am finding it natural, and rewarding, to meet customers. I feel that I am down to earth, enjoying it, and can be a vital part of the business process.

Many large companies, on the other hand, may have problems finding a simple vision. Rather, the corporate center in such large firms often becomes a stimulant for anonymous bureaucracy and delays, clearly not intentional, but still the case. In contrast, smaller firms with their clear foci often offer their leaders relatively more influence. And don't forget, a lot of employees want to see and feel their CEOs with a simple but clear vision on the topics of today.

37

Introduction to Leadership and Self: Now to You

We just covered how critical the persons running the business are to ensure the success of a business. Let us take a deeper look at leadership now and move towards examination of the "self" of the leader. Is leadership a case of nature or nurture? Are we born leaders? Or can we grow to become good leaders? There have been endless dialogues about this issue, and even research— for example, testing children in psychological settings and following them through adulthood, even testing fish to see what we can learn about leadership in schools of following fish (Nakayama, 2013). Some claim that most leaders are extroverts, or bolder and more active (Campbell, 2019). Others say leadership can evolve, especially with positive feedback (Kuisma and Meltovaara, 2021). We may not have the answer to this dilemma, and it is probably a bit of both; however, we shall still be able to discuss how important keeping an eye on "self" is, as we take on more and more managerial responsibilities. And we shall see that it is key that we effectively cannot lead our organizations if we do not understand ourselves and do not take care.

Business factors identified for this chapter are the following: open-mindedness and listening capabilities, effective coaching, and preparation for "life after" work. With these factors, many discussions may arise. For example, how can leaders develop themselves to be more open-minded and better listeners? How can coaching as a process be improved? And how can leaders use it— can they be coaches themselves? Do they need coaches as they lead? What is the role of experience as a leader leads? What are other skills, hobbies, and interests that can be cultivated along a leader's career, and how may those be used for better self-understanding throughout the employment period and eventually pursued after employment?

Readers will notice that there are no executive interviews in this section. The reason for this decision is that the book reviews we selected already offer us, we believe, such deep levels of transparency, authenticity, and self-exposure. Also, it is now time for self-reflection. Savor that space. Enjoy that opportunity. What are you as a leader? How do you lead? What are your own leadership goals?

Here are some takeaways that you might expect from this Part:

1. Stretch, never give up, improve over time. Push oneself!
2. Open-mindedness: Allow experimentation; inquire; generalist: prepare for the next phase as a leader.
3. Take advantage of crises; to unfreeze/change, to motivate!

38

Essential Books to Learn about Leadership and Self: Now to You

Warren Berger, (2016), A more Beautiful Question: The Power of Inquiry, Bloomsbury Trade (reviewed March 2020)

To be curious seems to be central in this publication, and to be able to practice this in less structured settings appears equally important. The objective seems to encourage being bold enough to practice "questioning the question." To properly focus questions requires patience and the ability to be creative. To practice the art and science of good questioning might lead to positive improvement of our businesses, and of our own lives as well!

This book deals with the role critical questioning plays in enabling people to innovate, solve problems, and move ahead in their careers and lives. Questioning seems essential for successful entrepreneurship and innovation. How can we get better at asking good questions? And why does our ability to come up with impactful questions seem to weaken as we get older?

The author argues that, as things get more complex, good questions become essential for producing effective workable answers. However, such solutions often tend to be counterintuitive. Why do we slow down, even stop to question as we grow older? Why does nonintuitive questioning—a great source of creativity—gradually diminish? Can the conventional school system be to blame? A certain shyness might for instance become more prevalent as students grow older. They simply do not want to make fools of themselves in the eyes of fellow students by raising nonconventional questions. But schools' curricula may also contribute to the issue: "closed" approaches, overrepresented in the curricula, may leave little to no room for deep questioning. The disproportionate emphasis on "correct" answers discourages creativity and reduces the students' interest in many subjects. Such a phenomenon is much less prevalent, say, in Montessori schools, which tend to adopt a less structured curriculum, more aimed at discovering and nurturing each student's individual interests.

Why do many smart businesspeople screw up when it comes to finding better ways? The author recommends that an essential component of creativity is to take a step back and see things more with a "beginner's mindset." Being a good listener and developing mindfulness can also help. All these factors facilitate better questioning, which might in turn provide leads towards new nonintuitive approaches. This way of working is a characteristic of institutions such as IDEO, TED, and MIT's Media Lab. This is also how Edwin H. Land worked when he came up with the Polaroid camera. He asked: "Why can we not get to see photos immediately?" "Why do we have to send exposed films away to be developed in darkrooms somewhere else?" Mr. Land came up with the idea to "put the darkroom into the camera." And then the Polaroid camera became a reality!

The key objective is to frame questions in a way that might lead to innovative answers. In raising the question, "Why do I need to carry this heavy piece of luggage," the roller bag was developed. "How can we build an 18-hole golf course on a relatively small island, where space limitations might represent a real constraint?" The "answer" was the development of the so-called shorter-range golf ball. "How can I charge my mobile phone when there might be a shortage of electric outlets?" Cordless and solar charging answered this question.

Patience, perseverance, and constant "questioning the question" are crucial. To allow one's inconvenience to play a role can be a door-opener to a better solution. Daydreaming can have the same effect. Considering in particular the roles of questioning in business, let us take as a starting point that which most of us are familiar with thanks to Harvard Professor C. Christenson's concept of disruptive innovations. To trigger a disruptive innovation, one should think outside the "normal" area of competence defining a particular business. What business are we in? How can I compete successfully with myself? How can I make a plan, which implies that I am a start-up (again)? In short, businesses need to have a culture of inquiry to drive such disruptive innovations.

What about the questioning that could lead to a positive improvement in our lives? The basic premise is that we, cum humans, must strive to live in line with the questions we raise. From this premise, it follows that, when framing a question, one must maintain a strong sense of focus. An individual should focus on a question only if one can accept and live with the implications that would stem from posting questions and answering them. This does not mean that a question should be easy. Uncomfortable questions should also be raised, perhaps valuable, as they may help individuals discover themselves more realistically and then achieve a big positive change in one's lives. This book might be of interest not only to entrepreneurs but to business executives in general, as well as to all who are concerned with how to improve education.

Breakthrough ideas are critical for success! Such ideas need to be generated on an even faster and more regular basis, hence investigative questioning.

William MacAskill, (2016), Doing Good Better: Effective Altruism, Avery (reviewed October 2019)

What is altruism? Associated concepts are giving (money and/or time), development aid, and social entrepreneurship. The author argues that this should be done in a clear, focused manner; strategy means choice, as does doing good even better. So effective altruism is central, especially to assess specific potential charities: purpose, cost-effectiveness, robustness, and financial needs. Critical are proper analysis, research and evaluation, and to be open about what seems to be effective. All of this should be candidly discussed.

This book addresses the two issues of managing incremental improvements and becoming better at setting priorities. Surprisingly, altruism is part of these two key challenges too! Steven Pinker recently stated that "effective altruism represents one of the great new trends of the twenty-first century." Altruism deals with giving (money and/or time), providing development aid, and engaging in social entrepreneurship. This book deals first with five main questions regarding effective altruism, followed by four key issues about the effective implementation of altruism, that is, "altruism in action."

The author poses the critical question of how might one do the most good? Why does one need to be mindful regarding this? First, in terms of making the difficult trade-offs regarding how many people benefit and by how much, a simple cost-benefit analytical approach might help us to reflect.

What would be the most effective use of one's resources? Issues such as corruption, ineffectiveness, and minor donations arise at this point. Another logical question follows: Is a specially chosen area a relatively neglected one?

According to the author, such neglected areas often yield the most tangible results.

The final question the author raises relates to probabilities: What are the chances of success for a cause that is being supported? Expected net value calculations might help here. But let us all remember that according to the Fukushima atomic energy plant manual, "from an engineering standpoint, an accident occurring is practically unthinkable!" Even if this statement were correct, the potential negative effect of such an accident should be calculated using the expected value.

A next issue is to come up with a way to delineate which actual charities might make the most difference. A first attempt at this evaluation might be to assess how much a given charity might spend on administration as well as on compensation for the charity's CEO and other senior leaders. So how large a percentage of donation will actually end up in a given project? Another possibly rather meaningful method for evaluating the effectiveness of donations might be: What does a given charity do?, how cost-effective does each program area seem to be?, how robust is the performance evidence claimed behind each program?, how well is each program implemented?, and does this charity need additional funds for a given project? In the end, it is of course up to each individual donor to assess how to weigh each of these criteria.

Difficult moral issues might arise when trying to give, as well. For instance, aid sometimes entails controversial topics around sweatshops, child labor, animal cruelty, rainforest depletion, or pollution. Poor communities may at times suffer from such activities. The fact that we, in the more economically developed part of the world, see such activities as controversial does not automatically make these types of dilemmas go away. Realism, more than emotion or dogmatism, is perhaps called for when assessing these types of projects.

Several criteria are given for young people's educational choices so that youths can be better prepared to play more effective roles in today's altruism movement. Entrepreneurship, research, and/or politics all make good sense as educational areas of pursuit.

The effective altruist must thus accept grappling with four overriding key issues: Proper analysis, research, and evaluation should be a habit of regular giving; one should write down how to incorporate effective altruism in one's own context; to join the community of effective altruism, none the least to be able to debate how to handle major dilemmas in giving; and finally to tell others about effective altruism, be explicit by avoiding an overly discreet profile.

Petter A. Stordalen, (2019), Endelig Mandag (Finally Monday), Pilar (reviewed January 2020)

This book, in Norwegian, is written by a successful entrepreneur who founded and built a hotel chain, Choice Hotels. Having obviously been hit hard by the COVID-19 pandemic, his business has bounced back under his inspiring leadership, consisting of ten principles. Perhaps most critical of all, it seems, is to stay "low key," play down one's ego, and appear naïve or even dumb at times! To work hard, with focus, is always important, but 80% is enough!

One of the most successful Nordic entrepreneurs, Petter A. Stordalen, entitled his book "Endelig Mandag" ("Finally Monday"). The author sees several guiding principles for achieving success, summarized as a positive mental attitude and elaborated into the following:

Do what is best without attempting to be a hero, i.e., to have the courage to make one's own choices in life, not be influenced by how one might want to be perceived by others.

80% is more than enough as an acceptable completion ratio for projects. And reaching this point typically requires, say, only 50% of one's energy. The remaining 50% can be used for other things. High productivity turns out to be crucial.

To be naïve is a superpower, i.e., be naïve and honest especially when negotiating deals. This attitude will create a sense of confidence on the other side. Although this may initially result in a less favorable and more expensive outcome, in the long run, this approach tends to be beneficial.

Do not follow your dreams, but think "outside the box." In this age of digitalization, where robots are gradually taking over what has traditionally been more routine-driven human tasks, the deferential factor is unconventional thinking.

Building a new airport does not guarantee air traffic, i.e., do not brag about how little sleep one might need, but instead that success is not necessarily correlated with little sleep. The recipe for success is to go to bed early and get enough sleep! One should relish the small events, above all, by keeping the big picture in mind.

Read fewer newspapers. Despite all of the negative news that tend to be out there, the author argues that the world is better than ever before. Progress is likely linked to one human trait, namely that we tend to have a strong faith in what we can "see" as the future. This "can do" attitude is the differentiating factor regarding success in business, far more important than having a great idea or seed capital. Obviously, the willingness to make an effort is also a prerequisite for success. The paradox is that while there is more progress than ever before, most sources of news are typically negative.

Appear to be dumb. First, when hiring new executives, it seems important to hire candidates who demonstrate strong attributes. Advances take place faster than ever, and highly intelligent people are typically in the best position to quickly internalize such new wisdom. On top of this, to go for diversity within one's management team tends to stimulate others to learn faster.

Second, achieving high performance stems from the fact that while many executives may have excessive self-confidence, which is not necessarily backed by a high degree of knowledge, thus ending up on "Mount Stupid," they are regrettably overconfident but under-skilled. The author deals with this issue by doing the so-called "cross bearings," which implies meeting with key executives individually, listening a lot, and not revealing his own preferences when it comes to the particular question at hand. In this way, he is able to get a broader set of input factors to base his decision on. And it should be observed that no group meetings seem to achieve this.

Third, while not necessarily appearing dumb, one should maintain friendships. This humble levelheadedness does not exclusively mean to keep old, loyal friends but to get new ones as well. Friends that are active tend to enrich us and stimulate further development. Again, we see diversity at work! The author also refers to how children seem to excel, not only due to strong genes but also by having strong groups of friends.

Utilize the entire world arena. In today's ever-changing world, a fundamental question that all corporations ask is how to successfully adapt to change. This represents a particular conundrum given that innovations typically come from "the sidelines," from smaller and younger firms rather than from the more established players, many of which will eventually disappear. Traditions and conservative thinking, so common in established firms, might jeopardize a corporation's ability to solve problems effectively. How might one ameliorate tendencies to resist change? Again, the recipe, in the author's view, is diversity. New solutions are often linked to diversity. As a result, one should always try to create the broadest possible diversity.

Brush your teeth every day, and you will be rewarded. This chapter deals with developing those competence profiles that might be particularly desirable. So, do not complicate things unnecessarily. For instance, what are the most critical competencies to look for when hiring a new employee? If faced with a choice among three candidates, one has an exceptionally high IQ score, the second has a high propensity for being creative, and the third being highly organized and systematic, the author recommends choosing the third, because of this person's likely strong ability to deliver and get results. The author also values endurance. He makes a claim that a high degree of this might also make the candidate better prepared to cope with failures, never giving up. Good routines should support the building up of one's resilience. Self-control is also key. This is probably more important to have than charisma. An often-overlooked self-control habit that is critical to develop is promptly responding to e-mails. This is widely appreciated amongst most people, and it also tends to lead to more respect.

When at the top, turn around and look back. The Nordic countries are among the wealthiest in the world. This is not only a result of oil revenues but likely also associated with the emerging societal dynamism that came about from extensive deregulations in many sectors. The governments in the Nordic countries are generally efficient and predictable. Even though taxes are relatively high in such welfare state regimes, the Nordic governments are generally not antibusiness orientated, nor are they anti-capitalistic. The Nordics' national happiness surveys are high, none the least due to the free education provided in these states. Diversity might be seen as another contributing factor to the high ranking of the Nordic states. After all, money is not all but a "way to keep score."

This young entrepreneur's thinking is perhaps different from what we may expect from most other successful capitalists. Success in today's societal context might call for an emphasis on new dimensions compared to in the past: teams, diversity, utilization of emerging technology, and to create a highly motivated organizational context.

Erling Kagge, (2021), The Philosophy of an Explorer, Penguin Random House (reviewed June 2022)

The author is more than an accomplished business executive— a well-known publisher running his own publishing firm, and an authoritative art collector. He is also the first person in the world who has gone to the North and South Poles on skis, singlehandedly, and has been to the top of Mount Everest as well. This book sets out 16 principles for explorers attempting this type of journey. A "can do" attitude, i.e., never give up, makes the odds seem starkly against one-self, but equally, to "swallow" pride by turning around in certain cases is key, often a matter of life and death. Stupid risks should be avoided! And learn to be alone, a lesson that top leaders should acknowledge!

Mr. Erling Kagge, the Norwegian explorer, author, art collector, entrepreneur, lawyer, and politician, was the first person in the world to reach the "triple poles": the North Pole, South Pole, and the summit of Mount Everest on foot. Based on these experiences, he has come up with a set of useful principles mostly having much broader applications to guide many of us in business as well as to live more meaningful lives. There are many implications for entrepreneurs, especially. Human endurance is the main thread that runs through it all, positive, full of optimism and fulfillment.

The author stresses, "set your own compass": Major choices must be made by oneself, based on opportunities as one sees them, and not to worry too much about potential obstacles. One should follow one's own dream. There might be great benefits in setting such targets.

"Get up early" is the next "principle." This has a lot to do with discipline, and not putting things off. "Train yourself in optimism" is also recommended. This may call leaders to philosophize and push for an optimistic angle. It may also encourage them to be better prepared, with a positive attitude. Many of us simply fail to relish in the strengths we have, and we are in effect often making excuses for these! The author takes a dramatically different view, namely, pleading that we should not undervalue ourselves. This "can-do" attitude is fundamental, and it is not about bragging. The author claims that to think this way may also make it easier for many of us to acknowledge the greatness in others, i.e., not to "talk others down." There is a difference between what is completely impossible and what is almost impossible, according to the late philosopher and mountain climber Arne Naess. The author has labeled this "don't mistake probability for possibility"! However, "don't take stupid risks" either. Be courageous, not reckless! It may be braver in the end, to withdraw from activities that are turning out to be entirely off limits. One should not give up too easily though. When giving up, always "have something to lose" in mind. While we all need challenges, we should also be prepared to say stop, although never until absolutely necessary!

The author now turns more towards philosophizing about life, the life side of the work—life eq. A good life is about using senses, seeking knowledge, living in fellowship with others, and being engaged. It encompasses finding variety in the meanings of life. Yet this must come about naturally, not through frantic activities or even panic. "Don't choose happiness, let it choose you." To "learn to be alone" is a central feature when it comes to this. While many of us need togetherness and to receive recognition from others, this being perhaps deeply ingrained as part of the human condition, we might all nevertheless benefit from the realization that we should also be able to survive alone and also that we can prosper in this way.

The trip to the South Pole taught him to value small pleasures, such as formations of snow and ice, different shades of white, and so on. "Enjoy small helpings," the author says. Less can be more! Closeness to nature can often manifest this, observing and appreciating many of the "small wonders" that can be found in nature.

The author now takes a turn to discuss failure. "Accept failure," he states, success and failure are not necessarily mutually exclusive. Sometimes an early failure might open up for a successful path at a later stage. Humility, respect, and acknowledging the value of experience are all central here. While some success might be good, too much of it, perhaps coming too quickly, and/or too easily may indeed lead to dysfunctionality. We see this in many settings. Many so-called "early bloomers" may typically have a hard time following up later.

Responsibility is the critical factor to a freer life; the author claims: "Find freedom in responsibility." Only this consistent path makes success achievable, in contrast to a "make it easy for me" attitude.

"Make flexibility a habit" is of course also central here. While routine may be good, above all in the sense that this may help us to free up time, which we could then make better use of, routine should not be taken too far. If it is routine, then there is little left to take responsibility for. While habits and routines are indeed necessary, they must not become "resting pillows."

The issue of luck is discussed, it being claimed that to try hard and prepare thoroughly may also increase one's luck: "Don't leave luck to chance"! Preparations to achieve systematic luck entail doing the necessary homework, foreseeing difficulties, and thinking positively. While unforeseen difficult situations will almost always arise, the question is whether one has been prepared beforehand to cope with such events.

Our real goals are the ones that are constantly in the background, namely, "Allow your goals to pursue you." For the author to become an explorer was like following a predestined path.

After achieving what might be seen as success, a question that may arise is, "so, what's next?", the so-called "Champion's Dilemma." The author discusses how to "reset your compass," having experienced success after success and always having been able to come back! It is not a matter of fulfillment of single goals as something finite, Mr. Kagge thinks, but to learn from a success, so as to be able to pursue the next one(s).

In the end it is perhaps a matter of pushing, in business as well as in the personal agenda. Push for things! First, be kind. Leave one's "campsite" in the same condition or better than when one arrived. While most of us might not be inclined to pursue extreme targets to explore, contrary to what the author did in the cold, icy, and windy climatic realities of the far north, south or heights, ocean storms, and so on, we may nevertheless learn a great deal when it comes to slightly less extreme undertakings that we embark on, such as being well prepared in business, or when we hike, ski, or sail, for instance.

The book has a much broader application than just addressing prospective explorers or the rest of us embarking on expeditions somewhat less adventurous. Most of us are struggling with how to find more happiness in life. For instance, we may feel lonely, even when surrounded by people. To observe nature, to set realistic ambitions, to acknowledge that a so-called failure is nothing more than a license to learn more, and to be content with even the small things, are insights that the author offers us. As he says, these and other insights "came about" while he was undertaking his extreme struggles in hostile conditions, but these insights are perhaps even more important for busy top executives.

There is another set of implications that might be seen as even more fundamental, namely for how family-owned firms, with entrepreneurs in charge, may learn from the book. Family-owned firms often seem to perform relatively better than their publicly owned counterparts. Why? They are able to take a longer-term focus, and to reinvest in the firm, rather than pay it all out as dividends. But this assumes that the top management in such firms is competent and wise. The executives need to be driven and motivated. But how? The stock market, with its call for steady, quarterly dividends, is not there. So, what drives those who are leading privately owned firms? Mr. Kagge has an answer: to go for some risk, calculated gambles, and to recognize that by failing one has a lot to learn. For us, this "inner drive" that the author calls for seems to be absolutely essential, especially when it comes to being in charge of successful family businesses.

So, this book helps us to better understand what drives successful leaders in all business sectors, but perhaps particularly when it comes to family businesses, where there might be little to no pressures from top managers' inner drives.

39

Closing Remarks to the Part

Securing health and well-being has proven to be helpful to all individuals, and we shall even dare to exclaim that they are essential to leaders at the head of organizations. As airline safety videos so vividly show, "put your oxygen mask on before you help others with or around you with theirs," you cannot lead without giving yourself the nurture and caring you deserve as a human being.

A careful look at self means examining the physical, mental/emotional, and relational sides we have. It is not just about what we do or how we lead others that counts, but, even more, our awareness and our feelings. The general topic of self is so vast! In this Part, we have of course not attempted to cover it all, but we hope that some of the earlier readings and interviews have triggered a curiosity for our readers to learn more… about themselves! An additional hope is that more of these topics also shall find their ways into what is being taught at business schools.

Thus, striving to arrive at a reasonable balance between what is one's leadership job versus other private activities is central to this discussion. It is thus a matter of developing and maintaining a somewhat broader and deeper horizon than what might come about when exclusively working, working, working. Why is it so important to have an eclectic sphere of interests? We shall highlight three reasons in the following:

Joy with resilience. A good leader shall enjoy what he/she is doing, and not run him/herself down, with no more "energy in the tank," to quote New Zealand's outgoing Prime Minister, Jacinda Ardern. A harmonious balance between work and other activities seems fundamental. Steve Jobs was also known to favor this notion of enjoyment—using instead the word "passion"— namely, that to be good at what one does requires passion.

Proactivity in learning. To be an active learner is, of course, a central part of this— and is at the core of this book. Embrace, own, and steward your learning! Meaningful learning typically calls for a wider horizon of interests. A too-narrow focus, on the other hand, often leads executives down blind paths, consequently then missing major or critical shifts in the environment.

Preparation for all stages. It is essential for a good leader to prepare for what shall come after the leader steps down. To use an analogy from mountaineering, the way down must be prepared for! And, as many experienced rock climbers know, the way down is often the hardest, none the least due to less intensity in the level of adrenaline, less ability to concentrate, fatigue, and so on. Thinking about the way up too, or the way down, in other words, the steps or phases, can be a big advantage. Being aware and mindful during the entire process is important.

What many leaders experience after they step down is often not easy to handle. To prepare for this phase is thus critical: cultivate hobbies, adopt long-term thinking, etc. A good test when it comes to whether an ex-leader is successful and is staying "fresh" might be whether he/she is invited by their successor to provide advice. If no longer on top of key issues, then it shall be unlikely that the new leader shall want to ask for such advice, not wanting to "waste their time." Strong leaders therefore can become excellent sources of inspiration, wisdom, mentoring, coaching, or advising even after they leave the firm or retire outright.

Part IX

Conclusions

And whatever we do, let's be ambitious.
   - Dr. Alan Finkel, neuroscientist, educator, philanthropist

Education is the most powerful weapon which you can use to change the world.
   - Nelson Mandela, anti-apartheid activist, politician, author

40

Practice Insights from Arnoud De Meyer, PBM, Business Academic at Lee Kong Chian School of Business, Singapore Management University

How to Steer Universities and Business Schools Through Turbulent Times

Business schools face a turbulent environment. The combination of the growing challenge to traditional forms of learning, whether it is for young adults or mid-career professionals; the influence of AI-based support systems; the rise of capable and professional EdTech companies, of which some deliver high-quality and high-touch degree programs; the emergence of predatory journals and conferences; the growing competition from Asian schools and universities, etc. render the environment in which business schools operate all the more unpredictable and volatile. How should academic leaders steer their organizations?

From my recent study on how Singapore has been able to build in less than 30 years a system of higher education that is considered to be on top of its league, I can make five suggestions.[1]

First, ensure that you have clarity in purpose. Determine why you exist as an academic institution. And how do you translate this in practical key performance indicators (KPI)? This sounds like a mundane and straightforward step in the strategy development and implementation for a business school. But in my many years associated with EQUIS, the European accreditation organization for business schools, I have observed that quite a few organizations seem to have forgotten why they exist. Continuation of their existing

---

[1] De Meyer A with J. Ang. 2022. Building Excellence in Higher Education: Singapore's Experience. Routledge, New York.

activities or pure survival seems to drive them, rather than a deep reflection on why they were created and why they exist. Many business schools have become quasi-commercial organizations and may have forgotten that they were created to support the local or national economic development and its business community. In the case of Singapore, the development of the system of higher education from one to six universities and five polytechnics was a response to the developing and variegated needs of the Singapore economy. "Fit for purpose" is an expression that is often used to explain its development. And this clear purpose is translated in a clear KPI: the cohort participation rate, or the percentage of young adults of a particular age cohort to join institutions of higher learning.

Second, embrace innovation in learning and research. Be audacious and experiment with new ideas. When I was President of Singapore Management University, we rarely hesitated to work with our students, as partners, in implementing new forms of learning. Often, these innovations were based on digital applications, but one of our most successful innovations is what is called SMU-X or the experiential learning. This approach to learning recognizes that students can learn a lot of concepts on their own from online resources, e.g., online courses and YouTube, but that effective and long-lasting learning happens when a student applies these concepts to real-world problems, under the guidance of faculty and mentors from practice. In experimenting with innovations like this, you must focus on the core issue: how do you improve the student's learning (and not simply on how we teach better). And like with any innovations, you have to prepare to fail. Failure is part of innovation, so do it fast and cheaply.

Third, I am convinced that the development of academic institutions requires an intelligent and well-implemented governance system. I have had the privilege of working in different countries or regions, e.g., Belgium or France in Continental Europe, the UK, Singapore, and more recently Hong Kong. Based on that experience I am convinced that a governance system that finds the right balance between autonomy for the university and an intelligent alignment with the strategic priorities of the country or the region is for most academic institutions optimal. Academic institutions need the managerial autonomy to develop their own identity, grow their own strengths, and diversify themselves from their colleagues and competitors. But they will develop most optimally when they can align themselves in their research and learning programs with the strategic objectives of their financial backers, i.e., in most cases the governments, national research foundations, and partners from industry and the nonprofit sector. It is not sufficient to design such a system. The experience of countries like Singapore, the Republic of Korea, and Japan indicated that it is the intelligent implementation of such a governance system that ultimately makes the difference.

Fourth, learn from partners. Most if not all business schools and universities are now developing an international academic network. They engage with partners for student exchanges and the development of joint educational and research programs. In most cases these are simple collaboration agreements, but sometimes they develop into joint ventures or alliances. However, it would be inappropriate to compare these with commercial partnerships. Risking simplifying too much, I would argue that commercial partnerships will survive if the partners make profits and perceive they get their fair share from these profits. But in academia the ultimate goal of partnerships is to learn from each other. All universities in Singapore have developed and grown with overseas partners. I have observed that these partnerships came to a natural end when one of the partners felt that there was limited learning. Thus, to be successful, invest in learning and ensure that your ecosystem of partners is one that promotes joint and continued learning.

Finally, be flexible. In the turbulent world that I mentioned higher up, you will not be able to predict the next disruption or envisage the coming disaster. You may have a clear purpose, a good governance system, and a willingness to innovate and learn, but you never really know when the next pandemic or war will disrupt all this. Yes, you can have good sensors and antennae to pick up early signals of disruption, but you also need to be very flexible in adjusting your plans. The investment in physical assets is often the biggest brake on flexible adjustment. Would it be better to share these assets and develop together capabilities? Yes, I envisage the future academic institution to be one that works in an educational ecosystem, i.e., a loosely coupled network of partners that innovate together, that coevolve their capabilities and roles, and align their investments so as to create additional learning and research outcomes. That is a very different type of organization than what we are used to. But turbulent times require creative solutions.

41

Conclusions on Accelerated Learning for Business Success

We wish to briefly come back to the beginning of the book when we first presented the concept of an accelerated process for business learning. We recall that first, a general realization that a topic is of interest or importance is identified. Then we suggested that the learner review relevant book reviews and executive interviews on this topic, in this book. At each of these short intervals, we recommend that the learner engage in the process of topic absorption—small pauses that may help to ascertain that the perspectives, insights, and inputs presented have been captured, reflected upon, and processed by the reader.

Let us remind ourselves once again about the three fundamental premises of this book. It is all about fast learning. This has at least three main implications:

- We as individuals. For each of us, learning seems to be a stepwise process, but where we never reach a final step! Learning is a continuous process, and so-called relearning is key. To "dismantle" old axioms is part of this, so that we actually might be able to absorb what new there is to learn. This has been discussed extensively in the literature, see Lewin (1947), Kolb (1984), Bower (1966), Quinn (1980), Burch (1970), Maslow (1970), Argyris and Schön (1978), Schein (2010) and others.
- Various experts may have different views regarding what might be important. To be able to better appreciate such differences, we have reviewed what leading practitioners have stated in books and interviews. We have deliberately avoided the inclusion of inputs from academicians. There seems to be a tendency among many such academicians to stick to what

they initially have come to believe, through their training, research, and collegiate discussions. We did not wish to introduce such a potentially "consuming" element into our book. To try to see patterns in what various open-minded practitioners might believe in is a major premise of this book.
- Business schools and other executive training institutions bear primary responsibility for what is being taught, i.e., for what we, the students, might learn. Thus, such institutions' curricula become important. The specific recommendations provided for each of the previous chapters are paramount. We shall summarize all of this on page 8. This might be seen, indeed, as a blueprint for curriculum design for business schools of the future.

The process of learning is thus often challenging, but as one becomes more aware of one's own unique learning process and personal role in the relationship equation that runs from information to knowledge to wisdom, transformative learning or regenerative learning can occur. Here is where we authors ask for your serious commitment to learning.

The type of learning we promote should be not just about setting daily or weekly routines to learn, but also with which intention the readers actively, proactively, and deeply enter into their learning process. Passion is key, at the very least, curiosity. And by embracing new information, with a purposeful, mindful intention, we believe the best learning can occur. Transformative learning is one theory of learning with a focus on adult education and young adult learning. Transformative or transformation learning (Mezirow, 1995) relies on the premise that learners can adjust their thinking based on new information, which is fundamentally what learning brings in terms of advantage—new learnings, new insights, new thinking (Argyris, 1978)!

We have already mentioned that learning can be a conscious transformation, whereby as reinforcement, we need to think that transformation is the act or process of changing completely. Our readers must buy into this process themselves so that the learning shift can help to align us with our highest potential as leaders. To be even more specific, we are responsible for our own learning. Responsibility, responding with ability, accountability, and ownership all play a role in the process of executive education.

Regenerative (borrowed perhaps from the world of sustainability) learning is particularly interesting for leadership development and seems to be getting more and more attention in business, leadership, and self-help publishing and media outlets. We have seen projects involving regenerative leadership, which encourages business leaders to address two processes simultaneously: crossing boundaries and the loss of connectedness. Business publishing includes a

41 Conclusions on Accelerated Learning for Business Success

tremendous amount of materials on how to better self-connect and connect to others and to nature (this can also imply the general external business environment, which does include nature and climate).

Supporters and practitioners of regenerative leadership enjoy the nourishment from deep connection to self, others and nature, "thereby holding the potential to serve the wellbeing of the entire ecosystem: self, team and organization… To become regenerative leaders, we need deep skills. Skills like listening truly, following curiosity, building trust, showing up full, questioning ourselves and our mindsets constructively." (Favretti & Freud, 2022).

The authors believe that this book may help students and participants of executive education programs to both transform and regenerate, for better performance; transform through new information that influences their thinking and business decisions and regenerate through creating deeper connections to themselves, others, and the external environment which are all critical to the outcomes of business choices made and directions pursued.

We also encourage cross-functional thinking, as stated in the beginning. We can learn how to search for ways to align self, team, and departments with overall organizational objectives. Technology can help. Coming together with different types of expertise, education, and experiences to achieve a common goal can make us better business leaders.

A note here on how this book might lead up to courses (at IMD or elsewhere, but we shall make use of IMD as an example):

1. First, quick scan regarding particular sections in the book. This should provide a quick set of insights into the "basics."
2. Then, if interested in more, read one or more of the book reviews or books, or one or more of the extra readings referred to in each of the executive interviews.
3. Then, if still interested, consider a (short) course at IMD or elsewhere.
4. If still interested, consider a longer course (EMBA; IMD's Orchestrating Winning Performance) and/or a course with broader focus.
5. Finally, constant renewal; continuous learning. Go back and take more courses. Always.

What are the major curricular implications from the previous sections? We have presented many perspectives, examples, experiences, and visions from business book authors, academicians, practitioners, and leaders. But if our readers are also business school executives, what may be some key points and topics they may consider useful as takeaways? Clearly, each book review and executive interview will provide another point of view, but what may not be as evident is how that summary or profile can convert to a specific input or impulse for changes in the business school curriculum.

We have covered many principal learning issues throughout the book: silos, speed, open-mindedness, listening capability, coaching, preparation for what comes after stepping down, long-term focus, human resource, and talent management. Consequently, such elements make the overall question of progress in executive leadership, learning, and education more complex. In the end, are we looking at a matrix or road map for learning? How do we, both learners and business schools, deal with new technologies and virtuality, advances in finance, organizational configurations, green strategies, value chain disruption, branding, quality, pricing, and more?

What are some of the overriding challenges for developing stronger curricula in the end? In our opinion the main concern and test is to better understand the dynamics of adaptation. How might students be taught the appropriate skills here? And what is relevant? Two types of skills come to mind in particular: listening and dialogue. How might we train and be trained to listen better? How might we learn and maintain the open-mindedness that would be required? How might we better communicate, debate, and discuss with more open minds, and less potential dogmatism and preset ideas? Thus, skills such as observation, reflection, awareness, and mindfulness are more critical than they have ever been before. Life, personal and business, is impermanent. Adapting is the only way forward.

Here is the alphabetical summary of the key learning issues identified in Parts 2–9, totally 24 themes. We strongly recommend that these themes become central in curriculum design in business schools of the future:

- Artificial intelligence (AI).
- Compromise: wins for each party.
- Crises: take advantage of such.
- Cycle management, exits, and "nos."
- Environment.
- Family as owners.
- Generalist view; open-mindedness.
- Impact investing; geographic expansion.
- Joint ventures, cooperation.
- Long-term focus.
- Membership/subscription economy.
- Mistakes; early recognition of such.
- New ventures and start-ups.
- People: the best.

41 Conclusions on Accelerated Learning for Business Success

- Portfolio of businesses, but still simple.
- Public versus private (government versus business).
- Relevance to customers. Cost/benefit.
- "Responsible": regarding growth, aid, close downs, …
- Risk-taking; expert teams; analysis.
- Scale-ups, rapid expansion.
- Social conflicts.
- Stretch: improve over time.
- Sustainable growth.
- Vision: clear, inspirational.

We thus have concluded our journey for accelerated learning by emphasizing a few critical implications for business schools and have offered some recommendations for the design of a modern curriculum for such executive education establishments.

In summary, what we have tried to discuss and show here in this book is:

(a) The importance of lifelong learning.
(b) That learning should not just be the responsibility of the educational institution but rather is a commitment that should be embraced by the learner, whereby the learner him/herself becomes almost his/her own owner or steward, taking full accountability and responsibility to learn continuously.
(c) That learning is a joint journey—responsibility and accountability of professor and student, and of establishment and learner.
(d) That all "parties" to this process must be fully connected with industry—in other words, practitioner-oriented.
(e) That learning should take place in a "space" we will say is free of silos, biases, prejudices—or as much as possible.
(f) That business schools must commit to being future-oriented in terms of topics, courses, programs, materials, and means (i.e., virtual, and AI) and to listening to business leaders for input.
(g) That learning, like science, is an impermanent concept—its methods, approaches, and goals, for instance, evolve and transform and will continue to do so forever.
(h) That the relationship between deliverable or lesson, and learning is very much a question of timing and speed.
(i) The "dynamic of opposites" comes into play—long programs mixed with short; on campus with virtual; dependent study and work assignments with independent; small group with large group; professor to student

with peer to peer; traditional materials with new, fresh or virtual; thought leadership-driven with thought "follow-ship"-driven, and so on.

Some of our recommendations for the design of the modern curriculum are listed above. In theory what we propose is quite similar to what entrepreneurs and founders go through when planning or founding their start-ups—business schools need to define their product/service-market-team fit. We would add to that the importance of not only identifying the need in the market and building the solution that the customers, in this case of course business leaders, want to buy, followed by the right team to bring this all to reality, but to also be extremely anticipatory, placing utmost priority on trying as hard as possible to foresee future trends, cycles, and changes that may impact the business environment and thus in one way, defining also the client's future needs, needs that he/she may not even expect, ever.

References

Acemoglu, D., & Robinson, J. A. (2012). *Why nations fail: The origins of power, prosperity and poverty*. Profile Books, Cop.
Amabile, T., & Kramer, S. J. (2011, May). *The power of small wins*. Harvard Business Review.
Andersen, T. (1994). *Asger Jorn, En Biografi, Sohn*. Silkeborg.
Argyris, C., & Schön, D. (1978). *Organizational learning: A theory of action perspective*. Addison Wesley.
Barnes, J. (1982). *The presocratic philosophers*. Routledge & Kegan Paul.
Ben-Ghiat, R. (2020). *Strongmen: Mussolini to the present*. Norton.
Bennis, W., & Nanus, B. (1985). *Leaders: Strategies for taking charge*. Harper Business.
Berger, W. (2019). *The book of beautiful questions*. Bloomsberg.
Bower, M. (1966). *The will to manage: Corporate success through programmed management*. McGraw-Hill.
Burch, N. (1970). Conscious competence learning model: Four stages of learning theory - unconscious incompetence to unconscious competence matrix and other theories and models for learning and change.
Burgers, J. (2006). *Customers are just like regular people*. Academic Services.
Campbell, D. (2019). Extroverts enjoy four key advantages according to a new UTSC study, University of Toronto Scarborough, May 29, 2019.
Collins, J. (2001). *Good to great: Why some companies make the leap … and others don't*. Penguin Random House.
De Pree, M. (2004). *Leadership is an art*. Currency.
Favretti, M., & Freud, B. (2022). Regenerative learning and rediscovering our relationship to all living systems [online]. https://www.gettingsmart.com/podcast/maggie-favretti-and-benjamin-freud-phd-on-regenerative-learning/. Accessed 20 June 2022.

Finkel, A. (2017, November 14). Human intelligence 2.0: How will we get there? Speech given at creative innovation conference, Melbourne.
Frankl, V. E. (1946). *Man's search for meaning*. Beacon Press.
Gage, R. (2012). *Risky is the new safe*. Wiley.
Hawken, P. (2021). *Regeneration: Ending the climate crisis in one generation*. Penguin Random House.
Iniguez, S., & Lorange, P. (2021). *Executive education after the pandemic*. Palgrave.
Jaffe, D. T. (2020). *Borrowed from your grandchildren: The evolution of 100-year family enterprises*. Wiley.
Jhajharia, S. (2017). *SPARKS: Ideas to ignite your business growth*. Panoma Press.
Kolb, D. A. (1984). *Experiential learning: Experience as the source of learning development*. FT Press.
Kuisma, K., & Meltovaara, K. (2021). Positive feedback culture sparks learning, motivation and performance. [online] LAB Focus. Available at: https://blogit.lab.fi/labfocus/en/positive-feedback-culture-sparks-learning-motivation-and-performance/. Accessed 3 March 2023.
Lewin, K. (1947, June). Frontiers in group dynamics: Concept, method and reality in social science. *Social Equilibria and Social Change, Human Relations, 1*, 5–41.
Lorange, P. (2002). *New vision for management education: Leadership challenges*. Pergamon.
Lorange, P. (2019a). *The business school of the future*. Cambridge University Press.
Lorange, P. (2019b). *Adaption and flexibility in the family firm: A brief history of S. Ugelstad Invest, Smøyg*.
Lorange, P. (2021), Reinventing the family, firm .
Lowe, J. C. (2007). *Warren buffett speaks*. John Wiley & Sons.
Mandela, N. (1990, June 23). Speech given at Madison Park high school, Boston.
Maslow, A. H. (1970). *Motivation and personality* (2nd ed.). Harper & Row.
Mattis, J., & West, B. (2019). *Call sign chaos: Learning to lead*. Penguin Random House.
Mazzucato, M. (2018). *Value of everything: Making and taking in the global economy*. Public Affairs.
Merkel, A. (2014). 1st European family business summit, Berlin. http://www.bundesregierung.de/Content/DE/Rede/2014/11/2014-11-25-familienunternehmerkonferenz.hhml;jsessionid-EC40486B8DEF40B565B49C5620F601B.sl1z.
Mezirow, J. (1995). Transformation theory of adult learning. In M. Welton (Ed.), *In defense of the lifeworld: Critical perspectives on adult learning* (pp. 37–90). State University of New York Press.
Mintzberg, H. (2003). *The strategy process: Concepts, contexts, cases*. Pearson Education.
Morton, B. (2011, August 30). *Falser words were never spoken*. The New York Times.
Nakayama, S. (2013). Leaders are born, not made, fish study finds, [online] Scientific American. Available at: https://www.scientificamerican.com/article/leaders-are-born-not-made-fish-study-finds/. Accessed 3 March 2023.

Nielsen, J. (2007). Long versus short articles as content strategy [online]. https://www.nngroup.com/articles/content-strategy-long-vs-short/. Accessed 20 June 2022.

Perdue, M. (2018). You want your family business to last? Five tips for getting there [online]. Available at: https://www.noln.net/articles/2941-you-want-your-family-business-to-last-five-tips-for-getting-there. Accessed 14 Febuary 2023.

Polman, P., & Winston, A. S. (2021). *Net positive how courageous companies thrive by giving more than they take*. Harvard Business Review Press.

Quinn, J. B. (1980). *Strategies for change: Logical incrementalism*. R.D. Irwin.

Rachman, G. (2022). *The age of the strongman*. Penguin Random House.

Raworth, K. (2017). *Doughnut economics: Seven ways to think like a 21st-century economist*. Penguin Random House Business Books.

Reeves, M., Haanaes, K., & Sinha, J. (2015). *Your strategy needs a strategy*. Harvard Business Review Press.

Schein, E. H. (2010). *Organizational culture and leadership*. Jossey-Bass.

Schwarzkopf, N. (1993). *It Doesn't take a hero: The autobiography of general H*. Norman Schwarzkopf, Bantam.

Sekulich, T. (2020). Compaxo: The balance between what was and what will be. [online] Tharawat Magazine. https://www.tharawat-magazine.com/stories/compaxo-the-balance/. Accessed 14 February 2023.

Siilasmaa, R. (2018). *Transforming Nokia*. McGraw Hill.

Tett, G. (2022). *Anthro-vision: A new way to see in business and life*. Avid Reader Pr.

Thomas, H., Lorange, P., & Sheth, J. (2013). *The business school in the twenty-first century*. Cambridge University Press.

Thunberg, G. (2022). *The climate book*. Allen Lane.

Toffler, A. (1970). *Future shock*. Penguin Random House.

Tzu, L. (1996). *Tao Te Ching* (A. Waley, Trans.), Wordsworth Editions.

van Tulder, R., & van Mil, E. (2022). *Principles of sustainable business*. Taylor & Francis.

Wade, M., Bonnet, D., Yokoi, T., & Obwegeser, N. (2021). *Hacking digital: Best practices to implement and accelerate your business transformation*. McGraw-Hill.

Warrell, M. (2020). Learn, Unlearn & Relearn: What got you here Won't get you there [online]. Accessed June 20, 2022, from https://www.forbes.com/sites/margiewarrell/2020/06/12/learn-unlearn%2D%2Drelearn-what-got-you-here-wont-get-you-there/?sh=934076320a6d.

Warren, B., & Nanus, B. (1987). *Leaders: Strategies for taking charge*. Harper Collins.

Welch, J., & Welch, S. (2005). *Winning*. Harper Business.

Wilde, O. (1891). *The picture of Dorian gray*. Ward, Lock & Co.

Further Readings

Anker, P. (2020). *The power of the periphery*. Cambridge University Press.
Baron, J., & Lachenauer, R. (2021). *Family business handbook*. Harvard Business Review Press.
Baxter, R. K. (2015). *The membership economy*. McGraw Hill.
Berger, W. (2016). *A more beautiful question: The power of inquiry*. Bloomsbury Trade.
Blas, J., & Farchy, J. (2021). *The world for sale*. Penguin Random House.
Breiding, J. (2019). *Too small to fail*. Harper Collins.
Bremmer, I. (2022). *The power of crisis: How three threats – And our response – Will change the world*. Simon & Schuster.
Browder, B. (2015). *Red notice*. Simon & Schuster.
Browder, B. (2022). *Freezing order*. Simon & Schuster.
Brown, D. J. (2013). *The boys in the boat*. Penguin Random House.
Carreyrou, J. (2018). *Bad blood: Secrets and lies in a Silicon Valley startup*. Alfred A. Knopf.
Chouinard, Y. (2016). *Let my people go surfing*. Penguin Random House.
Clark, D. (2021). *The long game*. Harvard Business Review Press.
Clyne, A. H., & Jaffe, D. (2021). *Finding her voice and creating legacy*. Pitcairn.
Dalio, R. (2017). *Principles*. Simon & Schuster.
Dewar, C., Keller, S., & Malhotra, V. (2022). *CEO excellence*. Simon & Schuster.
Epstein, D. (2019). *Range: How generalists triumph in a specialist world*. Penguin Random House.
Flesner, P. (2021). *Fastscaling*. Self-Published.
Gelfand, M. (2018). *Rule makers, rule breakers*. Simon & Schuster.
Gergen, D. (2022). *Hearts touched with fire: How great leaders are made*. Simon & Schuster.
Goldstein, J. (2021). *Money: From bronze to bitcoin*. Atlantica.
Green, W. (2021). *Richer, Wiser, Happier*. Simon & Schuster.
Greenblatt, J. (2010). *The little book that still beats the market*. Wiley.
Gunther, M. (1985). *The Zürich axioms*. Harriman Classics.
Hill, A. (2019). *Ruskinland: How John Ruskin shapes our world*. Pallas Athene.
Hoffman, R., Cohen, J., & Triff, D. (2021). *Masters of scale*. Penguin Random House.
Hoffman, R., & Yeh, C. (2018). *Blitzscaling*. Penguin Random House.
Hokemeyer, P. (2019). *Fragile power*. Hazelden.
Janzer, A. (2017). *Subscription marketing: Strategies for nurturing customers in a world of churn*. Cuesta Park Consulting.
Johnson, S. (2018). *Farsighted: How we make the decisions that matter the most*. Hodder & Stoughton.
Kagge, E. (2021). *The philosophy of an explorer*. Penguin Random House.
Khanna, R. (2022). *Dignity in a digital age: Making tech work for all of us*. Simon & Schuster.

Konovalov, O. (2021). *The vision code: How to create and execute a compelling vision*. Wiley.
Lavin, F. (2021). *The smart business guide to China E-commerce*. Independent Publishing Group.
Peter Lorange, (2021), Reinventing the family, firm .
MacAskill, W. (2016). *Doing good better: Effective altruism*. Avery.
Mattis, J., & West, B. (2021). *Call sign chaos*. Penguin Random House.
McAfee, A. (2020). *More from less*. Simon & Schuster.
McCullough, T., & Whitaker, K. (2018). *Wealth of wisdom: The top 50 questions wealthy families ask*. Wiley.
McKibbon, B. (2020). *Falter*. Henry Holt & Company.
Mitchell-Blitch, M. (2020). *In the company of family: How to thrive when business is personal*. Eredita Consulting LLC.
Mounk, Y. (2022). *The great experiment*. Penguin Random House.
Nadella, S. (2017). *Hit refresh*. Harper Business.
Nir, E. (2014). *Hooked: How to build habit-forming products*. Redline.
Pabrai, M. (2007). *The Dhandho investor*. Wiley.
Perdue, M. (2021). *The frank Perdue way: Simple steps*. Super Success, Tremendous.
Pinker, S. (2018). *Enlightenment now: The case for reason, science, humanism and progress*. Allen Lane.
Plender, J. (2016). *Capitalism: Money, morals and markets*. Biteback Publishing.
Polman, P., & Winston, A. (2021). *Net positive: How courageous companies thrive*. Harvard Business Review Press.
Prashantham, S. (2022). *Gorillas can dance*. Wiley.
Rachman, G. (2022). *The age of the strongman: How the cult of the leader threatens democracy around the world*. Bodley Head.
Rosling, H. (2018). *Factfulness*. Sceptre.
Rüsen, T. A., Kleve, H., & von Schlippe, A. (2021). *Managing business family dynasties*. Springer.
Schmidt, E., Rosenburg, J., & Eagle, A. (2020). *Trillion Dollar coach*. Hodder & Stoughton.
Schwab, K., & Malleret, T. (2020). *Covid-19: The great reset*. Agentur.
Schwarzman, S. A. (2019). *What it takes*. Simon & Schuster.
Schwass, J., & Glemser, A.-C. (2016). *Wise family business*. Springer.
Sethi, A. (2016). *From science to start-up*. Springer.
Siilasmaa, R. (2019). *Transforming Nokia: The power of paranoid optimism to head through colossal changes*. McGraw Hill.
Spier, G. (2014). *The education of a Value investor*. MacMillan Education.
Stordalen, P. A. (2019). *Endelig Mandag (finally Monday)*. Pilar.
Svensen, D. F. (2005). *Unconventional success: A fundamental approach*. Simon & Schuster.
Tamaseb, A. (2021). *Super founders: What data reveals about billion-Dollar startups*. Redline.

Thomas, H., & Hedrick-Wong, Y. (2019). *Inclusive growth*. Emerald.
Wapshott, N. (2021). *Samuelson Friedman: The Battle over the free market*. W. W. Norton & Company.
Weil, P. J. (2019). *Woes of the rich*. Self-Published.
Westover, T. (2018). *Educated*. Penguin Random House.
Williams, R., & Pressier, V. (2010). *Preparing heirs*. Robert Reed.
Yunus, M. (2018). *A world of three zeros – A world of social engagement, public affairs*.
Zell, S. (2017). *Am I being too subtle? Straight talk from a business rebel*. Portfolio.

GPSR Compliance

The European Union's (EU) General Product Safety Regulation (GPSR) is a set of rules that requires consumer products to be safe and our obligations to ensure this.

If you have any concerns about our products, you can contact us on

ProductSafety@springernature.com

In case Publisher is established outside the EU, the EU authorized representative is:

Springer Nature Customer Service Center GmbH
Europaplatz 3
69115 Heidelberg, Germany

www.ingramcontent.com/pod-product-compliance
Lightning Source LLC
LaVergne TN
LVHW010333260326
834688LV00036B/694